DUMBARTON OAKS
MEDIEVAL LIBRARY

Jan M. Ziolkowski, General Editor

THE LIFE OF SAINT SYMEON
THE NEW THEOLOGIAN

NIKETAS STETHATOS

DOML 20

The Life of Saint Symeon
the New Theologian

NIKETAS STETHATOS

Translated by

RICHARD P. H. GREENFIELD

*D*UMBARTON OAKS
*M*EDIEVAL *L*IBRARY

HARVARD UNIVERSITY PRESS
CAMBRIDGE, MASSACHUSETTS
LONDON, ENGLAND
2013

Library of Congress Cataloging-in-Publication Data
Niketas, ho Stethatos, ca. 1000–ca. 1090.
  The life of saint Symeon the new theologian / Niketas Stethatos ;
translated by Richard P.H. Greenfield.
      p. cm. — (Dumbarton Oaks medieval library ; 20)
  Greek text with English translation.
  Includes bibliographical references and index.
  ISBN 978-0-674-05798-2 (alk. paper)
  1. Symeon, the New Theologian, Saint, 949–1022.   2. Orthodox Eastern
Church—Biography.   I. Title.
  BX395.S9N55 2013
  270.3092 — dc23
  [B]   2012030827

Contents

Introduction

Symeon the New Theologian, who lived from ca. 949 to 1022
CE, was a Byzantine mystic, a prolific writer, and a monastic founder and leader who is now revered as a saint by the
Orthodox Church. His reputation has grown widely in recent years, to the point where he is considered by contemporary Orthodoxy to be one of its most influential spiritual
thinkers, sharing only with John the Evangelist and Gregory of Nazianzos the epithet "the Theologian." In his own
time, however, Symeon was more than just a religious figure:
a member of a powerful aristocratic family, he and his work
cannot be disengaged from the complex social and political world of Constantinople during the late tenth and early
eleventh centuries. Moreover, during his lifetime and indeed
long afterward, a cloud of controversy and suspicion hung
around him, something which tainted his reputation and
prevented his work from becoming widely known until the
later twentieth century. The work entitled *The Life and Conduct of Our Father among the Saints Symeon the New Theologian,
Elder and Superior of the Monastery of Saint Mamas Xerokerkos*,
written by his disciple Niketas Stethatos more than thirty
years after his death, may thus be considered interesting and
important simply because of its principal subject, but it is
also an unusually valuable piece of Byzantine hagiography in

other ways, providing glimpses into the often bitter politics of monasticism and the considerable ambivalence that lay behind the construction of sanctity and the negotiation of orthodoxy at the zenith of the medieval Byzantine Empire.

NIKETAS STETHATOS AND HIS *LIFE OF SYMEON*

Niketas Stethatos, the author of *The Life of Symeon,* was born early in the eleventh century, perhaps around 1005.[1] As an adolescent, probably at the monastery of Stoudios in Constantinople, Niketas copied the rough drafts of work that Symeon, who was then nearing the end of his life, would send him,[2] but it was evidently not until some sixteen years later, when he was around thirty, that he was himself inspired to take up writing by two significant visionary experiences.[3] The largest and most important portion of Niketas's literary output involved the edition and publication of Symeon's numerous writings and, eventually, the composition of the present *Life.* His other surviving work includes three *Centuries* of chapters (which found a place in the popular and influential collection of Orthodox spiritual writings, the *Philokalia*),[4] some theological and polemical treatises,[5] and various short pieces, letters, and some liturgical compositions.[6] Niketas is thus now recognized as one of the most significant Byzantine theological authors and editors of the early eleventh century, although at one time he was best known to modern scholarship only as a minor character in the disputes surrounding the so-called schism of 1054, having written a criticism of Latin ecclesiastical practices.[7] His literary output continued into his extreme old age, when, it would appear, renowned for his own asceticism[8] and with

his youthful battles forgotten, he became superior of the Stoudios monastery. This would place his death before 1092; he was probably over eighty when he died.[9]

As Irénée Hausherr cogently argued in his introduction to the original edition and French translation, internal evidence suggests that Niketas composed *The Life of Symeon* at the earliest in 1052, but more likely sometime between 1054 and his death ca. 1090.[10] Written in good, generally straightforward Byzantine ecclesiastical Greek, the *Life* is logically constructed, in chronological order with some asides. It seems possible that some of the miracle stories toward the end of the work, notably the segment supplied by the eyewitness Nikephoros/Symeon, were added to an earlier version or draft.[11] Niketas adds authority—and sometimes complexity—to his writing by including a substantial number of biblical quotations and references; he also draws upon a fairly standard range of patristic works. In most ways, then, the *Life* is a conventional, somewhat stylized piece of hagiography. Niketas drew on his deep knowledge (and editorial manipulation) of the autobiographical accounts embedded in Symeon's own works, on some additional eyewitness accounts of Symeon's later life, on traditional hagiographical stereotypes, and, finally, on his own extremely limited personal experience of his hero.[12]

In the *Life* Niketas is at pains to underline the depth of his own relationship with Symeon.[13] He describes himself as his disciple (μαθητής)[14] and tries to demonstrate, by his inclusion in the text of a letter he received from Symeon, that he was the latter's deliberately chosen literary trustee,[15] not merely the youthful copyist of the venerable author's work. Yet the picture is not so straightforward. As also seems clear

from the *Life*, any direct relationship between the two men can have been of only short duration and conducted largely at long distance—probably during the last three years of Symeon's life, when he was living across the Bosporus and Niketas was still a youth in Constantinople.[16] Further, by Niketas's own admission, when Symeon died Niketas forgot about him, turning to the collection and publication of his writings only a decade and a half later. Niketas's inclusion in the *Life* of a miracle story in which the deceased Symeon is witnessed offering advice to him about drafts of his work[17] also surely indicates the existence of suspicion about Niketas's part in the creation of the works attributed to Symeon.[18] Symeon was still a controversial figure decades after his death,[19] and during his lifetime opponents had raised doubts about his skill with words.[20] Important questions must thus still arise today concerning Niketas's actual role in the production of the entire corpus of Symeon's writing as it has survived. The real problem here is that Niketas not only wrote the *Life* but was also the editor of all of Symeon's surviving works.[21] Despite the willingness of some scholars to ignore or play down the issues this raises and thus to believe that Symeon's "own" writings may be distinguished from and even treated as more reliable than the *Life*,[22] it remains true that our present image of Symeon comes entirely through the more or less active filter of Niketas's editorial and authorial work.[23]

It is thus important to remember that the present *Life* is carefully constructed hagiography, not academic biography, and that in it the reader may be learning almost as much about Niketas as about Symeon. Indeed, more than eighty years ago, Hausherr drew attention to the way in which

Niketas constructed here a careful and skillful work of apologetic, indeed polemic, designed to demonstrate Symeon's sanctity.[24] Niketas, in other words, wrote to convince the skeptic or, perhaps more realistically, to sustain the faith of believers in the face of criticisms still being raised by those who remained unconvinced of Symeon's sanctity more than thirty years after his death.[25] In doing so he also drew on earlier hagiographic models that his original readers would have been expected to recognize.[26] Before taking too much at face value, the modern reader of the *Life* should thus always be ready to consider the issue of Niketas's control over the surviving record of Symeon and what effect this may have had.

Symeon's Life

The early chapters of the *Life* record that Symeon was born, probably in 949 CE, to an aristocratic family from the village of Galati in Paphlagonia, some 300 miles east of Constantinople in north-central Anatolia.[27] Symeon's grandparents were well connected at the imperial court, and his unnamed paternal uncle held an influential position there as chamberlain (κοιτωνίτης). As a young boy, Symeon, whose baptismal name was almost certainly George,[28] was sent to the capital by his parents to receive a suitable education.[29] It would seem that he enjoyed a privileged lifestyle and came to occupy a position of quite high rank and responsibility, suitable to someone of his background and age. If the *Life* is to be trusted, however, he resisted attempts by his uncle to introduce him directly into the inner imperial circle, and there are indications in his poetry that he always felt himself

to be something of a misfit.[30] Then, at some point while he was still a youth (perhaps when he was only fourteen, perhaps when he was twenty), his uncle came to a violent end, possibly in 963 or 969 during one of the changes of imperial regime.

Symeon now sought admission to the venerable Stoudios monastery in Constantinople, where his spiritual father, the notable ascetic Symeon Eulabes ("the Pious," also known as "the Stoudite"), resided.[31] At first the elder Symeon rejected his application to become a monk and Symeon remained in the secular world, where it appears he continued to manage the affairs of a prominent household and occupy a position in the administration which required regular attendance at court and travel on imperial business.[32] The *Life* states that he had abandoned his secular education after the primary level, while mastering shorthand and calligraphy, but now, under Symeon Eulabes's direction, he turned his attention to the study of spiritual works and the pursuit of an increasingly ascetic and contemplative mode of life. At this time Symeon experienced the first of the many ecstatic visions of divine light that would profoundly mark the course of his life and characterize his mystical legacy. But the elder Symeon continued to refuse his young disciple permission to enter the monastic life. For six more years Symeon was forced (or chose) to pursue his regular occupation while developing his ascetic spirituality in private until Symeon Eulabes yielded and Symeon was formally admitted to the monastery of Stoudios as a novice.[33]

Symeon entered the monastery, perhaps in 977 at the age of twenty-seven or twenty-eight and possibly in response to the political upheavals at the court in 976.[34] Although he

now experienced a second and perhaps defining vision of the divine light,[35] his stay at Stoudios was evidently brief. For a combination of reasons which seem to have included overly zealous ascetic conduct and excessive devotion to his spiritual father, as well as pressure exerted by his family, Symeon was soon expelled.[36] Symeon Eulabes now secured admission for him at the nearby monastery of Saint Mamas, where the younger Symeon was tonsured as a monk and for two years practiced and developed his asceticism and spirituality under the continuing direction of his spiritual father. At this point the superior of Saint Mamas died and Symeon, who was now about thirty-one, was elected in his place and ordained priest by the patriarch, probably in 980.[37]

If Niketas's account is to be believed, Symeon took what was essentially a dilapidated and spiritually run-down monastery and recreated it, physically and spiritually, according to his own vision of the true monastic life.[38] But not all his recruits, or those who remained from the previous regime, were happy with this new situation or with Symeon's style and message. Whatever the reason for the discontent,[39] things evidently became so strained that thirty of the brethren, probably a significant percentage, staged an open revolt, threatened Symeon with physical violence, and complained to the patriarch Sisinnios I (996–998).[40] Symeon did his best to smooth things over and continued as superior at Saint Mamas for about another decade, until, perhaps in 1005, he resigned his position, ostensibly to focus on his own contemplative regime and inspired writing but perhaps as a result of growing opposition.[41]

Symeon Eulabes had died by this time, and Symeon was clearly determined that the memory of his spiritual father,

one challenged by others, should not be allowed to fade.[42] Symeon's literary compositions thus included hymns, encomia, and a *Life* of Symeon Eulabes, which were evidently intended for the lavish annual celebrations he began to organize at the monastery in his spiritual father's memory. He also commissioned an icon of the deceased holy man and venerated it.[43] However, for reasons that are now at least partially unclear, a senior adviser to the patriarch and former metropolitan of Nikomedia, the *synkellos* Stephen of Alexina, took exception to Symeon's activities and the implicit sanctification of his spiritual father, or at least used this as an excuse for going after Symeon.[44]

Stephen, whose career spanned at least the years between 976 and 1011, was widely regarded as one of the preeminent scholars of his day and was respected by some (though clearly not Niketas) for his virtue and even his sanctity.[45] He was a skilled theologian who is known to have written several theological and hagiographical works, but he was also an accomplished "astronomer,"[46] as well as a skilled diplomat "possessing the ability of calming rough and wild minds by persuasion."[47] As such he not only was a close associate of the patriarch but also was employed on occasion in challenging situations by the emperors John Tzimiskes and Basil II.[48] Stephen evidently pursued a number of avenues as he sought determinedly to discredit Symeon, including an awkward theological trap, which the latter skillfully dodged while further antagonizing his opponent.[49] In the end, however, after years of persistent attacks on Symeon Eulabes's reputation and on the younger Symeon's veneration of him, Stephen managed to engineer condemnation of the latter. Icons of Symeon Eulabes were destroyed while Symeon was

sentenced to exile, perhaps in 1009, and had his property confiscated.[50]

Stephen was, however, not the only one who possessed that all-important commodity in the Byzantine world, influence. Throughout his life Symeon had evidently enjoyed strong support from members of the aristocratic and court elite to which his family belonged, and now he rallied his powerful backers behind him. Pressure was put on the patriarch and the synod and Symeon was soon recalled, exonerated, and offered his old monastery back, as well as a bishopric and a seat on the synod.[51] He declined such distractions, however, and returned to the small monastic community, dedicated to Saint Marina, that he was in the process of founding at Chrysopolis across the Bosporus from Constantinople. There, despite some local opposition, he lived out the last decade or so of his life in relative peace, fully able to devote himself at last to his contemplation and writing. He could also once more foster the growing cult of Symeon Eulabes, although after his death his own cult seems to have eclipsed that of his mentor. He died on March 12, probably in 1022. Thirty years later, as Niketas recounts, in August 1052, his remains were translated in triumph to Constantinople.[52]

SYMEON'S CONTEXT

Symeon was perhaps fortunate that he lived through the seven decades, from the 960s to the 1020s, that in most ways represent the zenith of the medieval Byzantine Empire. At the time of his death in 1022, three years before that of Basil II, the empire directly controlled an expanse of ter-

ritory which embraced parts of southern Italy, almost the entire Balkans and Greece, the Aegean, Anatolia, and much of Syria; its sphere of political and cultural influence stretched even wider. Symeon's view of the world from within this ancient but still flourishing, sophisticated, and deeply cultured empire was thus very much one of Byzantine supremacy. Here the traditional triumphalist understanding that the Christian God was supporting and guiding His people in His empire (while occasionally testing their faith and punishing their wrongdoings through setbacks and dissension) could be maintained without serious challenge.

One aspect of the Byzantine resurgence was especially important in the present context: the establishment of effective control over the islands, coasts, and waters of the northeastern Mediterranean and the Aegean in the 960s largely put an end to the Arab piracy which had made those areas dangerous and had had a crippling effect on the regional economy. In consequence the later tenth and early eleventh centuries witnessed a spurt of monastic foundations. Most obvious and long-lasting was the development of Mount Athos from 963, but across the Byzantine world relative security and an increase in disposable wealth fueled similar patterns of monastic restoration and development. Symeon's experience at Saint Mamas of rehabilitating a relatively dilapidated monastic house and at Saint Marina of founding a new one, both apparently with substantial financial support from wealthy and powerful supporters, typifies what was going on in many other places during these decades.

Such growth, however, also brought questions about what constituted the ideal or even an appropriate monastic way of life. During Symeon's lifetime and in the subsequent cen-

tury, monastic founders and leaders attempted to improve and regularize the running of their establishments. Debate remains as to how unified they were in their goals, how widespread or connected their attempts, how much their efforts owed to spiritual or more mundanely economic considerations, and whether such activity, collectively or individually, can ever usefully be described as a "reform." But what is clear is that such attempts at improvement often met with stubborn resistance, just as Symeon's did at Saint Mamas and in the world beyond.[53]

The quite rapid expansion of monasticism in this period also raised political and economic concerns and difficulties. Imperial and provincial administrators lost tax revenues and jurisdiction over considerable tracts of land, while at the other end of the social spectrum the growth of monastic estates threatened to squeeze out villagers and small-scale landowners.[54] It is in this context that the verbal and physical abuse Symeon received at Saint Marina is likely best understood.[55] The vivid image of a disgruntled neighbor lobbing a rock through Symeon's window, within inches of his head, provides a healthy reminder that he and the many others like him across the Byzantine world, who came subsequently to be revered as monastic founders and even gained a reputation for sanctity, tended to be figures of considerable ambivalence in their own day.[56]

SYMEON'S WRITINGS AND FLUCTUATING REPUTATION

In the *Life,* Niketas describes how, inspired by the Holy Spirit, Symeon felt an irresistible compulsion to write.[57] His output was prolific, and thanks to Niketas, the great majority has survived, filling more than eight substantial volumes

in modern editions. His principal works consist of his *Catechetical, Theological,* and *Ethical Discourses,* his *Hymns,* and his *Theological, Gnostic, and Practical Chapters.* Most, if not all, appear to have been intended primarily for use in the monastic church context and are thus relatively brief or are divided into a number of shorter subsections. After his death, and despite Symeon's apparent hopes and Niketas's efforts,[58] his works did not enjoy great popularity,[59] and knowledge of them remained largely confined to a monastic readership. Nevertheless, Symeon's ideas had considerable, if sporadic, influence across the later Orthodox world, most notably on the Hesychast movement prior to and during the fourteenth century.[60]

That Symeon did not gain more widespread popularity may certainly be ascribed to the controversy that surrounded him during his life and persisting doubts about his orthodoxy. It is thus notable that in the seventeenth century, the Bollandists refused to publish *The Life of Symeon* in the *Acta sanctorum* on the suspicion that he was a heretic.[61] At the end of the eighteenth century a Modern Greek version was published as part of the substantial collection of Symeon's works assembled by the Athonite monk Dionysios of Zagora,[62] but it was not until 1928 that the original Greek text of the *Life* was finally published in full by Irénée Hausherr and made available to a wider audience through Gabriel Horn's French translation.[63] More recently, in 1994, Symeon Koutsas published a new edition with a Modern Greek translation.[64] The publication history of Symeon's own writings is very similar, with critical editions and translations appearing only in the 1960s and early 1970s.

Since then, however, Symeon not only has become well known to academics but is widely venerated, with an ever-

spreading cult in the Orthodox Church.[65] Indeed, such has been the reverence for Symeon's visionary spirituality over the past thirty years that there seems to be some danger that nuanced scholarly judgment of him may be overwhelmed by the tide of faith. Even doubts perhaps implicit in the name "the *New* Theologian," by which Symeon is now generally known, appear to be in danger of being forgotten.[66]

This should remind the reader of the present volume that Niketas's goal was to compose a work of hagiography, not biography. It was a work written about a controversial subject and in a distinctly polemical and apologetic tone, by a man who devoted much of his life to having Symeon recognized as a divinely inspired holy man. While on one level it may thus provide a rich source of interest to those seeking enlightenment about one of the great spiritual fathers of the Orthodox Church, it may at the same time also afford, for the academic, not only fascinating and lively glimpses of the social and religious history of this important period in Byzantine history, but also some sharp insight into the complex and often distinctly murky process by which orthodoxy was negotiated in the Byzantine world.

NOTE ON THE TRANSLATION

The present translation of *The Life of Saint Symeon the New Theologian* is the first in English, although a few short passages have appeared in a number of works on Symeon and in various collections.[67] The original version of the *Life* has to this point been available to those unable to read Greek or Slavonic only in the parallel French translation of Gabriel Horn which accompanied Hausherr's text.[68] As early as 1790, Dionysios of Zagora published a paraphrased transla-

tion in Modern Greek at Venice (with a second edition published at Syros in 1886); this was reproduced in a number of nineteenth-century collections. Koutsas's edition also includes an excellent Modern Greek translation. My aim in the present translation is to make the *Life* available to both a general and a specialist audience in clear, readable, contemporary English that will stand the test of time. While colloquialisms have thus been avoided and I have attempted to remain faithful to the Greek, I have steered away from an overliteral adherence to its constructions, and hence an archaic English style, by breaking up long sentences, for example, and using names more frequently than in the original. I have created English titles at the beginning of each new section to help orient the reader. Direct quotations from the Bible and Church fathers are italicized in both Greek text and English translation; biblical citations are referenced in the Greek text, patristic citations in the Notes to the Translation. Passages which clearly reflect biblical language but do not quote directly are not italicized, but are referenced in the Greek text.

This volume would not have been possible without the encouragement and very real help of a number of people. My first debt is to Alice-Mary Talbot, the series editor, who not only suggested that I undertake the project in the first place but has been the source of innumerable corrections and helpful suggestions during every aspect of its preparation. I am likewise indebted to Derek Krueger for carefully reading the translation, proposing numerous improvements, and providing many helpful references. While remaining errors and infelicities are, of course, my own, without the benefit

of their great and generously shared erudition this would be a far less accomplished piece of work. In practical terms I would like to thank Noah Mlotek for his skillful assistance with preparation of the electronic Greek text. My own scholarship will always be illuminated by that of Philip Sherrard and Donald Nicol, and my thanks are also due to John Smith at Christ's Hospital, who not only managed to teach me some Greek but first took me to the land itself. Above all, however, I need to thank, first, Anne Foley, my wife, not only for her careful reading of the drafts and her help on many occasions in finding the right word, but for her patient endurance in listening for years to my ramblings about Symeon, Niketas, Lazaros, and many others far distant in time and place from the ancient Argolid; and second, my daughters, Justine and Emilienne, who have always filled my world with light. To them this volume is dedicated.

R. P. H. G.
Kingston, Ontario
February 2012

NOTES

1 Darrouzès, *Nicétas,* 8. Hausherr, *Vie,* xxiii, suggests 1000.

2 *Life of Symeon,* Chaps. 131–33 (hereafter cited by chapter number).

3 Chaps. 133–35, 140.

4 *On the Practice of the Virtues, On the Inner Nature of Things and on the Purification of the Intellect,* and *On Spiritual Knowledge, Love, and the Perfection of Living, Patrologia Graeca* 120.851ff; *The Philokalia,* trans. G. E. H. Palmer, P. Sherrard, and K. Ware, vol. 4 (London, 1995), 76–174.

5 The trilogy *On the Soul, On Paradise,* and *On the Angelic and Ecclesiastical Hierarchy,* Darrouzès, *Nicétas,* 56–365; *On the Limits of Life,* ibid., 366–411; *Against the Jews,* ibid., 412–43; *On the Girdles of Stoudite Deacons,* ibid., 9, 13, 486–95 (cf. also Krausmüller, "Stoudios and St. Mamas," 69–70); and the

unpublished *Against the Armenians*. Although his words do not survive, Niketas also took the emperor Constantine IX Monomachos publicly to task for his moral conduct; see I. Thurn, ed., *John Skylitzes, Synopsis Historion* (Berlin, 1973), 21.7 (interpolation), 434; *John Skylitzes. A Synopsis of Byzantine History, 811–1057*, trans. J. Wortley (Cambridge, 2010), 409.

6 On the latter see Krausmüller, "Private vs. Communal." He is also known to have written some other pieces that did not survive, including his early works on Symeon and a longer version of the *Life;* see Chaps. 113, 150. On his work in general, see Darrouzès, *Nicétas,* 11–14 and Koutsas, *Life,* 20–22. For discussion of his theology and spirituality, see Darrouzès, *Nicétas,* 25–39; also Hausherr, *Vie,* xxv–xxxvii.

7 A. Michel, *Humbert und Kerullarios, Quellen und Studien zum Schisma des XI. Jahrhunderts,* vol. 2 (Paderborn, 1930), 322–42.

8 Skylitzes; see above, n. 5.

9 Darrouzès, *Nicétas,* 10, 444; cf. Krausmuller, "Private vs. Communal," 309–10.

10 Hausherr, *Vie,* xvi–xxiii; cf. also Koutsas, *Life,* 19.

11 Chaps. 116–27.

12 Hausherr, *Vie,* lvii–lxvii. Cf. Krivochéine's comments, *Catechetical Discourses,* vol. 1, 16, and Alfeyev's development of them, *St. Symeon,* 27–28; also Koutsas, *Life,* 30–32. Hausherr discusses at some length Niketas's compositional process in regard to Symeon's written response to Stephen's tricky theological question (see below), which is preserved in two different versions as *Hymn* 21; see also Koder, *Hymns,* vol. 1, 47–50.

13 Chaps. 131–33.

14 Chap. 130; γνήσιον μαθητὴν, Chap. 149.

15 Chaps. 132–33.

16 Hausherr, *Vie,* lvi–lvii. There appears to be no basis for the assertion that Niketas frequently visited Symeon; see Krivochéine, *Light of Christ,* 61; cf. also Koutsas, *Life,* 16.

17 Chap. 150.

18 Cf. here Krivochéine's comments on this episode, *Catechetical Discourses,* 60–61.

19 Chap. 140.

20 Chaps. 74–78.

21 So, for example, the well-known passages concerning "George" in *Catechetical Discourses,* 22.

22 So Alfeyev, *St. Symeon*, 28; McGuckin, "Symeon the New Theologian," 27 (cf. 19 n. 4); 17–18, cf. 31–32.

23 See Marc Lauxtermann, review of A. Markopooulos, ed., "*Τέσσερα κείμενα για την ποίηση του Συμεών του Νέου Θεολόγου*," *Byzantina Symmeikta* 19 (2009): 292, commenting on Koder, "Ο Συμεών ο Νέος."

24 Hausherr, *Vie*, xxi, lxvii.

25 Cf. McGuckin, "Symeon the New Theologian," 17. In contrast Koutsas, *Life*, 24, suggests that we could not have a better biographer for Symeon than Niketas.

26 For example, Niketas clearly had the model of the life of Theodore the Stoudite in mind: Koder, "Ο Συμεών ο Νέος," 4–6.

27 Although its outlines are clear, establishing the precise chronology of Symeon's life is fraught with difficulties and has been the subject of some debate. See, e.g., Hausherr, *Vie*, lxxx–xci; Krivochéine, *Light of Christ*, 55–58; Koutsas, *Life*, 33–37; McGuckin, "Symeon the New Theologian," 17–32; Turner, *Spiritual Fatherhood*, 16–36; Alfeyev, *St. Symeon*, 27–42. The alternative dating first proposed by Panagiotes Chrestou, Νικήτα Στηθάτου μυστικὰ συγγράμματα (Thessalonica, 1957), has been widely criticized.

28 See above, n. 21.

29 McGuckin, "Symeon the New Theologian," 18, dates this to 960. On his education see Turner, *Spiritual Fatherhood*, 37–39.

30 Koder, "Ο Συμεών ο Νέος," 3; compare McGuckin, "Symeon the New Theologian," 18.

31 Cf. McGuckin, "Symeon the New Theologian," 19. Further on Symeon Eulabes, see Alfeyev, *St. Symeon*, 19–27, 102–15; cf. Hausherr, *Vie*, xxxviii–li. His *Ascetical Discourses* are edited by Hilarion Alfeyev and Louis Neyrand, *Syméon le Studite, Discours ascétiques*, SC 460 (Paris, 2001).

32 *Catechetical Discourses*, 22; chap. 6. Cf. McGuckin, "Symeon the New Theologian," 19; Turner, *Spiritual Fatherhood*, 24–27.

33 Chaps. 6–11.

34 Hausherr, *Vie*, lxi, lxxxvii; McGuckin, "Symeon the New Theologian," 22–23.

35 So McGuckin, "Symeon the New Theologian," 20–22.

36 Chaps. 16–17, 21; Hausherr, *Vie*, lxxxxvii; Turner, *Spiritual Fatherhood*, 30–31; cf. McGuckin, "Symeon the New Theologian," 24.

37 Chaps. 29–30. There are issues with the dating at this point. Cf. McGuckin, "Symeon the New Theologian," 24–25.

38 Chaps. 34–35. Cf. the interpretation of McGuckin, "Symeon the New Theologian," 26. On the monastery's subsequent history, see R. Janin, *La géographie ecclésiastique de l'empire byzantin, 1: Le siège de Constantinople et le patriarcat oecuménique, 3: Les églises et les monastères,* 2nd ed. (Paris, 1969), 314–19.

39 See here McGuckin, "Symeon the New Theologian," 27, 33; cf. Krausmüller, "Stoudios and St. Mamas," 85.

40 Chaps. 38–39. For a rather different interpretation, see McGuckin, "Symeon the New Theologian," 28. On factionalism, see *Catechetical Discourses* 4, ll.247–83, 334–38, and also Krausmüller, "Stoudios and St. Mamas," 72–73.

41 Chap. 59. Koder, "Ο Συμεών ο Νέος," 6, suggests his resignation was connected with his condemnation by the synod, as does McGuckin, "Symeon the New Theologian," 30.

42 For a brief discussion of the issues, see Alfeyev, *St. Symeon,* 21–27.

43 Chap. 72.

44 Hausherr discusses this at length, *Vie,* lxvii–lxxx. See also Alfeyev, *St. Symeon,* 39 n. 131; McGuckin, "Symeon the New Theologian," 29.

45 Hausherr, *Vie,* lii, and in general on Stephen, li–lvi. See further Dirk Krausmüller, "Religious Instruction for Laypeople in Byzantium: Stephen of Nicomedia, Nicephorus Ouranos, and the Pseudo-Athanasian *Syntagma ad quendam politicum," Byzantion* 77 (2007): 239–50.

46 Leo the Deacon, *Leonis Diaconi Caloënsis historiae libri decem,* ed. C. B. Hase (CSHB Bonn, 1828), 169; Alice-Mary Talbot and Denis Sullivan, trans., *The History of Leo the Deacon: Byzantine Military Expansion in the Tenth Century* (Washington, D.C., 2005), 211–12.

47 Skylitzes, *Synopsis* (as in n. 5), 317; Skylitzes, trans. (as in n. 5), 301–2.

48 See the two previous notes.

49 Chaps. 75–77 and Hymn 21, *Hymns,* vol. 2, 130–69; cf. vol. 1, 47–50, and Hausherr, *Vie,* lxiii–lxvii. For the long-term importance of this document, see McGuckin, "Symeon the New Theologian," 29. On its theology, see Alfeyev, *St. Symeon,* 151–54.

50 Chaps. 87–99.

51 Chaps. 100–104.

52 Chap. 129.

53 See above and McGuckin, "Symeon the New Theologian," 32–35.

54 As, for example, Basil II's *Novel* of 996 clearly suggests. For an Eng-

lish translation of the relevant paragraph, see P. Charanis, "The Monastic Properties and the State in the Byzantine Empire," *Dumbarton Oaks Papers* 4 (1948): 63–64.

55 Chaps. 110, 112, 123–24.

56 See, for example, Richard Greenfield, "Shaky Foundations: Opposition, Conflict and Subterfuge in the Creation of the Holy Mountain of Galesion," in Peter Soustal, ed., *Heilige Berge und Wüsten: Byzanz und sein Umfeld* (Vienna, 2009), 25–40.

57 Chap. 131; cf. 111.

58 Chap. 132.

59 Symeon is, for example, absent from the *Synagoge* of Paul of Evergetis: John Wortley, "The Model and Form of the *Synagoge*," in M. Mullett and A. Kirby, eds., *Work and Worship at the Theotokos Evergetis 1050–1200* (Belfast, 1997), 166–77; Joseph Munitiz, "Writing for the Heart, the Spiritual Literature of Byzantium," in Paul Stephenson, ed., *The Byzantine World* (London, 2010), 250, 254.

60 Hausherr, *Vie,* xi–xii. For Symeon's influence in Russia and on later Orthodoxy, see Alfeyev, *St. Symeon,* 276–83.

61 Hausherr, *Vie,* vii.

62 See Hausherr, *Vie,* ii; Alfeyev, *St. Symeon,* 281. This version was translated into Russian and Romanian in the nineteenth century; see Hausherr, *Vie,* vi.

63 Hausherr, *Vie;* on earlier publication projects that never came to fruition, see ix.

64 Symeon Koutsas, Άγιος Συμεών ο Νέος Θεολόγος (Nea Smyrne, 1994).

65 Alfeyev, *St. Symeon,* 286.

66 Alfeyev, *St. Symeon,* 1. Note that he appears in the *Oxford Dictionary of Byzantium,* ed. A. Kazhdan et al. (New York, 1991), s.v., only as Symeon the Theologian. For further summary of the discussion, see Turner, *Spiritual Fatherhood,* 36 n. A. In contrast, cf., e.g., the introductory note on Symeon in the English translation of the *Philokalia,* 12–13, and numerous official Orthodox websites.

67 So Alfeyev, *St. Symeon;* Krivochéine, *Light of Christ;* Deno J. Geanakoplos, *Byzantium, Church, Society, and Civilization Seen through Contemporary Eyes* (Chicago, 1984), 182.

68 For the Slavonic translation, made in the early nineteenth century, see Alfeyev, *St. Symeon,* 283.

THE LIFE OF
SAINT SYMEON
THE NEW THEOLOGIAN

Βίος καὶ πολιτεία τοῦ ἐν ἁγίοις πατρὸς ἡμῶν Συμεὼν τοῦ νέου Θεολόγου, πρεσβυτέρου καὶ ἡγουμένου μονῆς τοῦ ἁγίου Μάμαντος τῆς Ξηροκέρκου. Εὐλόγησον πάτερ.

I

Χρῆμα θερμὸν ἀρετή, καὶ δεινὸν μὲν ἐμφυσῆσαι τοῦ πόθου τοὺς ἄνθρακας καὶ πῦρ αὐτόχρημα τὴν ψυχὴν ἀπεργάσασθαι, δεινὸν δὲ πτερῶσαι νοῦν ἀπὸ γῆς καὶ πρὸς οὐρανοὺς ἐπᾶραι τῷ Πνεύματι καὶ Θεὸν ὅλον ἀποδεῖξαι τὸν ἄνθρωπον. Ἐπεὶ οὖν καὶ Συμεὼν οὗτος ὁ μέγας ὁ νῦν εἰς ὑπόθεσιν ἡμῖν προτεθείς, ταύτης ἐργαστὴς[1] θερμότατος γεγονώς, εἰς περιφανὲς ὕψος τῆς κατ' αὐτὴν δόξης εἴπερ τις ἄλλος ἀνέδραμε, φέρε διηγητέον πᾶσι τοῖς παροῦσι τὰ ἐκείνου σαλά, ὅσα τε αὐτῷ ἐκ γένους καὶ πατρίδος ὑπῆρχε πλεονεκτήματα, καὶ ὅσα ἐκεῖνος ἱδρῶσι καὶ πόνοις ἀσκητικοῖς καὶ τοῖς ὑπὲρ ἀρετῆς ἄθλοις καὶ ἀγωνίσμασιν ἐκτήσατο κατορθώματα.

2

The life and conduct of our father among the saints Symeon the new theologian, elder and superior of the monastery of Saint Mamas Xerokerkos. Bless me, Father.

1. Introduction; Symeon's Early Life

Chapter 1

Virtue is an ardent thing, able to breathe upon the embers of desire and immediately set the soul on fire, able also to give the mind wings to soar with the Spirit from earth to heaven and to make man wholly God. Since this great man Symeon, who forms the subject of our present narrative, was a most ardent practitioner of virtue and, more than anyone else, rose to the pinnacle of fame on account of it, his merits should certainly be described to everyone here: the advantages that accrued to him from his birth and his homeland, and the success he achieved by his ascetic efforts and labors and by his struggles and contests for virtue.

2

Οὗτος² Συμεὼν ὁ τὴν ἀρετὴν περιβόητος ἔφυ μὲν ἐκ χώρας τῆς Παφλαγόνων ὡς εὐθαλές τι καὶ καρποφόρον φυτόν, βρῖθον τοῖς καρποῖς ἐξ ἁπαλῶν ὀνύχων τοῦ Πνεύματος [cf. Gal 5:22]. Ἔσχε δὲ πατρίδα κώμην τὴν οὕτω κατ᾽ ἐγχωρίους καλουμένην Γαλάτην, τοὺς δέ γε φύντας ἐξ εὐγενῶν καὶ πλουσίων, Βασίλειος δ᾽ ἦσαν καὶ Θεοφανώ, οἳ παρωνύμως καὶ Γαλάτωνες ὠνομάζοντο. Ἐπειδὴ δὲ ἁπαλὸς ὢν ἔτι τὴν ἡλικίαν τῇ Κωνσταντίνου παρὰ τῶν γεννητόρων ὡς χρῆμά τι διακομίζεται πολλοῦ ἄξιον, καὶ αὐτοῖς ἀνασῴζεται τοῖς προγόνοις ἐνδόξοις οὖσι τηνικαῦτα ἐν βασιλείοις, γραμματιστῇ παραδίδοται καὶ τὴν προπαιδείαν ἐκδιδάσκεται. Συνετὸς δὲ ὢν καὶ γέμων φρονήσεως ἐκ νεότητος, εἶχε μὲν σπουδαίως πρὸς τὰ μαθήματα, τάχει δὲ φύσεως τὴν ἐκεῖθεν ὠφέλειαν εὐφυῶς τε καὶ λογικῶς ἀνελέγετο, εἰ δέ τι παιδαριῶδες καὶ ἄσεμνον ἐν τοῖς παισὶν ἑώρα πραττόμενον, συστέλλων ἑαυτὸν ἅτε δὴ τὴν φρόνησιν πολιός, καὶ τὸν νοῦν ὅλον ἐπιστρέφων πρὸς τὰ μαθήματα μακρὰν τῶν ἀφρονούντων ἐγίνετο.

2   Ἤδη δὲ τῆς τελεωτέρας ἁπτόμενος ἡλικίας καὶ τῶν τελεωτέρων ἥπτετο θερμότερον³ μαθημάτων, ὅθεν καὶ κάλλιστα τὰ τῶν ταχυγράφων ἐν βραχεῖ τῷ χρόνῳ κατωρθωκὼς ὡραῖα γράφειν λίαν μεμάθηκεν, ὡς τὰ ὑπ᾽ ἐκείνου γραφέντα βιβλία πιστοῦται σαφῶς τὸ λεγόμενον. Ἐλείπετο δὲ αὐτῷ ἐξελληνισθῆναι τὴν γλῶτταν τῇ ἀναλήψει παιδείας τῆς θύραθεν καὶ λόγου εὐμοιρῆσαι ῥητορικοῦ.

Chapter 2

Symeon, this man so renowned for his virtue, was born in the region of Paphlagonia and, like some flourishing and fruitful plant, was laden from childhood with *the fruits of the Spirit*. His home was a village called Galati by the local inhabitants. His parents, who were of noble and rich stock, were Basil and Theophano, known by the surname Galatones. While still at a tender age, he was taken to Constantinople by his parents, like some precious object, and entrusted to his grandparents who were at that time well known at the imperial court. He was also handed over to a schoolteacher and taught the elementary curriculum. Because he was intelligent and full of good sense from his youth, he was eager for his lessons and, with his natural quickness, cleverly and logically derived benefit from them. But if he saw the other children doing something childish and inappropriate, he would draw back, as though he were already an old man in terms of his good sense, and turn his mind wholly to his lessons, distancing himself from those who were acting foolishly.

When he had reached a more advanced age, he reached 2 more ardently for more advanced lessons, and so, after he had successfully mastered shorthand in a very short time, he learned calligraphy, as the books copied by him clearly prove. He never hellenized his speech by assimilating secular learning, however, nor mastered rhetoric. Rather, since

Ἀλλὰ τοῦτο μὲν ἐκ παιδὸς ὁ ἀνὴρ πολὺς τὴν σύνεσιν ὢν καὶ τὸν μῶμον ἐκφεύγων εἰ καὶ μὴ καθόλου ὅμως οὐχ εἴλετο, ἄκροις δὲ ψαύσας δακτύλοις τῆς ἐκεῖθεν ὠφελείας καὶ μόνην μεμαθηκὼς τὴν οὕτω λεγομένην γραμματικήν, τὸ λοιπὸν ἢ καὶ τὸ πᾶν ὡς εἰπεῖν τῆς ἔξωθεν ἀπεσείσατο παιδείας, καὶ τὴν ἐκ τῶν συμφοιτητῶν βλάβην ἐξέφυγεν.

3

Ὁ τοίνυν πρὸς πατρὸς αὐτοῦ θεῖος ὡς ἑώρα κάλλει σώματος καὶ ὡραιότητι τῶν πολλῶν αὐτὸν διαφέροντα, ἐπεὶ πολλὴ παρρησία εἰς τοὺς τότε τὰ σκῆπτρα τῆς βασιλείας κατέχοντας ἦν αὐτῷ (Βασίλειος δ' ἦσαν καὶ Κωνσταντῖνος οἱ ἐκ τῆς πορφύρας ὁμόστεφοι καὶ αὐτάδελφοι) τὰ τῶν κοιτωνιτῶν διαπρέποντι, σκέπτεται τῷ αὐτοκράτορι αὐτὸν δοῦναι καὶ οἰκειώσασθαι. Ἀλλ' ἐπεὶ θρήνοις ἐκεῖνος τὸ τοῦ θείου ἀπεκρούσατο βούλημα, τοῖς κρατοῦσι τότε μὴ βουληθεὶς γνώριμος καταστῆναι, ἵνα μὴ ζημιωθῇ Θεὸν ἐν τῷ κερδαίνειν τὰ μηδενὸς ἄξια, μόλις πείθεται παρ' αὐτοῦ τῇ τοῦ σπαθαροκουβικουλαρίου τιμῇ διαπρέψαι καὶ εἰς τῆς συγκλήτου γενέσθαι βουλῆς.

2   Ἀλλ' ὅρα μοι τὴν ἀληθινὴν εὐγένειαν, πῶς οὐ κρατεῖται δεσμοῖς καὶ δουλείᾳ πραγμάτων βιωτικῶν ἢ τοῖς λαμπροῖς ἥττηται τοῦ βίου τούτου καὶ ἐπιζήλοις! ὡς γὰρ ὁ μὲν ἔσπευδε λαμπρὸν ἀποδεῖξαι[4] τὸν ἄνδρα διὰ τῆς ῥεούσης

Symeon was very intelligent from his boyhood, he fled this <learning> and its defilement and, even if he did not totally avoid it, only brushed with his fingertips what was beneficial in it. Thus, when he had completed what is known as primary education, he avoided what remained, or rather the entirety of secular education, and fled the harmful influence of his schoolfellows.

Chapter 3

Symeon's paternal uncle occupied the distinguished position of a chamberlain,[1] and thus had considerable access to those who held imperial power at that time (they were Basil and Constantine, the brothers who had been born in the purple and now shared the crown).[2] When his uncle saw that Symeon stood out from others in his physical beauty and handsomeness, he planned to present him to the emperor and introduce him into his circle. But after Symeon had sorrowfully rejected his uncle's plan (not wanting to become an intimate of the current rulers, so that he might not lose God in gaining things of no value), he was reluctantly persuaded by him to accept the distinguished rank of *spatharokoubikoularios*[3] and become a member of the senate.[4]

But let me demonstrate for you how true nobility is not 2 bound by the chains and servitude of worldly affairs, nor is it overcome by the splendors and ambitions of this life! His uncle thus strove to make Symeon a man resplendent

7

δόξης, ὁ δὲ τὸ μὲν σοφῶς ἀπεκρούσατο τὸ δὲ πρὸς καιρὸν οἰκονομικῶς κατεδέξατο καὶ τὸ μέλλον ἐκαραδόκει, αἴφνης[5] ὁ περιφανὴς ἐκεῖνος ἀνὴρ ἐξαισίῳ θανάτῳ τῆς παρούσης ζωῆς ἐκβάλλεται. Ἁρπάζει οὖν ὁ Συμεὼν τὸν καιρὸν καὶ *πάντα καταλιπὼν* [Lk 5:28] φεύγει κόσμον καὶ τὰ ἐν κόσμῳ εὐθὺς καὶ προστρέχει Θεῷ· οὕτω[6] πᾶσα ψυχὴ τρωθεῖσα τῶν οὐρανίων τοῖς κάλλεσι καὶ τῆς ἐκεῖθεν δό-ξης ἐν ἐπιθυμίᾳ γενομένη, καὶ τῆς λαμπρότητος τῆς τῶν ὁρωμένων ἀπάτης εὐκόλως καταφρονεῖ, καὶ ὅλη τῶν ἐκεῖ-θεν ἐλπίδων καὶ ἀπολαύσεων γίνεται, τὰς νοερὰς ἑαυτῆς αἰσθήσεις τῷ ἡδεῖ τῶν νοουμένων καθ᾽ ἑκάστην γλυκαινο-μένη καὶ ζητοῦσα τελεώτερον[7] τοῦ ποθουμένου τυχεῖν.

4

Γίνεται τοιγαροῦν ἐπὶ τὴν περιώνυμον τοῦ Στουδίου μο-νήν. Ζητεῖ τὸν ἐκ νεότητος αὐτοῦ χρηματίσαντα πατέρα πνευματικὸν καὶ διδάσκαλον· ὁ δὲ ἦν Συμεὼν ὁ μέγας τὴν ἀρετὴν καὶ τὴν ἄκραν ἀπάθειαν εἴπερ τις ἄλλος κατωρθω-κώς, ᾧ καὶ τὴν εὐλάβειαν ἡ πρὸς Θεὸν εὐσέβεια καὶ σε-μνοτάτη καταστολὴ[8] τῶν ἠθῶν παρωνύμως προσέθετο. Ὑπαντᾶται αὐτῷ, γνωρίζει τὰ τοῦ σκοποῦ, ἀξιοῖ δεχθῆναι παρ᾽ αὐτοῦ καὶ τὸν βίον ἐξ αὐτῆς[9] ἀλλάξασθαι καὶ συγκα-ταταγῆναι τοῖς μοναχοῖς. Ὁ δέ, οἷα δὴ ἔμπειρος τοῦ μονα-

8

through transitory glory, while Symeon on the one hand wisely rejected this but on the other conditionally accepted it for the time being as he waited for what was to come. But when that illustrious man was suddenly cast from the present life by a violent death, Symeon seized this opportunity and thus, *leaving everything* behind, immediately fled the world and worldly things and hastened toward God. In this way, every soul that is smitten by the beauties of heaven and comes to desire its glory also readily despises the splendid delusion of visible things. Such a soul becomes entirely focused upon heavenly hopes and joys and, with its noetic perceptions being sweetened each day by the pleasure of spiritual thoughts, it seeks more perfectly to gain that which it desires.

Chapter 4

So Symeon arrived at the famous monastery of Stoudios,[5] and sought out the man who had been his spiritual father and teacher from his youth. This was the great Symeon, who, more than anyone else, had achieved virtue and attained the very summit of dispassion. His piety toward God and most reverent sobriety gave him the surname "the pious [Eulabes]." Symeon met with him, let him know his objective, and asked to be received by him so that he might immediately change his way of life and join the ranks of the

δικοῦ βίου καὶ τῶν τοῦ Πονηροῦ ἐπιθέσεων, τό γε νῦν
ἔχον οὐ κατανεύει, ἀναχαιτίζει δὲ τοῦτον ἔτι νέον ὄντα καὶ
τὸν τεσσαρεσκαιδέκατον ἄρτι[10] χρόνον τῆς ἡλικίας ἀνύο-
ντα τῆς τοιαύτης ὁρμῆς, καὶ τὸν τῆς τελεωτέρας αὐξήσεως
ἐκδέξασθαι ὑποτίθεται χρόνον.

2   Ἐπεὶ δὲ διάγων ἦν ἐκεῖνος ἐκ νέου τῷ τοῦ θείου οἴκῳ
τὴν φλόγα ὑποτυφομένην ἔχων τοῦ θείου[11] πόθου, πρὸς
τοῖς ἄλλοις ἐπεμέλετο προσευχῆς σπουδαίως ἄγαν καὶ
ἀναγνώσεως. Ὅθεν καί ποτε βίβλον λαβὼν ἐκ τῶν τοῦ
διδασκάλου χειρῶν Μάρκου καὶ Διαδόχου τῶν θεσπεσίων
ἀνδρῶν καὶ ἀναπτύξας αὐτήν, εὗρεν εὐθὺς λέγουσαν διὰ
τῶν γεγραμμένων αὐτῷ· Ζητῶν ὠφέλειαν ἐπιμέλησαι τῆς
συνειδήσεως καὶ ὅσα λέγει ποίησον καὶ εὑρήσεις ὠφέλειαν. Τοῦτο τοίνυν οἷα δὴ ἐκ στόματος ἀκούσας Θεοῦ,
ἐπιμελεῖσθαι τῆς ἑαυτοῦ συνειδήσεως ἤρξατο· ἡ δὲ θεῖόν
τι ἐν ἀνθρώποις πρᾶγμα ὑπάρχουσα καθ᾽ ἑκάστην αὐτῷ ἐν
θέρμῃ τοῦ Πνεύματος ὑπετίθει τὰ κρείττονα καὶ τὴν ἐπί-
δοσιν ηὔξανε τοῦ καλοῦ, ὡς ἐντεῦθεν ἐπαυξηθῆναι αὐτῷ
τὰ τῆς προσευχῆς καὶ μελέτης μέχρις ἀλεκτρυόνων ᾠδῆς.[12]
Εἶχε καὶ γὰρ τὴν δίαιταν συνεργοῦσαν αὐτῷ ἐκ μόνων τῶν
ἀναγκαίων εἰς τὴν τῆς προσευχῆς καὶ ἀναγνώσεως παρά-
τασιν, καὶ πρὸ τῆς ἀποταγῆς τὸν τῶν ἀσωμάτων ἐν σώματι
καὶ τούτῳ[13] τρυφερῷ καὶ νεάζοντι βίον ἠσπάζετο. Ἔνθεν
τοι οὐδὲ περιόδων πολλῶν ἐτῶν ἐδεήθη εἰς τὸ παντελῶς
ἐκδημῆσαι τῶν ὁρωμένων καὶ ἐν τοῖς ἀοράτοις Θεοῦ γενέσθαι θεάμασι· μετὰ γὰρ ὀλίγου χρόνου παρέλευσιν ἡ
χάρις τοῦ Πνεύματος, εὑροῦσα τὴν ἐκείνου ψυχὴν ἐλευθέ-
ραν τῆς ὕλης καὶ τῷ πόθῳ πυρπολουμένην τοῦ Κτίσαντος,

monks. But Symeon Eulabes, who was experienced in the monastic life and the deceptions of the Evil One, did not assent for the present. Instead he restrained Symeon from such an impulsive step because he was still young and had only just reached fourteen years of age, and suggested that he should wait until he was more mature.

But since the flame of divine desire had smoldered secretly within Symeon since boyhood while he was living in his uncle's house, he devoted himself eagerly to prayer and reading, as well as other pursuits. On one occasion, then, when he received from the hands of his teacher a book by those divinely inspired men Mark and Diadochos, he opened it and at once came across the following passage: *When you are looking for help, examine your conscience, and if you do what it says, you will find it.*[6] He heard this as though it came from the mouth of God, and so began to examine his conscience. And each day this conscience, which is something divine in human beings, suggested to him in his spiritual fervor what was best, and increased his progress in what was good, so that in consequence he prolonged his prayers and studies until cockcrow. For his mode of life, which he had restricted to the bare necessities, enabled him to prolong his prayer and reading, and even before his renunciation of the world he embraced the life of the incorporeal <angels>, even though he was young and his body delicate. He thus did not need the passage of many years to depart completely from what is visible and arrive at the invisible contemplation of God. For after a short time passed, the grace of the Spirit, finding his soul free of matter and inflamed with desire for the Creator, *caught him up* from earth on the wings of desire for intellectual

ἥρπασεν αὐτὴν ἀπὸ γῆς πτερώσασα τῇ τῶν νοητῶν ἐπιθυμίᾳ καὶ πρὸς ὀπτασίαν καὶ ἀποκαλύψεις Κυρίου [cf. 2 Cor 12:1–4] ἀνύψωσε.

5

Τοίνυν καὶ ὡς ἱστάμενος ἦν εἰς προσευχὴν ἐν μιᾷ τῶν νυκτῶν καὶ νοῒ καθαρῷ τῷ Πρώτῳ συναπτόμενος Νῷ, φῶς ἄνωθεν εἶδε λάμψαν ἐξαίφνης ἐξ οὐρανῶν ἐπ’ αὐτὸν εἰλικρινές τε καὶ ἄπλετον τὸ πᾶν τε καταφωτίσαν καὶ καθαρὰν ὥσπερ ἡμέραν ἀπεργασάμενον, ὑφ’ οὗ δηλαδὴ καὶ αὐτὸς φωτιζόμενος ἐδόκει τὸν οἶκον ἅπαντα σὺν τῇ κέλλῃ ἐν ᾗ ἱστάμενος ἔτυχεν ἀφανισθέντα καὶ εἰς τὸ μὴ ὂν εὐθέως χωρήσαντα, ἑαυτὸν δὲ ἁρπαγέντα [2 Cor 12:2; cf. 1 Th 4:17] ἐν τῷ ἀέρι καὶ τοῦ σώματος ὅλως ἐπιλαθόμενον. Οὕτως οὖν ἔχων χαρᾶς, ὡς ἔλεγεν οἷς τὰ τοιαῦτα ἐθάρρει καὶ ἔγραφε, τηνικαῦτα πολλῆς ἐπληρώθη καὶ δακρύων θερμῶν· καὶ τὸ ξένον τοῦ τεραστίου ἅτε τῶν τοιούτων ἀποκαλύψεων ἔτι ἀμύητος καταπλαγεὶς φωναῖς ἀπαύστοις τὸ "Κύριε ἐλέησον" μεγάλως ἐβόα, ὡς ἐν ἑαυτῷ γενόμενος ὕστερον ἔγνω· τότε γὰρ οὐκ ᾔδει ὅλως ὅτι φωνῇ φθέγγεται ἢ ἔξωθεν ἡ λαλιὰ αὐτοῦ ἐξακούεται. Ἐν γοῦν τῷ τοιούτῳ φωτὶ ἐνεργούμενος εἶδε, καὶ ἰδοὺ εἶδος φωτεινοτάτης νεφέλης [cf. Mt 17:5] ἀμόρφου τε καὶ ἀσχηματίστου καὶ πλήρους ἀρρήτου δόξης Θεοῦ εἰς τὸ ὕψος τοῦ οὐρανοῦ,

12

apprehension and exalted him to the *vision and revelations of the Lord.*

Chapter 5

While he was standing in prayer one night, with his own pure intellect communing with the Prime Intellect, he suddenly saw a pure and immense light shining on him from the heavens above, illuminating everything and making it bright as day. He too was illuminated by it, and it seemed that the whole building, along with the cell in which he was standing, vanished and all at once dissolved into nothingness, but he himself was *caught up* into the air and completely forgot about his body. When this happened to him, as he said and wrote to his confidants in such matters, he was filled with great joy and shed warm tears. He was astounded by the strangeness of this marvel because he was still uninitiated in such revelations, and began shouting out continuously, "Lord, have mercy,"[7] although he only realized this later when he came to himself; for at the time he was completely unaware that he was speaking aloud or that his words could be heard outside his cell. While he was in the midst of this light, then, he looked, and behold, in the vault of heaven there was a kind of very *bright cloud* without any form or shape and full of the ineffable glory of God. And—oh, what

ἐκ δεξιῶν δὲ τῆς τοιαύτης νεφέλης ἱστάμενον ἑώρα τὸν
ἑαυτοῦ πατέρα Συμεώνην τὸν Εὐλαβῆ—ὢ τοῦ φρικτοῦ
ὁράματος!—ἐν τῇ συνήθει ταύτῃ στολῇ ἣν περιέκειτο ζῶν,
ἐνατενίζοντά τε ἀκλινῶς τῷ θείῳ ἐκείνῳ φωτὶ καὶ αὐτοῦ
ἀπερισπάστως δεόμενον. Ἐπὶ πολὺ οὖν οὕτως ἐν ἐκστάσει
ὢν καὶ τὸν αὐτοῦ πατέρα ἐκ δεξιῶν παρεστῶτα τῆς δόξης
ὁρῶν τοῦ Θεοῦ [cf. Act 7:55–56], οὐκ αἰσθάνετο κἄν τε ἐν
σώματι τὸ τηνικαῦτα ἦν κἄν τε ἐκτὸς τοῦ σώματος [cf. 2 Cor
12:2–3], ὡς διεβεβαιοῦτο καὶ ἔλεγεν ὕστερον. Ὀψὲ δέ ποτε
τοῦ φωτὸς ἐκείνου κατὰ βραχὺ[14] συσταλέντος πρὸς ἑαυτό,[15] πάλιν ἐν τῷ σώματι καὶ τῆς κέλλης ἐντὸς ἑαυτὸν κατ-
ενόησε, καὶ οὕτω τὴν μὲν καρδίαν ἑαυτοῦ πεπληρωμένην
εὗρεν ἀφάτου χαρᾶς, τὸ δὲ στόμα μεγάλα κρᾶζον ὡς εἴρηται τὸ "Κύριε ἐλέησον," καὶ ὅλον κατάβροχον ἑαυτὸν τοῖς
ὑπὲρ μέλι [Ps 118(119):103] καὶ κηρίον γλυκυτέροις δάκρυσιν. Ἐκ δὴ τούτου λεπτὸν καὶ κοῦφον οἷάπερ πνευματικὸν
τὸ σῶμα αὐτοῦ γενόμενον ᾔσθετο, καὶ ἐπὶ πολὺν χρόνον
οὕτω διετέλεσεν ἄν. Τοιοῦτον ἡ καθαρότης καὶ τοσοῦτον
ὁ θεῖος ἔρως ἐν τοῖς σπουδαίοις ἔργον ἐργάζεται!

6

Τ αύτην οὖν ὡς ἑώρακε τὴν θεωρίαν ὁ θαυμάσιος Συμεών, ἐπυρπολεῖτο τὰ ἔνδον ἔτι πλέον ὑπὸ τοῦ θείου πυρὸς
καὶ τοῦ ἀποκεῖραι αὐτὸν παρακαλῶν τὸν πατέρα προσ-
έκειτο. Ἐκεῖνος δὲ προβλεπτικῷ τῷ ὄμματι ἐπιτήδειον

an awesome sight!—to the right of this cloud he saw his own spiritual father, Symeon Eulabes, standing in the usual clothes which he wore in life, gazing unwaveringly at that divine light and praying continually. Being in this state of ecstasy for a long time and seeing his own spiritual father *standing at the right hand* of the glory *of God,* as he later affirmed and said, he could not tell whether he was *in his body* at that time or *out of his body.* Sometime later the light gradually faded and he came back to himself in his body and in his cell. He found his heart was full of unspeakable joy, his mouth was loudly calling out "Lord, have mercy," as has been said, and he was soaked with tears that were *sweeter than honey* and honeycomb. From then on he had the feeling that his body had become light and airy as though it were imbued with the Spirit and this lasted for a long time. Such is the effect that purity and divine love produce in those who are good![8]

Chapter 6

After the wondrous Symeon had seen this vision, he was even more inflamed by the divine fire within him, and he pleaded with his spiritual father, pressing him to tonsure him. But that man, *foreseeing* the appropriate time *with his*

καιρὸν προορῶν, ἀλλὰ καὶ τὸ ἁπαλὸν τῆς νεότητος ἀβέβαιον εἶναι πρὸς τὸ τραχὺ τῆς ἀσκήσεως, τοῦτο ποιεῖν τηνικαῦτα οὐκ ἔκρινε. Ἐπεὶ οὖν μετὰ περίοδον ἓξ ἐτῶν τῆς φοβερᾶς θεωρίας ἐκείνης πρὸς τὴν ἰδίαν πατρίδα ὁ Συμεὼν δι' αἰτίαν τινὰ ἔσπευδεν ἀπελθεῖν, συντάξασθαι παραγίνεται τῷ θείῳ τούτῳ¹⁶ πατρὶ ἐν τῇ περιωνύμῳ τοῦ Στουδίου μονῇ. Ὁ δὲ θαυμάσιος ἐκεῖνος ὡς εἶδεν αὐτόν· "Καιρὸς ἰδού, τέκνον," ἔφη, "καθ' ὃν εἰ βούλει τὸ σχῆμα καὶ τὸν βίον ἀλλάξασθαι δεῖ." Ἄνθραξ πυρὸς [cf. Ez 1:13, 10:2] ὁ λόγος εἰς τὴν καρδίαν τοῦ νέου ἐγένετο, καί· "Ἵνα τί μὴ τάχιον," ἔφη, "τοῦτο πρὸς ἐμὲ τὸ τέκνον σου εἴρηκας, πάτερ; Ἀλλά γε καὶ νῦν ἤδη κόσμῳ καὶ τοῖς ἐν αὐτῷ πᾶσιν ἀποτάσσομαι [cf. Lk 14:33], καὶ ἐπεὶ τῇ προφάσει τῆς ἐγχειρισθείσης μοι βασιλικῆς δουλείας ἀπαίρειν ἤδη πρὸς τὴν ἰδίαν πατρίδα ἐπείγομαι, ἰδοὺ πάντα τὰ ἐκεῖσε προσόντα μοι ἀναλαβόμενος ὑποστρέφω καὶ εἰς χεῖρας πάντα καὶ ὅλον ἐμαυτὸν παραθήσομαι τῆς σῆς ἁγιότητος."

2   Εἶπε καὶ τῆς ἐκεῖσε φερούσης ἁψάμενος πρὸς τὰ οἰκεῖα διὰ τάχους ἐγίνετο. Ἐπεὶ δὲ τὸ τηνικαῦτα ὁ καιρὸς ἐπέστη τῶν νηστειῶν, ὅλον ἐξέδοτο ἑαυτὸν πρὸς τοὺς ὑπὲρ ἀρετῆς¹⁷ ἀγῶνας. Ἔνθεν τοι καὶ τὴν ἐκ προγόνων ἐρευνήσας βιβλιοθήκην λαμβάνει τὴν Κλίμακα τοῦ θεσπεσίου Ἰωάννου ἐκεῖθεν, ᾗ καὶ προσομιλῶν ὡς γῆ τις ἀγαθὴ τὸν σπόρον τοῦ λόγου ἐν τῇ καρδίᾳ ἐδέχετο καὶ αὐξάνειν ὁσημέραι καὶ καρποφορεῖν ἑαυτὸν παρεσκεύαζε [cf. Lk 8:5–15]. Τοίνυν καὶ ἐπεὶ σμικρότατον ἦν κελλίον πρὸς τῇ εἰσόδῳ τοῦ ἐκεῖσε εὐκτηρίου, μονώτατος εἰσελθὼν ἔμενεν ἐν αὐτῷ· ὅθεν καὶ νυκτὸς μὲν τὰς θύρας ἑαυτῷ κλείων τοῦ

prophetic eyes,[9] and also judging that, because of Symeon's tender years, he was still too unsteady for the harsh life of asceticism, decided not to do so at that time. But then, six years after that awesome vision, when Symeon was getting ready to travel to his homeland for some reason, he came to say goodbye to this holy father in the famous monastery of Stoudios. As soon as that wondrous man saw him, he said, "See, my child! The time has come for you to change your garb and your way of life, if you so wish." His words became a *fiery coal* in the young man's heart and he said, "My father, why didn't you say this earlier to me, your spiritual child? I'll renounce the world and everything in it right now. But look, since I'm already in a hurry to leave for my homeland on this imperial mission that I've been assigned, when I've retrieved all my possessions there, I'll come back and place everything, including myself, into the hands of your holiness."

With these words Symeon set off on his journey and 2 swiftly reached his home. Since it was Lent at that time, he gave himself over entirely to his struggles for virtue. While he was there he searched through his family library and took out the *Ladder* of the divine John.[10] He studied this and, like some *good soil,* received *the seed of the word in his heart* and prepared himself day by day to grow and *bear fruit.* And since there was a tiny room by the entrance to the chapel there, he used to go into it and remain in complete solitude. At night he would close the doors of the chapel[11] and pray for

εὐκτηρίου ἐπὶ τρισὶν ὥραις προσεύχετο [cf. Mt 6:6; 4 Kings 4:33; Is 26:20], ἡμέρας δὲ ποτὲ μὲν ηὔχετο *ἐν τῷ κρυπτῷ τῷ οὐρανίῳ Πατρί* [Mt 6:6], ποτὲ δὲ προσωμίλει τῇ θείᾳ γραφῇ. Τὰς γοῦν ὑπερφυεῖς ἀνδραγαθίας τῶν ἐν ὑπακοῇ διαπρεψάντων ἁγίων ἀκούων καὶ τὴν ἐγγινομένην προκοπὴν τοῖς θερμῶς μετερχομένοις αὐτὴν ἐπεπόθει καὶ αὐτὸς τὸν ἴσον ἐκείνοις θέσθαι ἀγῶνα. Διὸ καὶ τῇ εἰρημένῃ βίβλῳ προσομιλῶν εὗρεν ἐπὶ λέξεως οὕτως ἔχουσαν· *Ἀναισθησία ἐστὶ νέκρωσις ψυχῆς καὶ θάνατος νοὸς πρὸ θανάτου σώματος.* Τοῦτο ὡς ἀνέγνω τὸ ῥῆμα ὁ Συμεὼν τὴν θεραπείαν ἐν τῇ τοιαύτῃ βίβλῳ ζητήσας καὶ εὑρών, προσηύχετο ἐν σοροῖς ἀγρυπνῶν, εἰκόνα νεκρῶν ζωγραφῶν ἐν τῇ καρδίᾳ αὐτοῦ καὶ ὅλον τὸν κατ᾽ αὐτῆς ἤρετο πόλεμον, νηστείᾳ μὲν εὐτονωτέρᾳ χρησάμενος καὶ ἀγρυπνίᾳ, μνήμῃ δὲ θανάτου καὶ κρίσεως ἀδολεσχῶν.

7

Οὕτω τοιγαροῦν ποιοῦντος αὐτοῦ, ἐν μιᾷ προσευχομένου νυκτὸς ἔνδον τοῦ εὐκτηρίου ἐν ᾧ καὶ σορὸς ἦν σωμάτων νεκρῶν,[18] τῶν θυρῶν κεκλεισμένων οὐσῶν κατὰ τὸ σύνηθες, συρρεύσαντα μετὰ ἀπειλῆς πλήθη δαιμόνων ὥρμησαν κατὰ τοῦ εὐκτηρίου, καὶ ἀθρόον τὰς θύρας ὠθήσαντες, ἤνοιξαν τοῦ ἁρπάσαι αὐτόν, τοιοῦτον ψόφον ἀπεργασάμενοι ὡς νομίσαι αὐτὸν πρὸς τοὺς ἐξ ἑκατέρου

three hours, while in the daytime he would sometimes pray *in secret to his* heavenly *Father,* sometimes study the holy scripture. When he heard about the extraordinary acts of valor of the saints who were distinguished by their obedience and about the progress made by those who fervently pursue this, he too longed to engage in the same contest as they. And then, while he was studying the aforementioned book, he found this sentence there: *Insensitivity is the demise of the soul and the death of the intellect before the death of the body.*[12] When he read this saying, Symeon found the treatment that he sought in that book, and he began praying among tombs while he kept vigil, painting an image of the dead upon his heart. He also began an all-out war against this insensitivity, engaging in more rigorous fasting and vigils and meditating on the remembrance of death and the judgment to come.

Chapter 7

One night, while he was doing this, he was praying inside the chapel in which there was also a tomb full of dead bodies. Although the doors were closed as usual, a menacing crowd of demons ganged up and rushed toward the chapel.[13] Pushing on the doors all together, they burst them open so as to grab Symeon, and made such a crash that he thought the doors had been smashed as they were slammed against

τοίχους προσαραχθείσας[19] συντριβῆναι τὰς θύρας. Ὁ δὲ
φόβῳ μεγάλῳ [Lk 8:37] ληφθεὶς διαπετάσας τὰς χεῖρας εἰς
οὐρανὸν [cf. 3 Kings 8:22; 2 Chr 6:13] τὴν θείαν ἐκεῖθεν ἐπε-
καλεῖτο βοήθειαν [cf. Jdt 6:21; Lam 3:57]. Ὡς οὖν εἶδον
αὐτὸν τὰ τῆς πονηρίας πνεύματα [cf. Eph 6:12] οὕτως
ἀμετακίνητον ἐπὶ ἱκανὰς ὥρας ἱστάμενον, ἡττηθέντα ὑπ-
ανεχώρησαν. Ἀλλὰ τῷ πολλῷ τανυσμῷ[20] αἱ χεῖρες ἐκείνου
ἀποξηρανθεῖσαι οὐκ ἐκάμπτοντο, μόλις δὲ μετ' ὀδύνης
πολλῆς συστείλας αὐτὰς καὶ κεκλεισμένας τὰς θύρας ἰδὼν
ἐθαύμασεν.

2   Ἔκτοτε τοίνυν πλείονα προσλαβόμενος ἀνδρείαν κατὰ
δαιμόνων εἰς οὐδὲν τὴν ἔφοδον αὐτῶν ἔθετο, πληροφο-
ρίαν λαβὼν ὡς οὐδεμίαν ἔχουσιν ἰσχὺν καθ' ἡμῶν, εἰ μὴ
ἐγκαταλειφθῶμεν ὑπὸ Θεοῦ. Οὕτως οὖν ἔχων καὶ οὕτω
ποιῶν πάσης ἀπείχετο μερίμνης βιωτικῆς, μόνης δὲ τῆς
προσευχῆς καὶ τῆς ἀναγνώσεως ἐπεμέλετο, εἴ που δὲ ὑπὸ
ἀκηδίας ἠνωχλήθη, πρὸς τοὺς ἐν οἷς ὑπῆρχον μνήματα
τόπους ἀπήρχετο, καὶ καθήμενος ἐπάνω αὐτῶν τοὺς ὑπὸ
γῆν νεκροὺς νοερῶς ἀνιστόρει, καὶ ποτὲ μὲν ἐπένθει, ποτὲ
δὲ θρηνώδεις ἐν δάκρυσιν ἡφίει φωνάς, διὰ πάντων τούτων καὶ τῶν τοιούτων τὸ κάλυμμα τῆς ἀναισθησίας[21] μη-
χανώμενος περιᾶραι τῆς καρδίας αὐτοῦ. Τοιοῦτος ἦν ἐκ
προοιμίων ὁ ἀγὼν τοῦ θαυμαστοῦ Συμεὼν καὶ τοιαύτη ἡ
ἐκείνου ἐργασία ἔτι τελοῦντος ἐν λαϊκοῖς. Ἀμέλει καὶ ἐπὶ
τοσοῦτον ἡ τοῦ Θεοῦ χάρις ἐνήργησεν εἰς αὐτόν, ὅτι καθάπερ ἐγγεγραμμένη τις εἰκὼν ἐν τοίχῳ οὕτως ἡ θέα τῶν
νεκρῶν ἐκείνων σωμάτων ἐν τῷ νοΐ ἐνετυπώθη αὐτοῦ. Οὐ
μὴν ἀλλὰ[22] καὶ πᾶσαι αἱ αἰσθήσεις αὐτοῦ ἠλλοιώθησαν, ὡς

the walls on either side. He was seized *with great fear* and *stretched up his hands to heaven* and *called for* divine *help* from there. When those *spirits of wickedness* saw him standing motionless like that for hours, they went away defeated, but he could not bend his arms, which had become stiff from being stretched out for so long. However, when he had lowered them with much difficulty and pain, he was astounded to see that the doors were shut.

From then on he plucked up more courage against the demons and paid no attention to their assaults, being assured that they have no power against us unless we are abandoned by God. And so, while all this was happening and he was doing this, he separated himself from all worldly cares and engaged only in prayer and reading. If he was ever troubled by spiritual boredom, he used to go off to places where there were tombs and, sitting on them, would picture in his mind the dead beneath the ground. Sometimes he would mourn, and sometimes he would utter tearful cries of grief, but in such ways he constantly contrived to strip away the veil of insensitivity from his heart. This was how the wondrous Symeon undertook the struggle from the beginning, and this was the sort of activity in which he engaged while he was still a layman. And indeed, the grace of God worked in him to such an extent that the sight of those dead bodies was imprinted on his mind as though it were an image painted on a wall. Not only that, but all his senses were also

2

ἐντεῦθεν βλέπειν αὐτὸν παντὸς ἀνθρώπου πρόσωπον καὶ
πᾶν κάλλος ὡραῖον καὶ πᾶν κινούμενον ζῷον ἐν ἀληθείᾳ
νεκρόν.

8

Ἐπεὶ δὲ καὶ ὁ καιρὸς τῆς πρὸς τὴν μεγαλόπολιν αὐτοῦ
ἀποδημίας ἐνειστήκει καὶ σπεύδοντα τοῦτον ὁ γεγεννη-
κὼς ἑώρα καὶ τὰ πρὸς τὴν ὁδὸν παρασκευαζόμενον, ὡς
οὐκ ἴσχυσε τοῦτον τοῦ κατὰ Θεὸν ἀνακόψαι σκοποῦ, πάντα λίθον ἐπὶ τούτῳ κινήσας, λαμβάνει κατ᾽ ἰδίαν αὐτὸν καὶ
οὕτω μετὰ δακρύων παρακαλεῖν ἤρξατο· "Μὴ ἐάσῃς με,
τέκνον, παρακαλῶ ἐν τῷ γήρει μου· ἰδοὺ γὰρ ὡς ὁρᾷς τὸ
τέλος τῶν ἡμερῶν μου ἐγγύς, καὶ ὁ καιρὸς οὐ μακρὰν τῆς
ἐμῆς ἀναλύσεως [2 Tim 4:6]· ὅτε οὖν ἐν τῷ τάφῳ καλύψεις
τὸ σῶμά μου, τότε βάδιζε ἔνθα ἂν βούλῃ καὶ πορεύου ὁδὸν
ἣν ἂν ἐθέλῃς· τὰ νῦν δὲ μὴ ἐπιπολὺ τῷ χωρισμῷ σου
λυπῆσαί με θελήσῃς· οἶδας γὰρ ὅτι σε μόνον βακτηρίαν
τοῦ γήρους μου καὶ τῆς ἐμῆς ψυχῆς παραμύθιον κέκτημαι·
ὅθεν καὶ τὴν σὴν στέρησιν θάνατον οἰκεῖον λογίζομαι."
Ταῦτα καὶ τούτων πλείονα ἔλεγεν ὁ πατὴρ λιβάδας κατα-
φέρων δακρύων. Ὁ δέ γε υἱὸς ὡς ὑπερβὰς ἤδη τῆς φύσεως
τοὺς θεσμοὺς καὶ τὸν οὐράνιον Πατέρα ἀντὶ τοῦ ἐπιγείου
προτιμησάμενος· "Ἀδύνατόν μοι," ἔφη, "τὸ παραμεῖναι τοῦ
λοιποῦ ὑπάρχει τῷ βίῳ, πάτερ, κἂν πρὸς βραχὺν χρόνον,

transformed so that from that time on he used to see every human face, every beauty, and every living thing as actually being dead.

Chapter 8

Then the time came for Symeon's departure for the capital. His father was powerless to deter him from his divine intention, despite leaving no stone unturned, but when he saw that Symeon was eagerly preparing for his journey he took him aside and began to plead tearfully with him. "My child, please don't leave me in my old age. The end of my days is near, as you see, and *the time of my passing* isn't far off. When you've buried my body in the grave, then you may go wherever you want and travel whatever road you wish. But for now you surely don't want this separation from you to grieve me so, when you know that you alone are the staff of my old age and the comfort for my soul; for I think that losing you will be the death of me." Symeon's father said these words and many more while he shed streams of tears. But his son, who had already transcended the bonds of nature and preferred the heavenly Father to his earthly one, said, "It's impossible for me to continue in this kind of life in the future, father, even for a short time, for we do not know

οὐ γὰρ οἴδαμεν *τί τέξεται ἡ ἐπιοῦσα* [Prov 3:28, 27:1], καὶ τὸ προτιμήσασθαι ἄλλο τι τῆς τοῦ Κυρίου δουλείας σφαλερὸν ἔμοιγε οὖν καὶ ἐπικίνδυνον."

9

Ταῦτα ἔφη, καὶ ἅμα πάσῃ τῇ ἐπιβαλλούσῃ αὐτῷ ἐκ γονέων περιουσίᾳ ἐγγράφως εὐθὺς ἀπετάξατο. Τοίνυν καὶ μόνα τὰ ἑαυτοῦ πράγματα, οἰκογενεῖς καὶ ὅσα ἐξ ἑτέρων πόρων αὐτῷ προσεγένοντο ἀναλαβόμενος καὶ ἐπιβὰς τοῦ ἵππου ἔφευγεν ἀκρατῶς ἐλαύνων ὥσπερ ὁ Λώτ, μὴ ἐπιστραφεὶς ὅλως *εἰς τὰ ὀπίσω* [Gen 19:17] πρὸς τοὺς θρήνους τῶν συγγενῶν ἢ τῆς καταπιστευθείσης αὐτῷ φροντίσας τοῦ δημοσίου δουλείας· οὕτω δριμύτερός ἐστι παντὸς ἄλλου πράγματος καὶ αὐτῆς ἅμα τῆς φυσικῆς πρὸς τοὺς τεκόντας στοργῆς ὁ διακαὴς ἔρως τοῦ οὐρανίου Πατρός· οὐδὲ γὰρ οἶδεν ἀνάγκης τινὸς φυσικῆς σχέσεως ἢ ἀνθρώπων ἡττᾶσθαί ποτε ἀπειλῆς, τὸ χεῖρον τοῦ κρείττονος ἐκνικήσαντος[23] καὶ τῆς παγκοσμίου αἰσθήσεως τὸν αὐτοκράτορα λογισμὸν ἀπορρήξαντος. Ἔνθεν τοι καὶ οὕτως ἔχων ὁ θαυμαστὸς Συμεὼν τοὺς μὲν παῖδας προάγειν ἐκέλευσεν, ἐκεῖνος δὲ ποτὲ μὲν ὑπομένων ὄπισθεν εἵπετο πενθῶν, ποτὲ δὲ τοσοῦτον προῆγεν αὐτοὺς ὅσον μὴ ἐξακούεσθαι τοὺς θρήνους αὐτοῦ. Διὸ καὶ ὀδυρμῶν μὲν τὰ ὄρη γοερῶν δὲ[24] φωνῶν τὰς νάπας πληρῶν τὸν εἰς Θεὸν

what tomorrow may bring. Thus to prefer something other than the service of the Lord would be perilous and dangerous for me."

Chapter 9

Symeon said this and at the same time renounced in writing with immediate effect all the property that would come to him from his parents. Then, taking with him only his own possessions, his personal servants, and whatever he had acquired from other income, he mounted his horse and galloped wildly away. Like Lot,[14] he never looked *back* toward the laments of his family, nor gave any thought to the public service that had been entrusted to him. Thus the searing, intense longing for the heavenly Father is fiercer than anything else, even than the natural affection for parents. For <this longing> knows no constraint from any natural relationship, nor is it ever thwarted by any human threat, since the better conquers the worse and frees the sovereign mind from the world of the senses. Because he was in this state then, the wondrous Symeon ordered his men to go on ahead. Sometimes he himself would hang back and follow behind them while he grieved, but sometimes he would go so far ahead of them that they could not hear his laments. And in this way, filling the mountains with his mournful lamentations and the valleys with his cries, he found some fulfill-

ἔρωτα παρεμυθεῖτο ποσῶς. Ἀλλὰ γὰρ οὕτως ἐν μιᾷ προ-
άγοντα καὶ κατὰ μέσον ὄρους γενόμενον περιαστράπτει
αὐτὸν δίκην πυρὸς αἴφνης ἡ χάρις τοῦ Πνεύματος ἄνωθεν
καθὰ δὴ καὶ Παῦλόν ποτε [cf. Act 9:3, 22:6], καὶ ὅλον
ἀρρήτου χαρᾶς καὶ γλυκύτητος ἔπλησεν, ἐπαυξήσασα τὴν
ἀγάπην αὐτῷ τοῦ Θεοῦ καὶ τὴν πίστιν εἰς τὸν πνευματικὸν πατέρα αὐτοῦ.

10

Οὕτω τοίνυν δι᾽ ἡμερῶν ὀκτὼ τὴν προκαθεζομένην
τῶν ἄλλων καταλαβὼν πόλεων, ὥσπερ διψῶσά τις ἔλαφος
ἐπὶ τὰς τῶν ὑδάτων τρέχει πηγάς [Ps 41(42):1], οὕτω πρὸς
τὸν θεῖον ἐκεῖνον γέροντα καὶ οὗτος σπεύσας ἀπέδραμε,
καὶ ὡς αὐτῷ προσέπεσε τῷ Δεσπότῃ Χριστῷ, πάντα προθεὶς τὰ ὑπάρχοντα αὐτῷ παρὰ τοὺς πόδας αὐτοῦ [cf. Act
4:34–35, 37]. Ὁ δὲ φιλοστοργότατος ἐκεῖνος τῷ ὄντι πατὴρ
τὴν εἰς βάθος ταπείνωσιν καὶ πίστιν αὐτοῦ θεασάμενος,
ἐλεύθερον μὲν τὸν μαθητὴν ἀπέδειξε τῆς ἐκείνων μερίμνης πάντα διασκορπίσας τοῖς πένησι [cf. Mt 19:21], μεθ᾽
ἑαυτοῦ δὲ τοῦτον λαβὼν εἰς τὸ μοναστήριον ἀπεδύσατο
πρὸς τοὺς ὑπὲρ αὐτοῦ πειρασμούς. Προῄδει γὰρ τῷ προβλεπτικῷ ὄμματι τὰ μέλλοντα συμβήσεσθαι αὐτῷ ὑπὲρ
τούτου κακά.

ment for his intense desire for God. One day, however, when he had gone on ahead and was somewhere in the mountains, the grace of the Spirit *suddenly flashed about* him like fire from above, just as it once did with Paul, and it filled him with indescribable joy and sweetness, increasing his love for God and his faith in his spiritual father.

Chapter 10

So Symeon reached the capital city in eight days. There, just as the thirsty *hart* runs to *flowing streams,* so he ran eagerly to that divine elder [Symeon Eulabes] and prostrated himself before him, as before Christ the Master, and laid *at his feet* everything he had. When the father, who really was a very loving man, saw the depth of Symeon's humility and faith, he freed his disciple from worry over these possessions by distributing everything to the poor, and then took him with him into the monastery. There Symeon Eulabes stripped himself for the trials <he would face> on the younger Symeon's behalf,[15] for *he had foreseen with his prophetic eyes*[16] the evils that were going to befall him on behalf of this man.

II

Τῇ οὖν ἐπαύριον λαβὼν τὸν γενναῖον προσφέρει τῷ προεστῶτι, Πέτρος δὲ ἦν ὁ τὸ μέγα τοῦτο ποίμνιον τῶν Στουδίου²⁵ τότε ἰθύνων, καὶ δύο καταβαλόμενος τῇ μονῇ λίτρας χρυσίου ἐνδύει τὸν σάκκον αὐτῷ τῆς γυμνασίας τῶν ἀρετῶν. Ἐπεὶ δὲ κελλίον οὐκ ἦν σχολάζον εἰς ξενίαν τότε τοῦ νέου, παρατίθεται αὐτὸν ὁ καθηγούμενος τῷ μεγάλῳ τούτῳ πατρί, οὕτω δεῖν κεκρικότων ἀμφοτέρων διὰ τὸ νέον τῆς ἡλικίας τοῦ Συμεών. Ὁ δὲ λαβὼν ὃν ἐξ ἁπαλῶν ὀνύχων τῇ διδασκαλίᾳ τοῦ λόγου ἐξέθρεψεν, ὑπὸ τὴν κλίμακα τῆς κέλλης αὐτοῦ δέδωκε καταμένειν αὐτὸν καὶ φιλοσοφεῖν ἐκεῖσε τὰ τῆς στενοτάτης ὁδοῦ [cf. Mt 7:13–14; Lk 13:23–24]· ὑπῆρχε γὰρ ταφοειδές τι κελλίον ἐν αὐτῇ, εἰς ὃ μετὰ στενοχωρίας πολλῆς εἰσδύνων ἐκάθευδεν. Ἅπτεται τοιγαροῦν ὁ μὲν τῶν ὑπὲρ ἀρετῆς τελεωτέρων πόνων, ὁ δὲ τῆς πρὸς αὐτὸν ἐντέχνου διδασκαλίας. Καί φησι πρὸς αὐτὸν ὁ πατήρ· "Βλέπε, τέκνον, εἰ βούλει σωθῆναι²⁶ καὶ τὰς ἐνέδρας διαδρᾶναι τοῦ Πονηροῦ, σεαυτῷ μόνῳ πρόσεχε καὶ μὴ προσομιλεῖν ἀκαίρως οὕτω τινὶ τῶν ἐνταῦθα ἐν ταῖς θείαις συνάξεσιν ἀνάσχῃ, μηδὲ ἀπὸ κέλλης εἰς κέλλαν εἰσέρχεσθαι, ἀλλὰ ξένος καὶ ἀπαρρησίαστος ἀπὸ παντὸς

2. Symeon's Monastic Life at Stoudios

Chapter 11

The next day Symeon Eulabes took the noble Symeon and presented him to the abbot Peter, who was directing the great flock of the monks of Stoudios at that time. He deposited two pounds of gold for the monastery and then dressed Symeon in the coarse tunic of training in the virtues.[17] There was no vacant cell to accommodate the young man at that time, and so the superior entrusted him to that great father [Symeon Eulabes], since both of them judged this necessary because of Symeon's youth. The father took Symeon, whom he had reared from infancy in the teaching of the word, and told him to stay under the stairs of his cell and reflect there upon the meaning of the most narrow way. For there was a sort of cell in it, like a tomb, and Symeon would squeeze into this with much difficulty and sleep there. And so, while he tackled the more advanced exercises in the pursuit of virtue, his spiritual father coached him in the necessary technique. The father said to him, "Look, my child, if you want to be saved and escape the ambushes of the Evil One, concentrate only on yourself.[18] Make sure you don't talk inappropriately to anyone here during the divine services, or go around from cell to cell, but rather remain aloof and don't get on familiar

ἀνθρώπου γενοῦ, τὰς ἁμαρτίας σου ἐννοῶν καὶ τὰς αἰωνί-
ους ἀναλογιζόμενος τιμωρίας, ἀμετεώριστον ἀεὶ τὸν νοῦν
διατήρει ἀπὸ τῶν ἔξωθεν, καὶ μεγάλην ταῦτα φυλάξας
εὑρήσεις ὠφέλειαν."

12

Ταῦτα ὡς ἐκ στόματος Θεοῦ ἀκούων ὁ Συμεὼν ἀπαρά-
τρωτα πάντα ἐφύλαττε. Πλείονας[27] δὲ τοὺς στεφάνους
αὐτῷ βουλόμενος προξενεῖν ὁ γυμνάζων πατήρ, τὰς ἐν τῷ
κελλίῳ αὐτοῦ εὐτελεστάτας διακονίας προσέταττε τούτῳ
ποιεῖν, ὁ δὲ ἅπαξ ἑαυτὸν δουλώσας[28] τῷ γέροντι πάντα
προθύμως ἐποίει δοῦλον ἑαυτὸν καὶ ξένον ἡγούμενος,
προπαρεσκευασμένος γὰρ ἦν ὡς κἂν ἐν καμίνῳ πυρὸς [cf.
Dn 3:6–26; Mt 13:42, 50] κἂν ἐν θαλάσσης βυθῷ ἑαυτὸν
ἐμβαλεῖν προστάξῃ, μετὰ χαρᾶς τοῦτο καὶ προθυμίας ποι-
ήσει. Ποιῶν οὖν πάσας τὰς[29] διακονίας καὶ σφόδρα κο-
πιῶν οὐδὲ νηστείας καὶ ἀγρυπνίας ἠμέλει, ἀλλ᾽ ὡς εἰδὼς
τὸ ἐκ τούτων ὠφέλιμον ἀκρατῶς ἐβάδιζεν ἐν αὐταῖς. Ὁ δὲ
γέρων ἐκκόπτειν θέλων τὸ ἐκείνου θέλημα τὰ ἐναντία
πολλάκις τούτῳ ποιεῖν προσέταττε καὶ τραπέζῃ χρῆσθαι
καὶ ὕπνῳ ἠνάγκαζεν, ὅπερ εἰ καὶ σφόδρα ἐλύπει τὸν Συμεώνην, ἀλλ᾽ ὅμως ἔφερε πολυτρόπως ἐγγυμναζόμενος,
σοφὸς γὰρ ὢν ὁ γέρων ἐκεῖνος ὁ θεῖος ποτὲ μὲν τὰ τῆς
ἀτιμίας καὶ τοῦ κόπου μεταχειρίζεσθαι τοῦτον ἐποίει, ποτὲ

terms with anyone. Reflect upon your sins, reckon up your eternal punishment, and always keep your mind free from external distractions. If you follow these instructions, you will find great benefit."

Chapter 12

Symeon listened to these instructions as though they came from the mouth of God and kept them all impeccably. The father, who was training him, would order him to do the most menial jobs in his cell because he wanted to procure more garlands for him, and Symeon, who had subjected himself to the elder once and for all, would do everything eagerly. For he regarded himself as a slave and a stranger, and even if he were ordered to cast himself into a *fiery furnace* or into the depths of the sea, he would have been prepared to do so joyfully and eagerly. Even though he was doing all these jobs and was exhausted, he did not neglect his fasts or vigils, but continued with them to the full, for he knew the benefit that came from them. The elder, however, because he wished to eradicate Symeon's will, would often order him to do the opposite of this and would force him to eat and to sleep. Even if this greatly saddened Symeon, he nevertheless put up with being trained in a variety of ways. For that divine elder was a wise man and would sometimes make him undertake demeaning and tiring tasks but at others would

δὲ τὴν τιμὴν καὶ τὴν ἄνεσιν οὗτος ἐκείνῳ προσέφερε, καὶ
ἀμφοτέρωθεν³⁰ μισθοὺς αὐτῷ προξενεῖ³¹ τῷ θελήματι ἀντι-
πίπτων αὐτοῦ.³²

2   Οὕτως οὖν ἐγγυμναζόμενος παρὰ τοῦ πατρὸς ὁ ἀνὴρ
καὶ οὕτω τὴν ἀρίστην πλάσιν μεταπλαττόμενος εἰς τοσοῦτον ηὔξησε τὴν πρὸς τὸν πατέρα πίστιν αὐτοῦ καὶ εὐλάβειαν, ὡς εὐλαβεῖσθαι πατεῖν καὶ τὴν γῆν ἐν ᾗ τοῦ πατρὸς
οἱ πόδες ἐβάδιζον· ὅθεν πάντα τόπον ἔνθα ἂν ἱστάμενον
καὶ προσευχόμενον αὐτὸν ἐθεώρει ὡς ἅγιον ἁγίων ὑπερε-
τίμα, καὶ πρὸς αὐτὸν πίπτων ἐκυλινδεῖτο καὶ κατεφίλει
αὐτόν, καὶ ταῖς χερσὶ τὰ τοῦ διδασκάλου δάκρυα ἐξ αὐτοῦ
ἀνεμάσσετο καὶ ὡς ἴαμα παθῶν τῇ ἑαυτοῦ κεφαλῇ καὶ τῇ
καρδίᾳ προσέφερε, προσψαῦσαι δέ τινος τῶν αὐτοῦ ἐνδυ-
μάτων ἀνάξιον ὅλως ἑαυτὸν ἐλογίζετο.

13

Ἐν τούτῳ οὖν ὁρῶν ὁ Ἐχθρὸς τῷ ὕψει ἀναδεδραμηκό-
τα τὸν Συμεώνην, ἔβρυχε τοὺς ὀδόντας αὐτοῦ κατ' αὐτοῦ
[Act 7:54] καὶ καθελεῖν αὐτὸν πολυτρόπως ἐπείρα. Ἀλλ' ὁ
πυρινὸς τῆς προσευχῆς στῦλος [Ex 13:21–22 inter al.] τοῦ
γέροντος σκέπη ἦν τῷ Συμεὼν κραταιά. Ἵνα δὲ ἡ δύναμις
ἐλεγχθῇ τῆς κακίας αὐτοῦ εἰς οὐδὲν ἰσχύουσα, συγχω-
ρεῖται μικρὸν προσβαλεῖν τῇ ἀσθενείᾳ τῷ Συμεών. Ἔνθεν
τοι καὶ πρῶτα διὰ τοῦ ὕπνου τούτῳ προσέρχεται, καὶ δὴ

offer him praise and relaxation, procuring rewards for him in both ways by thwarting his will.

As a result of being trained by the father in this way and thus being refashioned by the best coaching, Symeon developed such faith and reverence toward his father that he would avoid walking on the ground which his father's feet had trod; indeed, he would venerate as the holy of holies every place where he saw him stand and pray, and would prostrate himself and grovel upon it and kiss it. He would also wipe away his teacher's tears from it with his hands and would apply them to his own head and heart as a cure for ills. But he considered himself completely unworthy to touch any of his father's clothes.

Chapter 13

When the Enemy saw that Symeon had quickly attained this high level of conduct, he *ground his teeth against him* and tried to throw him down in many ways. But the *fiery column* of the elder's prayer was a strong protection for Symeon. In order to prove that the power of his evil had no strength, however, the Enemy was allowed to attack Symeon's weakness a little. And so he first set upon him with sleepiness and

ῥαθυμίαν ἐμβάλλει σκότωσίν τε τῇ κεφαλῇ καὶ βάρος ὅλῳ τούτου τῷ σώματι, ὡς δόξαι τὸν Συμεώνην ἀπὸ κεφαλῆς καὶ μέχρι ποδῶν σάκκον βαρὺν ἐνδεδύσθαι καὶ μήτε ἵστασθαι μήτε ἀνανεῦσαι μήτε μὴν τὸ στόμα δύνασθαι διανοῖξαι αὐτοῦ ἢ ἀκούειν ἐν ἐκκλησίᾳ τῶν ψαλλομένων. Γνοὺς οὖν ὁ γενναῖος τὴν τοῦ Ἐχθροῦ προσβολὴν ἀντιπαρατάσσεται διὰ καρτερίας αὐτῷ[33] καὶ τῶν ὅπλων τοῦ Πνεύματος, μὴ ἐνδοὺς ὅλως ἢ τοῦ τόπου οὗ ἵστατο μεταστάς. Τὴν καρτερίαν τοίνυν καὶ τὴν πολλὴν ἔνστασιν τοῦ Συμεὼν φέρειν μὴ δυνηθεὶς ὁ Ἐχθρὸς ἡττηθεὶς φεύγει τὴν πάλην τρόπῳ τοιῷδε·

2 Ἱσταμένου τοῦ Συμεὼν ἐν μιᾷ ἐν τῇ ἀρχῇ τῶν ἑωθινῶν ὕμνων, ἔδοξεν ἀπὸ τοῦ ἄκρου τῶν ποδῶν αὐτοῦ οἱονεὶ τοῦ σάκκου τὸ βάρος συστέλλεσθαι καὶ ἐπὶ τὰ ἄνω προσαποδύεσθαι.[34] Τὰ μὲν οὖν ὅθεν ἀφίστατο μέρη τοῦ σώματος ἐλεύθερα κατελίμπανεν, ἐφ᾽ ἃ δὲ συνωθεῖτο μεῖζον τὸ βάρος ἐποίει τοῦτον αἰσθάνεσθαι· εἶτα ὡσεὶ νέφος παχὺ ἐν πνεύματι βιαίῳ ἀπέστη πρὸς ἀέρα, καὶ τηνικαῦτα ὥσπερ κοῦφον καὶ λεπτότατον γενόμενον ἑαυτὸν ᾔσθετο ὁ γενναῖος καὶ ὅλον οἷα πνευματικόν. Χαρᾶς οὖν ἀφάτου πλησθεὶς ἐβόησε καὶ αὐτὸς μετὰ τοῦ Δαυίδ· "Διέρρηξας τὸν σάκκον μου, Κύριε, καὶ περιέζωσάς με εὐφροσύνην[35] [Ps 29 (30):11]." Ἄνωθεν οὖν ἔκτοτε δύναμιν λαβὼν ἐν ταῖς συνάξεσι πάσαις οὐδόλως ἐκάθητο, ἀλλὰ τὸν ἑαυτοῦ διδάσκαλον ἐκμιμούμενος διήνυε πάσας ἱστάμενος.

induced a feeling of lethargy and dizziness in his head and of heaviness throughout his body, so that Symeon felt as if he were dressed from head to foot in a heavy tunic and was unable to stand or look up or open his mouth or hear the singing in church. But the noble one realized this was an attack by the Enemy and held his ground through his steadfastness and the weapons of the Spirit, not giving in at all or being shifted from where he stood. Thus the Enemy could not bear Symeon's steadfastness and his stubborn resistance and he fled the wrestling match after being defeated in the following way:

One day, when Symeon was standing at the beginning of 2 the morning hymns, he felt as though the weight of his tunic were being drawn back from the top of his feet and stripped away upward. The parts of his body from which it was lifted were left free, but it made those where it was gathered together feel as though there were a heavier weight on them. Then, like a thick cloud in a stiff breeze, it lifted into the air, and the noble one felt himself become light and very airy and as though he were wholly spiritual. Filled with unutterable joy, he cried out like David, *"Thou hast loosed my tunic,* Lord, *and girded me with gladness."* From then on he received strength from above so that he never sat down during any of the services but, imitating his teacher, remained standing throughout.

14

Οὕτω τοίνυν τοῦ πονηροῦ τῆς ἀκηδίας[36] πνεύματος ἡττηθέντος, οἱ τῆς δειλίας δαίμονες νυκτὸς αὐτῷ ἐπανέστησαν, καὶ ὅτε μὲν ηὔχετο, τὴν κέλλαν ἐκεῖνοι κατέσειον, ψόφους ἀποτελοῦντες καὶ φοβερὰς φαντασίας, ὅτε δὲ πρὸς ὕπνον ἐτρέπετο, ὡς Αἰθίοπες αὐτῷ ἐπεφαίνοντο πῦρ ἀπὸ τῶν[37] ὀφθαλμῶν καὶ τῶν στομάτων αὐτῶν ἐκπέμποντες καὶ εἰς τὸ πρόσωπον αὐτοῦ ἀνθρακώδη ἐμπνέοντες καὶ ὅλην ὅμου τὴν κέλλαν πληροῦντες, ποτὲ δὲ καὶ μετὰ φλογερῶν ὅπλων ἐφαίνοντο ἀλαλάζοντες καὶ πυρινὸν τὸ ἔδαφος ἔνθα ἔκειτο καὶ τοὺς τοίχους ἀποτελοῦντες. Καὶ οἱ μὲν οὕτω τὰ συνήθη ἐποίουν, ὁ δὲ ἐφ' ἑκάστῃ προσβολῇ ἀνιστάμενος ηὔχετο, καὶ εὐθὺς εἰς φυγὴν ἐκεῖνοι ἐτρέποντο.

15

Εἶτα τί; ἐφ' ἑτέραν ἔρχονται πάλην οἱ μὴ ἠρεμεῖν εἰδότες ποτέ, καὶ τῶν ἄλλων ὡς κραταιότεροι οἱ τῆς πορνείας αὐτῷ ὑπεισέρχονται. Ἔνθεν τοι καὶ καθ' ἑκάστην νύκτα δεύτερον ἢ καὶ τρίτον αὐτῷ ταῖς φαντασίαις προσέβαλλον, ὥστε κἂν ἡδονῇ μίξεως τρῶσαι τὴν καρδίαν αὐτοῦ. Ὁ δὲ τοσαύτην κατὰ δαιμόνων ἔλαβε τὴν χάριν ἀπὸ Θεοῦ, ὥστε

Chapter 14

When the wicked spirit of spiritual boredom had been defeated in this way, the demons of cowardice rose up against Symeon at night. They would shake his cell when he was praying, producing loud noises and horrible apparitions,[19] and when he was falling asleep they would appear to him as Ethiopians, emitting fire from their eyes and mouths, breathing hot coals in his face and filling his entire cell. Sometimes, too, they would appear with blazing weapons, shouting war cries, and would make the walls and the ground where he lay seem fiery. But while they thus exhibited their usual behavior, he would get up at each attack and pray, and they would immediately turn and flee.

Chapter 15

Then what? Those demons, who never know how to keep still, came for another bout, and now the demons of fornication, who are stronger than the others, came upon Symeon unawares. In this way they would launch two or even three apparitions upon him every night in order to wound his heart with sexual pleasure. But he received such grace from God against the demons that even in his sleep it was as

καὶ ἐν τοῖς ὕπνοις αὐτοῖς ὡς ἐγρηγορὼς ὅλος διέκειτο καὶ πλεῖον μᾶλλον αὐτοῖς ἀντεμάχετο ἢ ὅτε ἔξυπνος ἦν.

16

Ὡς οὖν πάλιν καὶ ἐνταῦθα ἡττήθησαν, οὐκέτι μὲν αὐτῷ προσβαλεῖν[38] τοιούτῳ τρόπῳ ἐτόλμησαν, ἐκμαίνονται δὲ ἰταμῶς, καὶ τῷ ὅπλῳ τοῦ φθόνου τούς τε ἀμελεστέρους τῶν ἀδελφῶν καὶ αὐτὸν ὡς οὐκ ὤφελεν Πέτρον τὸν καθηγούμενον ὁπλίζουσι καὶ διεγείρουσι κατ' αὐτοῦ. Ἀλλ' ὁ γενναῖος πύκτης Χριστοῦ τὸν θώρακα καὶ τὴν περικεφαλαίαν τοῦ Πνεύματος περικείμενος [cf. Is 59:17; 1 Th 5:8; Eph 6:14–17], οὐδὲ πρὸς θέαν τινὸς ἢ ὁμιλίαν τῶν βασκαινόντων ἐπιστραφῆναι ἠνείχετο, ἔφευγε δὲ πάντας ἄλλους ἀνθρώπους ἀμίσως, καὶ ὡς νήπιον Χριστοῦ ἐν τελείῳ φρονήματι ἐν μόναις ταῖς πνευματικαῖς ἀγκάλαις τοῦ θείου πατρὸς ἐκείνου προστρέχων ἐπανεπαύετο, ᾧ καὶ τὰ τῆς ψυχῆς ἀνεκάλυπτε πάντα, καὶ καθοπλιζόμενος πρὸς μάχην ἐξήρχετο τῶν δαιμόνων.

2   Διὸ καὶ ἐν ταῖς θείαις συνάξεσιν οὕτως ἵστατο ὡς στήλη τις ἢ ἀνδριὰς ἄψυχος, ἀμετεωρίστους ἔχων τοὺς ὀφθαλμούς, ὅθεν καὶ δακρύων ἐξέφερε πηγὰς ἐξ αὐτῶν ὁσημέραι μηδενὸς τῶν ὁρώντων λόγον ποιούμενος. Οὕτω τοιγαροῦν ὁρῶντες αὐτὸν οἱ μοναχοὶ ἐν τοιαύτῃ καταστάσει διάγοντα, οἱ μὲν ἔχαιρον δοξάζοντες τὸν Θεόν, ὅσοι

though he were wide awake and he would fight back against them even more than when he was <actually> awake.

Chapter 16

As the demons were again defeated on this occasion, they no longer dared attack Symeon in this way. Instead, in their raving madness, they armed with the weapon of envy the more easygoing brothers and even Peter the superior (who ought not to have been vulnerable), and they stirred them up against him. But the noble boxer of Christ, clad in *the breastplate* and *helmet* of the Spirit, refused to have anything to do with the sight or the company of those who were jealous of him. Instead he avoided all other men (without hating them) and, being a child of Christ with a perfectly developed mind, went running into the spiritual arms of his holy father and came to rest there. He disclosed to him everything in his soul and, thus armed, went out to battle with the demons.

And so he would stand like a column or a lifeless statue   2
during the divine services, without letting his eyes wander, and he would also shed streams of tears from them every day without paying any attention to those who saw him. When the monks saw him acting in this fashion, those who strove for piety rejoiced and gave glory to God, but those who

εὐλαβείας ἀντεποιοῦντο, οἱ δὲ οὐκ ἔφερον ὁρᾶν αὐτόν,
ἔλεγχον γὰρ τῆς ἑαυτῶν ῥαθυμίας τὸν ἐκείνου βίον
ἡγοῦντο, ὅσοι πονηρίᾳ προσέκειντο. Ἔνθεν τοι καὶ μέγας
ἐκ τούτων πειρασμὸς ἐπεγείρεται τῷ γενναίῳ, καὶ δὴ
ἀγῶνα καὶ σπουδὴν τίθενται αὐτοί τε οἱ μὴ φέροντες ὁρᾶν
τοὺς ὑπερφυεῖς ἀγῶνας αὐτοῦ καὶ ὁ προϊστάμενος αὐτῶν,
ἢ τῆς προθέσεως αὐτὸν μεταστῆσαι καὶ τῆς πρὸς τὸν
πνευματικὸν[39] πατέρα πίστεως ἀποσπάσαι καὶ πεῖσαι τῷ
ἐκείνων φρονήματι ἐξακολουθεῖν, ἢ τέλεον ἐξῶσαι αὐτὸν
τῆς μονῆς τοῖς λόγοις αὐτῶν μὴ πειθόμενον πειθαρχῆ-
σαι.

17

Μόνους δὲ ἄρα τούτους ἐξεπολέμωσαν τῷ Συμεώνῃ
ὥσπερ τῷ Ἰωσὴφ τοὺς ὁμαίμονας οἱ ἐχθροί [cf. Gen 37];
Οὔμενουν! Ἀλλὰ καὶ ἀπὸ τῶν ἔξω τινὰς καὶ αὐτὸν τὸν γεγεννηκότα πατέρα, καὶ ἦν ἰδεῖν ξένην συμπλοκὴν καὶ μάχην ἐν ἀμφοτέροις· τῶν μὲν ἔξωθεν σπουδαζόντων πρὸς
τὰ οἰκεῖα πάλιν μεταστρέψαι τὸν Συμεὼν καὶ τὸν κόσμον
ὃν ἔφυγε, τῶν δὲ ἔσωθεν τῆς πνευματικῆς καταστάσεως
ἀποκινῆσαι καὶ ὠφελείας καὶ ἢ σύμφρονα αὐτὸν ἑαυτοῖς
ἀπεργάσασθαι ἢ μὴ πειθόμενον ἀπορρῆξαι παντάπασι καὶ
τῆς ξυναυλίας αὐτῶν. Ἀλλὰ τίς ἡ σοφία τῶν σοφῶν [cf. Is
29:14] καὶ τὰ τούτων κατ’ ἐκείνου ἐπιχειρήματα; Θωπεῖαι
καὶ ἀπειλαί, ψόγοι καὶ εὐφημίαι, διαβολαὶ καὶ ὑποσχέσεις,

tended toward wickedness could not bear to see him, for
they considered that his mode of life was a condemnation of
their own laxity. As a result, then, the demons created a great
trial for the noble one, for those who could not bear to see
his extraordinary efforts, along with their abbot, made a determined effort either to have him give up his determination, abandon his faith in his spiritual father, and agree to
follow their ideas, or else to expel him from the monastery
for good if he could not be persuaded to obey their orders.

Chapter 17

Did the demons make only these monks hostile to Symeon, as they did Joseph's brothers? On the contrary! For they
also <recruited> some from outside the monastery and even
his own natural father. Thus a strange alliance could be seen,
fighting him from both sides. Those from outside were eager to have Symeon return to his family again and the world
that he had fled, while those within <the monastery wanted>
to depose him from his spiritual condition and its benefits
and either get him to agree with them or, if he could not be
persuaded, break all ties with their community. But what
was *the wisdom of the wise,* what did these people attempt
against him? Flattery and threats, blame and acclaim, slanders and promises, so that with one of these they might

ὡς ἑνί γε τούτων κατασείσωσι τὸν κατὰ τῶν δαιμόνων ἱστάμενον· τοῖς[40] μὲν γὰρ ἕλκοντες αὐτὸν ἦσαν εἰς δεῖπνον καὶ πότους καὶ ὁμιλίας καὶ τὰ παρ' αὐτοῖς σεμνὰ ὑπισχνούμενοι. Τίνα δὴ ταῦτα; Διακονίας καὶ κέλλας λαμπρὰς καὶ χειροτονίας· τοῖς[41] δὲ ἀπωθούμενοι καὶ τὴν ξένην αὐτῷ ἐπισείοντες. Τίνος ἔνεκεν; Ἵνα Θεὸν ἀθετήσῃ καὶ ἀρετὴν καὶ πατέρα ἀρνήσηται.

18

Τί οὖν ὁ γενναῖος ἐκεῖνος καὶ *ὑπὲρ πρεσβυτέρους συνιών* [cf. Ps 118(119):100], καὶ εἰδὼς διακρίνειν καλῶς τὸ κρεῖττον ἀπὸ τοῦ χείρονος; Ἐμαλακίσθη ταῖς θωπείαις; Ὑφῆκε ποσῶς τῆς συντόνου ἀσκήσεως; Ἀντηλλάξατο τῆς στενῆς τὴν εὐρύχωρον; [cf. Mt 7:13–14] Οὐδαμῶς! Ἀλλ' ὥσπερ τις ἀήττητος ἀθλητὴς ἁρπάζει τῇ καλῇ ἀπειθείᾳ[42] τὰ δόκιμον αὐτὸν ἀπεργαζόμενα, τὰς διαβολάς, τὸν *διωγμόν*, τὰς *θλίψεις* [cf. Mt 13:21; Mk 4:17; 2 Th 1:4], τὰς συκοφαντίας, καὶ παρατρέχει τὰ πολλοῖς ἀσπαζόμενα. Τίνα ταῦτα; τοὺς ἐπαίνους, τὰς εὐφημίας, τὴν τιμήν, τὰς προεδρίας καὶ διακονίας καὶ εἴ τι ἄλλο τοῖς περὶ ταῦτα σπουδαίοις ἀσπάζεται. Ἀλλὰ τί τὸ ἐντεῦθεν; Ἤλειφε τὸν ἀθλητὴν ὁ γέρων ταῖς νουθεσίαις εἰς ἀνδρείαν καὶ καρτερίαν τῶν πειρασμῶν καὶ λόγοις ἐχρῆτο τοιούτοις πρὸς αὐτόν· "Φέρε, τέκνον ἐμόν, γενναίως τοὺς ἐκ τῶν δαιμόνων ἐπεγειρομένους σοι

shake Symeon from his stance against the demons. On the one hand, then, they were enticing him to meals, drinking bouts, and socializing, and were promising the things that they themselves valued. And what were they? Positions of responsibility, nice cells, and ordinations. And on the other they were driving him away and threatening him with expulsion. To what end? In order that he might break his faith with God and renounce both his virtue and his spiritual father.

Chapter 18

What then was the response of that noble man who *understood more than the aged* and knew well how to distinguish the better from the worse? Was he softened by their flatteries? Did he moderate the intensity of his asceticism in any way? Did he exchange the narrow path for the broad? Certainly not! Rather, like an invincible athlete, by his virtuous refusal to yield he overpowered the things that were being used to test him: the slanders, *the persecution, the afflictions,* and the calumnies, and he disregarded what most people embrace. And what are they? Compliments, acclaim, honor, high rank, positions of responsibility, and anything else coveted by people who are eager for such things. But what happened then? The elder prepared his athlete with advice to motivate his courage and perseverance in his trials, using words something like this to him: "My child, endure nobly the trials that are stirred up for you by the demons, because

πειρασμούς, ὅτι τὸ δοκίμιον ἡμῶν ἐν τούτοις ἐστίν. Ἴσθι
γὰρ ἀκριβῶς ὅτι ὅσα ἂν καὶ κοπιᾶσαι εἰς ἀγῶνας γενναίως
προθυμηθῶμεν, νηστεῦσαί τε καὶ ἀγρυπνῆσαι [cf. 2 Cor
6:5] ἢ ἄλλο τι ἀσκήσεως εἶδος ἐνδείξασθαι εἰς κενὸν ἡμῖν
γίνονται, ἐὰν μὴ ἄκακον, ἁπλῆν, ἀπερίεργον, ταπεινὴν καὶ
πραεῖαν ψυχὴν ἀγωνισώμεθα κτήσασθαι. Ἐν γὰρ τῇ τοιαύτῃ ἐπισπένδει καὶ ἐμπνεῖ καὶ ὡς εἰς οἶκον τερπνότατον
ἡ χάρις τοῦ θείου Πνεύματος ἐγκατοικεῖ, ἄλλως δὲ οὐκ ἔνι
ταύτην ἢ ἰδεῖν ἢ λαβεῖν τινα."

19

Ταῦτα ὡς ἤκουσεν ὁ σοφώτατος Συμεὼν τὴν χάριν ἐπι-
ποθῶν τοῦ Ἁγίου Πνεύματος λήψεσθαι, πίπτει πρηνὴς καὶ
τῶν ποδῶν ἐκείνου ἅπτεται τῶν ἁγίων, ἐκδυσωπῶν θερμῶς
εὐχαῖς αὐτοῦ μᾶλλον τὴν χάριν λαβεῖν καὶ μὴ ἐξ ἔργων
οἰκείων ἢ πόνων ἀξιωθῆναι ταύτην ἐπιζητεῖν. Κάμπτεται
πρὸς οἶκτον ὁ συμπαθὴς πατὴρ καὶ κειμένῳ τῷ μαθητῇ
λέγει· "Ἀνάστα, τέκνον, κἀγὼ αὐτὸς ἄνθρωπός εἰμι, πλὴν
εἰς τὴν τοῦ Θεοῦ θαρρῶν⁴³ φιλανθρωπίαν σοι λέγω, ὅτι
διπλῆν τὴν χάριν αὐτοῦ δωρήσεταί σοι ὑπὲρ ἐμέ." Τοῦτο
τὸ ῥῆμα ὑπερθαυμάσας ὁ Συμεὼν καὶ μετὰ πίστεως ἀδια-
στάκτου δεξάμενος ἀνέστη, δακρύων πλήρεις ἔχων τοὺς
ὀφθαλμούς, ὃν ἀσπασάμενος ὁ γέρων ἀπέλυσεν ἐν εἰρήνῃ
[cf. Lk 2:29], ὥρας ὡσεὶ τρίτης οὔσης τῆς νυκτός.

it is in these that we are proven. But understand clearly that, however eager we may be to toil nobly in our contests, to fast and keep vigil or display some other kind of asceticism, that counts as nothing for us unless we also strive to have a soul that is without guile, simple, uncomplicated, humble, and gentle. For the grace of the divine Spirit pours into such a soul, breathes upon it, and dwells in it as in a most pleasant abode, but otherwise there is no way to see or receive this grace."[20]

Chapter 19

When the most wise Symeon heard these words, he desired to receive the grace of the Holy Spirit and so fell on his face and clasped his father's holy feet. He begged him fervently that he might receive this grace through his prayers and not be required to seek it by his own deeds and labors. The father, who was sympathetic, was swayed toward compassion and said to his disciple as he lay there, "Get up, child. I'm also a man myself. But because I'm confident in God's love for humanity, I tell you that you'll be given double the grace I have from Him." Symeon was astonished by his words, but accepted them with unhesitating faith and stood up, his eyes filling with tears. After the elder had embraced him, he *let* him *depart in peace,*[21] around the third hour of the night.

2 Τῷ δὲ κατερχομένῳ πρὸς τὴν ἰδίαν κέλλαν—ὦ τῆς τα-
χείας Θεοῦ *ἀντιλήψεως* [cf. Ps 21(22):19]!—πρώϊμον ἀνα-
τέλλει τὸ φῶς καὶ δὴ αἴφνης *φῶς ἄνωθεν αὐτὸν περιέλαμ-
ψεν* [Act 26:13] ἀστραπῇ ὅμοιον, ὃ καὶ περιδραξάμενον τοῦ
νοὸς αὐτοῦ καὶ ὅλον συναρπάσαν αὐτὸν ἡδυτάτης εὐφροσύνης πεπλήρωκεν· ἡ δὲ πτεροῖ πρὸς ἔρωτα Θεοῦ πλείονα
τὴν ἐκείνου ψυχήν, καὶ τῇ ζέσει τοῦ Πνεύματος ἐν συντε-
τριμμένῃ καρδίᾳ προσπίπτει Θεῷ καὶ τὴν εὐχαριστίαν
ἐξομολογούμενος ἀπονέμει, καὶ δὴ γίνεται θαῦμα φρικτὸν
ἐπ᾿ αὐτῷ κάτω κειμένῳ καὶ κλαίοντι· ἅμα γὰρ τῷ προσπε-
σεῖν αὐτὸν τῷ Θεῷ καὶ ἰδοὺ *φωτοειδῆ νεφέλην* [cf. Mt 17:5]
ὅλον ἐπιπεσοῦσαν αὐτῷ ἐθεάσατο νοερῶς, πᾶσάν τε ἡδο-
νὴν καὶ γλυκύτητα ἐμποιήσασαν αὐτοῦ τῇ ψυχῇ καὶ ἐμπλή-
σασαν θείας χάριτος, τοῦ δὲ σαρκικοῦ φρονήματος τὸ
γεῶδες πάχος εἰς τέλος ἀπολεπτύνασαν.

20

Ἐντεῦθεν οὖν ἐπὶ πλεῖον τῇ πρὸς τὸν πατέρα πίστει
προέκοπτε καὶ *τοῖς ἔμπροσθεν ἐπεκτείνετο* [Phlp 3:13]· πρὸς
γὰρ τὸν πόθον τῆς φανείσης αὐτῷ ὄψεως ὅλως ἐκκρεμα-
σθεὶς ἀέναον ἐκτήσατο τὴν κατάνυξιν. Ἐδόθη δὲ⁴⁴ αὐτῷ
καὶ λόγος ἐκεῖθεν σοφίας καὶ γνώσεως, ὡς πάντας θαυμά-
ζειν ἐπὶ τῇ συνέσει καὶ τοῖς λόγοις αὐτοῦ καὶ οὕτω λέγειν
ἐκπληττομένους· "*Πόθεν ἡ τοιαύτη τούτῳ σοφία* [Mt 13:54]

46

But as soon as Symeon was back in his own cell—oh, how 2
swift is God's aid!—it grew light ahead of time, for *a light*
from above suddenly *shone around him* like lightning. This
took hold of his mind and completely carried him away, filling him with the sweetest gladness. It uplifted his soul even
more in its intense longing for God, and with the boiling
heat of the Spirit in his contrite heart, he prostrated himself
before God, confessing his gratitude and giving thanks. And
while he was lying there weeping, an awesome wonder befell
him. For at the same moment as he prostrated himself before God, *behold,* he saw with his intellect a *bright cloud* descending upon him. It produced an exquisite pleasure and
sweetness in his soul, filling it with divine grace, and it completely refined the earthly solidity of his corporeal thought.

Chapter 20

After this Symeon developed even more faith in his spiritual father and *strained forward to what lies ahead.* For he was
so completely obsessed with longing for the vision that had
appeared to him that his contrition became ceaseless. He
also received from it such wisdom and knowledge in his
speech that everyone was amazed by his intelligence and his
words and *they were* thus *astonished and said, "Where did this*

καὶ γνῶσις παιδείαν μὴ μεμαθηκότι τὴν θύραθεν;" Ἀλλ'
ἔλαθεν αὐτοὺς ὅτι Σοφία ὢν ὁ Θεὸς καὶ Γνῶσις τελεία, ἐν
οἷς ἂν περιπατήσῃ καὶ μονὴν ποιήσῃ [cf. John 14:23; Col
1:9–10], σοφίας καὶ γνώσεως ἀπορρήτου πληροῖ τοὺς μετόχους αὐτοῦ καὶ πάντων σοφῶν καὶ ῥητόρων σοφωτέρους
[Prov 30:24] ὡς τοὺς αὐτοῦ μαθητὰς καὶ ἀποστόλους ἐργάζεται. Οὐ μόνον δέ, ἀλλὰ καὶ ἐπὶ τῇ ταπεινώσει καὶ τῇ
διηνεκεῖ κατανύξει αὐτοῦ ἐξεπλήττοντο ἅπαντες· εἰς τοσοῦτον γὰρ ὕψος αὐτὸν ἡ σύντονος ἄσκησις δι' ὀλίγου ἀναδραμεῖν ἀπειργάσατο, ὡς ὑπερελάσαι καὶ αὐτοὺς τοὺς
ἐγχρονίσαντας ἐν τοῖς ἀγῶσι τῆς ἀρετῆς καὶ γενέσθαι
τοῦτον ἐκείνων⁴⁵ διδάσκαλον κατὰ τὸν μέγαν Δανιὴλ τὸν
προφήτην, καὶ τοῦτο γνώσεται πᾶς ὁ βουλόμενος ἐξ ὧν
παρ' ἐκείνων ἐρωτώμενος ἀντέγραφεν αὐτοῖς καὶ ταῖς ἐπι-
στολαῖς κατέπληττεν ὑπερβαλλόντως αὐτούς.

21

Ἀλλὰ γὰρ οὐ πολὺ τὸ ἐν μέσῳ, καὶ οὕτω βλέποντες
αὐτὸν τῇ προκοπῇ τῶν ἀρετῶν καὶ τῇ πρὸς τὸν πατέρα
πίστει ἔτι μᾶλλον ἐπεκτεινόμενον οἱ βασκαίνοντες, προσ-
ελθόντες τῷ ἡγουμένῳ ἐμφυσῶσι δεινότερον⁴⁶ κατὰ τοῦ
ἀνδρὸς τοὺς ἄνθρακας τοῦ θυμοῦ αὐτοῦ. Ὁ δὲ ἐπεὶ προσκαλεσάμενος τὸν γενναῖον εἰς λόγους συνῆλθεν αὐτῷ, καὶ
τοῦτο μὲν ὑποσχέσεσι, τοῦτο δὲ καὶ ἀπειλαῖς ἔσπευδεν

man get such wisdom and knowledge, when he hasn't had a secular education?" But they were forgetting that God, being Wisdom and perfect Knowledge, fills with ineffable wisdom and knowledge those with whom He lives and makes His abode, and He makes those who partake in Him *wiser than* all *the wise* men and teachers of rhetoric, as He did His disciples and apostles. They were also all astonished not only by this but also by his humility and his ceaseless contrition, for his intense asceticism resulted in his rising, in a short time, to such a high level that he even surpassed those who had spent a long time striving for virtue, and he became their teacher like the great Daniel the prophet.[22] Anyone who wishes may understand this from his written responses to questions, for he completely astounded them by his letters.

Chapter 21

Not long afterward, however, those who were jealous of Symeon went to the superior and fanned the embers of his anger toward him more fiercely, because they saw that he was still making progress in the virtues and developing even more faith in his spiritual father. The superior summoned the noble Symeon and had a conversation with him during which he strove, partly by promises, partly by threats, to

ἀποσπάσαι αὐτὸν τοῦ διδασκάλου καὶ πρὸς ἑαυτὸν ἐπι-
σπάσασθαι· ἦν γὰρ φθόνον ἔχων ὡς οὐκ ὤφελε κατ' ἐκείνου τοῦ μεγάλου γέροντος ὁ προεστώς. Ὡς⁴⁷ εἶδε τὸ φρόνημα τοῦ Συμεὼν ἀταπείνωτον καὶ τῆς πρὸς τὸν γέροντα
πίστεως ἀμετακίνητον, ἡττηθεὶς τῇ πυκνότητι καὶ σοφίᾳ
τῶν λόγων αὐτοῦ ἐκέλευσεν εὐθὺς καὶ ἐξωθοῦσι τὸν μακάριον τῆς μονῆς.

22

Ἰδὼν οὖν τὸν φθόνον ὁ μέγας ἐκεῖνος πατὴρ τοῦ ἡγουμένου καὶ τῶν λοιπῶν, λαβὼν τὸν ἑαυτοῦ μαθητὴν φοιτᾷ
πρὸς Ἀντώνιον ἐκεῖνον τὸν τηνικαῦτα τῇ ἀρετῇ περιβόη-
τον ἡγούμενον ὄντα τῆς ἀγχοῦ παρακειμένης μονῆς τοῦ
ἁγίου Μάμαντος, καὶ τούτῳ ὡς θησαυρὸν τῶν καλῶν
παρατίθεται τὸν Συμεών. Τί δαί; Ἡρέμησε ποσῶς ἐπὶ τούτοις ὁ Πονηρὸς καὶ ὑφῆκε τοῦ φθόνου καὶ τῶν κατὰ τοῦ
ἀνδρὸς πολέμων; Οὐδαμῶς! Ἀλλ' ἐγείρει πάλιν τὸν κατὰ
σάρκα τούτου πατέρα καὶ τῶν τῆς συγκλήτου τινὰς καὶ
σπουδὴν τίθενται κωλῦσαι τοῦ μὴ ἀποτάξασθαι τῷ κόσμῳ
καὶ τοῖς ἐν κόσμῳ [cf. Lk 14:33] τὸν Συμεώνην. Ἀλλ' ὁ

distance him from his teacher and win him over to his side; for the abbot was envious, as he should not have been, of the great elder. But when he realized that Symeon's mind was not going to be changed and that his faith in the elder was immovable, defeated by the shrewdness and wisdom of Symeon's words, he gave immediate orders to expel the blessed one from the monastery.

3. Symeon's Life and Work as Monk and Superior at Saint Mamas

Chapter 22

When that great spiritual father [Symeon Eulabes] saw the envy of the abbot and the others, he took his disciple and went to see Antony, who was renowned at that time for his virtue and was superior of the nearby monastery of Saint Mamas.[23] He entrusted Symeon to this man like a treasury for all that is good. Then what? Did the Evil One keep quiet for a while after this and give up his envy and his attacks on Symeon? Certainly not! For now he stirred up his natural father again and some members of the senate and they tried to prevent Symeon from renouncing the world and those in the world. But the noble athlete of Christ remained

γενναῖος ἀθλητὴς τοῦ Χριστοῦ ἀκατάσειστος καὶ ἀταπεί-
νωτος ἔμενε πυρπολούμενος τῷ ἔρωτι τοῦ Θεοῦ.

23

Διὸ καὶ τῷ κατὰ σάρκα ἐπιστέλλει πατρὶ λόγους οὓς
ἐκεῖνον ἔδει πρὸς τὸν υἱὸν ἐπιστέλλειν καὶ νουθετεῖν μηδὲν
τῆς ἀγάπης προτιμᾶν τοῦ Χριστοῦ. Ἀλλ᾽ ἐνταῦθα γενο-
μένῳ πάλιν ἄλλη τις θεοσημεία γράφοντι αὐτῷ ἐπιφαίνε-
ται· ὡς γὰρ ἔγραψε τῷ πατρὶ τὰ τῆς παραινέσεως θέλων
διδάξαι αὐτὸν πῶς δεῖ γράφειν πρὸς ἄνδρας ἁγίους συν-
εῖρε καὶ τοῦτο· "Τὴν δὲ πρὸς τὸν ἅγιόν μου πατέρα ἐπιστολὴν οὕτως ἐπιγράψεις·" καὶ σὺν τῷ λόγῳ—ὦ τῶν
καινῶν σου μυστηρίων, Χριστὲ Βασιλεῦ!—αἴφνης οὐρανό-
θεν ἐπέλαμψεν αὐτῷ φῶς ἄπειρον καὶ οἱονεὶ τὴν στέγην
τοῦ δώματος[48] διασχὸν καὶ χαρᾶς ἀφάτου καὶ ἡδονῆς πάλιν ἐπλήρωσεν αὐτοῦ τὴν ψυχήν, ὡς τῷ ἀπλέτῳ τοῦ φωτὸς
ἐκείνου[49] καὶ τὸν φαίνοντα λύχνον (νὺξ γὰρ ἦν) εἰς ἅπαν
ἀμαυρωθῆναι. Καὶ ἰδοὺ ἐκ τοῦ θείου φωτὸς ἐκείνου φωνὴ
ταῦτα λέγουσα [Mt 17:5]· "Τῷ ἀποστόλῳ καὶ μαθητῇ τοῦ
Χριστοῦ καὶ μεσίτῃ καὶ πρέσβει ἡμῶν τὰ πρὸς τὸν Θεόν."
Ταῦτα ὡς ἤκουσε παρ᾽ ἐλπίδα[50] πᾶσαν ὁ Συμεὼν ἐξέστη τῇ
διανοίᾳ [Gen 45:26] καὶ τὰ αἰσθητήρια ἔφριξεν [Dn 7:15]·
ἐξώμνυτο γὰρ τὸν ἐπιφανέντα αὐτῷ Θεόν, ὅτι "Τῷ θείῳ
φωτὶ ὅλος," φησί, "καταυγαζόμενος καὶ λιβάδας καταχέ-
ων[51] δακρύων ὥσπερ τινὸς ᾐσθόμην ἑτέρου κουφίζοντός

unshaken and invincible, inflamed with his intense longing for God.

Chapter 23

Symeon thus wrote his natural father a letter (one that *he* should have been sending to his son), warning him to value nothing above the love of Christ. But at the very moment he was doing this, he received another sign from God while he was in the act of writing. For as he was writing words of advice to his father, wanting to explain to him how he should write to holy men, he added, "You should address the letter to my holy father as follows." But at those words—oh, how strange are your mysteries, Christ the King!—an all-encompassing light suddenly shone on him from heaven. It seemed to pass right through the roof of the building and it again filled his soul with ineffable joy and pleasure. The light was so immense that the lamp that was burning (for it was night) could no longer be seen at all. And *lo, from* that divine light *a voice said* these words: "To the apostle and disciple of Christ, to our mediator and ambassador to God." When he heard these words so unexpectedly, Symeon *lost control of his mind* and his senses *shuddered.* For he used to swear by the God who had appeared to him that, as he said, "while I was completely illuminated by the divine light and shedding streams of tears, I felt as if someone else was lifting up my

μου τὴν χεῖρα καὶ πρὸς τὸ γράφειν συνωθοῦντος καὶ καθ-
οδηγοῦντος αὐτήν· οὐ γὰρ συνεχωρούμην αἰσθητῶς ὁρᾶν
ὅτε τὴν ἄνωθεν ῥηθεῖσαν ἐπιγραφὴν ἔγραφον."

24

Ἐπεὶ δὲ τὸν μαθητὴν ὁ καλὸς ποιμὴν [John 10:11, 14]
συνεχέστερον ἐπεσκέπτετο καὶ ὅλον αὐτὸν τῷ θείῳ πυρ-
πολούμενον ἔρωτι καὶ τῇ ἐπιθυμίᾳ τοῦ ἁγίου σχήματος
φλεγόμενον κατεμάνθανεν, ἀποκείρει καὶ τὸν χιτῶνα τῆς
εὐφροσύνης [Is 61:10] αὐτῷ περιτίθησι. Ἐντεῦθεν εἰς
ἀγῶνας μείζονας τῶν προλαβόντων ὁ θερμὸς εἰς ἀρετὴν
Συμεὼν ὑπεισέρχεται καὶ ζώννυται μὲν ἐν φρονήσει νοὸς
τὴν ὀσφὺν τῇ τῆς σωφροσύνης[52] ζώνῃ καὶ τῆς ἀνδρείας,
αἷς ἐξ ἁπαλῶν ὀνύχων συνηυξήθη τε καὶ συνέζησεν. Ἅπτεται δὲ τῶν τελειοτέρων ἔργων τῆς δικαιοσύνης καὶ τῶν
ἄλλων πάντων, σχολάσας μόνῃ προσευχῇ καὶ ἡσυχίᾳ, καὶ
τῇ μελέτῃ τῶν θείων[53] ἑαυτὸν δίδωσι καὶ συνάπτεται Θεῷ
τελεώτερον ἐν φωτὶ θεωρίας, ᾧ καὶ πρὸ τῆς χρίσεως ἔζη
καὶ ὑφ' οὗ δαψιλῶς ἀπὸ σπαργάνων ἐλάμπετο.[54]

hand and pressing on it and guiding it to write; for I was physically unable to see when I was writing the form of address spoken from above."

Chapter 24

When the *good shepherd* [Symeon Eulabes], who used to visit his disciple quite frequently, observed that he was completely inflamed with his intense longing for God and burned with desire for the holy habit, he tonsured him and *dressed* him in the *robe of gladness*. From then on Symeon, who was so ardent for virtue, entered into even greater contests than before. With his intellectual understanding he girded his loins with the girdle of self-control and courage, virtues that he had developed and lived by from his early childhood. And he tackled the more advanced works of righteousness and all the other virtues. Spending his time only in prayer and spiritual solitude, he gave himself up to the study of the divine scriptures and drew closer to God in the light of his meditation,[24] in which he had lived even before he was anointed, and by which he was abundantly illuminated from infancy.

25

Τοίνυν καὶ δίαιτα μὲν ἦν αὐτῷ ἡμερήσιος εἰς ἄκρον ἐκκαθαρθέντι ὁ ζωοποιὸς ἄρτος καὶ τὸ αἷμα τὸ τίμιον τοῦ Χριστοῦ καὶ βοτάναι τῶν ἐδωδίμων καὶ σπέρματα. Τούτοις γὰρ συνεῖχε τὴν ζωὴν τοῦ σώματος ἑαυτοῦ, μηδενὸς ἑτέρου πλὴν τῶν κυριακῶν κατά γε τὰς ἑξῆς τῆς ἑβδομάδος ἡμέρας μεταλαμβάνων, ἐν δὲ ταῖς τῶν ἑορτῶν ἡμέραις τοῖς ἀδελφοῖς συνεκοινώνει τραπέζης ἐν κατηφείᾳ προσώπου καὶ διηνεκεῖ κατανύξει, εἶτα εὐχαριστῶν συνανίστατο καὶ φεύγων εἰς τὴν κέλλαν ἔκλειεν ἑαυτῷ τὰς θύρας καὶ ἵστατο εἰς προσευχήν. Εἶτα μικρὸν ἀναγνοὺς μετελάμβανε μικρᾶς ἀναπαύσεως κατακλινόμενος εἰς τὴν γῆν· οὐ γὰρ ἦν αὐτῷ κλίνη καὶ στρώματα καὶ ἄλλη τις ὑπηρεσία σωματική, ἀλλὰ κλίνη μὲν αὐτῷ ἐστρωμένη ψιάθῳ καὶ κωδίῳ φιλοτίμως τὸ ἔδαφος ἦν, ὅπερ οὐδὲ καθ' ἑκάστην εἶχεν αὐτὸν ἐπ' αὐτῷ κείμενον, ἐν γὰρ κυριακῇ καὶ ἑορτῇ ἐπισήμῳ ἄϋπνον εἶχεν αὐτὸν ἡ κέλλα ἀπὸ ἑσπέρας ἕως[55] πρωΐας καὶ οὐδ' οὕτως ὡς ὁ μέγας ἐκεῖνος Ἀρσένιος μετελάμβανεν ὕπνου, ἀλλ' εὐθὺς αὐγάζοντος τοῦ ἡλίου εἰς εὐχὴν ἵστατο δάκρυσι θερμοτάτοις ὑπεραντλούμενος· οὐδὲν γὰρ ἕτερον τῆς τοῦ Θεοῦ ὁμιλίας ἐτίθετο προτιμότερον. Καὶ τοῦ μὴ ῥῖψαι ῥῆμα ἀργὸν [Mt 12:36] διὰ πολλῆς εἶχε σπουδῆς· ᾔδει γὰρ ἀκριβῶς, ὅτι καὶ τῆς δοκούσης ἐλαχίστης ἐντολῆς τοῦ Χριστοῦ ἡ παράβασις οὐ μικρὸν τῇ ψυχῇ τὸν κίνδυνον ἐν τῷ μέλλοντι προξενεῖ.

Chapter 25

When he reached this degree of purification, his daily diet consisted of the life-giving bread and precious blood of Christ together with vegetables and grains. With these he sustained life in his body, taking nothing else on all the days of the week except Sundays. On feast days he would join the brothers for the refectory meal with his face averted and with ceaseless contrition. After the thanksgiving, he would get up with them and escape to his cell, where he would shut the doors upon himself and stand in prayer. Then, after reading for a while, he would take a little rest, lying down on the ground. For he had no bed, or bedclothes, or any other physical comfort; instead his bed, lavishly made up with a rush mat and a sheepskin, was the floor! And he did not even lie on that every night, for on Sundays and major feast days he would stay awake in his cell from dusk until dawn. Even then he would not partake of sleep, as the great Arsenios did,[25] but would stand in prayer as soon as the sun rose, drenched in the most fervent tears. For nothing was more precious to him than conversing with God. He also took great care not to utter *a careless word,* for he knew very well that even the transgression of the seemingly least important of Christ's commandments would constitute a significant danger for his soul in the future.

26

Ἦν οὖν ἰδεῖν αὐτὸν ὡς ἐν σταδίῳ καθ' ἑκάστην ἡμέραν εὐψύχως καὶ ἐν ζέοντι πνεύματι τρέχοντα τὸν δρόμον τῶν ἐντολῶν [cf. Ps. 118(119):32] τοῦ Χριστοῦ πρὸς μηδένα τῶν ἀνθρώπων ἐπιστρεφόμενον, ὅλον προσοχῆς, ὅλον θέρμης πεπληρωμένον τοῦ Πνεύματος καὶ ὅλον θείων ἀποκαλύψεων καὶ ἐλλάμψεων. Ἔνθεν τοι καὶ πᾶσαν μὲν τὴν ἡμέραν ἐγκεκλεισμένον ὁ καρτερικώτατος εἶχεν ἑαυτὸν ἐν τῇ κέλλῃ καὶ τὸ παράπαν ἀπρόϊτον. Εἰργάζετο δὲ καθήμενος ἔνδον τὸ μέλι τῆς ἀρετῆς, καὶ τὰ κηρία ὡς μέλιττα φιλεργὸς συνετίθει καλῶς ἑκάστης τῶν ἀρετῶν, ἵν' ἔχῃ τροφὴν ἀδάπανον εἰς τὸ μέλλον καὶ προσφόρως τὸν ἑαυτοῦ καρπὸν ἀποδώσει τῷ Βασιλεῖ καὶ Θεῷ αὐτοῦ τῆς ἐπουρανίου τραπέζης ἐπάξιον.[56]

2 Διὸ καὶ πρῶτα μὲν ὅλον ἑαυτὸν συνάγων ἀπὸ τῶν ἔξω εἰς προσευχὴν ἵστατο κατ' ἀρχὰς τῆς ἡμέρας, ὡς εἴρηται, ἄνω τὸν νοῦν ἁρπάζων καὶ ἀΰλως τῷ ἀΰλῳ Θεῷ συγγινόμενος ὑπ' οὐδεμιᾶς φροντίδος τὴν διάνοιαν ἔχων περισπωμένην ἢ μεριζομένην ἐν ταῖς αἰσθήσεσιν, αὐτὸ δὲ τὸ Θεῖον τῶν ἐκείνου εὐθὺς ἀντελαμβάνετο δεήσεων καὶ τῷ ἐμφύτῳ φωτὶ περιλαμβάνον τὸ νοερὸν αὐτοῦ τῆς ψυχῆς καὶ ἀναχωνεῦον εἴ τι χοϊκὸν ἑαυτῷ, ἐπλήρου θερμοῦ πνεύματος καὶ πάσης εὐφροσύνης τὴν καρδίαν αὐτοῦ. Ὅθεν καὶ ὡς ἀπὸ βαλανείου λελουμένος τοῖς δάκρυσι καὶ ὅλος ὡς φλὸξ ἀπὸ τῆς[57] προσευχῆς ἐπὶ τὸ κάθισμα τοῦ κελλίου ἐξήρχετο,

SECTION 3

Chapter 26

One could thus see Symeon running the course of Christ's commandments every day as though he were in a stadium. He did so courageously, boiling with spiritual energy, and paying no attention to any human concern. He was completely focused, completely filled with the fervor of the Spirit and with divine revelations and illuminations. Thus that most obdurate man spent the whole day enclosed in his cell and never came out. As he sat inside he would produce the honey of virtue and, like a busy bee, carefully construct the wax comb of each of the virtues, so that he might have inexhaustible nourishment for the future, and so that he might fittingly offer to his King and God his own produce that was worthy of the heavenly banquet table.

He would thus first collect his thoughts completely, 2 <turning them> away from all external distractions, and would stand in prayer at daybreak, as has been said, lifting his intellect heavenward and uniting himself immaterially with the immaterial God. When his mind was free from any mental distraction or any diversion by his senses, the Divinity Himself would immediately receive his entreaties and, encompassing the intellectual part of his soul with His inherent light, would also melt away any earthly vestige in him, and would fill his heart with spiritual fervor and every kind of gladness. And afterward, washed by his tears as though he had been in a bath, and wholly like flame from his prayers, he would come out of his cell for the reading of the psalter.[26]

εἶτα ταῖς θείαις ὡμίλει γραφαῖς καὶ τοὺς τῶν προασκησάν-
των βίους ἀναγινώσκων τὰ ἐκείνων εἰς ἑαυτὸν συνελέγετο
κατορθώματα.

27

Μετὰ δὲ τὴν ἀνάγνωσιν ἥπτετο τοῦ ἐργοχείρου γράφων τὰς δέλτους τῶν θεοπνεύστων γραφῶν· ἦν γὰρ ἄγαν
εὐφυῶς γράφων, ὡς ἡδονῆς πληροῦσθαι πάντα τὸν τὰ
ἐκείνου βλέποντα γράμματα. Τοῦ ξύλου δὲ κρούοντος
εὐθὺς ἀνίστατο εἰς ὑμνῳδίαν Θεοῦ, καὶ τελουμένης τῆς
θείας ἀναφορᾶς αὐτὸς ἐν ἑνὶ τῶν τοῦ ναοῦ εὐκτηρίων μετὰ
τὴν τοῦ Εὐαγγελίου ἀκρόασιν ἑαυτὸν ἀποκλείων ἵστατο
εἰς προσευχὴν καὶ ὡμίλει μετὰ δακρύων Θεῷ ἕως οὗ τὸν
ἄρτον ὁ ἱερεὺς ὕψωσεν. Εἶτα ὅλος θείου πυρὸς ἐξερχόμενος τῶν ἀχράντων μετελάμβανε μυστηρίων καὶ ἅμα σιωπῶν ἀπέτρεχε πρὸς τὴν κέλλαν αὐτοῦ, τῆς μετρίας ἐκείνης
δὲ καὶ ἀπραγματεύτου μεταλαμβάνων τραπέζης, εἴχετο
συνήθως τῆς ἰδίας ἐργασίας, ὡς εἴρηται. Ἀλλὰ γὰρ τῆς
ἑσπέρας καταλαβούσης καὶ τῆς νυκτὸς ἀρχομένης ἦν ἰδεῖν
αὐτὸν ὡς ἀκοίμητον ἄλλον ἀστέρα δᾳδουχοῦντα τὸ νύχος
αὐτῆς καὶ μέχρι μεσονυκτίου εἰς προσευχὴν ἱστάμενον καὶ
ὁμιλίαν τῶν θείων γραφῶν, ἔσθ' ὅτε καὶ ταῖς ἱεραῖς ἐξιστά-
μενον[58] θεωρίαις καὶ μυστικῶς τῷ Θεῷ συναπτόμενον.

Then he would devote himself to the holy scriptures and, reading the Lives of those who had practiced asceticism in the past, would store up their virtuous actions in himself.

Chapter 27

After his reading Symeon would engage in manual labor, copying manuscripts of the divinely inspired scriptures; for he used to write so elegantly that anyone who saw his handwriting was filled with pleasure. When the wooden *semantron*[27] sounded, he would immediately get up to sing God's praise. While the divine eucharistic liturgy was being celebrated, he would shut himself off in one of the church's chapels after the Gospel reading and would stand in prayer, tearfully communing with God, until the priest elevated the bread. Then he would emerge, filled with divine fire, and would partake of the sacred mysteries before hurrying away to his cell in silence. After he had eaten his modest and simple meal, he would usually do his own work, as has been described. But when dusk arrived and night fell, one would see him illuminating its darkness like an unsleeping star, standing in prayer and meditation upon the divine scriptures until the middle of the night, or sometimes falling into the ecstasy of his holy visions and being joined in mystical union with God.

28

Τοῦ ξύλου τοίνυν κατὰ ἑβδόμην κρουομένου τῆς νυκτὸς ὥραν ἀνίστατο τῆς γῆς ἐν ᾗ κατακλινόμενος ὀλίγης κομιδῇ μετελάμβανεν ἀναπαύσεως καὶ τοὺς ἑωθινοὺς ὕμνους σύναμα τοῖς ἀδελφοῖς ἀπονέμων Θεῷ ὄρθιος διατελῶν ἦν καθ' ὅλον⁵⁹ τὸν ὄρθρον μέχρι τῆς αὐτοῦ ἀπολύσεως, οὐδὲ γὰρ ἐκάθητο τῶν θείων ἀναγινωσκομένων γραφῶν, ἀλλ' εἰς ἓν τῶν τοῦ ναοῦ εἰσερχόμενος εὐκτηρίων ἵστατο ἀσάλευτος τῆς ἀναγνώσεως ἀκροώμενος καὶ τοῖς δάκρυσι καταρραίνων τὸ ἔδαφος· ἀλλὰ τῆς εἰωθυίας τελεσθείσης ἀκολουθίας μόνος πάντων ὄπισθεν ἐν σιωπῇ τοῦ ναοῦ ἐξερχόμενος ἀνέτρεχεν εἰς τὴν κέλλαν αὐτοῦ καὶ εἴχετο τῶν ἱερῶν ἀγώνων αὐτοῦ. Οὗτος ὁ δρόμος τῶν ἀσκητικῶν ἀγώνων τῆς ὅλης ἡμέρας τε καὶ νυκτὸς τοῦ θαυμαστοῦ Συμεών· τὰς δέ γε τῆς ἁγίας τεσσαρακοστῆς ἡμέρας ἄσιτος μικροῦ διετέλει τὰς ὅλας ἑκάστης ἑβδομάδος ἡμέρας πλὴν σαββάτου καὶ κυριακῆς, ἐν ταύταις γὰρ ταῖς δυσὶν κοινῆς τραπέζης δι' ὀσπρίων καὶ λαχάνων ἑφθῶν μετελάμβανεν. Ἐπὶ πλευροῦ δὲ οὐδαμῶς ἔπιπτεν, ἀλλ' εἴ που καὶ τὴν φύσιν ὀκλάσασαν ἔγνω, κλίνων τὴν αὐτοῦ κεφαλὴν ὡς ἐκάθητο εἰς ἀγκῶνα περικεκομμένην τινὰ καὶ ὀδύνης μεστὴν παρεῖχεν αὐτῇ ἀνάπαυσιν καὶ ψευδόμενον ὕπνον ἕως ὥρας μιᾶς. Τοιαύτη ἦν ἡ ἐργασία τῶν εἰσαγωγικῶν καὶ μέσων πόνων τῆς νομίμου τούτου ἀθλήσεως [cf. 2 Tim 2:5].

Chapter 28

When the *semantron* sounded at the seventh hour of the night,[28] Symeon would get up from the ground, on which he was lying to take just a little rest, and offer the early morning hymns to God along with the brothers. He used to remain upright for the whole of matins until the dismissal, for he would not sit down during the reading of the holy scriptures, but rather would go into one of the church's chapels and stand motionless while he listened to the reading and sprinkled the floor with his tears. When the usual service was finished, he would silently come out of the church alone, after everyone else, and hurry back to his cell, where he would engage in his holy contests. This was the course that the wondrous Symeon's ascetic contests took all day and night. During the days of holy Lent, however, he went almost entirely without food all day every week, except for Saturday and Sunday, on both of which days he partook of the communal meal of pulses and boiled vegetables. He would never fall asleep on his side, but if ever he felt his nature succumbing, he would lay his head in the crook of his arms while he sat and allow himself some fitful and uncomfortable rest and a semblance of sleep for an hour. This was the sort of work that constituted the introductory and intermediate exercises for this athlete, who competed according to the rules.

29

Ἐπεὶ δὲ οὕτως ἔχων ἐπὶ δυσὶ χρόνοις τὸ μέσον καλῶς ὑπερκύψας⁶⁰ ἐπὶ τὸ τέλειον διὰ σοφίας ἀνέδραμε, καὶ τὰς φύσεις τῶν ὄντων ὄμματι θεωρίας κατασκοπήσας τοὺς λόγους ἔγνω τούτων δι' οὓς ἄνωθεν ἔσχον τὴν κίνησιν, τρανοῦται τὴν γλῶτταν ὑπὸ τοῦ Πνεύματος καὶ λόγους ἀγαθοὺς [cf. Ps 44(45):1] ἐπιστέλλων ἐρεύγεται μέσον τῆς ἐκκλησίας Χριστοῦ. Ἀλλὰ γὰρ οὕτω τὸν μαθητὴν ὁ ποιμὴν καὶ διδάσκαλος ὡς ἔγνω συντόμως τῇ θέρμῃ τοῦ Πνεύματος εἰς ἄνδρα τέλειον εἰς μέτρον ἡλικίας ἀναδραμόντα Χριστοῦ [Eph 4:13], σκέπτεται καλῶς ὡς λύχνον ἤδη καιόμενον ἐπὶ τὴν λυχνίαν θεῖναι τῆς τῶν πιστῶν ἐκκλησίας, ἵνα φαίνῃ πᾶσι τοῖς ἐν αὐτῇ ὃ ἑαυτὸν ἐφώτισε φῶς γνώσεως [cf. Mt 5:15–16].

30

Τοιαῦτα δὴ οὖν τοῦ ἱεροῦ ἐκείνου ἀνδρὸς περὶ τοῦ Συμεὼν σκεπτομένου, βραχὺς ὁ μεταξὺ χρόνος καὶ ὁ προεστὼς τῆς ἐκείνου μονῆς πρὸς Κύριον ἐξεδήμησε τὰ κάτω λιπών. Ψήφῳ τοίνυν Νικολάου τοῦ Χρυσοβέργη τοῦ πατριάρχου καὶ τῶν μοναχῶν τοῦ ἁγίου Μάμαντος εἰς τὸν θρόνον ἀνάγεται⁶¹ διδασκαλικὸν καὶ ἱερεὺς χειροτονεῖται

Chapter 29

After living in this way for two years he graduated with honors from the intermediate training and, in his wisdom, hurried on to the advanced course. Because he had carefully studied the nature of living beings with the eyes of spiritual contemplation, he understood the inner principles which, coming from heaven above, produced their activity. His speech was also clarified by the Spirit and he used to deliver eloquent addresses in the middle of Christ's church. But when his shepherd and teacher [Symeon Eulabes] realized that his disciple had thus hurried swiftly on in the fervor of the Spirit *to mature manhood, to the measure of the stature of Christ,* he observed correctly that he should place Symeon, like *a lamp* that has been lit, *on the lamp stand* in the church of the faithful, so that *the light* of knowledge enlightening him might shine out upon *all* there.

Chapter 30

A short time after that holy man made this observation about Symeon, the abbot of his monastery [Saint Mamas] left this world and departed to the Lord. And so Symeon, that concelebrant with the heavenly powers, was elevated to the teacher's chair and ordained priest by the decision of Nicholas Chrysoberges[29] and the monks of Saint Mamas.

ὁ συλλειτουργὸς τῶν ἄνω δυνάμεων, οὐκ ἀμογητὶ μὲν καὶ δίχα τῆς ἐπαινετῆς ἐνστάσεως, ἣν ἐν ταπεινώσει καρδίας σφοδρῶς ἐνίστατο εὐλαβούμενος τὸ τῆς ἱερωσύνης ἀξίωμα καὶ τὸ βάρος τῆς ἀρχῆς ἀπωθούμενος διὰ δειλίαν ἐπαινουμένην καὶ κρείττονα. Χρίεται οὖν τὸ τῆς ἀγαλλιάσεως ἔλαιον [Ps 44(45):7] καὶ τὴν εἰρήνην ἐπιφωνεῖ τοῖς λαοῖς [cf. Ps 84(85):8] ὁ μεγαλοφώνως ἄξιος μαρτυρηθεὶς ὑπὸ πάντων ἱερεὺς καὶ τῶν τοῦ Θεοῦ μυστηρίων ὑφηγητής, ὁ θεατὴς τῶν φρικτῶν ὀπτασιῶν, ἃς Χερουβικοῖς οὗτος ὀφθαλμοῖς ἐθεώρει.

2 Ἐπειδὴ γὰρ ἐτελεῖτο παρὰ τοῦ ἀρχιερέως τὸν ἱερέα ὁ σοφώτατος Συμεών, καὶ ὁ μὲν τὴν εὐχὴν ἐποίει ἐπ' αὐτῷ, ὁ δὲ τὸ γόνυ καὶ τὴν κεφαλὴν ὑποκλινόμενα εἶχε τῷ μυστηρίῳ, εἶδε καὶ ἰδοὺ τὸ Πνεῦμα τὸ Ἅγιον δίκην ἀπείρου φωτὸς ἁπλοῦν καὶ ἀνείδεον κατελθὸν ἐκάλυψε τὴν πανίερον αὐτοῦ κεφαλήν, ὃ καὶ λειτουργῶν ἔβλεπε τοῖς τεσσαράκοντα ὀκτὼ χρόνοις τῆς αὐτοῦ ἱερουργίας κατερχόμενον ἐν τῇ ἀναφερομένῃ παρ' αὐτοῦ θυσίᾳ τῷ Θεῷ, καθὼς αὐτὸς πρός τινα ὡς περὶ ἄλλου τινὸς ἔλεγεν ἑαυτὸν ὑποκρύβων καὶ γέγραπται ἐν τοῖς αὐτοῦ ἀποφθέγμασι.

31

Τίς οὖν ἐν τῇ γενεᾷ ταύτῃ εἰς τοσοῦτον ἀνῆλθε περιωπῆς ὡς ὁρᾶν ἀεὶ καθαρῶς τὸ Πνεῦμα τὸ Ἅγιον καὶ ἀκούειν λαλοῦντος αὐτοῦ καὶ ἐνεργοῦντος καὶ κινουμένου

This did not occur without a struggle nor some praisewor-thy resistance. For Symeon, being humble at heart, vigor-ously resisted because of his reverence for the dignity of the priesthood and refused the burden of leadership due to a commendable and proper reluctance. In the end, however, this man, whose worthiness to be a priest and officiator in God's sacraments was loudly confirmed by everyone, this seer of awesome visions that he contemplated with eyes like those of the Cherubim, was *anointed with the oil of gladness* and proclaimed *peace to the peoples.*

When the most wise Symeon was being ordained priest 2 by the patriarch and the latter was saying the prayer over him while he was bending his knee and bowing his head for the sacrament, Symeon beheld the Holy Spirit, pure and formless like boundless light, coming down and covering his most holy head. Indeed, during his forty-eight years as a priest, when he was celebrating the liturgy, he also used to see this light descending upon the eucharistic sacrifice he offered up to God. He would recount this story, but as though he were talking about someone else in order to conceal himself, and this has been recorded among his sayings.[30]

Chapter 31

Who, then, in this generation, has risen to such a level of contemplation that they can always clearly see the Holy Spirit and hear it speaking and feel it working and moving?

αἰσθάνεσθαι; ἐντεῦθεν εἰς βάθη ταπεινοφροσύνης ἐλη-
λακὼς ἔσπευδεν ἑαυτὸν ὑποκρύβειν⁶² καὶ λανθάνειν εἰ
οἷόν τε καὶ αὐτοὺς τοὺς συνόντας αὐτῷ, τὴν ἀνθρωπίνην
δόξαν ἀποστρεφόμενος. Διὰ δὴ τοῦτο πολλάκις παρά τινων ἐρωτώμενος ὁποῖος εἶναι ὀφείλει ὁ ἱερεύς, μόλις μετὰ
κατανύξεως ἀπεκρίνατο στένων· "Οἴμοι, ἀδελφοί, τί με
περὶ τοιούτων ἐρωτᾶτε; καὶ τὸ πρᾶγμά ἐστι φρικτὸν καὶ
νοούμενον. Ἐγὼ μὲν ἱερεὺς εἶναι οὐδαμῶς εἰμι ἄξιος, τὸ
φρικτὸν τῆς ἱερᾶς ἐννοῶν ἀξίας· πλὴν ὅμως ἀσφαλῶς ὁ
ταπεινὸς οἶδα ποταπὸς ὀφείλει εἶναι ὁ ἱερεύς· πρῶτον μὲν
ἁγνὸς οὐ τῷ σώματι μόνον ἀλλὰ πολλῷ μᾶλλον καὶ αὐτῇ
τῇ ψυχῇ. Οὐ μόνον δὲ ἀλλὰ καὶ πάσης ἁμαρτίας ἀμέτοχος,
καὶ τῷ μὲν ἔξωθεν ἤθει ταπεινός, τῷ δὲ ἔσωθεν⁶³
καταστήματι συντετριμμένος. Ὅτε δὲ τῇ ἱερᾷ τραπέζῃ
παρίσταται, νοερῶς μὲν τὴν θεότητα, αἰσθητῶς δὲ τὰ προ-
κείμενα δῶρα ὀφείλει ὁρᾶν καὶ αὐτὸν τὸν ἐν τοῖς δώροις
ἀοράτως παρόντα γνωστῶς κεκτῆσθαι ἐν τῇ καρδίᾳ αὐτοῦ, ἵνα μετὰ παρρησίας δύναται τὰς ἱκετηρίας προσφέρειν
καὶ ὡς φίλος φίλῳ διαλέγεσθαι τῷ Θεῷ καὶ Πατρὶ καὶ
ἀκατακρίτως λέγειν, 'Πάτερ ἡμῶν ὁ ἐν τοῖς οὐρανοῖς,' ὡς
τὸν ἀληθινὸν Θεὸν καὶ φύσει ὄντα Υἱὸν τοῦ Θεοῦ ἔχων
οἰκοῦντα ἐν ἑαυτῷ διὰ τοῦ οἰκοῦντος Ἁγίου Πνεύματος ἐν
αὐτῷ."

Symeon, who had reached the depths of humility, thus tried to hide himself away and, if he could, even escape the attention of his companions, because he shunned human praise. Indeed, for this reason, although people often asked him what sort of man a priest should be, he would sigh and reply reluctantly and contritely, "Alas, brothers, why are you asking me about such things? This is an awesome subject even to consider. I myself am in no way worthy to be a priest, when I consider how awesome the priestly dignity is. However, even I, your humble servant, certainly do know what sort of person a priest should be. First, he should be pure not only in body, but even more so in his soul. Moreover, he should also be free from all sin, outwardly humble in disposition, and inwardly contrite in character. When he stands at the holy altar table, he should see the divinity intellectually at the same time that he sees with his senses the offerings that are set out there. He should thus maintain a clear conception in his heart of the One who is present invisibly in the offerings, so that he can address his supplications confidently, and converse, as friend to friend, with his God and Father, and say irreproachably, 'Our Father who art in heaven,' because he has the true God and He who is by nature the Son of God dwelling in him through the Holy Spirit that dwells in him."[31]

32

Ταῦτα λέγων ἡφίει δακρύων λιβάδας καὶ ἕκαστον τῶν συνόντων ἠξίου μὴ ἐφίεσθαι μηδὲ ἀναξίως ἐπιτρέχειν πρὸ τοῦ διὰ πόνων ἐλάσαι πολλῶν εἰς τοιαύτην κατάστασιν τῷ ὑψηλῷ καὶ ἀγγέλοις φοβερῷ μυστηρίῳ, ἀλλὰ πονεῖν μὲν καθ᾽ ἑκάστην εἰς τὴν ἐργασίαν σπουδαίως τῶν ἐντολῶν τοῦ Χριστοῦ, μετανοεῖν δὲ[64] καθ᾽ ὥραν ὡς εἰπεῖν ὑπὲρ ὧν πλημμελοῦμεν ἄνθρωποι ὄντες ἡμεῖς οὐ μόνον διὰ σαρκὸς ἀλλὰ καὶ διὰ μέσου νοὸς καὶ τῶν ἀφανῶν τῆς ψυχῆς λογισμῶν, καὶ οὕτω μᾶλλον ἐν συντετριμμένῳ τῷ πνεύματι καθ᾽ ἑκάστην θυσίαν ἀναφέρειν Θεῷ ὑπέρ τε ἑαυτῶν καὶ τῶν πλησίον εὐχὰς καὶ δεήσεις μετὰ δακρύων τὴν μυστικὴν ἱερουργίαν ἡμῶν, ᾗ καὶ Θεὸς ἥδεται καὶ ἣν προσδεχόμενος εἰς τὸ ἅγιον καὶ ὑπερουράνιον καὶ νοερὸν αὐτοῦ θυσιαστήριον ἀντιδίδωσιν ἡμῖν τὴν τοῦ παναγίου Πνεύματος δωρεάν.

33

Οὕτω τοίνυν τοῖς πυθομένοις ἀποκρινόμενος καὶ οὕτως ἐν καταστάσει τοιαύτῃ ὁ τῶν ἄνω τάξεων συλλειτουργὸς καθεσθεὶς ἐν καθέδρᾳ τῶν πρεσβυτέρων [cf. Apc 4:4, 11:16] τὴν ἀναίμακτον ἀεὶ τῷ Θεῷ θυσίαν προσέφερεν ἐν ὀπτασίᾳ τοῦ Πνεύματος καὶ ἀγγελομόρφῳ τοῦ προσώπου

Chapter 32

As he uttered these words, Symeon would shed streams of tears and would demand that each of those present not desire or unworthily seek that sublime mystery, which is fearful even to the angels, before they had achieved through much labor the spiritual condition described above. Rather they should work hard every day at carrying out Christ's commandments, and repent all the time, so to speak, for the offenses which we, being human, commit, not only in the flesh but also in the mind and in the secret thoughts of our souls. Thus too, in a state of spiritual contrition, they were to offer up prayers and tearful supplication on behalf of themselves and their neighbors at each sacrifice to God, at our mystical sacred rite. For God is also pleased by this sacrifice and, receiving it upon His holy, celestial, and intellectual altar, repays us with the gift of His all-holy Spirit.

Chapter 33

So this would be Symeon's response to those who asked. And it was in this very condition that this man who was a concelebrant with the heavenly ranks, seated on the elders' chair,[32] would always offer the bloodless sacrifice to God, experiencing the vision of the Spirit and with his face re-

μορφῇ. Οὐδὲ γὰρ εἰ καὶ σταθερός τις ἦν τὴν ψυχὴν ὁ πρὸς
αὐτὸν ἀτενίζων ἐν τῷ καιρῷ τῆς λειτουργίας αὐτοῦ ἠδύνατο ἀτενῶς ὁρᾶν εἰς τὴν λαμπρότητα τοῦ προσώπου
αὐτοῦ ὁπηνίκα τῷ λαῷ τὴν εἰρήνην ἐδίδου, ὑπὸ τῶν ἐκ-
πεμπομένων ἐκεῖθεν ἀκτίνων τοὺς ὀφθαλμοὺς σκοτιζόμε-
νος, ἀλλὰ καθάπερ ὁ πρὸς τὸν δίσκον αἴφνης ἰδὼν τοῦ
ἡλίου καὶ τὸ προσὸν αὐτῷ φῶς ἀμαυροῖ οὕτω πάσχων
πρὸς ἑαυτὸν συνεστέλλετο· ἡ γὰρ χάρις τοῦ Πνεύματος
ὅλη ἐν ὅλῳ διαδοθεῖσα τῷ τούτου σώματι[65] ὅλον ὡς πῦρ
αὐτὸν ἀπειργάσατο καὶ σχεδὸν ἀπρόσιτος ἦν ἀνθρωπίνοις
ὀφθαλμοῖς ἐν τῷ καιρῷ τῆς λειτουργίας αὐτοῦ.

2   Ἔλεγε δὲ καὶ Συμεὼν ὁ Ἐφέσιος, μαθητὴς τοῦ ἀνδρὸς
καὶ αὐτὸς γεγονὼς καὶ τὰ ἐκείνου τισὶ διηγούμενος, ὅτι τέ,
φησί, "Συλλειτουργῶν τῷ ἁγίῳ, τοὺς νοεροὺς ὀφθαλμοὺς
ἀποκαλυφθεὶς εἶδον αὐτὸν κατὰ τὸν καιρὸν ἐκεῖνον τῆς
λειτουργίας αὐτοῦ ἔνδον τοῦ θυσιαστηρίου μετὰ ὠμοφο-
ρίου πατριαρχικὴν στολὴν περικείμενον καὶ τοῖς θείοις
ἐνασχολούμενον μυστηρίοις." Ἐμὲ δὲ ὡς καὶ Μελέτιος ὁ
ὑπὸ τῶν ἐκείνου χειρῶν ἀποκαρεὶς ἐβεβαίωσεν, ὅτι "Νεφέλην φωτεινὴν[66] πολλάκις," φησίν, "ἑωρῶμεν καλύπτουσαν
ὅλον αὐτὸν ἱστάμενον ἐν τῷ βήματι τῷ καιρῷ τῆς ἁγίας
ἀναφορᾶς." Καὶ εἰκότως, οἱ γὰρ τῷ ὕψει τῶν ἀρετῶν δια-
πρέποντες καὶ τῆς ἐνθέου δόξης καταξιοῦνται.

sembling that of an angel. Indeed, not even someone who was spiritually sturdy, and who stared directly at him when he was celebrating the liturgy, was able to gaze directly into the brightness of Symeon's face when he offered the peace to the congregation; for his eyes would be blinded by the rays that were given off by it, and just as when someone suddenly looks at the disk of the sun and is blinded by its light, so the person who experienced this would shrink away. For, since the grace of the Spirit had been distributed throughout his entire body, it made him like fire, and the human eye could scarcely look at him when he was celebrating the liturgy.

Symeon of Ephesus, who had also been the man's disciple, would say, when he was telling people stories about him, "When I was concelebrating with the saint, my intellectual eyes were opened and I saw him, at the moment when he was celebrating the liturgy in the sanctuary, with an *omophorion* and wearing a patriarch's stole,[33] engrossed in the divine mysteries." And Meletios, who was tonsured at his hands, confirmed to me that "we would often see a luminous cloud completely enveloping him when he was standing in the sanctuary at the time of the holy eucharistic prayer." And rightly so, for *those who become eminent for reaching the summit of the virtues are also worthy of the glory of God.*[34]

2

34

Ἐπεὶ δὲ τὴν τοῦ ποιμνίου φροντίδα τῶν λογικῶν προβάτων Χριστοῦ ἀνεδέξατο τῷ χρόνῳ δεκάτῳ ἐσαθρώθη τὸ μοναστήριον, καὶ οὐχὶ μοναστῶν καταγώγιον ἢ ποίμνιον ἦν, ἀλλὰ κατάλυμα κοσμικῶν καὶ νεκρῶν σωμάτων πολυάνδριον ἐχρημάτιζεν, ἐν ὀλίγοις τοῖς καταμένουσι καὶ αὐτοῖς ἀγεωργήτοις λιμώττουσι τὸν λιμὸν τοῦ Λόγου ἐξ ἀκαρπίας, πρῶτα μὲν τὰς ὀλίγας ἐκείνας καὶ πιστευθείσας αὐτῷ τρέφει ψυχὰς τροφῇ ἀθανάτῳ τοῦ Λόγου, καὶ τοῦ λιμοῦ ἀνακτᾶται καὶ ζωῆς ἀπογεύει τῆς κρείττονος. Εἶτα *συνάγει μετὰ Ἰησοῦ* [cf. Mt 12:30, Lk 11:23] καὶ προστίθησι τὸν ἀριθμὸν τῶν προβάτων καὶ αὐξάνει τοῦτον εἰς πλῆθος καὶ μαθητῶν λογάδα συνίστησι καὶ ἐκ μιᾶς ῥαγὸς ἢ ἀτελοῦς καὶ ἀώρου τοῦ βότρυος πολλοὺς τῇ Δεσποτικῇ ληνῷ πλήρεις βότρυας ἐναποτίθεται *ἄνδρας ἐπιθυμιῶν* [cf. Dn (Theodotion) 9:23; 10:11, 19] τῶν τοῦ πνεύματος.

2   Ἀλλὰ γὰρ ἐπεὶ πολλῆς ἐδεῖτο βοηθείας εἰς ἀνάκτησιν ἡ μονή, τὰ μὲν συμπεπτωκότα καὶ κάτω κείμενα ἐκφορεῖ τοῦ μέσου ὡς ἄχρηστα καὶ ὅλον τὸ μοναστήριον πλὴν τοῦ ναοῦ ἐκ βάθρων φιλοτίμως ἀνοικοδομεῖ. Τὸν δέ γε ναόν, ὃν Μαυρίκιον λέγεται κτίσαι τὸν αὐτοκράτορα, τῶν νεκρῶν σωμάτων ἀποκαθαίρει πάλαι πολυάνδριον γεγονότα, καὶ τὸ ἔδαφος αὐτοῦ μαρμάροις καταστρωννύει καὶ καλλωπίζει τοῦτον τοῖς ἀναθήμασιν εἰκόσιν ἱεραῖς ἁγίων⁶⁷ καταλαμπρύνας. Πρὸς τούτοις καὶ βίβλων ἐν αὐτῷ ποιεῖται ἀπόθεσιν ἱερῶν ἐνδυτῶν καὶ λοιπῶν ἄλλων σύναμα

74

Chapter 34

When Symeon took up responsibility for the flock of Christ's spiritual sheep, the monastery had been dilapidated for a long time. It was not a shelter for monks or a flock, but a lodging for laypeople and a place for burying the dead. The few still living there were not being cultivated and so were not yielding fruit and were famished with hunger for the Word. First of all, then, Symeon nourished those few souls who had been entrusted to him with the eternal food of the Word, revived them from their hunger, and gave them a taste of the better way of life. He then *gathered* with Jesus, added to the number of the sheep, increased this number greatly, and assembled a chosen group of disciples. From one grape, or rather from an imperfect and unripe bunch of grapes, he deposited many full bunches in the Master's winepress, *men full of desire* for spiritual things.

The monastery itself needed a lot of attention if it was to   2
be restored. The parts that had collapsed and were lying on the ground were useless, so he dug them out from the center and lavishly rebuilt the whole monastery from the foundations up, except for the church. As for the church, which the emperor Maurice[35] is said to have built originally and which had long since become a burial place, he cleared it of the bodies and then paved the floor with marble slabs. He beautified it with votive offerings, and made it resplendent with holy icons of the saints. He also created a place in it for storing books, sacred vestments, and other such things, and adorned it with windowpanes made from turned disks of

LIFE OF SAINT SYMEON

τοῖς φωταγωγοῖς ἐξ ὑέλου τετορνευμένοις καὶ θαυμασίοις
τὸ κάλλος πολυκανδήλοις.

35

Οὕτω δὲ τὸ ὅλον ὁ Συμεὼν ἀνοικοδομήσας φροντι-
στήριον ἅπτεται λοιπὸν καὶ τῆς τῶν μαθητῶν ἀνακτήσε-
ως, κατηχῶν καὶ διδάσκων αὐτοὺς τὴν τέχνην τῶν τεχνῶν
καὶ τὴν ἐπιστήμην τῶν ἐπιστημῶν τὴν πολιτείαν τῶν μοναχῶν, λόγῳ μὲν ὀλίγα, ἔργῳ δὲ διεγείρων τὰ πλείω πρὸς
τὴν τῶν ἐντολῶν ἐργασίαν ἑαυτὸν αὐτοῖς ὑπογραμμὸν
προτιθεὶς καὶ λέγων· "Ἀπ' ἐμοῦ ὄψεσθε καὶ οὕτω ποιήσετε
[Jdg 7:17]." Ἔνθεν οὖν καὶ τράπεζαν κοινὴν ἑαυτῷ καὶ
τοῖς⁶⁸ μαθηταῖς ἐτίθει τὰ ἐφθὰ λάχανα καὶ τὰ σπέρματα,
ὧν οἱ μὲν ἀρκούντως μεταλαμβάνοντες μετ' εὐχαριστίας
ἀνίσταντο, ὁ δὲ πολλάκις καὶ αὐτῶν ἀπεχόμενος μόνοις
ἠρκεῖτο λαχάνοις ὠμοῖς καὶ ὕδατι μεμετρημένῳ, ὁμοῦ τε
ὑποπιάζων καὶ δουλαγωγῶν [cf. 1 Cor 9:27] ἑαυτὸν καὶ τοῖς
φοιτηταῖς ὑπόδειγμα παρέχων τῆς στενωτάτης καὶ τεθλιμ-
μένης ὁδοῦ [cf. Mt 7:14] ἐν ἑαυτῷ.

2   Οὕτω τοίνυν ποιοῦντι καὶ οὕτω διδάσκοντι ἐπαυξάνε-
ται⁶⁹ αὐτῷ τὸ τῆς κατανύξεως ἄνωθεν χάρισμα διὰ ταπεινοφροσύνης ὑπερβολήν, ὃ καὶ διὰ παντὸς αὐτῷ τοῦ βίου
ἄρτος καὶ πόμα ἦν, ὡς λέγειν μετὰ Δαυὶδ καὶ αὐτόν· "Ἐψώ-
μισας ἄρτον δακρύων [cf. Ps 79(80):5] καὶ ἐπότισας ἡμᾶς

76

glass[36] and with candelabra that were amazing in their beauty.

Chapter 35

After he had rebuilt the whole monastery, Symeon then also undertook the reformation of his disciples. He instructed and taught them *the art of arts and the science of sciences,*[37] that is, the monastic way of life, encouraging fulfillment of the commandments to some extent by word, but more so by deed, setting himself before them as an example and saying, *"Look at me and do likewise."* He thus established communal meals for himself and his disciples consisting of boiled vegetables and grains. They received plenty to eat and would rise <from the table> with gratitude, but Symeon himself would often abstain even from those things and would be satisfied with only raw vegetables and a measure of water. So, at the same time as he *pummeled and mortified* himself, he presented himself to his disciples as a model of the *most narrow and hard way.*

While he acted and taught in this way, the heavenly gift 2 of compunction developed in him through his extreme humility. Throughout his life this gift was his bread and drink, so that he too could say with David, "You have *fed us the bread of tears* and *have given us the wine of compunction to drink.*" Of

οἶνον κατανύξεως [Ps 59(60):3]." Ἀμέλει καὶ τρεῖς ἑαυτῷ
καιροὺς τῆς ἡμέρας εἰς τοῦτο τὸ ἔργον ἐτάξατο καθάπερ
εἴρηται· τὸν τῆς πρωΐας μετὰ τοὺς ὕμνους τοὺς ἑωθινούς,
τὸν τῆς ἁγίας ἀναφορᾶς καθ' ὃν ὁ Υἱὸς τοῦ Θεοῦ σφαγι-
άζεται καὶ τὸν τῆς ἑσπέρας μετὰ πᾶσαν ἄλλην ὑμνολογίαν.
Ἐν γὰρ τοῖς τρισὶ τούτοις καταμόνας ἱστάμενος εἰς εὐχὴν
μόνος μόνῳ μετὰ δακρύων προσωμίλει Θεῷ.

36

Τοιαύτην οὖν ἐν τῷ λεληθότι καθ' ἑκάστην ἔχων ὁ γενναῖος τὴν ἐργασίαν, ἐν μιᾷ ὡς ἵστατο ἐν νυκτὶ καὶ ἀπεδί-
δου τὰς εὐχὰς αὐτοῦ τῷ Κυρίῳ, εἶδε καὶ ἰδοὺ νεφέλη φωτὸς
[cf. Mt 17:5] ἐξ οὐρανοῦ κατελθοῦσα τῆς στέγης ἀρθείσης
τοῦ οἴκου ἐκάθισεν ἐπάνω τῆς αὐτοῦ τιμίας κεφαλῆς, καὶ
καλύψασα ὅλον ἐφ' ἱκανὰς ὥρας θερμοτάτης αὐτὸν καὶ
ἀρρήτου τινὸς πεπλήρωκεν ἡδονῆς ἀνεκφράστου τε εὐφροσύνης καὶ θυμηδίας, ὡς καὶ μυστικῆς ἐκεῖθεν ἀκοῦσαι
φωνῆς ξένα τινὰ καὶ κεκρυμμένα μυστήρια διδαξάσης
αὐτόν. Διὰ δὴ τοῦτο καὶ ἀπαναστάσης αὐτῆς εὗρε τὴν
καρδίαν αὐτοῦ ἐν σοφίᾳ Θεοῦ τὰ τῆς θείας χάριτος βρύ-
ουσαν νάματα, καὶ τοῦ λοιποῦ οὐκ εἶχεν αὐτὸς ἑαυτόν,
ἀλλ' ἡ τοῦ Θεοῦ χάρις ὅλον αὐτὸν πρὸς ἑαυτὴν ἐπισπάσα-
σα τὴν μὲν γλῶτταν αὐτοῦ κάλαμον ὀξυγράφου [Ps 44(45):1],
τὴν δὲ διάνοιαν πηγὴν σοφίας [Bar 3:12] Θεοῦ ἀπειργάσατο. Διὰ τοῦτο καὶ ἀμαθὴς ὢν πάντη τῶν θύραθεν

course he also set aside for himself three times of the day for this labor, as has been mentioned: first thing in the morning after the hymns of matins, at the holy eucharistic prayer when the Son of God is slain, and in the evening after all the other hymn singing. For at these three times he would stand by himself in prayer and would converse through his tears, one on one with God.

Chapter 36

Such was the practice in which the noble man used to engage every day in private. On one occasion, however, while he was standing during the night <vigil> and offering up his prayers to the Lord, lo and behold, the roof of the house was lifted away and a *cloud of light* came down from heaven and settled above his venerable head. It covered him completely for many hours and filled him with a most intense and indescribable kind of pleasure, an ineffable happiness and delight, so that he heard in it a mystical voice which taught him certain strange and hidden mysteries. As a result, even when the cloud had lifted again, he discovered that, in the wisdom of God, his heart was bursting with the streams of divine grace. From that time forward he was no longer his old self, but rather the grace of God drew him completely into itself, and formed his tongue into *the pen of a swift writer,* his mind into a *fountain of* divine *wisdom.* As a result, although he was totally uneducated in secular learn-

μαθημάτων, ὡς ὁ ἠγαπημένος ἐθεολόγει καὶ τὰ τῆς θεολογίας ὅλαις νυξὶν ἀνετάττετο.

37

Καὶ πᾶσαν μὲν[70] φύσιν τὴν τῆς παρούσης ζωῆς μετέχουσαν δαμάζειν τὸν ὕπνον ἀκούομεν, ἐκείνου δὲ ἡ ψυχὴ τῶν ἀναγκῶν ἐκδῦσα τοῦ σώματος οὔτε τῷ ὕπνῳ μὴ βουλομένη εἴα τὸ σῶμα κάμπτεσθαι, οὔτε κόπου αἰσθάνεσθαι τῆς ὁλονύκτου ἀγρυπνίας καὶ στάσεως, οὔτε πείνης ἢ δίψης ἀνάγκαις ταπεινοῦσθαι καὶ καταπίπτειν, ἀλλ᾽ ὥσπερ οἱ ἁβροδίαιτον ἔχοντες βίον ἀνθηρὸν τὸ χρῶμα καὶ ἐρυθρὸν περιφέρουσιν ἐν εὐεξίᾳ, οὕτως ἐν κακοπαθείᾳ πάσῃ ὁ Συμεὼν ἑαυτὸν ἐδείκνυ φαιδρότατόν τε καὶ ἀγγελόμορφον. Ἀλλὰ τοιοῦτος ἀποτελεσθεὶς παρὰ τῆς ἄνωθεν χάριτος καὶ ἀποστολικῆς ἀξιωθεὶς δωρεᾶς, τοῦ λόγου τῆς διδασκαλίας φημί, ὄργανον ἦν καὶ ὡρᾶτο τοῦ Πνεύματος μυστικῶς κρουόμενον ἄνωθεν, καὶ πῇ[71] μὲν τῶν θείων ὕμνων τοὺς ἔρωτας ἐν ἀμέτρῳ μέτρῳ συνέταττε, πῇ[72] δὲ τοὺς λόγους τῶν ἐξηγήσεων ἐν πυκνότητι ἔγραφε νοημάτων, καὶ ποτὲ μὲν τοὺς κατηχητικοὺς συνεγράφετο λόγους, ποτὲ δέ τισιν ἐπιστέλλων ἐξάκουστος πᾶσιν ἐγίνετο.

ing, he would speak about God like the beloved <disciple John> and would devote whole nights to theological study.

Chapter 37

We hear that sleep conquers every creature that partakes of the present life, but since that man's soul had cast off the constraints of the body, it would not allow his body to be bowed down by sleep, unless it was willing, nor to feel weariness from keeping a standing vigil throughout the night, nor to be humbled by the constraints of hunger and thirst and to succumb to them. Rather, just as those who indulge in a life of luxury present a blooming and rosy complexion in their good health, so, in all his mortification, Symeon appeared most radiant and angelic. Because he had been made so perfect by grace from above and had been deemed worthy of the apostolic gift, I mean of the language of teaching, he was—and was seen to be—an instrument of the Spirit that was being mystically played upon from above.[38] And so he came to be known by everyone, for now he would compose in free meter his *Loves of Divine Hymns*,[39] now write exegetical works with great shrewdness of understanding, or at one time he would pen his *Catechetical Discourses*,[40] at another write letters to people.

38

Ἀλλὰ τί τὸ ἐντεῦθεν; Ἤρδευε μὲν οὖν ὡς ἔφην ἀεννά-
ως τοῖς λόγοις τὸ ποίμνιον, κἀκεῖνο καθ᾽ ἑκάστην ηὐξάνετο, οὐκ ἀπονητὶ δέ, οὐδὲ δυσχερείας πάσης ἐκτός, ἀλλὰ
μετὰ πολλοῦ πόνου καὶ τῶν πειρασμῶν τῶν παρὰ τοῦ
Ἐχθροῦ. Καὶ ἵνα ἐξ ἑνὸς καὶ τοὺς λοιποὺς τοὺς ἐπενεχθέν-
τας αὐτῷ πειρασμοὺς καταδήλους ἐργάσωμαι, τὸ γεγονὸς
εἰς αὐτὸν παρὰ τῶν μοναχῶν τῆς ἐκείνου μονῆς ἐν τῷ
καιρῷ τῆς συνάξεως διηγήσομαι. Τῆς ἑωθινῆς ἐν μιᾷ τελεσθείσης[73] δοξολογίας καθὼς ἔθος ἦν τῷ μακαρίῳ τοὺς
μαθητὰς κατηχεῖν, ὡς τῆς κατηχήσεως ἤρξατο νουθετῶν
ἐλέγχων παρακαλῶν κατὰ τὴν τοῦ ἀποστόλου παραίνεσιν
[cf. 2 Tim 4:2], αἴφνης ὡσεὶ τριάκοντα ἄνδρες τῶν μοναχῶν
τὰ ἑαυτῶν διαρρήξαντες παλλία,[74] ὡς οἱ περὶ Ἄνναν ποτὲ
καὶ Καϊάφαν [cf. Mt 26:65; Lk 3:2; John 18:13], κραυγαῖς
ἀσήμοις καὶ ὁρμήματι φονικῷ κινηθέντες καὶ τὴν ἐκκλησίαν πᾶσαν διαταράξαντες χεῖρας ἀνόμους [cf. Act 2:23]
τολμηρῶς ἦραν κατὰ τοῦ πατρὸς αὐτῶν, ὥστε συλλαβεῖν
καὶ ὡσεὶ θῆρες διασπαράξαι αὐτόν. Ὁ δὲ τὴν ἐξαίφνης ὡς
εἶδε τούτων ἀλλοίωσιν καὶ ὅπως ἀπηλλοτριώθησαν τοῦ
οἰκείου διδασκάλου τε καὶ πατρός, τὰς χεῖρας δεσμεύσας
πρὸς ἑαυτὸν καὶ εἰς οὐρανὸν ἄρας αὐτοῦ τὴν διάνοιαν, ἐπὶ
χώρας ἄσειστος ἔστη ὑπομειδιῶν καὶ φαιδρὸν ἀτενίζων
πρὸς τοὺς ἀλάστορας.

Chapter 38

But what happened then? As I have said, with the unceasing flow of his words Symeon continued to water his flock, and it increased every day. This did not happen without effort, however, nor without any difficulty, but rather by means of much toil and despite the trials instigated by the Enemy. So that I may elucidate by one example the other trials that ensued for him, I will narrate what happened to him during a service at the instigation of the monks in his monastery. It was the blessed one's custom to instruct his disciples after the doxology of the early morning service was finished. But on this one day, when he began his instruction, admonishing, persuading, and exhorting according to the apostle's advice, all of a sudden around thirty of the monks tore their cloaks, just as the followers of Annas and Caiaphas once did.[41] Then with incoherent shouts, moved by a murderous impulse, they threw the whole church into confusion and boldly raised *impious hands* against their father as they tried to grab him and, like wild animals, tear him to pieces. But when he saw their sudden transformation and how they had turned into enemies of their own proper teacher and father, Symeon clasped his hands firmly to himself and raised his thoughts to heaven, and stood there, motionless in his place, smiling and gazing radiantly at those vengeful men.

39

῾Ὡς δ᾽ ὥρμησαν κατ᾽ αὐτοῦ καὶ ταῖς ἀσήμοις κραυγαῖς τε καὶ βλασφημίαις κυνῶν ὑλακτούντων μανίαν καὶ ἀναίδειαν ἐπεδείξαντο, ἐκωλύοντο μὲν ἄνωθεν τὰς ἀνόμους χεῖρας ἐπιβαλεῖν αὐτῷ· πόρρωθεν γὰρ αὐτοὺς ἡ τῷ Συμεὼν ἐνοικοῦσα χάρις ἐποίει καὶ ἀπεπέμπετο. Ἀποροῦντες δὲ τί διαπράξονται, τῆς ἐκκλησίας δρομαίως ἐξέρχονται, καὶ τὰ κλεῖθρα τῆς πύλης τοῦ μοναστηρίου συντρίψαντες τὴν φέρουσαν εἰς τὸ πατριαρχεῖον ὥσπερ ἐξεστηκότες καὶ μαινόμενοι ἔθεον, μόνον τὸν μακάριον μετὰ τῶν ἐν εὐλαβείᾳ ζώντων ἐγκαταλείψαντες. Ὡς δὲ τὴν πρώτην πύλην εἰσῆλθον τῆς μεγάλης τοῦ Θεοῦ ἐκκλησίας ἄοπλοι, καὶ ταῖς κραυγαῖς τὸν ἀρχιερέα—Σισίννιος δὲ ἦν—κάτωθεν ὤχλουν, μεταστέλλεται τούτους ὁ πατριάρχης, καὶ μαθὼν τῆς ταραχῆς τὴν αἰτίαν καὶ τὸ καττυθὲν ὑπ᾽ αὐτῶν κατὰ τοῦ ἁγίου, δεινὴν μανίαν αὐτῶν καταγνούς, τῇ ἐπαύριον μεταστέλλεται καὶ τὸν ἅγιον.[75]

2   Εἰσελθὼν οὖν ὁ μακάριος σεμνῷ τῷ ἤθει καὶ ἱλαρῷ καταστήματι πρὸς αὐτόν, τὴν αἰτίαν πρὸς αὐτοῦ τῆς τῶν μοναχῶν μανίας διερωτᾶται. Ὡς δ᾽ ἐκεῖνος ἅπαντα διηγήσατο ἐν τῷ νοστίμῳ λόγῳ τῆς χάριτος τὰ τῆς συνήθους ὁμιλίας καὶ κατηχήσεως, εἶθ᾽ οὕτω τὰ τῆς ἀναιδείας αὐτῶν καὶ τοῦ φονικοῦ ἐκείνων ὁρμήματος, καὶ ὅπως τὰ κλεῖθρα καὶ τοὺς μοχλοὺς τῶν πυλῶν συντρίψαντες ἔφυγον, ἐξεπλάγη πρὸς ταῦτα ὁ πατριάρχης καὶ γνοὺς τὸν φθόνον

Chapter 39

As they rushed at him with their incoherent cries and
blasphemies, they displayed the same frenzy and reckless-
ness as barking dogs, yet they were stopped from on high
from laying impious hands on him, for from afar the grace
that dwelled in Symeon acted upon them and drove them
away. Not knowing what to do next, they went racing out of
the church, leaving the blessed one alone with the monks
who lived in <true> piety. They smashed the bolts of the
monastery gate and ran off along the road that led to the
patriarchate as though they had lost their minds and gone
mad. After they had entered unarmed through the first gateway of the great church of God and disturbed the high priest
[patriarch]—this was Sisinnios[42]—with their cries from below, the patriarch summoned them. When he learned the
cause of the commotion and what they had concocted
against the holy one, and had observed their terrible, fren-
zied state, he summoned the saint on the next day.

The blessed one came before him with a dignified man- 2
ner and cheerful demeanor and was interrogated about the
cause of the monks' frenzy toward him. The patriarch was
astounded when Symeon, using the wholesome speech of
grace, told him all about his customary homily and instruction, and then about their shamelessness and their murderous onslaught and how they had fled, smashing the bolts and
the bars of the gates. Recognizing the envy and frenzy of

αὐτῶν καὶ τὴν μανίαν τῶν ἀσυνέτων, θυμοῦ δικαίου πλησθεὶς ἐξορίαν πάντων καταψηφίζεται.

40

Εἴπερ οὖν ἄλλος τις ἦν ὁ ταῦτα πεπονθὼς ὑπ᾽ ἐκείνων,
οὐκ ἂν ἤσθη ἐπὶ τῇ ψήφῳ; Οὐκ εὐφράνθη κατὰ τὸν εἰρη-
κότα, ὅταν τοιαύτην εἶδεν ἐκδίκησιν [cf. Ps 57(58):10]; Ἀλλ᾽
οὐχ οὕτως ὁ ποιμὴν ὁ καλὸς [John 10:11, 14] καὶ τοῦ πρώ-
του ποιμένος μιμητὴς ἀκριβέστατος! Ἐπειδὴ γὰρ τοὺς
ἀπάξοντας ἑτοίμους εἶδεν ἐπὶ τὸ τοὺς ἀποστατήσαντας
συλλαβέσθαι, πίπτει πρηνὴς καὶ τῶν πατριαρχικῶν ἐκείνων ἅπτεται ποδῶν ὁ τὴν ψυχὴν συμπαθέστατος καὶ τιθεὶς
αὐτὴν ὑπὲρ τῶν προβάτων [John 10:11, 15] αὐτοῦ, καὶ θρήνοις τὴν συγγνώμην αἰτεῖται. Κάμπτεται μόλις ὁ πατριάρχης καὶ τὴν μὲν ὑπερορίαν ταῖς παρακλήσεσιν ἀναβάλλε-
ται, οὐ συγχωρεῖ δὲ τούτοις ἔτι τὴν εἴσοδον τῆς μονῆς.
Αὐτίκα γοῦν ἀπελαύνονται πάντες τῆς ἐκκλησίας καὶ μανίας πλησθέντες σκορπίζονται [cf. Mt 12:30] τῷ οἰκείῳ θελήματι ἕκαστος αὐτῶν ἐξακολουθῶν· ὧν οἱ μὲν ἐν κατη-
χουμένοις ἐκκλησιῶν, οἱ δὲ πρὸς ἑτέρας μονὰς ἀπερρίφησαν,
ὅσοι δὲ τῆς κάτω μοίρας καὶ τῶν εὐτελεστέρων ἦσαν ὧδε
κἀκεῖσε ὅπη ἕκαστος ἔτυχεν ἐσκεδάσθησαν.

those stupid men and filled with righteous anger, the patriarch condemned them all to exile.

Chapter 40

Now, if someone else had suffered in this way at the
hands of those men, would he not have been delighted at
the judgment? Would he not *have rejoiced,* in the words of
the psalm, *when he saw* such *vengeance?* Not this *good shepherd,*
this most faithful imitator of the first shepherd! For when
he saw that the men who were to arrest the rebels were ready
to lay hold of them, he prostrated himself and grasped the
patriarch's feet. Thus that most compassionate man also *laid
down his life for his sheep* and, with laments, asked that they
be pardoned. The patriarch was scarcely swayed, however,
and although he revoked their banishment as a result of
Symeon's pleas, he would still not allow them to return to
the monastery. So they were all driven straight out of the
church and, filled with their frenzy, were *scattered,*[43] each according to his own desire. Some were cast out into the *katechoumena* of churches,[44] some to other monasteries, while
the more useless ones and the worst of the lot were spread
around[45] here and there, wherever they ended up.

41

Τί οὖν ὁ ποιμὴν ὁ καλός; Μόνος εἰς τὸ μοναστήριον ὑποστρέφει τὰ σπλάγχνα ἐπὶ τῇ στερήσει τῶν προβάτων Χριστοῦ σπαρασσόμενος καὶ τοῖς δάκρυσι κατανтλούμενος. Καὶ βλέπε μοι ψυχῆς ἁγίας ἀκεραιότητα καὶ ἀνεξικακίαν δικαίου ἀνδρός! ἐπειδὴ γὰρ οὐκ ἦν αὐτῷ φορητὸν κενὴν καθορᾶν τὴν αὐλὴν τῶν προβάτων, τί ποιεῖ ὁ πάντα σοφὸς καὶ γενναῖος, ἵνα τὸ ποίμνιον ἑαυτῷ καὶ Θεῷ καταλλάξῃ καὶ πρὸς ἑαυτὸν συναγάγηται; Διερευνᾶται τοὺς τόπους τῆς πόλεως ἔνθα ἕκαστος αὐτῶν ἦν τῷ οἰκείῳ διάγων θελήματι, καὶ μαθὼν ἑκάστῳ τὰ πρὸς τὴν[76] χρείαν αὐτοῦ διαπέμπεται, λόγοις παρακλητικοῖς τὸ σκληρὸν μαλάσσων τῆς καρδίας αὐτῶν. Ὡς δὲ τοῦτο ἐπὶ πολλὰς ἡμέρας ἐπράττετο, καὶ ὁ καλὸς τῷ ὄντι ποιμὴν ἐν ταπεινῷ τῷ σχήματι παραγινόμενος ἑνὶ ἑκάστῳ αὐτῶν συνεκαθέζετο, καὶ τὰ πρὸς ἀγάπην ὡμίλει καὶ τὴν ὑποστροφὴν ἠτεῖτο μετὰ συγγνώμης, ὡς εἴ τις ἀδικήσας μᾶλλον ἢ ἀδικηθεὶς ὑπ' αὐτῶν, λόγοις διδασκαλίας κατεμάλαξεν αὐτῶν τὸ ἀντίτυπον καὶ σκληρὸν τῆς καρδίας, καὶ ἐν ὀλίγῳ πάντας συνήγαγεν *ὁ ποιμὴν ὁ καλός* [John 10:11, 14] *ὁ διὰ τῆς θύρας* τοῦ Ἰησοῦ *εἰς τὴν αὐλὴν εἰσελθὼν τῶν προβάτων καὶ οὐχ ὡς κλέπτης ἄλλοθεν ἀναβάς* [John 10:1–2] καὶ τὴν ἰδίαν αὖθις αὐλὴν τοῖς ἡμέροις καὶ πρὸ βραχέος ἀγριωθεῖσι προβάτοις ἐγέμισεν.

Chapter 41

What did the good shepherd do then? He returned alone to the monastery, wracked with distress at the loss of Christ's sheep and bathed in tears. But consider with me the great simplicity of a holy soul and the forbearance of a righteous man! Since he could not bear to see the fold empty of sheep, what did that man, who was wise and noble in every way, do to reconcile his flock to himself and to God and gather them to himself once more? He tracked down the places in the city where each of them was living according to his own desire. When he had located them, he sent each man whatever he needed and softened the hardness of their hearts with comforting words. After doing this for many days, that truly good shepherd went humbly to each one of them and sat down with him and talked about love. He would then ask each monk to return and forgive him, as if it were he, Symeon, who had wronged someone rather than having been wronged by them. With instructive words he softened the obstinacy and hardness of their hearts, and in a short time that *good shepherd,* who *enters the sheepfold through the door* of Jesus and not *as a thief climbing in another way,* gathered them all and filled his own fold again with docile sheep who a short time before had been running wild.

42

Ἀκουέτωσαν οἱ τοῦ νῦν αἰῶνος ποιμένες καὶ τὴν ἀρετὴν ἐκείνου μιμείσθωσαν, ἵνα καὶ τῆς χάριτος ἧς ἀπήλαυσεν[77] ἄνωθεν, εἴ γε βούλοιντο, κοινωνοὶ καὶ συμμέτοχοι γένωνται. Οὐ γὰρ ἡ σπουδὴ πᾶσα τῷ μακαρίῳ ἐκείνῳ κατὰ τοὺς ἄρτι ποιμένας καὶ διδασκάλους ὑπῆρχεν, ὥστε πᾶσαν αὐτοῦ πληρῶσαι θέλησιν εἰς ἀπολαύσεις τοῦ σώματος ἐν τῷ βίῳ, ἀλλὰ τὰ τῆς ἐπιθυμίας μᾶλλον ἐκκαύματα ἀναστέλλειν καὶ μὴ διδόναι τῷ χείρονι τὴν ῥοπὴν τῆς ψυχῆς, μόνῳ δὲ τῷ κρείττονι στοιχεῖν καὶ τῷ θείῳ θελήματι ἕπεσθαι. Διὰ ταῦτα τὴν μὲν δόξαν τῶν ἀνθρώπων ὡς αἰωνίου κολάσεως πρόξενον ἔφευγεν. Οὐδὲ γὰρ ἔπασχε[78] τὸ τῶν πολλῶν, οἳ μὴ ἔχοντες ὅπως ἐξ ἄκρας ἀρετῆς τοῖς ἄλλοις αἰδέσιμοι φαίνεσθαι τῷ αὐχένι καὶ τῇ ὀφρύι τὸ φοβερὸν κατὰ τῶν ὑπὸ χεῖρα ἐπιμορφάζονται· ἀλλ' ἐμιμεῖτο τὸν αὐτοῦ Θεὸν καὶ Δεσπότην συμμετριάζων ἐν πᾶσι τοῖς μαθηταῖς, ὅθεν ἡ μακαριζομένη πενία ὡς πλοῦτος ἄσυλος αὐτῷ καὶ ἡ ἀκτημοσύνη ἠσπάζετο, δι' ἧς καὶ τὸ ταπεινὰ φρονεῖν καὶ ἀεὶ συντετριμμένον εἶναι τῷ πνεύματι ἐκείνῳ καλῶς ἐπεγίνετο.

Chapter 42

Today's shepherds should listen and imitate that man's virtue so that they too may share in and partake of the grace which he received from above, if they really want to. Unlike shepherds and teachers nowadays, the whole object of that blessed man's attention was not to fulfill his every wish for bodily pleasures in this life. Rather it was to suppress the things that kindle desire and not give in to the soul's propensity for the worse, but only to assent to the better and follow the divine will. Accordingly he fled men's praise as something that leads to eternal punishment. Nor did he suffer from the fault of so many people who, because they are unable to appear worthy of the respect of others by the loftiness of their virtue, pretend to be formidable to their subordinates by their haughty attitude and demeanor. Instead he would imitate his God and Master by observing the same moderation in all things with his disciples, and thus he embraced blessed poverty and the lack of possessions as secure wealth. For this reason he was also properly humble-minded and always contrite in spirit.

43

Ἐντεῦθεν αὐτῷ τὰ ῥεύματα τῶν δακρύων ἐπήγαζεν, ἡ πραότης ἐπήνθει, ὁ ἔρως τῆς τοῦ Θεοῦ ἀγάπης καὶ δικαιοσύνης, ἡ πρὸς τὸν πλησίον συμπάθεια, ἡ καθαρότης τῆς καρδίας, ἡ πρὸς ἑαυτὸν καὶ πάντας εἰρήνη, ἡ ὑπομονὴ τῶν πειρασμῶν καὶ τὸ ἕνεκεν δικαιοσύνης διωγμὸν ὑπομεῖναι ὡς μέγα τι κέρδος ἀεὶ αὐτῷ ἐσπουδάζετο [cf. Mt 5:3–12]. Διὸ καὶ τῆς ἐφέσεως οὐ διήμαρτεν, ἀλλ᾽ εἰς ἔργον ἐξέβη αὐτῷ τὰ τῆς προθέσεως ἔσχατον, καὶ τὰ τῆς ὑπομονῆς ἐδείχθη ἐν τοῖς πράγμασιν, ὡς προϊὼν ὁ λόγος δηλώσει. Ἐκεῖνος οὖν καὶ γεγαννυμένον ὥσπερ εἶχεν ἀεὶ διὰ ταῦτα τὸ πρόσωπον, ὑπὸ τῆς ἔνδοθεν χαρᾶς τοῦ Πνεύματος εὐφραινόμενος κατὰ τὸν εἰρηκότα Σοφόν· *καρδίας εὐφραινομένης θάλλει πρόσωπον* [Prov 15:13].

44

Τοιοῦτος ἦν ὁ Συμεὼν καὶ τοιοῦτον εἷλκε τὸν βίον καὶ τοιαύτην ἀεὶ μετήρχετο τὴν ἐργασίαν τὴν ἔμπρακτον. Ὃς πρῶτα μὲν τῷ[79] κόσμῳ καὶ τοῖς ἐν κόσμῳ καλῶς ἀπετάξατο [cf. Lk 14:33], γυμνωθεὶς πάσης προσπαθείας τῶν ὁρωμένων· εἶτα γυμνὸς τῶν ἰδίων θελημάτων εἰς τὸ στάδιον

Chapter 43

Hence floods of tears welled up in him, and his meekness blossomed, while he always eagerly strove after passion for the love and righteousness of God, sympathy for his neighbor, purity of heart, peace with himself and everyone else, endurance of trials, and the patient endurance of persecution for the sake of righteousness as goals of great value. Indeed, he did not fail in his aim, for he ultimately turned his intentions into actual deeds, and demonstrated his patient endurance by his actions, as my narrative will make clear in due course. And, throughout everything, his face was always beaming because he was gladdened by the inner joy of the Spirit, just as Wisdom has said, *A glad heart makes a cheerful countenance.*

Chapter 44

This was the kind of person Symeon was, this the sort of life he led, and this the actual work he always did. First of all he truly renounced the world and those in the world; then, stripped of every emotional attachment to all that is visible and freed from personal desires, he entered the arena of the

εἰσελθὼν τῆς ἀσκήσεως γενναίως τὸν Πολέμιον ἐτροπώ-
σατο. Εἶθ' οὕτω[80] προκόψας ἐπὶ τὸν λόγον ἀπὸ τῆς ἡσυχίας ἐν καθέδρᾳ τῶν πρεσβυτέρων [Ps. 106(107):32] ἐκάθισε
καὶ τῷ λόγῳ τῆς διδασκαλίας τὸν καταπιστευθέντα λαὸν
αὐτῷ κατεφώτισε, καὶ πολλοὺς ἀξίους ἐξ ἀναξίων προσή-
γαγε τῷ Θεῷ αὐτοῦ, καὶ τέλος πολλοῖς πειρασμοῖς ἐπάλαι-
σεν ἕνεκεν δικαιοσύνης, καὶ μέχρι τέλους τὸ μαρτύριον
τῆς αὐτοῦ συνειδήσεως ἀήττητον διεφύλαξε. Καὶ τοιοῦτος
μὲν ὡς εἴρηται ὁ ἐκείνου βίος, ὡς εἰπεῖν συντετμημένῳ τῷ
λόγῳ, ὁ ἔμπρακτος θεωρητικώτατός τε καὶ ὑψηλότατος,
τελειωθεὶς ἐν λόγῳ θεολογίας καὶ μεγάλῃ σοφίᾳ Θεοῦ.
Τοιοῦτον δὲ καὶ τὸ ποίμνιον αὐτοῦ, ὡς εἶναι ἄλλην ἐκκλησίαν τῶν ἱερῶν Στουδιτῶν ἐν τύποις καὶ πράγμασι καὶ
αὐτῇ τῇ καταστολῇ καὶ τοῖς ἔθεσιν, ἢ μᾶλλον ἀγγέλων
εἰπεῖν ἀσωμάτων ψάλλουσαν συνετῶς [cf. Ps. 46(47):7] καὶ
λειτουργοῦσαν θερμῶς τῷ Θεῷ [cf. Ps 103(104):4; Heb 1:7,
14]. Οὕτως οὖν ἔχων καὶ οὕτω τὸ σῶμα τῆς ταπεινώσεως
ὑπεραναβὰς ὁ μακάριος ηὔξανέ τε καθ' ἑκάστην ἐπὶ τὸ
κρεῖττον ἐπεκτεινόμενος [cf. Phlp 3:13] καὶ ηὐξάνετο πρὸς
αὐτοῦ τὸ ποίμνιον τοῦ Χριστοῦ διὰ τῶν ἀποκειρομένων
αὐτοῦ μαθητῶν.

monastic life and nobly routed the Enemy. Next, after he had advanced in the word <of God> through his spiritual tranquillity, he sat *in the assembly of the elders* and enlightened with the words of his teaching the people entrusted to him. In this way he brought to his God many worthy people who had been worthless. Finally, he wrestled with many trials for the sake of righteousness and to the last kept unvanquished the martyrdom of his conscience. So, as has been said, this was the sort of life <he led>, one that was, to put it briefly, practical, very contemplative, profoundly spiritual, and accomplished in the study of theology and the great wisdom of God. And this also was the sort of flock he had, one that was, as it were, another church of holy Stoudites in its rule, its activities, even in its very dress and customs,[46] although one might rather say it was <a church> of incorporeal angels singing psalms intelligibly to God and ministering fervently to Him. So, being like this and having transcended his body through his humility, the blessed one grew every day as he strained toward the better, and he increased the flock of Christ through the disciples he tonsured.[47]

45

Ἀλλὰ γὰρ ἄξιον ἑνὸς ἢ δύο τῶν ἐκείνου μαθητῶν ἐπι-
μνησθῆναι τῆς ἀρετῆς καὶ ὡς ἐν παρόδῳ περὶ αὐτῶν διη-
γήσασθαι, ὡς ἂν καὶ ἐντεῦθεν ἐκδηλοτέρα γένηται πᾶσιν
ἡ τοῦ διδασκάλου αὐτῶν ἀρετή. Ἀνήρ τις καὶ αὐτὸς ἐκ
Παφλαγόνων ὁρμώμενος, τὸ σῶμα εὐνοῦχος, ταχυγράφος
τὴν ἐπιστήμην, ἄρτι τῆς ματαιότητος κατολιγωρήσας τοῦ
βίου, ἐπεὶ φήμη τις εἶχεν αὐτὸν τοῦ μακαρίου πατρός,
φοιτᾷ πρὸς αὐτὸν τῷ κόσμῳ πάντη ἀποταξάμενος [cf. Lk
14:33]. Ὡς οὖν εἶδε καὶ ἐξήτασεν αὐτὸν ὁ μακάριος Συμεών, καὶ πανταχόθεν[81] εὗρε μεμισηκότα τὸν κόσμον καὶ
θερμῶς προσπεφευγότα Θεῷ, ἔνδον[82] τῆς ἑαυτοῦ μάνδρας
αὐτὸν ὑποδέχεται, καὶ τὴν κοσμικὴν ἐσθῆτα τούτου περι-
ελόμενος ἀμφιέννυσι τό γε νῦν ἔχον τὸν τῆς δουλείας σάκκον, μὴ δοὺς αὐτῷ τὸν ἀρραβῶνα τοῦ σχήματος, ὡς ἂν[83]
εἰ καλῶς μετέρχοιτο τὰς ἐπιτασσομένας αὐτῷ δουλείας καὶ
τὸν κόπον πάσης ὑπομένοι προθύμως κακοπαθείας, εὐκαί-
ρως αὐτῷ δοθείη τότε καὶ ἡ καταστολὴ τοῦ ἁγίου σχήματος, καὶ τοῖς λοιποῖς ἀδελφοῖς τῆς αὐτῆς κοινωνήσει στά-
σεώς τε καὶ τάξεως. Δοὺς οὖν ἐν ὀλίγῳ τῆς ὑποταγῆς

4. Arsenios, Hierotheos, and Other Disciples
of Symeon at Saint Mamas

Chapter 45

It is worth recalling the virtue of one or two of his disciples and telling about them in passing so that, in this way, the virtue of their teacher may become clearer to everyone. One man, who also came from Paphlagonia, was a eunuch in body, a stenographer by profession. He had recently grown contemptuous of the vanity of this life and so, when the blessed father's reputation came to his attention, he went off to him and bade a complete farewell to the world. When the blessed Symeon met him and questioned him, he discovered that he had come to hate everything about the world and had fled ardently to God, so he received him into his own fold. He removed his worldly clothing and dressed him for the time being in the coarse tunic of servitude. He did not promise him the monastic habit, however, so that if he attended properly to the tasks assigned him and willingly endured the toil of every mortification, he might then also, when the time was right, receive the apparel of the holy monastic habit and share in the same standing and rank as the other brothers. After a short time, the man gave most excel-

αὐτοῦ ἀρίστην δοκιμὴν ὁ ἀνήρ, καὶ ὃν εἶχεν ἔρωτα εἰς τοὺς ὑπὲρ ἀρετῆς ἀγῶνας ἔργοις ὑποδείξας διὰ πασῶν τῶν ἀτιμοτέρων διακονιῶν διελθών, ἀποκείρεται πρὸς αὐτοῦ σὺν τῷ φαινομένῳ καὶ τὸν ἐντὸς ἄνθρωπον Ἀρσένιος ὀνομασθείς. Εἰσέρχεται τοίνυν εἰς τὸ στάδιον τῆς ἀσκήσεως, καὶ γυμνὸς τῶν τῆς ψυχῆς θελημάτων τῷ Ἀνταγωνιστῇ συμπλέκεται.

46

Κ̲αὶ ὅρα τὴν μέθοδον αὐτήν τε τοῦ Ἐχθροῦ καὶ τοῦ Ἀρσενίου τὸ πυκνόν τε καὶ φρόνιμον! ἐπειδὴ γὰρ ἡ τῶν γονέων στοργὴ δεσμός τίς ἐστι δυσδιάλυτος ὑπὸ τῆς φύσεως συσφιγγόμενος, καὶ ὀλίγοις ἡ ταύτης ἐφιλοσοφήθη ἀποφυγή, διὰ ταύτης πειρᾶται τὸν Ἀρσένιον καθελεῖν ὁ Ἐχθρός. Ἀλλὰ τὴν πίστιν ἔχων ἐκεῖνος πολλὴν εἰς τὸν μακάριον Συμεὼν ὡς ἱστὸν ἀράχνης ἐκ προοιμίων ταύτην διέρρηξεν, ὡς ἑξῆς δηλώσει τὸ ὑπ' ἐκείνου πραχθέν.

2   Μήτηρ ἦν ἔτι ζῶσα τῷ Ἀρσενίῳ καὶ αὐτὴ[84] κατὰ τὸν Εὔξεινον Πόντον τὴν οἴκησιν ἔχουσα. Ταύτην ὁ Παμμήχανος κινήσας παρεσκεύαζε διὰ τὸν τοῦ υἱοῦ πόθον πρὸς τὴν βασιλεύουσαν τῶν πόλεων εἰσελθεῖν. Τοίνυν καὶ εἰσελθοῦσα ἔμαθε[85] τὴν τοῦ υἱοῦ ἀποταγὴν καὶ καταμονήν, φοιτᾷ σπουδαίως ἐκεῖσε, καὶ πρὸς τὴν πύλην πεσοῦσα θρήνοις αἰτεῖται κατιδεῖν τὸν υἱόν. Ὁ οὖν πυλωρὸς τὴν

lent proof of his submission and, having performed all the more menial tasks, demonstrated by his actions his love of the spiritual contest for virtue. He was thus tonsured by Symeon and was given the name Arsenios, both outwardly and in respect to the inner man.[48] And so he entered the arena of the monastic life and, stripped naked of the desires of his soul, came to grips with his Opponent.

Chapter 46

And see the strategy of the Enemy, but also Arsenios's strength and intelligence! Since parental love is a bond that is hard to dissolve because it has been tied by nature, and few have contrived a way to escape it, it was through this that the Enemy tried to bring Arsenios down. But because he had great faith in the blessed Symeon, he tore this <strategy> apart like a spider's web right from the start, as his actions will now demonstrate.

Arsenios's mother was still alive, living by the Black Sea. 2 The Most Crafty One provoked this woman and arranged for her to come to the queen of cities because she was pining for her son. So when she arrived and learned about her son's renunciation <of the world> and tonsure, she rushed off there <to the monastery>. She cast herself down before the gate and, weeping and wailing, sought to see her son. The gatekeeper could not withstand the woman's violent insis-

βίαν μὴ φέρων τῆς γυναικὸς μηνύει ταύτην τῷ Ἀρσενίῳ, καὶ ὡς "Οὐκ ἀναστήσομαι," φησί, "τῶν ἐντεῦθεν, ἐὰν μὴ τὸν υἱόν μου ὄψομαι τὸν ποθούμενον." Τί οὖν ὁ ἀληθινὸς μαθητὴς τοῦ ἀληθινοῦ ποιμένος καὶ διδασκάλου; "Ἐγώ," φησί, "νεκρωθεὶς ἤδη τῷ κόσμῳ πῶς ἐπιστραφήσομαι, ἀδελφέ, εἰς τὰ ὀπίσω καὶ ὄψομαι ὥσπερ σὺ φῇς τὴν σαρκί με γεννήσασαν; ἔχω τὸν ἐμὲ κατὰ πνεῦμα γεννήσαντα, ἀφ᾽ οὗ τὸ ἄδολον θηλάζω καθ᾽ ἑκάστην τῆς τοῦ Θεοῦ χάριτος γάλα [cf. 1 Pt 2:2], τὸν ἐμὸν λέγω κατὰ Θεὸν πατέρα, ὃς καὶ μήτηρ μου χρηματίζει τῷ πνεύματί με γεννήσας, ὡς εἴρηται, καὶ κόλποις τῶν σπλάγχνων αὐτοῦ ὡς ἀρτιγενές με νήπιον περιθάλπει. Οὐκ ἀνέξομαί ποτε τοῦτον καταλιπεῖν καὶ πρὸς ἐκείνην αὐτομολῆσαι, εἰ καὶ ἀποψύξασαν ἐν τῷ πυλῶνι ἀκούσομαι." Ἤκουσεν ὁ πυλωρός, καὶ τῇ μητρὶ τοῦ Ἀρσενίου τὰ λαληθέντα μηνύει. Ἐν τῷ πυλῶνι οὖν μετὰ δακρύων ἐπὶ τρισὶν ἡμέραις ἐκείνη προσκαρτερήσασα, ἐπὶ τὴν ἐνεγκαμένην ὑπέστρεψεν μὴ ἡττηθέντα τὸν ἴδιον υἱὸν τῇ φυσικῇ στοργῇ κἂν ὅλως θεασαμένη.

47

Εἰ τοίνυν τοιοῦτος ἐκ πρώτης βαλβίδος ὁ γεννηθεὶς κατὰ πνεῦμα υἱός, ποταπὸς ἦν [cf. Mt 8:27] καὶ ὁποῖος ἄρα ὁ γεννήσας αὐτὸν τῷ ὕψει τῆς ἀρετῆς καὶ τῆς γνώσεως; Ἐκ γὰρ τῶν υἱῶν, φησὶν ὁ Σοφός, ἐπιγινώσκεται ὁ πατήρ

tence, so he sent word about her to Arsenios and <told him that> she was saying, "I'm not leaving here unless I see my beloved son." What did the true disciple of the true shepherd and teacher <reply>? "I've already died to the world, brother," he said, "so how will I turn back and see, as you say, the woman who gave birth to me in the flesh? I <now> have the man who has given birth to me in the spirit, from whom I suckle *the pure milk* of the grace of God every day, I mean my father in God. He is also to be reckoned as my mother because he has given birth to me in the spirit, as has been said, and nurtures me in the folds of his bosom[49] like a newborn babe. I'll never be able to leave him and desert to her, even if I hear she has passed away in the gatehouse." The gatekeeper heard this and reported Arsenios's words to his mother. She remained obstinately weeping in the gatehouse for three days, but then went back home without even laying eyes upon her son who was not defeated by her natural affection.

Chapter 47

If the spiritual son was like this, right out of the starting gate, then *what sort of man,* what kind of person was the one who had begotten him in the height of his virtue and knowledge? For the father is known by his sons, says Wisdom.

[cf. Sir 11:28]. Ἐπεὶ δὲ πρὸς τοὺς ὑπὲρ ἀρετῆς ἀγῶνας ἄρτι τὸν Ἀρσένιον ὁ μακάριος ἐγύμναζε Συμεών, καὶ σπουδαῖον εὗρεν αὐτὸν εἰς πᾶσαν ὑπακοήν, οὐκ ἐνέλειπε παρέχων αὐτῷ διψῶντι ἀφορμὰς εἰς ὠφέλειαν. Διὸ καὶ ποτὲ μὲν ἐπὶ τῇ δουλείᾳ τῶν ἡμιόνων, ποτὲ δὲ ἐπὶ τῇ τοῦ μαγειρείου ὑπηρεσίᾳ, ἄλλοτε ἐπὶ τῇ τοῦ ὕδατος καὶ ἐπὶ πάσῃ ἀτιμοτέρᾳ δουλείᾳ ὑπηρετεῖν αὐτὸν προετρέπετο. Ἐκεῖνος δὲ οὐ μόνον εἰς ταῦτα πρόθυμος ἦν, ἀλλὰ καὶ εἰς τὸ ἄλλως κακοπαθεῖν, νηστεύειν τε καὶ ἀγρυπνεῖν καὶ προσεύχεσθαι ὑπερενίκα [cf. Rom 8:37] πάντας τοὺς συνασκουμένους αὐτῷ μοναχούς. Ὅθεν καὶ ἐνστάσης κατ᾽ ἀρχὰς τῆς αὐτοῦ ἀποταγῆς τῆς ἁγίας τῶν νηστειῶν τεσσαρακοστῆς, πρεσβείαν πρὸς τὸν μακάριον ποιεῖται Συμεὼν ἄπειρος ἔτι τῆς ἀσκήσεως ὤν, τοῦ τὴν πρώτην ἑβδομάδα δι᾽ ὅλου ἄσιτον διελθεῖν. Ὁ δὲ ἅγιος τὸ μὲν ζέον ὁρῶν τῆς αὐτοῦ προθυμίας ἔχαιρέ τε ὡς εἰκὸς καὶ πρὸς ἀσκητικοὺς ἀγῶνας τοῦτον διήγειρεν, οὐκ ἐβούλετο δὲ στοιχεῖν τὸν Ἀρσένιον τῷ ἰδίῳ θελήματι, ἀλλ᾽ ἐκ τῆς ἐκκοπῆς μᾶλλον τοῦ θελήματος κερδαίνειν τὰ μείζω καὶ τελεώτερα. Διὸ καὶ οὐ κατανεύει τῷ τούτου θελήματι. Ὁ δὲ θερμὸς ἦν ἐπὶ τοῦτο καὶ ζητῶν ἐπέκειτο πληρωθῆναι τὴν αἴτησιν αὐτοῦ καὶ μὴ κωλυθῆναι τοῦ ἐγχειρήματος.

Once the blessed Symeon had stripped Arsenios in preparation for the spiritual contests for virtue, he found him eager for every act of obedience, and so he did not cease offering profitable opportunities to this man who was thirsting for them. He thus encouraged him to serve, whether in the task of <looking after> the mules, or in service in the kitchen, or otherwise in <fetching> the water and in every menial task. Arsenios was not only eager for this service, but he also *out-did* all the monks who were in training with him in mortifying himself in other ways, in fasting and keeping vigil, and in praying. So, toward the beginning of his submission, when the holy forty-day fast [of Lent] was starting, he made a request to the blessed Symeon to go the whole first week without food, even though he was still inexperienced in ascetic practice. The holy one probably rejoiced at seeing the fervor of his desire and would <normally> have encouraged him to ascetic contests, but as he did not want Arsenios to follow his own will but rather, from the excision of his will, to make greater and richer gains, he did not assent to his wish. But Arsenios fervently pressed his case as he sought to fulfill his request, and would not be hindered from the undertaking.

48

Ὡς δὲ πολλάκις μὲν ἀνέκοπτε τοῦτον τῆς ὁρμῆς ὁ μακάριος, πολλάκις δὲ ζητῶν ἐκεῖνος ἐπέκειτο γενέσθαι τὸ
αὐτοῦ θέλημα, φησὶ πρὸς αὐτόν· "Ἀρσένιε, καλὸν μὲν ἦν
καὶ λίαν ἐπωφελὲς μὴ στοιχεῖν τῷ ἰδίῳ θελήματι, πειθαρχεῖν δὲ μᾶλλον τοῖς ὑπ᾽ ἐμοῦ σοι ἐντελλομένοις· ἐπεὶ δὲ τὸ
ἐκτελέσαι τὸ ἴδιον θέλημα λυσιτελές σοι ἔδοξεν ἐν οἷς κέ-
κρικας, παρ᾽ ἐμοῦ μὲν εἰ καὶ ἀβουλήτως ὅμως ἐφεῖταί σοι
πρᾶξαι τὸ καταθύμιον. Ὅρα δὲ οἷον μέλλεις παθεῖν καὶ
οἵαν τὴν ἐπικαρπίαν τῆς ἀπειθείας[86] τρυγήσεις."

2   Εἶπε, καὶ τῆς πρώτης ἑβδομάδος ἐνστάσης ὡς εἶχε θέρμης ὁ Ἀρσένιος ἅπτεται τῶν τελειοτέρων ἀγώνων ἀκρίτως
εἰσαγωγικὸς ὢν ἔτι καὶ μετὰ θερμῆς τῆς[87] προθέσεως. Ὡς
δὲ τῶν ἄλλων ἁπάντων μετὰ τὴν ἐννάτην ἐπὶ τὸ δεῖπνον
εἰσερχομένων αὐτὸς μόνος ἔμενε προσκαρτερῶν ἄσιτος
πρὸς τὸν ἅγιον ἀφορῶν Συμεὼν καὶ τοῦτον μιμεῖσθαι
βουλόμενος, κατὰ τὴν ἀγρυπνίαν τῆς τετράδος μέσον τῶν
συμψαλλόντων ἱστάμενος ἐν νυκτὶ αἴφνης ὀλιγωρήσας
ὕπτιος ἐπὶ τὴν γῆν ῥίπτεται, πτῶμα παρακοῆς καὶ φόβου
τοῖς λοιποῖς ὑπόδειγμα φοβερώτατον.

3   Ὡς δὲ προγνοὺς ἦν τοῦτο ὁ ἅγιος καὶ ἑνὶ τῶν μαθητῶν
ἐπισκήψας προχείρως ἔχειν καυκάλιον οἴνου εἰς κρᾶσιν
καὶ ἄρτον ὀλίγον, νεύει τοῦ ἀγαγεῖν ἐπὶ μέσον τῆς συνάξεως ταῦτα τοῦ ὄρθρου, καὶ τούτου γεγονότος ἐν τάχει,
ἀναστῆσαι τὸν Ἀρσένιον προστάττει καὶ τούτοις θρέψαι
αὐτόν. Τραφεὶς οὖν ἐκεῖνος ἀνέστη μεθ᾽ ὅσης ἂν εἴποις τῆς

Chapter 48

Many times the blessed one checked Arsenios's impulsiveness, but just as often the latter insisted on having his own way. So after a while he said to him, "Arsenios, it would be a good thing and most advantageous for you not to follow your own will, but rather to obey my instructions to you. But since you think it useful to carry out your own will in your decision-making, you have my permission, albeit begrudgingly, to do what you want. But," he said, "watch out for what's going to happen to you and what sort of harvest you'll reap from your disobedience."

So, from the start of the first week, Arsenios engaged in 2 the more advanced contests as fervently as he could, but he did so ill-advisedly, for he was still a beginner, and hotheaded. As a result, when all the others went in to supper after <prayers at> the ninth hour, he alone remained fasting obstinately, looking to Symeon as his model and wishing to imitate him. During the Wednesday vigil, however, while he was standing among the choir brethren during the night, he suddenly felt faint and collapsed to the ground on his back, a fall caused by disobedience and a most fearsome example that frightened the others.

Because the holy one had foreseen this, he had instructed 3 one of the disciples to have ready a bottle of unmixed wine and a little bread. Symeon beckoned him to bring these in the middle of matins and, when he had quickly done so, ordered him to raise Arsenios up and feed him with them. After Arsenios had eaten, he stood up (you can imagine how

αἰσχύνης, ἀκούει δὲ παρὰ τοῦ μακαρίου· "Εἰ ὅμοιος κατὰ πάντα ἦσθα τοῖς ἀδελφοῖς, ἀνόμοιόν τι μέσον τούτων ἐν ἀγρυπνίᾳ οὐκ ἂν ἔπαθες, Ἀρσένιε. Ἐπεὶ δὲ τοῦ πλείονος ἐν οἰήσει καὶ ἀπειθείᾳ[88] ψυχῆς πρὸ καιροῦ τυχεῖν ἔσπευσας καὶ τὸ πρωτεῖον ἑλέσθαι κατὰ τῶν ἄλλων, καὶ τοῦ ἥττονος ἐνδίκως ἡστόχησας."

49

Ἐντεῦθεν οὐχ ἡ τυχοῦσα λαμβάνει μεταμέλεια τὸν Ἀρσένιον, ὡς ὑπὸ τῆς αἰσχύνης τοῦ συνειδότος εἰς βάθος ἐλάσαι αὐτὸν ταπεινώσεως. Καὶ ἵνα τῆς αὐτοῦ ταπεινώσεως τὴν[89] προκοπὴν ὁ λόγος δηλώσῃ, ἑνὸς ἢ καὶ δύο εἰς ἥδυσμά τι τῷ λόγῳ ἐκ τῶν εἰς αὐτὸν ὑπὸ τοῦ μακαρίου χάριν ταπεινώσεως γεγονότων διαμνημονεύσωμεν.

2   Τὴν τοῦ κελλαρίτου διακονίαν μετερχόμενος ὁ Ἀρσένιος, σῖτον ἐν μιᾷ ὕδατι πλύνας ἥπλωσεν αὐτὸν ἐν τῷ προνάῳ μίαν τῶν θυρῶν ἀνεῳγμένην καταλιπὼν τοῦ καταπνέεσθαι. Κορῶναι δέ ποθεν καταπτᾶσαι καὶ εἴσω χωρήσασαι κατετρύφων ὡς εἶχον τοῦ σίτου καὶ σκιρτῶσαι ἐφώναζον. Τῶν φωνῶν οὖν ἐνωτισθεὶς ὁ Ἀρσένιος καὶ ἅμα εἰσπεπηδηκὼς αὐτάς τε χανδὸν ἐμφορουμένας εὗρε τοῦ σίτου καὶ τὸν σῖτον διεσκεδασμένον ὧδε κἀκεῖσε. Τοῦτο τοίνυν ἰδὼν καὶ θυμοῦ κατὰ τῶν ὀρνίθων πλησθεὶς κλείει τὴν θύραν, καὶ πάσας κοντῷ συντρίψας ἐπ' ἐδάφους κατέρραξεν. Ὡς

ashamed he was) and heard the blessed one say: "If you had been like your brothers in every way, you would not have experienced anything different from them during the vigil, Arsenios. But since, in the self-conceit and disobedience of your soul, you have been eager to get the better of the others prematurely and win first place over them, you have justly failed to beat even the worst."

Chapter 49

An extraordinary repentance then came over Arsenios, for the shame of his conscience drove him to the depths of humility. And, so that my narrative may make clear the progress of his humility, let us call to mind, as a kind of spice to the story, one or two of the humiliations that befell him, thanks to the blessed one.

One day, while Arsenios occupied the office of cellarer, 2 he had washed some grain in water and then spread it out in the narthex of the church, leaving one of the doors open to let the breeze blow in. Some crows flew down from somewhere, went inside, and started enjoying as much of the grain as they could, hopping about and cawing. When Arsenios heard their cries, he rushed in at once and found them greedily gorging themselves on the grain, while the grain itself was scattered about here and there. At this sight he was filled with rage against the birds and shut the door before battering them all with a pole and beating them to pieces on

οὖν μέγα τι κατόρθωμα πεπραχὼς ἀπαγγέλλει ταῦτα τῷ μακαρίῳ.

3   Ὁ δὲ ὡς τοῦτο δῆθεν ἀποδεξάμενος, "Ἄγωμεν," φησί, "καὶ ἴδω κἀγώ, ὅπως ταῦτα καλῶς ποιήσας ἀπέκτεινας." Ἀπελθὼν οὖν ὁ ἅγιος καὶ τὰς ὄρνεις ἰδὼν ὅπως τῷ ἐδάφει νενεκρωμέναι κατέστρωντο, ἐστύγνασε λυπηθεὶς ἐπὶ τῷ ἀλόγῳ τούτου θυμῷ καὶ προσκαλεσάμενος ἕνα τῶν ὑπ᾽ αὐτὸν σπαρτίον ἐνεχθῆναι κελεύει, δεθῆναί τε πάσας καὶ ἐπὶ τὸν τράχηλον κρεμασθῆναι τοῦ Ἀρσενίου. Ὡς δ᾽ ἐγένετο θᾶττον λόγου τὸ προσταχθέν, σύρεσθαι προστάττει τοῦτον καὶ τὸ μοναστήριον περιάγεσθαι καὶ μέσον τῶν συνόντων θεατρίζεσθαι μοναχῶν. Ὁ δὲ οὕτως τὴν αἰσχύνην τοῦ δράματος καθυπέμεινε καταβεβλημένῳ φρονήματι, ὡς ποταμοὺς καταφέρειν δακρύων καὶ φονέα ἐπὶ τούτοις ἀποκαλεῖν ἑαυτόν. Ἱκανὰ τοίνυν τὰ εἰρημένα δεῖξαι ἀμφοτέρων τὴν ἀρετὴν καὶ τὸ ἐμφιλόσοφον ἔργον τῆς εὐσεβείας αὐτῶν.

50

Ἀλλ᾽ ἔτι προσθεῖναι καὶ ὃ μικροῦ διέδραμεν ἡμᾶς τοῖς εἰρημένοις χρεών. Φίλων ποτὲ τοῦ μακαρίου ἐγένετο πρὸς αὐτὸν παρουσία. Ἐπεὶ δὲ τούτων εἷς διὰ σωματικήν τινα νόσον ἐδέετο κρέατος μετασχεῖν καὶ τούτου περιστερῶν ἄρτι ἀνιπταμένων ἐκ νεοσσῶν, κελεύει ὁ συμπαθὴς Συμεὼν καὶ μακάριος ἐξοπτηθῆναι τὰ πετεινὰ καὶ τῷ χρείαν

the ground. He then announced this to the blessed one as though he had managed some great achievement.

Symeon, pretending that he approved of this, said, "Let's 3 go so that I can see how well you've done at killing them." So the holy one went off, and when he saw how the birds were strewn about dead on the ground, his expression became grim, for he was saddened by Arsenios's senseless rage. He summoned one of his subordinates and told him to bring a cord, tie all the birds to it, and hang it around Arsenios's neck. His instructions were no sooner said than done. He then instructed that Arsenios be dragged off and paraded around the monastery and be made a spectacle of in the midst of his fellow monks. But Arsenios submitted patiently to the shame of this public display, with his presumption so abased that he shed rivers of tears and called himself a murderer because of what he had done. My narrative is, then, sufficient to demonstrate the virtue of both men and the contemplative practice of their piety.

Chapter 50

But we must still add to our narrative an episode that we have almost omitted. At one time some friends of the blessed one were visiting him, and as a result of some physical illness, one of them had to eat meat, specifically pigeon. The blessed Symeon, who was sympathetic, ordered the birds to be roasted and served to the man who had this di-

ἔχοντι προστεθῆναι. Ὡς δ᾽ ὁ νοσῶν ἤσθιε, στυγνῶς αὐτὸν ὁ Ἀρσένιος κατενόει καὶ αὐτὸς ἐπὶ τραπέζης καθήμενος. Ἔγνω οὖν αὐτὸν ὁ μακάριος Συμεὼν οὕτως ἔχοντα, καὶ θέλων αὐτὸν διδάξαι μόνῳ ἑαυτῷ προσέχειν καὶ μηδὲν ἡγεῖσθαι τῇ μεταλήψει κοινοῦν—πάντα γάρ, φησί, καθαρὰ τοῖς καθαροῖς [Tit 1:15, cf. Rom 14:20] καὶ οὐκ ἔστιν ὃ δύναται κοινῶσαι ψυχὴν ἐκ τῶν ἔξωθεν εἰσρεόντων [cf. Mk 7:15,18]—ἅμα δὲ καὶ τὸ ὕψος τῆς ἐκείνου ταπεινώσεως βουλόμενος δεῖξαι τοῖς δαιτυμόσιν εἰς τὸ γνῶναι αὐτοὺς ὅτι καὶ ἔτι τέκνα τῷ Θεῷ ὑπακοῆς [1 Pt 1:14] εἰσι καὶ ἐργάται τῆς ἀρετῆς ἀληθεῖς, λέγει πρὸς αὐτόν· "Τίνος χάριν, Ἀρσένιε, οὐ σεαυτῷ μόνῳ προσέχεις, καὶ ἐν ταπεινώσει τὸν ἄρτον σου κάτω νεύων ἐσθίεις, ἀλλὰ τῷ τὸ κρέας ἐσθίοντι δι᾽ ἀσθένειαν προσέχων κάμνεις τοῖς λογισμοῖς καὶ πλέον οἴει κατ᾽ εὐσέβειαν ἔχειν ἐκείνου, ἐπεὶ λάχανα ἐσθίεις καὶ σπέρματα γῆς καὶ οὐχ ὥσπερ οἱ ἀετοὶ τὰς περιστερὰς καὶ τοὺς πέρδικας; Οὐκ ἤκουσας Χριστοῦ λέγοντος, ὅτι οὐ τὰ εἰσερχόμενα διὰ τοῦ στόματος κοινοῖ τὸν ἄνθρωπον, ἀλλὰ τὰ ἐκπορευόμενα ἐξ αὐτοῦ [cf. Mt 15:11], ἅτινά ἐστι πορνεῖαι, μοιχεῖαι, φόνοι, φθόνοι, πλεονεξίαι καὶ τὰ ἑξῆς [cf. Mk 7:20–22; Mt 15:17–19]; Τί μὴ συνετὸς εἶ καὶ ἐν γνώσει ὁρᾷς καὶ λογίζει, ἀλλ᾽ οὕτως ἀσυνέτως καθ᾽ ἑαυτὸν[90] κατέκρινας τὸν ἐσθίοντα, κατελεῶν δῆθεν τὴν σφαγὴν τῶν ὀρνίθων, καὶ ἐπελάθου τοῦ εἰπόντος· ὁ μὴ ἐσθίων τὸν ἐσθίοντα μὴ κρινέτω [Rom. 14:3]; Ἀλλὰ φάγε καὶ αὐτὸς ἐξ αὐτῶν, καὶ ἴσθι ὅτι πλέον ἔσχες τὴν κοίνωσιν ἐκ τοῦ λογισμοῦ ἢ ἐκ τῆς βρώσεως τῶν πετεινῶν!"

etary requirement. But while the sick man was eating, Arsenios, who was also sitting at the table, watched him with hostility. The blessed Symeon realized that he was doing this and wanted to teach him to concentrate only on himself and deem nothing defiled in the partaking of food—for, as it is said, *to the pure all things are pure,* and what enters *from outside is not able to defile* the soul. At the same time he wanted to demonstrate to his guests the extent of Arsenios's humility so that they would realize that there are still *children obedient* to God and true workers of virtue. So he said to him, "Why aren't you concentrating only on yourself, Arsenios, and humbly eating your bread with your head bowed? Why are you worrying yourself instead by concentrating on the man who is eating meat because of his infirmity and imagining yourself more pious than him, since you are eating vegetables and grain from the earth and not pigeons and partridges like the eagles? Haven't you heard Christ say that *not what goes into the mouth defiles the man, but what comes out of* it, such things as *fornication, adultery, murder,* envy, greed, and the rest? Why can't you be smart and see and think with real knowledge? Instead you stupidly pass judgment in your own mind in this way on the man who is eating, apparently condemning the slaughter of the birds and forgetting the one who says, *let not him who abstains pass judgment on him who eats.* Eat some of them yourself, and understand that you have defiled yourself worse by your thoughts than by eating the birds!"

51

Καὶ λαβὼν μίαν ἐκ τῶν ὀρνίθων ὁ ἅγιος ἔρριψε κατ᾽ αὐτοῦ ἐπιτιμήσας αὐτῷ τοῦ φαγεῖν. Ὁ δὲ ὡς ἤκουσε τούτων τὸ ἀθρόον καταπτήξας τοῦ ἐπιτιμίου, καὶ εἰδὼς ὡς κρεοφαγίας παρακοὴ χαλεπώτερον, μετάνοιαν βαλὼν⁹¹ καὶ τὸ εὐλόγησον αἰτησάμενος, λαβὼν ἤρξατο καταμασᾶσθαι καὶ μετὰ δακρύων ἐσθίειν τὸ πετεινόν. Ὡς δὲ εἶδεν αὐτὸν ὁ ἅγιος ἱκανῶς ἐκλεπτύναντα τοῖς ὀδοῦσι τὸ βρῶμα καὶ ἤδη μέλλοντα τοῦτο παραπέμψαι πρὸς τὴν γαστέρα· "Ἀρκεῖ σοί," φησίν, "ἀπόπτυσον τὸ λοιπόν! Ὡς γὰρ ἀπήρξω σὺ τοῦ ἐσθίειν γαστρίμαργος ὤν, οὐδὲ ὅλος ὁ περιστερὼν δύναταί σε κορέσαι καὶ τὴν ἐπὶ τοῦτό σου στῆσαι ὁρμήν." Οὕτω μὴ διακριθεὶς ὁ ἀοίδιμος μαθητὴς τοῦ μεγάλου τούτου πατρὸς πεπλήρωκε τὴν ὑπακοήν, ἣν μέχρι θανάτου φυλάξαι ἐνώπιον Θεοῦ ἐπηγγείλατο.

2   Ταῦτα τοιγαροῦν οὐχ οὕτως ἁπλῶς καὶ παρέργως μοι εἴρηται, ἀλλ᾽ ὥστε δεῖξαι⁹² τὴν ἐνάρετον ἐπιστήμην τοῦ διδασκάλου καὶ τὴν ἐκ προκοπῆς ταπείνωσιν τῶν αὐτοῦ μαθητῶν, καὶ οἷον ἦν τηνικαῦτα τῶν ἀμφοτέρων τὸ ἔργον τῆς εὐσεβείας ἐν τῇ γενεᾷ ταύτῃ, ἐν ᾗ τῶν πατέρων ἡ ἔνθεος ἠμελήθη ἐργασία τῆς ἀρετῆς καὶ ἀκρίβεια.

Chapter 51

Taking one of the birds, the holy one threw it to Arsenios and ordered him to eat it. When he heard these words all of a sudden, Arsenios cowered at his punishment, but knowing that disobedience was worse than eating the meat, he made his penitential prostration, asked for a blessing, and then, taking hold of the bird, began to chew it and eat it, weeping <as he did so>. However, when the holy one saw that Arsenios had chewed up the meat enough with his teeth and was about to swallow it down into his stomach, he said, "That's enough for you, spit out the rest! You're a glutton, so if you start eating, the whole pigeon won't be enough to satisfy you or put a stop to your desire for this." Without hesitating, the illustrious disciple of this great father fulfilled the vow of obedience that he had promised before God to keep until death.

I have thus related these stories not simply as a digres- 2 sion, but in order to display the virtuous discipline of the teacher and the increasing humility of his disciples; also to show the kind of piety practiced by both men, <even> in this present generation in which the fathers' godly and scrupulous practice of virtue has been neglected.

52

Ἀλλ᾽ εἰ δοκεῖ καὶ ἐφ᾽ ἕτερον τῶν αὐτοῦ μαθητῶν τὸν λόγον τρέψωμεν. Οὐκ ἄχαρι γὰρ ἀλλὰ καὶ ὠφέλιμον μετὰ τοῦ ἡδέος φανήσεται ὑμῖν τὸ διήγημα. Ἐπίσκοπός τις ἀπὸ τῶν δυτικῶν πάνυ θεοφιλὴς τὸν τρόπον καὶ τὸν βίον μετὰ τοῦ λόγου καθαρὸς καὶ ἐνάρετος, πτώματι δεινῷ τῷ τοῦ φόνου ἐκ φθόνου τοῦ Διαβόλου περιέπεσε. Τὸ δὲ ὅπως ἐντεῦθεν ὡς ἔχει τὸ πρᾶγμα ἐκδιηγήσομαι.

2 Ποτὲ ὁ ἐπίσκοπος καθεζόμενος περὶ τὴν στοὰν τῆς κέλλης αὐτοῦ καὶ βίβλον ἔχων ἐπὶ χεῖρας ἔκδιψος ὥσπερ ἐγένετο· ἑσπέρα δὲ ἦν. Ἐπεὶ οὖν ἀνέψιος ὑπῆρχεν αὐτῷ φιλούμενος ἄγαν, φωνεῖ τὸν παῖδα κρᾶσιν αὐτῷ ποιήσασθαι εἰς ποτήριον οἴνου. Ὁ δὲ τοῦτο σὺν τῷ λόγῳ ποιήσας ἄγει τὸ ποτήριον τῷ ἐπισκόπῳ καὶ θείῳ αὐτοῦ. Λαβὼν οὖν ὁ ἐπίσκοπος τοῦτο καὶ γευσάμενος ἀηδίας ἐπλήσθη διὰ τὸ εἶναι χλιαρὰν τὴν κρᾶσιν τοῦ οἴνου, καὶ κουφίσας ἣν ἐπὶ χεῖρας ἐπεφέρετο βακτηρίαν ἐκ μέσου ταύτην λαβὼν τοῖς δακτύλοις αὐτοῦ ἴθυνεν αὐτὴν⁹³ ἐπὶ τὸν παῖδα, ἐκδειματῶσαι τοῦτον βουλόμενος· ἡ δὲ—ὦ τῶν ἀφύκτων⁹⁴ κριμάτων σου Χριστέ!—ἐξ ἐνεργείας τοῦ Διαβόλου ἐκδραμοῦσα τῶν δακτύλων τοῦ ἐπισκόπου καὶ τὸν παῖδα κατὰ τοῦ μήνιγγος πλήξασα εὐθὺς ἀνάρπαστον τῆς παρούσης ζωῆς τοῦτον πεποίηκε, καὶ νεκρὸς ὁ παῖς ἐπ᾽ ἐδάφους καταβληθεὶς ἔκειτο. Ὁ οὖν ἐπίσκοπος ὡς εἶδε παρ᾽ ἐλπίδα⁹⁵ πᾶσαν τὸν ἀνεψιὸν⁹⁶ τεθνηκότα καὶ νεκρὸν ὡς ἐξ αἰτίας

Chapter 52

But <now>, if you like, let us turn our narrative to another of Symeon's disciples, for the tale will appear to be not without charm, and will be profitable to you, as well as pleasing. A bishop from the western regions, a most God-loving man whose way of life was pure and virtuous in accordance with the word <of God>, stumbled, because of the Devil's envy, into a terrible transgression, that of murder. I will tell you in detail how this affair happened.

The bishop was once sitting in the cloister outside his cell 2 with a book in his hands when he became very thirsty. It was evening <at the time>. Since he had a dearly beloved nephew with him, he called for the boy to make a mixture of water and wine for him in a wine cup. The latter did as he was told and brought the cup to his uncle the bishop. The bishop took it but, when he tasted it, was disgusted because the wine mixture was lukewarm. He raised a staff which he was holding in his hands and, gripping this in the middle with his fingers, aimed it at the boy because he wanted to frighten him. But the <staff>—O Christ, how inexorable are your judgments!—shot out of the bishop's fingers as a result of the Devil's contrivance and, striking the boy on the skull,[50] immediately snatched him from the present life. The boy fell to the floor and lay there dead. When the bishop saw his nephew dead so very unexpectedly and his body lying on

αὐτοῦ κείμενον ἐπὶ γῆς, ῥίπτει πρηνῆ ἑαυτὸν ἐλεεινολο-
γούμενος καὶ ζητῶν θρήνοις καὶ αὐτὸς παραδοῦναι τὴν
ἰδίαν ψυχήν.

53

Ἐπεὶ δὲ δῆλον ὁ θρῆνος τὸ πτῶμα πᾶσι πεποίηκε, συν-
άγεται ὁ κλῆρος τῆς τούτου ἐπισκοπῆς, θρηνεῖ καὶ κόπτε-
ται οὐ τὸν παῖδα, ἀλλὰ τὸν ποιμένα τὸν ἴδιον· καὶ γὰρ ἦν
τῷ κλήρῳ παντὶ ὁ ἀνὴρ ἀγαθός, πρᾶος, γαληνός, δίκαιος,
συμπαθής, ἐλεήμων, πάσης ἀρετῆς καὶ δικαιοσύνης ἐργάτης, ὅθεν καὶ τῆς σφοδρᾶς ἀθυμίας ἀνακτήσασθαι τοῦτον
βουλόμενοι ἠντιβόλουν, προσέπιπτον, πάντα ὑποίσειν
ὑπὲρ τούτου ἐβόων αὐτοί, ὅσα περὶ δουλείαν ἐπιτιμίων καὶ
κακοπάθειαν. Ὁ δὲ οἷα εἰς βάθος δεξάμενος τὴν πληγὴν
μηδὲ τὴν ἀκοὴν προσέχουσαν ἔχων τοῖς ὑπ᾽ αὐτῶν λεγομένοις, ἔωθεν ἀναστὰς καὶ τάφῳ τοῦ τεθνηκότος τὸ λεί-
ψανον παραδούς, ἁλύσει τὸν τράχηλον δεσμήσας αὐτοῦ
καὶ ἑνὶ τῶν οἰκετῶν τὸ ἄκρον αὐτῆς παραδοὺς ἐπὶ τὴν Ῥώμην ἕλκειν αὐτὸν βίᾳ προσέταξεν. Ὡς οὖν εἶδον οἱ περὶ
τὴν ἐπισκοπὴν μηδὲν ἀνύοντας ἑαυτούς, μηδὲ δυναμένους
τὸν εἰς βάθος τρωθέντα τοῦ λοιποῦ κρατῆσαι ἐπίσκοπον,
συγχωροῦσι μετὰ πολλῶν κοπετῶν τούτῳ τὴν ἀναχώρη-
σιν.

the ground due to his fault, he threw himself down, uttering pitiful words and seeking with laments that he too might surrender his soul.

Chapter 53

Since the bishop's lamentation had made his transgression known to everyone, the clergy of his diocese gathered, and they lamented and mourned not the boy but their own shepherd. For to all his clergy he was a good man who was gentle, serene, just, sympathetic, merciful, and someone who accomplished every virtue and righteousness. Because they wanted to help this man recover from his deep despair, they began imploring him and prostrating themselves, proclaiming that they would take upon themselves all kinds of servitude, penance, and mortification on his behalf. But the bishop had received such a heavy blow that he did not even listen to their words. In the morning he got up, laid the remains of the dead boy in a grave, and then bound his own neck with a chain. He handed the end of it to one of his servants and forcefully ordered him to lead him to Rome. When the men of the diocese realized that they were accomplishing nothing themselves and that they could no longer restrain the bishop who had been so deeply afflicted, they let him go with many loud cries of grief.

2   Διαδραμὼν οὖν τὸν τοσοῦτον δρόμον πεζῇ τῆς μακρᾶς ἐκείνης ὁδοῦ ὁ ἐπίσκοπος μετὰ κοπετῶν καὶ δακρύων καὶ τὴν Ῥώμην καταλαβὼν ὑπὸ τοῦ δούλου ἐν ἁλύσει ἑλκόμενος, ἐξομολογεῖται τὸ πτῶμα τῷ Πάπᾳ καὶ τοῖς ἐν Ῥώμῃ ἀρχιερεῦσι θρήνοις καὶ οἰμωγαῖς τὴν φωνὴν τῆς ἐξομολογήσεως ἐγκοπτόμενος. Τὴν ἄπειρον οὖν συντριβὴν εἰδότες τοῦ ἐπισκόπου καὶ τὴν ἐν πένθει τούτου μετάνοιαν, οὐ μόνον συγγνώμην ταχεῖαν τῷ πάθει διδοῦσιν, ἀλλὰ καὶ μυρίαις παρακλήσεσι τὸ κατώδυνον παρακαλοῦσιν αὐτοῦ τῆς ψυχῆς [cf. 1 Kings 1:10]. Ἀλλὰ τῷ περικαρδίῳ κρατούμενος ὁ ἐπίσκοπος πόνῳ ἀπαράκλητος ἔμενεν.

54

Ἐκεῖθεν οὖν πρὸς τὴν Κωσταντίνου μεγαλόπολιν τὸν ἕλκοντα ἀποστρέφει. Πεζῇ τοίνυν καὶ ταύτην ποιησάμενος τὴν πορείαν, καταλαμβάνει τὴν βασιλεύουσαν καὶ εἰς τὴν μεγάλην τοῦ Θεοῦ εἰσελθὼν ἐκκλησίαν ἐξομολογεῖται μετὰ δακρύων τῷ τε πατριάρχῃ καὶ τοῖς ἀρχιερεῦσι τὸ πτῶμα καὶ σὺν τῷ λόγῳ τὸ τῆς ἐπισκοπῆς ἀξίωμα μετὰ τῆς ἁλύσεως ἀποτίθεται.

2   Ἐπεὶ δὲ τῷ πατρικίῳ Γενεσίῳ κατὰ ψυχὴν ὑπῆρχε φιλούμενος ὁ ἐπίσκοπος, καὶ αὐτὸς ἐκεῖνον ἐπίσης ἐφίλει, ὡς τὰ κατ' αὐτὸν ὁ πατρίκιος ἐμεμαθήκει,[97] μεταστέλλεται τοῦτον ἐπὶ τὸν οἶκον αὐτοῦ, καὶ τὸν ἐπίσκοπον ἀσπασάμενος καὶ λόγοις παρακλητικοῖς παραμυθούμενος αὐτοῦ τὴν

So the bishop traversed the considerable length of that   2
long journey on foot with loud cries of grief and tears. When
he reached Rome, <still> being led on a chain by his slave, he
confessed his transgression to the pope and the prelates in
Rome, although his confessional statement was interrupted
by laments and sobs. When they saw the bishop's boundless
contrition and the repentance apparent in his grief, they not
only swiftly pardoned him for the unfortunate accident but
also offered countless consolations for the *deep distress of* his
soul. But the bishop, still gripped by the pain in his heart, remained inconsolable.

Chapter 54

From Rome the man who was leading him brought him
back to the great city of Constantine. After he had made
this journey on foot as well and reached the imperial city, he
went into the great church of God [Hagia Sophia], where he
confessed his transgression with tears to the patriarch and
his bishops. In the course of his account he set aside his
episcopal rank, along with his chain.

Now the bishop was regarded with spiritual affection by   2
the patrician[51] Genesios, and he likewise had affection for
Genesios, and so, when the patrician learned what had happened to him, he invited him to his house. After he had
greeted the bishop and attempted to provide spiritual comfort with consoling words, Genesios discussed with him the

ψυχήν, κοινολογεῖται αὐτῷ τὰ τῆς ἐναλλαγῆς⁹⁸ τοῦ βίου, καὶ μαθεῖν ἐρωτᾷ περὶ τούτου τὸν ἐκείνου σκοπὸν καὶ ὁποῖον αἱρεῖται τοῦ λοιποῦ ζῆσαι βίον κατὰ τὴν παροῦσαν ζωήν. Ὁ δέ· "Τὸν μονήρη," φησί, "καὶ τοῦτον ἐν ὄρεσιν ἢ σπηλαίοις⁹⁹ καὶ ταῖς ὀπαῖς τῆς γῆς [Hbr 11:38]." Ὁ οὖν πατρίκιος συνετὸς ὢν ἐς τὰ μάλιστα· "Οὐκ οἶμαι τοῦτο λυσιτελοῦν σοί, πάτερ," φησίν,¹⁰⁰ "ἀλλ᾽ εἴ τι μᾶλλον ἐμοὶ πείθῃ ὑποτιθεμένῳ σοι ἀγαθά, ἐν κοινοβίῳ τὸν μονήρη βίον ἀγάπησον διελθεῖν, καὶ οὐ μικρὰν εὑρήσεις ὠφέλειαν διὰ τῆς ἐκκοπῆς τοῦ ἰδίου¹⁰¹ θελήματος." Ὁ δέ· "Καὶ ποῦ ἂν εὕροιμι τοιοῦτον," φησί, "κύριέ μου, κοινόβιον ὑπὸ ποιμένος ποιμαινόμενον ἐπιστήμονος, ἵνα καὶ ἐμαυτὸν ὅλον ἐκδώσω εἰς ἑκούσιον θάνατον ὁ τῷ τοῦ ἀκουσίου ἐγκλήματος δυστυχῶς βαρυνόμενος;"

55

Ὁ οὖν Γενέσιος τὸν μακάριον Συμεώνην πατέρα κεκτημένος πνευματικὸν καὶ εἰδὼς οἷος ἐκεῖνος εἰς τὸ ποιμαίνειν καὶ θεραπεύειν ψυχὰς καὶ οἷον τὸ αὐτοῦ ποίμνιον, γνωρίζει τοῦτον αὐτῷ καί· "Εἴ γε," φησίν, "ἀληθινῆς ὠφελείας ἐρᾷς καὶ ἰδεῖν ἄλλον βούλει μέγαν Ἀρσένιον καὶ πάσης ἀντεχόμενον ἀκριβείας κοινόβιον, ἔρχου καὶ ἴδε [John 1:46, 11:35; Apc 6:1,5,7] καὶ ἰδὼν πιστώθητι." Εὐθὺς οὖν ὁ ἐπίσκοπος εἴπετο, ὁ δὲ προῆγε, καὶ καταλαβόντες ὁμοῦ τὸ

changes in his life; he also asked him about his aim in this and what mode of life he would be seeking to choose for the rest of his present life. "The solitary one," said the bishop, "and it will be *in mountains, or in dens or caves of the earth.*" But the patrician, who was an extremely intelligent man, replied, "I don't think that would be helpful to you, father. But if you were instead to be persuaded by some good advice that I can offer you, you would do well to pursue the monastic life in a cenobitic community, and you would derive no little benefit from the negation of your own will." "And where, my lord, might I find such a community," he asked, "guided by a wise shepherd, so that I, who am so miserably burdened by the <weight> of my involuntary crime, may surrender myself completely to a voluntary death?"

Chapter 55

Now Genesios had the blessed Symeon as his spiritual father, and knowing how good he was at shepherding and caring for souls and the sort of flock he had, he told the bishop about him. "If you really do crave genuine help and you want to see another great Arsenios[52] and a cenobitic monastery that strictly conforms in every way," he said, "*come and see* and, seeing, believe." So the bishop immediately followed, while Genesios led the way. They arrived

τοῦ μακαρίου κοινόβιον μηνύονται αὐτῷ καὶ ὑπ᾽ αὐτοῦ κατασπάζονται. Ἐπεὶ δὲ τὰ συμβεβηκότα τῷ ἐπισκόπῳ μάθοι ὁ ἅγιος, πανθάνει τὴν ψυχὴν καὶ ἐκ μόνης τῆς ἀκοῆς τοῦ συμβάντος, καὶ δακρύων καταφέρει πηγάς. Ὡς δὲ τὸ συμπαθὲς ἐθεάσατο τοῦ ἁγίου ὁ ἐπίσκοπος καὶ τὴν σύνεσιν τῶν χειλέων [cf. Job 33:3] τούτου ἀκήκοεν, πίπτει πρηνὴς ἐπὶ τοὺς πόδας αὐτοῦ καὶ αἰτεῖται τὴν ὑποδοχήν, τὴν ἐναλλαγὴν τῶν ἐκτὸς καὶ τὴν μετὰ τῶν μαθητῶν αὐτοῦ κατασκήνωσιν. Ὁ δὲ μακάριος τὴν θέρμην τούτου καταμαθὼν ἐξ ὀλίγου καὶ γνοὺς τῷ πνεύματι οἷον ἔμελλε σκεῦος Θεοῦ ἐκλεκτὸν χρηματίσειν, ὑποδέχεται αὐτὸν καὶ πάντα τελέσας ἐπ᾽ αὐτῷ τὰ τοῦ σχήματος Ἱερόθεον τὸν ἱερέα ἐπονομάζει Θεοῦ.

2   Ὁ δὲ Ἱερόθεος τῶν ἐπιθυμουμένων αὐτῷ τυχὼν ὡς ἐβούλετο παγκράτιον ἐξαυτῆς κατὰ τοῦ τρώσαντος συγκροτεῖ, νηστείαις μὲν καὶ κακουχίαις μακραῖς τὸ σαρκίον ἐκτήκων αὐτοῦ, ἀγρυπνίαις δὲ καὶ στάσεσιν ὁλονύκτοις ἐν προσευχαῖς καταδαμάζων ἑαυτὸν καὶ τῇ δουλείᾳ τῶν ἀδελφῶν τὸ πνεῦμα συντρίβων ἑαυτοῦ. Διὸ καὶ τῇ ἐπιθυμίᾳ τῶν θλίψεων παράφορά τινα ὑπεκρίνετο σκεύη πολλάκις ἐξεπίτηδες διαστρέφων ἢ καὶ συντρίβων, ἵνα ὕβρεις ἀκούσῃ, εἰ δέει δὲ καὶ κατὰ κόρρης ῥαπίσματα δέξηται. Διὰ δὴ τοῦτο ὑβριζόμενος ἔχαιρεν ὡς τοῦ ποθουμένου τυχών, καὶ μαστίγων ἐδίψα πεῖραν λαβεῖν, ἵνα τὸν ἔξω τυπτόμενος θύλακα τὸν ἐντὸς ἄνθρωπον ἐλευθερώσῃ τῆς ἐν τῷ μέλλοντι θλίψεως. Τοίνυν καὶ τοσαύτη κατάνυξις ἐντεῦθεν ἐδόθη αὐτῷ μετὰ πλήθους δακρύων, ὡς μὴ δύνασθαι ταῦτα ἐπισχεθῆναι παρ᾽ αὐτοῦ ἐν ἡμέρᾳ ἢ ἐν νυκτί.

together at the monastery of the blessed one, were announced to Symeon, and were greeted by him. The holy one suffered in his soul when he learned what had happened to the bishop, simply on hearing about the accident, and shed streams of tears. When the bishop saw the holy one's compassion and heard the *knowledge of his lips,* he fell on his face at Symeon's feet and sought to be admitted to the monastery, to change his outer garb, and to live with his disciples. The blessed one swiftly perceived the bishop's zeal and, understanding spiritually what sort of vessel chosen by God[53] he was going to be, received him. After performing all the ceremonies for taking the monastic habit, he gave the priest of God the name Hierotheos.[54]

Now that Hierotheos had what he wanted, he immediately joined in an all-out contest with the <Devil> who had wounded him, wasting away his flesh with lengthy fasts and mortifications, subduing himself with vigils and standing all night in prayer, and crushing his own spirit in servitude to the brethren. In his desire for affliction he would thus pretend to do crazy things, often intentionally damaging or even smashing vessels, so that he might become the target of insults or, if warranted, even be beaten about the head. Then, when he was insulted for this, he would rejoice because he had achieved his goal. He also thirsted to experience whippings, so that as the exterior sack <of his flesh> was beaten, his inner man might be freed from future punishment. He was thus given such a gift of compunction with an abundance of tears that he could not stop them by day or night.

56

Καὶ ἵνα ἐξ ἑνὸς δείξω τοῖς πᾶσι τὴν ἐκ μελέτης αὐτοῦ διὰ τὰς θλίψεις γενομένην καὶ τοὺς πειρασμοὺς ἐπιτήδευσιν, τοῦτο μόνον εἰπὼν ἐπὶ τὸν μακάριον αὖθις ἐλεύσομαι Συμεών. Τὴν τῆς ἀποθήκης ὁ Ἱερόθεος ἐπιτελῶν διακονίαν ἐπιτρέπεταί ποτε παρὰ τοῦ ἁγίου ἓν τῶν κούφων ἀγγείων ἀπὸ τοῦ πίθου γεμίσαι. Ὁ δὲ ὑπακούει ταχέως καὶ πρὸς τὸν πιθῶνα γίνεται. Ἀλλ' ἐπεὶ τούτῳ ἔθος ἦν τοῦ ἀεὶ ψάλλειν καὶ πενθεῖν κἂν διακονῶν ἐβάδιζε, καὶ ἅμα ἔνθα ἂν ἐτυποῦντο μορφαὶ ἁγίων ἢ τύπος σταυροῦ κατασπάζεσθαι ταῦτα κἂν μυριάδες ὑπῆρχον, ἔτυχεν εἶναι σταυρὸν καὶ περὶ τὴν καλύπτραν τοῦ πίθου, ὃν ἀνοίγων τὸν πίθον ἠσπάζετο καὶ σκέπων αὖθις ἐφίλει. Τοῦτον ἀσπασάμενος καὶ τὸν πίθον ἀνοίξας ἐγέμισε τὸ κοῦφον ἀγγεῖον καὶ ἐπὶ τὸν πίθον ἐπακουμβήσας εἴασεν· ἄρας οὖν τὴν καλύπτραν καταφιλεῖν ἤρξατο τὸν σταυρόν, καὶ στραφὲν εὐθὺς τὸ ἄγγος ἐκενοῦτο τῇ γῇ, αὐτὸς δὲ ὡς εἶδε τοῦτο κενούμενον γελάσας ἔφη· "Μὰ τὸν σαλὸν Ἱερόθεον, πονηρὲ δαίμων, ἕως οὗ τὸν σταυρόν μου φιλήσω, οὐ κρατήσω αὐτό, οἶδα γὰρ ὅτι δι' αὐτὸ τοῦτο καὶ τὸ δρᾶμα πεποίηκας." Ὡς δ' ἐκενώθη ὅλον, κενὸν τοῦτο ἀνελόμενος ἔδραμε, καὶ πάντα ὡς ἐγένετο τῷ μακαρίῳ πατρὶ διηγήσατο.

2   Ὁ δὲ ἅγιος τὴν ἐργασίαν τοῦ Ἱεροθέου εἰδὼς καὶ ὅτι πάντα εἰς τὸ προξενῆσαι ἀτιμίαν ἑαυτῷ ἐποίει, θέλων δὲ καὶ στεφάνους αὐτῷ διψῶντι παρέχειν, ἐντέλλεταί τι

Chapter 56

I will use one example to make clear to everyone the trials and tribulations he experienced as a result of his behavior, and after telling this single story I will return to the blessed Symeon. Once, while Hierotheos was performing storeroom duty, the holy one told him to fill one of the empty jugs from the storage jar. He quickly obeyed and went to the large jar. But it was his custom always to sing the psalms and grieve aloud all the time, even when he was going about his duties, and at the same time, wherever depictions of the saints or the sign of the cross were portrayed, he used to kiss them, even if there were thousands of them. There happened to be a cross on the lid of the storage jar, so when he opened the jar he used to kiss it, and when he covered it again he used to make the same display of affection. <On this occasion> he kissed the cross, opened the jar, filled the empty jug, and left it leaning against the storage jar. Then he took the lid and began kissing the cross, but the jug immediately rolled over and emptied itself onto the ground. But <Hierotheos> laughed when he saw it was empty and said, "By Hierotheos the fool,[55] you wicked demon, while I was kissing my cross I couldn't keep hold of the jug. I know that's why you've caused this problem." And as it was now completely empty, taking the empty jug he ran off and told the blessed father the whole story.

The holy one, however, understood Hierotheos's contriv- 2 ance and that he was doing everything to bring dishonor upon himself. And so, because he wanted to provide him

τοιοῦτον περὶ αὐτοῦ. Ἐπειδὴ γὰρ ἔτυχε κατ᾽ ἐκείνην τὴν ἡμέραν τὸν ἡμίονον[102] τῆς μονῆς κούφων πλῆθος ἐπιφορτίζεσθαι παρὰ τῶν ἐκεῖσε, τεθῆναι προστάττει ἐπάνω τούτων τὸν Ἱερόθεον, καὶ παρ᾽ ἄλλου σύρεσθαι μέχρι τοῦ Ξηρολόφου, καὶ οὕτω λέγειν τὸν ἕλκοντα· "Εἴ τις βεβλαμμένος ἔνι τὰς φρένας, τοιοῦτον καὶ τὸν θρίαμβον ὑπομένει."[103] Τούτου οὖν γεγονότος καὶ τοῦ Ἱεροθέου ἐπιφορτισθέντος τοῖς κούφοις, ὡς ὁ τὸν ἡμίονον ἕλκων ἃ προσετάγη μεγάλῃ τῇ φωνῇ ἔλεγε, συνεφώνει αὐτῷ ταῦτα καὶ ὁ θαυμαστὸς Ἱερόθεος προσαφιεὶς τοῖς λόγοις καὶ δακρύων πηγάς.

57

Ἵνα δὲ μή τις ὑπολάβῃ[104] οὕτω κακουμένου αὐτοῦ παρ᾽ ἐκείνου εἰς μῖσός τινας κατ᾽ αὐτοῦ τῶν μαθητῶν ἐμπεσεῖν, ἕτερόν τι γεγονὸς πρὸς τοῦ Ἱεροθέου εἰς βεβαίωσιν τῆς πίστεως ἧς εἶχε πρὸς τὸν μακάριον διὰ βραχέων διηγήσομαι. Ἀπεστάλη ποτὲ πρὸς τὸν ῥηθέντα πατρίκιον παρὰ τοῦ μακαρίου ὁ Ἱερόθεος χάριν ἐπισκέψεως. Ὡς δ᾽ ἐπιθυμῶν[105] αὐτὸν εἶδε καὶ κατησπάσατο ὁ πατρίκιος, συνεστιαθεὶς δεξιοῦται τὸν φίλον ἀποδέσμῳ χρυσοῦ· ὁ δὲ πρῶτα μὲν λαβεῖν τὸν ἀπόδεσμον οὐκ ἐπείθετο, χρείαν μὴ ἔχων αὐτοῦ ὁ μηδὲν πλὴν τοῦ τριχίνου ἐσθήματος ἐσχηκὼς πώποτε. Ἀλλ᾽ ὁ διδοὺς ἐπεὶ μεθ᾽ ὅρκων ἀνάγκην ἐπῆγεν, ἔλαβεν

with the garlands for which he thirsted, he prescribed something suitable for him. That day a number of empty jars were being loaded onto the monastery's mule by those who were there, so <Symeon> gave orders for Hierotheos to be set on top of these and led along by someone else as far as Xerolophos.[56] The man who was leading was to say, "If someone loses their wits, this is the kind of triumph that awaits them!" So this was done, and after Hierotheos was loaded onto the empty jars, while the muleteer called out in a loud voice what he had been told <to say>, the wondrous Hierotheos also joined in with him and supplemented his words with streams of tears.

Chapter 57

So that no one may get the idea that because Hierotheos was maltreated by Symeon in this way, some of his disciples came to hate him [Symeon], I'm going to recount briefly something else that happened to Hierotheos as confirmation of his faith in the blessed one. Hierotheos was once sent by the blessed one on a visit to the above-mentioned patrician [Genesios]. When he saw him, the patrician embraced him eagerly and, after he had dined with him, presented his friend with a bag of gold. At first Hierotheos did not want to accept the bag, because he had no need of it (he who had never possessed anything except his haircloth habit). But since the donor forced him with oaths, he did ac-

ὅμως αὐτὸν καὶ τὴν σκέπην ἄρας τῆς αὐτοῦ κεφαλῆς καὶ θέμενος αὐτῇ τὸν χρυσὸν ἐπὶ τῆς χειρὸς ἔφερε, καὶ τὸν βραχίονα ἐκτεταμένον ἔχων ἔτρεχεν ἐκεῖθεν ἐπὶ τούτου τοῦ σχήματος, ἕως οὗ τό τε μοναστήριον κατέλαβε, καὶ τὸν μακάριον ἐθεάσατο, καὶ τὸν ἀπόδεσμον τοῦ χρυσοῦ ἔβαλεν εἰς τὰς χεῖρας αὐτοῦ.

2 Τοιαύτην οὗτός τε ὁ ἀοίδιμος καὶ οἱ λοιποὶ τῶν μαθητῶν τοῦ ἁγίου, ὅσοις ἐγένετο ἀψευδὴς ἡ τοῦ κόσμου φυγή, εἶχον τὴν πίστιν εἰς αὐτὸν καὶ τὴν ἀγάπην βεβαίαν, εἰ καὶ πολυτρόπως ὑπ' αὐτοῦ ἐδοκιμάζοντο διὰ τῶν φαινομένων λυπηρῶν τε[106] καὶ πειρασμῶν, εἰ μή τις ἄρα τέκνον μωμητὸν καὶ διεστραμμένον [cf. Dt 32:5; Phlp 2:15] ἐκ δυστροπίας ἐφάνη, καὶ διὰ τὴν ἐνοῦσαν κακίαν τῷ πατρὶ ἀπηχθάνετο· εἰς γὰρ τοιαύτην ἀγάπην προέκοψε Θεοῦ μετὰ τῶν ἄλλων ἐκείνου μαθητῶν καὶ ὁ Ἱερόθεος οὗτος, ὥστε καί εἴ ποτε[107] βιβλίον ἀναγινώσκων ἦν, ὅπου δ' ἂν καὶ ἐν οἷς χωρίοις εὑρέθη[108] γεγραμμένον Θεὸς ἢ Χριστὸς ἢ Ἰησοῦς, ἐν αὐτῷ τῷ θείῳ ὀνόματι τὸν δεξιὸν ἐτίθει ἑαυτοῦ ὀφθαλμόν, εἶτα τὸν ἕτερον, καὶ εἰς τοσοῦτον ἔκλαιεν, ἕως οὗ καὶ τὴν βίβλον καὶ τὸν κόλπον αὐτοῦ δακρύων ἐγέμισε.

cept it; however, he took his hood off his head and, putting the gold in it, carried it in his hand. Holding his arm stretched out, he ran from there like this until he reached the monastery and, when he saw the blessed one, put the bag of gold into his hands.

Such was the faith and the genuine love that the renowned Hierotheos and the other disciples of the holy one (at least those who had truly fled from the world) had for Symeon, even if he tested them in all sorts of ways with apparent trials and tribulations. The only exception would perhaps be someone who was obviously *a child deserving rebuke, one perverted* by his wicked disposition, or who, through the evil dwelling in him, had become hostile to the father. This Hierotheos had developed such love for God, in common with Symeon's other disciples, that whenever he was reading a book, at all the places where he found "God" or "Christ" or "Jesus" written, he would touch the divine name to his right eye, then to the other, and he would weep so much that he would cover both the book and his lap with his tears.

58

Τοιούτων ἦν γεωργὸς χωρίων ὁ τρισόλβιος[109] καὶ μέγας πατὴρ ἡμῶν Συμεὼν καὶ τοιούτους ἐκτήσατο τοὺς αὐτοῦ μαθητάς. Εἰ γὰρ καὶ καθ' ἕνα τῶν ἐκλεκτῶν ἐκείνου[110] μαθητῶν διαμνημονεῦσαι πειράσομαι περί τε Λέοντος ἐκείνου τοῦ σοφωτάτου, ᾧ ἐπώνυμον[111] ἦν ὁ Ξυλοκώδων, Ἀντωνίου τε καὶ Ἰωαννικίου, Σωτηρίχου, Βασιλείου καὶ Συμεὼν καί τινων ἄλλων ἀνδρῶν ἐπιθυμιῶν [cf. Dn (Theodotion) 9:23; 10:11, 19] τῶν τοῦ πνεύματος, ἐπιλείψει με διηγούμενον, ἀποστολικῶς εἰπεῖν, ὁ χρόνος [Hbr 11:32] καὶ ὁ χάρτης αὐτὸς εἰς τὴν ἐκείνων διήγησιν. Ἀλλὰ τούτων μὲν ἅλις.

59

Ἐπεὶ δὲ καλῶς ἔσχε ταῦτα πάντα τῷ θαυμαστῷ Συμεώνῃ, καὶ καλῶς τὸ τοῦ Χριστοῦ ποίμνιον συνήγαγέ τε καὶ συνεκρότησε καὶ μαθητὰς ἀξιολόγους τῷ πνεύματι ζέοντας καὶ ὁλοψύχως τῷ Κυρίῳ δουλεύοντας [cf. Rom 12:11] ἀπετέλεσεν, ἐλύπει δὲ σφοδρῶς αὐτὸν τὰ πράγματα καὶ ἡ

Chapter 58

Such were the fields cultivated by our thrice happy and great father Symeon, and such were the disciples that he acquired. But if I were to try to recall his chosen disciples one by one <and speak> about Leontios, who was very wise and who was nicknamed "the wooden bell," about Antony and Ioannikios, Soterichos, Basil and Symeon, and some of the others who were *men full of desire* for spiritual things,[57] in the words of the apostle *time would fail me to tell,* and the paper itself would be insufficient for their tale. But enough of them.

5. Symeon's Instructions to Arsenios; His Life in Retirement after Resigning as Superior

Chapter 59

Everything had turned out well for the wondrous Symeon, for he had successfully gathered and organized the flock of Christ and had rendered his worthy disciples *fervent in the Spirit* and wholehearted *servants of the Lord.* But the business and administration of the community caused him much dis-

τούτων φροντὶς ἀποσπῶντα τοῦτον τῆς καλλίστης καὶ φίλης ἡσυχίας, σκέπτεται θείῳ κινούμενος Πνεύματι τοῦ
κοινοβίου καὶ τῶν μαθητῶν κατὰ τὴν παλαιὰν παράδοσιν
ποιήσασθαι πρόνοιαν καὶ τὸ ἀνενόχλητον ἑαυτῷ τοῦ λοιποῦ πραγματεύσασθαι καὶ τῆς φίλης ἡσυχίας ἐπαπολαύ-
ειν¹¹² αὖθις ὡς πρότερον. Ἐκράτει γὰρ τὴν ἐκείνου ψυχὴν
ὁ ἔρως τῆς ἡσυχίας, καὶ ἐν μέσῳ θορύβων ἀναστρεφόμε-
νον ἠλλοιωμένον εἶχεν αὐτὸν τῇ ἀλλοιώσει τῇ κρείττονι.

2   Κρίσει οὖν Σεργίου τοῦ πατριάρχου ὑπεξίσταται μὲν
ἑκουσίως τῆς ἡγουμενείας¹¹³ αὐτός, ἡγούμενον δὲ ἀντ᾽
αὐτοῦ τὸν μαθητὴν Ἀρσένιον προχειρίζεται τὴν κατὰ
Χριστὸν ἡλικίαν ἄρτι αὐξήσαντα καὶ εἰς ἄνδρα τέλειον [cf.
Eph 4:13] ἀναδραμόντα τῷ πνεύματι καὶ ποιμαίνειν δυνάμενον τὸ ποίμνιον τοῦ Χριστοῦ. Αὐτὸς δὲ μίαν ἑαυτῷ ἀφο-
ρίζει γωνίαν εἰς τὰς χεῖρας ἀποβλέπων [cf. Ps 122 (123):2]
τοῦ μαθητοῦ ὡς εἷς τῶν ἄλλων διὰ ταπείνωσιν χριστο-
μίμητον. Ἅπτεται τοιγαροῦν ἐντεῦθεν ὁ μὲν¹¹⁴ μαθητὴς
Ἀρσένιος τῆς φροντίδος τοῦ κοινοβίου· ὁ δὲ ποιμὴν καὶ
διδάσκαλος τῶν ὑπὸ τὴν μονὴν ἁπάντων τῆς καταμόνας
σχολῆς καὶ τῆς θεωρίας τῶν λόγων τῆς κτίσεως, ὡς ἄν¹¹⁵
ὁ μὲν τὸ ποίμνιον ἄγῃ, ὁ δὲ προσευχῇ στηρίζῃ τὸν ἄγοντα
καὶ τῶν ἄλλων ἀναθεωρῇ τὰς ἀφανεῖς κινήσεις καὶ ἰθύνῃ
ἐπὶ τὸ κρεῖττον καὶ τελεώτερον.

tress, for it distracted him from the spiritual tranquillity that he loved and found so beautiful. And so, moved by the divine Spirit, he prepared to make provision for the monastery and his disciples according to the old tradition,[58] and arrange for himself in future to be undisturbed \<by them\> so that he might, once again as before, enjoy his beloved tranquillity. For the desire for this tranquillity gripped his soul and, even while he was living amid this tumult, managed to change him by its power of transforming to the better.

Therefore, with the approval of the patriarch Sergios,[59] 2 Symeon voluntarily resigned from his position as superior and appointed in his place his disciple Arsenios. The latter had by now matured in Christ and had quickly developed *into a perfect* spiritual *man,* able to shepherd Christ's flock. But for himself, in his Christ-like humility, Symeon set aside an obscure corner, looking to the hands of his disciple just like one of the other \<monks\>. So from that time forward the disciple Arsenios took on the administration of the monastery, while Symeon, the shepherd and teacher of everyone in the monastery, \<undertook\> in solitude the study and contemplation of the principles of creation. The one would, as it were, lead the flock, while the other, by prayer, would both support the leader and carefully examine the private cogitations of the others and steer them toward the better and more perfect course.

60

Ἀλλὰ γὰρ πρῶτα μὲν συνειλεγμένων τῶν μαθητῶν παραινεῖ μέσον αὐτῶν τὸν θαυμαστὸν Ἀρσένιον καὶ τοιαύτῃ χρῆται πρὸς αὐτὸν διδασκαλίᾳ οὕτως εἰπών· "Τὰ μὲν πρός σέ μου σπλάγχνα καὶ τοὺς λοιποὺς τῶν ἐμῶν τέκνων καὶ ἀδελφῶν οἶδας καὶ αὐτὸς ἀκριβῶς, ὦ πάτερ καὶ ἀδελφέ, καὶ οὐκ ἂν ἐπιλήσμων τῆς ἐμῆς ἀγάπης, τῆς ἐμῆς προσπαθείας, τῶν ὑπὲρ ὑμῶν μου δακρύων, ὧν ἡμέρας τε καὶ νυκτὸς ἐπὶ χρόνοις εἴκοσι καὶ πέντε κεκένωκα ἐνώπιον τοῦ Θεοῦ γενήσῃ ποτέ, ἀλλὰ καὶ μνησθήσῃ τούτων, καὶ τῆς ἐμῆς πίστεως τῆς πρὸς τὸν πνευματικόν μου πατέρα καὶ πατέρα ὑμῶν, τὸν μακάριον λέγω Συμεών, μιμητὴς ἔσῃ, τὴν ἐμὴν εἰδὼς ἀναστροφήν, καὶ προηγήσῃ πιστῶς τῶν πατέρων καὶ ἀδελφῶν σου, καὶ ὡς οἰκείων φροντίσεις μελῶν [cf. 1 Cor 12:12–27], εἰ δέοι δὲ καὶ *τὴν ψυχήν σου θήσεις ὑπὲρ αὐτῶν* [cf. John 10:11,15], καὶ οὐ προτιμήσεις ἕτερόν τι τῶν τοῦ κόσμου πραγμάτων τῆς ἀγάπης αὐτῶν.

2 "Καὶ γὰρ ἐπεί σε τῶν ἄλλων ἁπάντων εἰς ἡγουμενείαν ἐξελέξατο τὸ Πνεῦμα τὸ Ἅγιον, καὶ διὰ τῆς ἐμῆς προέκρινε ταπεινώσεως, δεῖ σε κατὰ τὸν τοῦ Κυρίου καὶ Θεοῦ ἡμῶν λόγον *ἔσχατον πάντων* [Mk 9:35] εἶναι τῷ φρονήματι καὶ τῇ κατὰ Θεὸν ταπεινώσει σου, ἵνα ὡς μὲν δυνατὸς τὰ ἀσθενήματα βαστάζῃς τῶν ἀδυνάτων, ὡς δὲ ἰατρὸς τὰ νοσήματα τῶν ἀδελφῶν θεραπεύῃς, ὡς δὲ ποιμὴν *τὸ πλανώμενον* [Mt 18:12] ἐπιστρέφῃς, καὶ τὸ μὲν καλῶς ἔχον πολυτόκον[116] ἐργάζῃ ταῖς ἀρεταῖς, τὸ δὲ ψώρας γέμον καὶ

Chapter 60

But first, when the disciples were assembled, Symeon exhorted the wondrous Arsenios in their midst and offered him instruction of this sort: "My father and brother Arsenios, you yourself know well my feelings toward you and the rest of my children and brothers. You should never forget my love and my deep affection, or the tears that I have shed before God on your behalf night and day for twenty-five years, but should remember them. And, knowing my own conduct, you should imitate my faith in my spiritual father, and your father, I mean the blessed Symeon [Eulabes]. You should faithfully lead your fathers and brothers, taking care of them as if they were your own limbs, and *laying down* your *life for* them if necessary. You should value nothing in the world more than your love for them.

"Since the Holy Spirit has selected you from all the others for the position of superior and, through my humble self, has chosen you, you must, according to the word of our Lord and God, be *the last of all* in your opinion of yourself and in your humility before God.[60] In this way, as a strong man you may support the weakness of those who are without strength, as a doctor you may treat the illnesses of the brethren, and as a shepherd you may round up the sheep *that has gone astray,* make the good sheep prolific in virtue, but drive

ἀνιάτως ἔχον ἀφορίζῃς τῆς ἀγέλης σου τῆς λογικῆς, ἵνα μὴ καὶ τοῖς ὑγιέσι μεταδῷ τοῦ νοσήματος. Ἐγὼ δὲ ὡς ἤδη γηράσας καὶ πολλὰ καμὼν σχολάσω τῶν πόνων μικρὸν καὶ ἔσομαί σοι πρὸς Θεὸν εὐθύμῳ καὶ ἀνενοχλήτῳ ψυχῇ.

61

"Σπεῦδε οὖν, τέκνον ἐμὸν ἐν Κυρίῳ, τὸ τοῦ Κυρίου σου ποίμνιον ἐπαυξάνειν τῇ ἐπιμελείᾳ τῶν ἐν αὐτῷ λογικῶν προβάτων· μὴ πρὸς ἀνέσεις ἢ τρυφὰς ἐκκλίνῃς τοῦ σώματος, ἑαυτῷ μᾶλλον ἢ τοῖς ἀδελφοῖς σου τὰ τῆς μονῆς θησαυρίζων ἀπολαύσεως ἕνεκεν. Μὴ συνεχεῖς ἀγαπήσῃς τὰς προόδους ποιεῖσθαι· ἀρκετὸν γάρ σοι καὶ ἅπαξ τοῦ μηνὸς ἐξερχομένῳ τὰς ἀναγκαιοτέρας ἐκτελεῖν ὑποθέσεις τῆς κατὰ σὲ μονῆς, τὰς δ᾽ ἄλλας οἱ διακονοῦντες ποιήσουσιν τὸ ἀπερίσπαστόν σοι διατηροῦντες ἐν τῇ διακονίᾳ τοῦ Λόγου καὶ τῇ ἐπιμελείᾳ δηλονότι προσκαρτεροῦντι τῶν ἀδελφῶν. Μὴ ἑαυτῷ μὲν τραπέζας πολυτελεῖς ἑτοιμάζῃς, τοῖς δέ γε[117] ὑπὸ σὲ ἀδελφοῖς καταπεφρονημένας καὶ ταπεινὰς καὶ τὸν ὀξίνην[118] παρέχῃς οἶνον εἰς πόσιν αὐτοῖς, ἀλλὰ κοινὴ μὲν ἡ τράπεζα (ἄνευ ἀρρωστίας καὶ ὑπαντῆς φίλων) τῶν τοῦ αὐτοῦ σοι καὶ βίου καὶ φρονήματός σοί τε καὶ τοῖς τέκνοις ἔστω, εἴτε διὰ λαχάνων ἑφθῶν καὶ σπερμάτων, εἴτε διὰ ἰχθύων ἅπαξ τῆς ἑβδομάδος κατὰ κυριακὴν ἢ καὶ δεσποτικὴν ἑορτὴν παρὰ τοῦ κελλαρίτου κοινῶς ἑτοιμάζεται.

away from your spiritual flock the mangy and incurable one so that it may not spread its sickness to the healthy. I, however, who am already old and very weary, will rest a little from my labors and, with a cheerful and untroubled soul, be there for you before God.

Chapter 61

"Strive, my child in the Lord, to increase your Lord's flock by your care for its spiritual sheep. Do not turn to bodily indulgence or luxuries by saving up the resources of the monastery for your own pleasure rather than for your brethren. Do not take delight in frequent outings. It should be sufficient for you to go out once a month to take care of the more pressing affairs of your monastery, while the monastic officials may deal with the others, leaving you undistracted to devote yourself diligently to the service of the Word and, of course, to the care of the brethren. Do not prepare extravagant meals for yourself while providing wretched and miserable ones for the brethren under you and serving them vinegary wine to drink. Let there be instead a common meal for you and your children, except for those who are sick, and when you are entertaining friends who have the same mode of life and ideas as you. The meal should consist either of boiled vegetables and grains or of fish once a week on Sunday or on dominical feast days, prepared by the cellarer for everyone.

2   "Τὰς τῆς μονῆς σου διακονίας σαυτῷ μόνῳ οὐ κατα-
πιστεύσεις πάσας[119] ποιεῖν, ἀρκεῖ σοι γὰρ ἡ πρώτη καὶ
ἀναγκαία, ἡ τῶν ἀδελφῶν σου λέγω ψυχικὴ ἐπιμέλεια.
Ἑκάστῳ δὲ τῶν ἐν εὐλαβείᾳ ζώντων καὶ φόβῳ Θεοῦ τὰς
διακονίας διανεμεῖς τοῦ κοινοβίου σου, πασῶν δηλονότι
τούτων τοὺς λόγους ἐξετάζων αὐτὸς κατὰ τὴν τοῦ μάρτυ-
ρος Χριστοῦ καὶ ὁμολογητοῦ τοῦ πατρὸς ἡμῶν Θεοδώρου τοῦ Στουδίτου παράδοσιν, ἣν πατροπαραδότως εἰς
πλουσίαν κληρονομίαν ἐλάβομεν.

62

"Οὐκ ἔσῃ θυμῷ καὶ ὀργῇ κατὰ τῶν σῶν φερόμενος
τέκνων καὶ ἀδελφῶν ἄνευ τινὸς πράγματος κίνδυνον προ-
ξενοῦντος ψυχαῖς, ἠπίῳ δὲ λόγῳ μᾶλλον καὶ φθέγματι διδάξεις αὐτοὺς πῶς δεῖ περιπατεῖν καὶ ἀναστρέφεσθαι ἕκαστον μέσον τῆς ἀδελφότητος· τοὺς νέους καὶ ἀστηρίκτους
φείδεσθαι ἑαυτῶν καὶ τῶν λοιπῶν ἀδελφῶν, ἵνα μὴ πρόξε-
νοι βλάβης γίνωνται τοῖς ὁρῶσι διά τε τῆς παρρησίας καὶ
τῶν ἀτάκτων τῆς νεότητος ἐπιτηδευμάτων· τοὺς ἐν ἀσκήσει χρονίσαντας ἐν λόγῳ διδάξεις συνέσεως τὴν ὑπομονὴν
τῶν πειρασμῶν, τὴν ταπείνωσιν, τὸ πένθος, τὴν ἐπιμέλειαν
τῆς εὐχῆς καὶ τοῦ γίνεσθαι διὰ πράξεως τῶν ἐντολῶν τοῦ[120]
Θεοῦ εἰς ὠφέλειαν τῶν λοιπῶν· τοὺς ἱερεῖς τὴν εὐλάβειαν,
τὴν ἡσυχίαν, τὴν μελέτην τῶν θείων γραφῶν, τὴν γνῶσιν

"You should not give yourself the duties of your monas- 2
tery to do all by yourself, for the first and most important
duty, I mean the spiritual care of your brethren, is enough
for you. Rather, you should delegate the duties of your community to each of those who live in piety and the fear of
God, that is to say, yourself evaluating the rationale of all
of them, according to the tradition of our father the martyr and confessor of Christ Theodore of Stoudios, which
we have received as a rich inheritance passed down by our
fathers.[61]

Chapter 62

"You should not get carried away with anger or rage
against your children and brothers, unless it is a matter en-
dangering their souls, but rather should instruct them with
kind words and speech as to how each should live and com-
port himself in the midst of the brotherhood. <You should
thus instruct> those who are young and restless to have con-
sideration for themselves and the rest of the brethren so
that they do not cause harm, through their loose talk and
the unruly conduct of youth, to those who observe them.
Using wise words you should teach those experienced in asceticism about endurance of temptations, humility, contrition, diligence in prayer, and to help the rest by carrying out
God's commandments. And <you should instruct> those
who are priests about piety, tranquillity, study of the holy

τῶν ἀποστολικῶν κανόνων καὶ παραδόσεων, τὴν τῶν δογμάτων ἀκρίβειαν, τὴν καθαρότητα τῆς καρδίας, τὴν ἀένναον προσευχὴν καὶ κατάνυξιν, τὴν ἐπὶ τοῦ θείου βήματος ἐν φόβῳ παράστασιν, καὶ ἵνα διὰ λόγου καὶ πράξεως πάσῃ τῇ ἀδελφότητι καὶ τοῖς ἔξω ἅλας [Mt 5:13; cf. Mk 9:50; Lk 14:34] ὦσι θεῖον καὶ φῶς [cf. Mt 5:14; Phlp 2:15] λόγον ζωῆς ἔχοντες [cf. Phlp 2:16] ἐν ἑαυτοῖς. Εἰ δὲ καὶ κατὰ τῶν ἀτάκτων δεῖ σέ ποτε κινηθῆναι εὐλόγῳ θυμῷ ἐν ῥάβδῳ παιδείας [cf. Prov 22:15] πρὸς τὸ ἀνακοπήν τινα ποιήσασθαι τοῦ κακοῦ καὶ φαύλην ἀναστεῖλαι συνήθειαν οὐδὲ τοῦτο ξένον τῆς τῶν πιστῶν ἐκκλησίας· πᾶσα γὰρ πρᾶξις ἡμῶν ἡ κακίαν μὲν ἀναστέλλουσα δικαιοσύνῃ δὲ καὶ ἀρετῇ βοηθοῦσα ἐπαινετὴ καὶ θεάρεστος.

2   "Τὰ τῆς ἰδίας μονῆς οὐ γονεῦσι καὶ ἰδίοις σου ταμιεύσεις, ἅπαξ[121] τῶν τοιούτων ἀπορραγεὶς καὶ τῆς προσπαθείας ἀλογήσας αὐτῶν, ἀλλ' ὡς Δεσποτικοῖς προσέξεις πράγμασι, καὶ οὕτω ταῦτα φυλάξεις ὡς λόγον ὀφείλων καὶ ὑπὲρ οἰκτροῦ πράγματος ἀποδοῦναι τῷ Θεῷ, ἐκείνοις δὲ ὡς πενομένοις εἰ πένονται παρέξεις τὰ πρὸς τὴν ἀναγκαίαν χρείαν καὶ μόνην,[122] μὴ ἐν προσποιήσει πραότητος διὰ ἔπαινον τῶν ἀνθρώπων μικροῦ τινος πράγματος ἐφ' ὕβρει γινομένου τοῦ εὐαγγελικοῦ βίου καὶ τῆς τῶν μοναχῶν καταστάσεως καταφρονήσας, ἀλλὰ τὸν σὸν μιμούμενος Χριστὸν καὶ Θεόν, ἐμβριμώμενος[123] [cf. Mt 9:30; Mk 1:43; John 11:33] καὶ ἑαυτὸν ἀπαθῶς ἐκταράσσων, ἐκδίκησιν ποιοῦ τῶν ἐντολῶν τοῦ Θεοῦ.

scriptures, knowledge of the apostolic canons and tradi-
tions, correctness of doctrine, purity of heart, perpetual
prayer and compunction, and reverent attendance at the
holy altar. Thus *having the word of life* in themselves, they
may, by word and deed, become divine salt and light to the
whole brotherhood and to those outside it. But if ever you
do need to be moved with good reason by anger to use *the
rod of correction* on the unruly in order to check some evil
and remove a bad habit, that is not something alien to the
church of the faithful, for our every action that removes evil
and assists righteousness and virtue is laudable and pleasing
to God.[62]

"You should not hoard the resources of your monastery 2
for your parents or your family, for you have broken with
such people once and for all, and should have no regard for
your attachment to them. Instead you should take care of
<these resources> as you would your Master's property and
thus safeguard them, since you will have to provide an ac-
counting to God for even a trifling matter. But if <your rel-
atives> are poor, you should give them, like <other> poor
people, only what is strictly necessary. Do not, by feigning
kindness so that people may think well of you, disregard any
small matter that might besmirch the life of the Gospel and
the observance of the monks. Rather, in imitation of your
Christ and God, sternly admonishing and dispassionately
troubling yourself, defend the commandments of God.

63

"Ἔστω σοι μετὰ πάντων καὶ ἐπὶ τῇ ἐξετάσει τῶν λογισμῶν ἑκάστου ἀκρίβεια, ὡς ἂν¹²⁴ εἰδείης τίνες μὲν αὐτῶν
δέονται τῆς τῶν εὐχομένων καὶ κοινωνούντων συστάσεως,
τίνες δὲ ἀφορισμοῦ καὶ τῆς μετὰ τῶν μετανοούντων τάξεως, ἵνα μὴ τὴν ἐκκλησίαν Θεοῦ ἀντὶ ναοῦ ἁγίου *σπήλαιον
λῃστῶν* [Jer 7:11; Mt 21:13; Mk 11:17; Lk 19:46] ἢ *πορνεῖον*
[cf. Ez 16:31,39] ἐν γνώσει ἢ¹²⁵ ἀγνοίᾳ ποιήσῃς, καὶ τὸ φοβερὸν ἐπὶ τούτῳ κρῖμα οὐκ ἐκφεύξῃ τῆς ὀργῆς τοῦ Θεοῦ.
*Εὐλαβεῖς ποιήσεις κατὰ τὸ γεγραμμένον τοὺς πνευματικούς
σου υἱοὺς* [cf. Lv 15:31] καὶ διδάξεις εὐλαβεῖσθαι αὐτοὺς ἀπὸ
τῶν ἱερῶν τοῦ Θεοῦ τόπων ὁμοῦ καὶ σκευῶν τῆς λειτουργίας αὐτοῦ· μόνοις γὰρ ἴσθι τοῖς ἱερωμένοις καὶ εὐλαβεστά-
τοις τῶν μοναχῶν τοῖς καὶ τῶν μυστηρίων μετέχουσι τὸ
ἅπτεσθαι αὐτῶν παρὰ τῶν ἀποστόλων ἀφιερώθη. Διὰ
ταῦτα οὐ συγχωρήσεις πᾶσι καὶ τοῖς βουλομένοις τὴν τοῦ
θείου βήματος εἴσοδον, ἀλλ᾽ ἢ μόνοις ὡς εἴρηται τοῖς ἱερωμένοις καὶ ἡγιασμένοις τῶν ἀδελφῶν.

2   "Περὶ δὲ τῶν λοιπῶν τῶν λυσιτελούντων σου τῇ μονῇ
ἔχεις τὴν διδασκαλίαν καὶ τὸν πατροπαράδοτον τύπον
ἡμῶν ἐν τῇ θεοπνεύστῳ διατυπώσει τοῦ μεγαλομάρτυρος
Χριστοῦ καὶ ὁμολογητοῦ Θεοδώρου τοῦ κοινοῦ πατρὸς
καὶ διδασκάλου ἡμῶν τε τῶν δούλων αὐτοῦ καὶ τοῦ ὁσίου
πατρὸς ἡμῶν τοῦ Στουδιώτου. Ἐὰν οὕτω φυλάξῃς, οὕτω
δὲ¹²⁶ καὶ ποιήσῃς ὑπὲρ τῆς ἀγάπης τῶν σῶν ἀδελφῶν *τὴν
ψυχήν σου τιθείς* [cf. John 10:11,15], *πιστὸς ὁ Θεὸς* [1 Cor

Chapter 63

"Along with all these things, you must be exacting in the scrutiny of each person's thoughts, so that you may know which monks should be in the congregation of those who pray and take communion together, but also which ones require excommunication and classing with the penitents. For if you wittingly or unwittingly make the church of God *a den of robbers* or a *brothel* instead of a holy temple, you will not escape the terrible judgment of the wrath of God for this offense. You should *make your* spiritual *sons reverent,* according to scripture, and teach them to be reverential of the holy places of God, and likewise of the vessels of His liturgy. For you must know that the apostles have blessed the handling of these vessels only by those among the monks who are ordained and the most pious and who participate in the mysteries of the Eucharist.[63] For this reason you should not permit access to the divine sanctuary to all who want it, but, as I have said, only to the ordained and consecrated brothers.

"Concerning everything else that may be of benefit to 2 your monastery, you have the teaching and the paradigm handed down by our fathers in the divinely inspired rule of the great martyr of Christ and confessor Theodore, our common father, <who is> the teacher both of us his servants and of our blessed father the Stoudite [Symeon Eulabes]. If you observe these rules and act accordingly by *laying down* your *life* for love of your brothers, *the God* of your fathers will

1:9, cf. 10:13] τῶν πατέρων σου ὅτι πολὺς ἔσται ὁ μισθός σου ἐν τοῖς οὐρανοῖς [cf. Mt 5:12; Lk 6:23] καὶ ἡ κληρονομία σου μετὰ Ἰησοῦ Χριστοῦ [cf. Eph 5:5; Col 3:24; 1 Pt 1:4] τοῦ ἀρχιποιμένος [1 Pt 5:4] τῆς ἐκκλησίας ἡμῶν τῶν πιστῶν, ἡ δὲ ἐν τῷ μέλλοντι ἀνάπαυσίς σου μετὰ Ἀντωνίου, Εὐθυμίου, Συμεὼν καὶ Θεοδώρου τῶν μακαρίων πατέρων ἡμῶν. Αὕτη μέν, ὦ πάτερ ἀδελφὲ καὶ ἡγούμενε, ἡ πρὸς σέ μου διδασκαλία καὶ ὑποτύπωσις.

64

"Δεῦτε τοιγαροῦν καὶ ὑμεῖς, ὦ τέκνα καὶ ἀδελφοὶ καὶ πατέρες μου, οὓς ἐπισυνήγαγον [cf. Mt 23:37; 12:30; Lk 11:23] μετὰ Ἰησοῦ Χριστοῦ τοῦ Θεοῦ μου καὶ οὓς διὰ Πνεύματος Ἁγίου ἐν τῇ διδασκαλίᾳ τοῦ Λόγου ἐγέννησα [cf. 1 Cor 4:15], καὶ ἀκούσατέ μου τοῦ ἀναξίου πατρὸς καὶ διδασκάλου ὑμῶν, καὶ ἐμοὶ μὲν ὡς κεκοπιακότι δότε τόπον σχολῆς καὶ μικρᾶς τῶν πόνων ἀνέσεως, ἵνα μικρὸν ἀναψύξω καὶ ἐμαυτὸν ἐπισκέψωμαι, τῷ δέ γε παρὰ τῆς ἄνωθεν χάριτος καὶ τῆς ἐμῆς ταπεινώσεως προκριθέντι εἰς ἡγούμενον ὑμῶν κλίνατε τὸ γόνυ καὶ τὰς καρδίας ὑμῶν, παρακαλῶ ὑμᾶς ἐν Χριστῷ Ἰησοῦ, καὶ δέξασθε αὐτὸν ὡς ἐμὲ τὸν καὶ αὐτὸν καὶ ὑμᾶς γεγεννηκότα διὰ τῆς ἄνωθεν χάριτος, καὶ ταπεινώθητε ἐνώπιον τῆς κραταιᾶς χειρὸς τοῦ Θεοῦ [1Pt 5:6] καὶ αὐτοῦ τοῦ γεγονότος ἤδη ποιμένος ὑμῶν διὰ τῆς ἐκλογῆς

be *faithful* to you. *Great will be your reward in heaven,* and your inheritance will be with Jesus Christ, *the chief shepherd* of the church of us his faithful, and your repose in the future will be with our blessed fathers Antony, Euthymios, Symeon, and Theodore. This, then, is my teaching and rule for you, my father, brother, and superior.

Chapter 64

"Come then also you my children, my brothers and fathers whom I have *gathered up* with my God Jesus Christ[64] and whom *I have begotten* through the Holy Spirit in the teaching of the Word; listen to me, your unworthy father and teacher. Since I have toiled and grown weary, allow me an opportunity for leisure and a little relaxation from my labors so that I may refresh myself a little and engage in some self-reflection. But kneel before the man who has been selected as your superior by heavenly grace and by my humility, and <offer> your hearts to him, I ask you in Christ Jesus. Receive him as you would me, who have begotten both him and you through heavenly grace, and *humble yourselves* before *the mighty hand of God* and of him who has now become your

ὑμῶν τῆς ἁγίας. *Μηδεὶς οὖν ἐξ ὑμῶν τῆς αὐτοῦ καταφρο-*
νείτω νεότητος [cf. 1 Tim 4:12], μηδεὶς τοῦ ἀπλάστου λόγου
καὶ τῆς διδασκαλίας αὐτοῦ· *εἰ γὰρ καὶ ἰδιώτης ὑπάρχει τῷ*
λόγῳ, ἀλλ' οὐ πάντως καὶ τῇ γνώσει τῆς χάριτος [2 Cor 11:6].
Ὁ γὰρ ἔμπρακτος λόγος τὴν γνῶσιν ἔχων τὴν ἄνωθεν
σοφώτερός ἐστι τῆς μεμωραμένης τῶν ἀνθρώπων σοφίας
[cf. 1 Cor 1:20–25], καθ' ὃ τῶν ἀστέρων λαμπρότερος καὶ
κρείττων ὑπάρχει ὁ ἥλιος.

65

"Διὰ δὴ τοῦτο κλίνατε τὸ οὖς ὑμῶν εἰς τὰ ῥήματα τοῦ
στόματος αὐτοῦ καὶ φθέγξεται ὑμῖν προβλήματα ἀπ' ἀρχῆς,[127]
ὅσα ἤκουσέ τε καὶ ἔγνω καὶ οἱ πατέρες αὐτοῦ διηγήσαντο
αὐτῷ [cf. Ps 77(78):1–3]. Ἡ γὰρ ἀληθὴς ταπείνωσις ἔνθεν
τοῖς καλῶς ὁρῶσι τῶν τε μαθητευομένων καὶ παντὸς ἑτέρου γνωρίζεται, ἐκ τοῦ ὑπέχειν τὸ οὖς εἰς τὸ ἀκοῦσαι τί
αὐτῷ λαληθήσεται καὶ διὰ στόματος τῶν διδασκάλων
τούτῳ γνωσθήσεται. Οὕτω γὰρ πᾶς ἄνθρωπος δέχεται τὸν
σπόρον τοῦ Λόγου τῷ ἀδελφῷ ταπεινούμενος, καὶ οὕτω
καρποφορεῖν οἶδεν *ἐν τριάκοντα καὶ ἐν ἑξήκοντα*[128] *καὶ ἐν*
ἑκατὸν [Mk 4:20; cf. Mk 4:8; Mt 13:8] τὸν τέλειον καρπὸν
τοῦ ἁγίου Πνεύματος. Μηδεὶς ἀντιλέγων ἢ ἀπειθῶν ἔστω
ἐνώπιον αὐτοῦ, μηδεὶς ἀνυπότακτος ἢ θρασύς, ἀλλὰ πάντες ὑπήκοοι, πάντες εὐπειθεῖς, πάντες ὑποτασσόμενοι γί-

shepherd by your holy decision. *Let none of you despise his youth,* none his unformed speech and his teaching, for *even if he is unskilled in speaking,* he is *not* at all unskilled *in the knowledge* of grace. For practical speech that contains heavenly knowledge is wiser than the foolish wisdom of men, just as the sun is brighter and greater than the stars.

Chapter 65

"So *incline your ears to the words of* his *mouth and he will utter problems* to you *from of old, things that he has heard and known, that* his *fathers have told* him. For true humility, both in those who are in training and in everyone else, is recognized by perceptive people, when someone listens carefully to what is being said and what is made known to him through the speech of his teachers. Every person thus receives the seed of the Word by being humble before his brother, every person thus knows how *to bear* the perfect fruit of the Holy Spirit *thirty-, sixty-, and one hundredfold.* So let no one contradict or be disobedient to him, no one insubordinate or insolent. Instead, you must all be obedient, all compliant, all

νεσθε τῷ πατρὶ ὑμῶν τῷ πνευματικῷ, ἐπειδὴ κατὰ τὸν θεῖον
ἀπόστολον αὐτὸς *ἀγρυπνεῖν* ὀφείλει καὶ εὔχεσθαι *ὑπὲρ τῶν
ψυχῶν ὑμῶν, ἵνα μετὰ χαρᾶς τοῦτο ποιῇ καὶ μὴ στενάζων·
ἀλυσιτελὲς γὰρ ὑμῖν ἔσται τοῦτο* [cf. Hbr 13:17] κατὰ τὴν
παροῦσαν ζωήν. Τοὺς ὑπὸ τῶν δαιμόνων *σπειρομένους*
ὑμῖν *λογισμοὺς* [cf. Mt 13:25] πίστει φερόμενοι ἐξομολο-
γεῖσθε αὐτῷ, ἐπειδὴ κατὰ τὸ εἰρημένον *μώλωπες θριαμβευ-
όμενοι οὐ προκόψουσιν ἐπὶ τὸ χεῖρον.* Ὥσπερ γὰρ οἱ ὄφεις,
μέχρις ἂν ἔνδον ὑπὸ τῶν ἰδίων φωλεῶν κρύπτωνται, ζῶσί
τε καὶ γεννῶσιν ὄφεις πολλούς, ἐπὰν δὲ τῶν φωλεῶν ἐξελθόντες σύροντες φανερῶς¹²⁹ ἑαυτούς, αὐτοὶ δι᾿ ἑαυτῶν
ἐμφανίζονται τοῖς ἀνθρώποις καὶ ὑπ᾿ αὐτῶν ἀναιροῦνται,
τὸν αὐτὸν τρόπον καὶ οἱ πονηροὶ λογισμοὶ στηλιτευόμενοι
παρ᾿ ἡμῶν καὶ τοῖς πατράσιν ἡμῶν φανερούμενοι ἀναιροῦνται *τῇ μαχαίρᾳ τοῦ θείου Λόγου* αὐτῶν¹³⁰ [cf. Eph 6:17]
καὶ οὐ γεννῶσιν ἐν ἡμῖν τὰς συγκαταθέσεις, δι᾿ ὧν ἐπὶ τὰ
φαῦλα ἡ πρᾶξις ἐξάγεται.

66

"Εἰ δὲ καὶ εἰς ἔργον ἐκ ῥαθυμίας ἐκβῇ τὰ τῶν φαύλων
ἐννοιῶν καὶ πράξομέν τι τῶν ἀνθρωπίνων ἀπονυστάξαν-
τες, ἀλλὰ παρακαλῶ μηδὲ οὕτως ἐν τῷ γεγονότι χρονίσω-
μεν· δράμωμεν¹³¹ σπουδαίως καὶ τοῖς ποσὶ προσπέσωμεν
τοῦ πατρὸς ἡμῶν καὶ τὸ ἔργον ἀνεπαισχύντως μετὰ

submissive to your spiritual father, since, in the words of the holy apostle, he must *keep watch over* and pray for *your souls* and must *do this joyfully and not sadly, for that would be no advantage to you* in the present life. You must confess confidently to him the thoughts that are sown in you by the demons because, according to the saying, *wounds that are exposed will not fester.*[65] For just as snakes survive and breed many <more> snakes as long as they remain hidden in their own holes, but whenever they come slithering out of their holes into the open they reveal themselves to people and are destroyed by them, in the same way, when we publicly display our wicked thoughts and make them known to our fathers, they are destroyed by the sword of the divine Word itself, and do not breed in us the acquiescence through which our actions lead us to the bad.

Chapter 66

"But if, from our carelessness, our bad ideas do turn into action, and having become drowsy, we do something from human weakness, please let us not then waste time on what has happened to us; rather let us run eagerly, fall at the feet of our father, and, having no cause for shame, tearfully de-

δακρύων ἐκφαυλίσωμεν τοῦ κακοῦ καὶ δεξώμεθα ἐν μετα-
νοίᾳ θερμῇ τὰ στυπτικὰ ἢ καὶ καίοντα φάρμακα παρ' αὐτοῦ,
καὶ ταχέως τευξόμεθα τῆς ἰάσεως. Ἐν τοῖς ὑπ' αὐτοῦ πρατ-
τομένοις καὶ λεγομένοις¹³² μὴ ἀπαρέσκεσθε, ἀλλ' εἰ καὶ
παρὰ τὸ δοκοῦν τοῖς πατράσιν εἰσίν, ὑποκλίνετε τό γε νῦν
ἔχον αὐτῷ τὰς κεφαλάς. Εἶτα εἴ τινες ἐξ ὑμῶν χρόνῳ καὶ
βίῳ καὶ λόγῳ τῶν λοιπῶν διαφέρουσι, κατ' ἰδίαν γνωριζέ-
τωσαν αὐτῷ τοῦ κεκωλυμένου τὸν λόγον, καθὼς καὶ ὁ μέγας ὑπετυπώσατο Βασίλειος. Ὑπομείνατε αὐτὸν ἐν ἡμέρᾳ
ἐπαγωγῆς [Sir 5:8] καὶ πικρίας διὰ τὸν Κύριον, μηδαμῶς
αὐτῷ ἀντιλέγοντες ἢ ἀνθιστάμενοι· ὁ γὰρ ἀντιλέγων ἢ
ἀνθιστάμενος αὐτῷ τῇ τοῦ Θεοῦ ἐξουσίᾳ ἀνθέστηκεν [cf.
Rom 13:2], ὥς φησι Παῦλος· ἐν ὅσοις γὰρ οὐκ ἔστι παράβασις Θεοῦ ἐντολῆς ἢ ἀποστολικῶν κανόνων καὶ διατάξεων,
ἐν πᾶσιν ἀνάγκη πᾶσα ὑπακούειν αὐτῷ¹³³ ὀφείλετε καὶ ὡς
τῷ Κυρίῳ πείθεσθαι· ἐν ὅσοις δὲ κινδυνεύει τὸ τοῦ Χριστοῦ
Εὐαγγέλιον καὶ οἱ νόμοι τῆς ἐκκλησίας αὐτοῦ, οὐ μόνον οὐ
δεῖ πείθεσθαι τούτῳ παραινοῦντι ὑμῖν καὶ διατασσομένῳ,
ἀλλ' οὐδὲ ἀγγέλῳ ἄρτι ἀπ' οὐρανοῦ κατεληλυθότι¹³⁴ καὶ
ὑμῖν εὐαγγελιζομένῳ παρ' ὃ οἱ αὐτόπται τοῦ Λόγου εὐηγ-
γελίσαντο [cf. Gal 1:8.; Lk 1:2].

nounce the evil deed. Let us then receive from him, with fervent repentance, astringent or even caustic remedies, and so bring about our cure. Do not be displeased with his actions or words, but even if they are contrary to the opinion of the fathers, bow your head in subjection to him for the time being. Then, those of you who are distinguished from the rest in age, manner of life, and speech can make known to him in private the reason for stopping him, just as the great Basil has ordained.[66] For the Lord's sake, submit patiently to him on a *day of calamity* and bitterness, in no way contradicting or resisting him. For as Paul says, the person who contradicts or resists him *resists the authority of God*. In all those matters in which there is no deviation from God's commandment or from the apostolic canons and regulations, you must absolutely obey him in them all and trust in him as you would in the Lord. But in those matters in which the Gospel of Christ and the laws of His church are jeopardized, you must not only not follow the orders of the person who suggests this to you or orders it, but must not do so even if an angel has come down from heaven and is preaching something to you contrary to what those who were eyewitnesses to the Word have preached.

67

"Φυλάξατέ μοι ταῦτα καὶ ἃ ἰδίᾳ καὶ καταμόνας ἕκαστον ὑμῶν ἐξεδίδαξα εἰς κατόρθωσιν ἀρετῆς, τέκνα μου καὶ ἀδελφοί, ὡς παρακαταθήκην [cf. 1 Tim 6:20] Θεοῦ ἐν τοῖς ταμιείοις τῶν καρδιῶν ὑμῶν. Οὐ μόνον δέ, ἀλλὰ καὶ ἐπεργάσασθε αὐτοῖς καὶ πολυπλασιάσατε ὡς καλοὶ δοῦλοι Χριστοῦ, ἵνα διὰ τῆς φυλακῆς καὶ ἐργασίας τῶν ἐλαχίστων τούτων ταλάντων ἐπὶ πολλῶν ἀγαθῶν τῆς τοῦ Θεοῦ βασιλείας ἀπόλαυσιν ἀποκατασταθῆτε τῇ τοῦ Χριστοῦ χάριτι[135] [cf. Mt 25:14–30], καὶ αὐτῷ συμβασιλεύσητε καὶ κληρονομήσητε τὴν ἡτοιμασμένην τοῖς δικαίοις τοῦ Θεοῦ βασιλείαν ἀπὸ καταβολῆς κόσμου [Mt 25:34; cf. Apc 13:8, 17:8]. Ἀσπάσασθε οὖν ἐμέ τε καὶ τὸν πατέρα ὑμῶν τὸν κύριν[136] ἡγούμενον ἐν φιλήματι ἁγίῳ [cf. Rom 16:16], καὶ ὁ Θεὸς ἡ εἰρήνη ἡ πάντα νοῦν ὑπερέχουσα [Phlp 4:7] βραβεύσοι ὑμῖν[137] τὴν εἰρήνην [cf. Col 3:15] αὐτοῦ καὶ ὁδηγήσοι ὑμᾶς[138] εἰς τὴν ὁδὸν τῶν αὐτοῦ ἐντολῶν [cf. Ps 118(119):35] καὶ αὐξήσοι ὑμᾶς τὸ αὐτοῦ ποίμνιον φυλάττοντας τὴν πίστιν εἰς τοὺς κατὰ Θεὸν πατέρας ὑμῶν εἰς πλῆθος ἅγιον, εἰς λαὸν περιούσιον καὶ εἰς βασίλειον αὐτοῦ ἱεράτευμα [1 Pt 2:9] ἐν Χριστῷ Ἰησοῦ."

Chapter 67

"My children and brothers, keep safe for me in the treasuries of your hearts, like something entrusted to you by God, these matters as well as what I have taught each of you in private and individually concerning the successful practice of virtue. Moreover, like good servants of Christ, cultivate these teachings and multiply them in order that, by preserving and employing the least of these talents, you may be reimbursed by the grace of Christ with the enjoyment of the many good things of the kingdom of God, and you may rule with Him and *inherit the kingdom that has been prepared* for the righteous people of God *from the foundation of the world.* So *kiss* me, and your father the lord superior, *with a holy kiss,* and may God, *the peace which passes all understanding,* let His *peace rule over* you and lead you in the way of His commandments and increase you, who are His flock and who keep faith with your fathers in God, into a holy multitude, into a superior people, into a *royal priesthood* in Christ Jesus."

68

Ταῦτα τοιγαροῦν καὶ πλείονα τούτων ἕτερα παραινέσας αὐτῷ τε τῷ θαυμαστῷ Ἀρσενίῳ τῷ ἡγουμένῳ καὶ τῇ λοιπῇ ἀδελφότητι ὁ ἅγιος[139] πατὴρ ἡμῶν Συμεών, τὸ τῆς ἡσυχίας ἐργαστήριον ὑπεισέρχεται καὶ τῆς φίλης αὖθις φιλοσοφίας μετὰ πλείονος τῆς προθέσεως ἅπτεται. Ὡς[140] οὖν αὐτῷ μὲν ὁ μακρὸς τῆς ἀσκήσεως δίαυλος διηνύετο, προέκοπτον δὲ αἱ πρὸς τὸ κρεῖττον ἐν αὐτῷ ἐπιδόσεις, ἐπὶ τὸ ὑψηλότερον καὶ θεοειδέστερον ἀναγομένης αὐτοῦ[141] τῆς ψυχῆς, καὶ οἱ μὲν πόνοι τῶν ἱερῶν ἀγώνων ἐπὶ τὸ ἄπονον ἢ μᾶλλον ξένως εἰπεῖν ἐπὶ θεοπρεπεῖς ἀνέσεις τῶν ἀσωμάτων δυνάμεων μετηλλάττοντο, ἡ δὲ φύσις τοῦ σώματος ἠλλοιοῦτο πρὸς ἀφθαρσίαν ἐξισταμένη δυνάμει κρείττονι τῆς ἑαυτῆς ταπεινώσεως, *εἰς ὀπτασίας αὖθις καὶ ἀποκαλύψεις Κυρίου* [2 Cor 12:1] ἡρπάζετο καὶ τῶν μελλόντων προεθεώρει τὴν ἔκβασιν.

69

Τοίνυν καὶ ἐν μιᾷ ὡς εἰς προσευχὴν ἱστάμενος ἦν καθαρὰν καὶ προσωμίλει θεῷ, εἶδε καὶ ἰδοὺ ὁ ἀὴρ ἤρξατο διαυγάζειν αὐτοῦ τῷ νοΐ, ἔνδον δὲ ὢν τοῦ κελλίου ἐδόκει αἴθριος ἔξω διατελεῖν· νὺξ δὲ ἦν περὶ πρώτην αὐτῆς φυλακήν.

Chapter 68

When Symeon, our holy father, had given this advice and more besides to that wondrous Arsenios the superior and to the rest of the brethren, he entered the workshop of spiritual tranquillity and engaged once again with even greater eagerness in his beloved ascetic philosophy. Since he had already completed the long course of asceticism, however, his spiritual gifts increased as his soul ascended to a higher and more divine state. Thus, while the labors of his sacred struggles became easy for him, or rather, strange to say, were transformed into the divine recreation of the incorporeal powers, the nature of his body was changed to incorruptibility, being altered by the superior power of his humility. And once again he was caught up in *visions and revelations of the Lord,* and he foresaw the outcome of future events.

Chapter 69

On one occasion then, while he was standing in pure prayer and conversing with God, he saw with his intellect the air start to shimmer, and although he was inside his cell, he seemed to be outside in the open air. It was nighttime,

Ὡς δὲ φαίνειν ἄνωθεν ἤρξατο δίκην αὐγῆς πρωϊνῆς—ὢ τῶν φρικτῶν ὄψεων τοῦ ἀνδρός!—ἡ οἰκία καὶ πάντα παρήρχοντο καὶ ἐν οἴκῳ οὐδόλως εἶναι ἐνόμιζεν. Ὡς ἐξίστατο δὲ ὅλως ὅλῳ κατανοῶν τῷ νοῒ ἐκεῖνο τὸ δεικνύμενον φῶς, ηὔξανέ τε κατὰ μικρὸν αὐτὸ καὶ τὸν ἀέρα ἐποίει λαμπρότερον φαίνεσθαι καὶ ἑαυτὸν ἔξω τῶν γηΐνων σὺν ὅλῳ τῷ σώματι κατενόει γινόμενον. Ἀλλὰ γὰρ ἐπεὶ τρανότερον ἔτι φαιδρύνεσθαι τὸ φῶς ἐκεῖνο προσέθετο, καὶ ὡς μεσημβρία ἡλίου ἄνωθεν ἐπιλάμποντος αὐτῷ ἑωρᾶτο, μέσον ἱστάμενον τοῦ φαινομένου ἑαυτὸν κατενόει καὶ ὅλον ἐν ὅλῳ τῷ σώματι ἀπὸ τῆς ἐκεῖθεν[142] ἐγγινομένης ἡδύτητος αὐτῷ χαρᾶς καὶ δακρύων ἔμπλεων.

2   Ἀλλὰ γὰρ καὶ αὐτὸ παραδόξως τὸ φῶς ἁπτόμενον[143] ἔβλεπε τῆς σαρκὸς αὐτοῦ καὶ κατ᾽ ὀλίγον γινόμενον ἐν τοῖς μέλεσιν αὐτοῦ. Τὸ παράδοξον οὖν τοῦ ὁράματος τούτου τῆς προτέρας αὐτὸν θεωρίας ἀπέστησε καὶ μόνον κατανοεῖν ἐποίει τὸ ἐν αὐτῷ πανεξαισίως τελούμενον. Ἔβλεπεν οὖν ἕως οὗ κατ᾽ ὀλίγον ὅλον ὅλῳ τῷ σώματι αὐτοῦ, τῇ καρδίᾳ καὶ τοῖς ἐγκάτοις αὐτοῦ ἐδόθη καὶ πῦρ ὅλον καὶ φῶς αὐτὸν ἀπετέλεσεν. Ὥσπερ δὲ πρότερον τὴν οἰκίαν, οὕτω τηνικαῦτα τὸ σχῆμα, τὴν θέσιν, τὸ πάχος καὶ τὸ εἶδος τοῦ σώματος ἀγνοῆσαι τοῦτον πεποίηκε, καὶ δακρύων ἐπαύσατο. Φωνὴ οὖν ἐκ τοῦ φωτὸς ἐπ᾽ αὐτῷ γίνεται καί φησιν· "Οὕτως ἀλλαγῆναι τοὺς ζῶντας καὶ περιλειπομένους ἁγίους ἐν τῇ ἐσχάτῃ σάλπιγγι κέκριται καὶ οἱ οὕτως γενόμενοι ἁρπαγήσονται, καθὰ καὶ Παῦλός φησιν [cf. 1 Th 4:16–17]."

about the first watch. As it began to get light overhead like the glimmer of daybreak—oh, the awesome visions of this man!—the building and everything else disappeared and he seemed no longer to be inside. While he was in this state of complete ecstasy and was contemplating with his whole intellect the light that was appearing, it gradually increased. It made the air seem brighter, and he felt himself and his whole body transcending this earthly existence. The light continued to get brighter and brighter and seemed to be shining down on him from above like the sun at midday. As it did so, he felt himself standing in the midst of this manifestation and his whole body was completely filled with joy and tears from the sweetness that emanated from it.

Then he saw the light taking hold of his flesh in a strange 2 way and gradually merging into his limbs. The strangeness of this sight distracted him from his earlier vision and caused him to contemplate only what was happening within him in this completely extraordinary way. Thus he watched until, little by little, the light was imparted to his whole body, to his heart and his internal organs, and rendered him wholly fire and light. And just as had happened before with the building, so now it caused him to lose awareness of the form, the structure, the mass, and the shape of his body, and he stopped weeping. Then a voice came to him from out of the light, saying, "This is how it has been determined that the holy ones *who are alive* and *who remain* are to be transformed *at* the last *trumpet,* and in this state *caught up,* as Paul says."[67]

70

Ἐπὶ πολλὰς τοίνυν ὥρας οὕτω¹⁴⁴ διατελῶν καὶ ἱστάμενος ὁ μακάριος, καὶ μυστικαῖς τισιν ἀκαταπαύστως¹⁴⁵
ἀνυμνῶν φωναῖς τὸν Θεόν, κατανοῶν τε τὴν περιέχουσαν
αὐτὸν¹⁴⁶ δόξαν καὶ τὴν δοθῆναι μέλλουσαν αἰωνίως τοῖς
ἁγίοις μακαριότητα, ἤρξατο λογίζεσθαι καὶ λέγειν ἐν ἑαυ-
τῷ· "Ἆρά γε πάλιν ἐπιστρέψω εἰς τὸ πρότερον σχῆμα τοῦ
σώματος, ἢ οὕτω διάγων ἔσομαι;" ὡς οὖν τοῦτο διελογί-
σατο, αὐτίκα ὥσπερ σκιὰν ἢ ὡς πνεῦμα τέως ἔγνω τὸ
σχῆμα περιφέρειν τοῦ σώματος· φῶς γὰρ ὅλον ἑαυτὸν
ἀνείδεον ἀσχημάτιστόν τε καὶ ἄϋλον ὥσπερ εἴρηται κατενόει γενόμενον σὺν τῷ σώματι, καὶ τὸ μὲν σῶμα ἐγίνωσκε
συνεῖναι αὐτῷ, πλὴν ἀσώματόν πως καὶ ὡς πνευματικόν·
βάρος γὰρ ἢ παχύτητα τέως οὐδόλως ἔχειν τοῦτο ὑπώ-
πτευε καὶ ἐθαύμαζεν ὁρῶν ἑαυτὸν ἐν σώματι ὡς ἀσώμα-
τον. Ἀλλὰ γὰρ τῇ προτέρᾳ φωνῇ πάλιν τὸ ἐν αὐτῷ λαλοῦν
φῶς οὕτως ἔλεγε· "Τοιοῦτοι μετὰ τὴν ἀνάστασιν ἐν τῷ
αἰῶνι τῷ μέλλοντι ἔσονται πάντες οἱ ἅγιοι περιβεβλημένοι
ἀσωμάτως πνευματικὰ σώματα ἢ κουφότερα καὶ λεπτότε-
ρα καὶ ὑψιπετέστερα ἢ παχύτερα καὶ βαρύτερα καὶ χαμαι-
πετέστερα, ἐξ ὧν ἡ στάσις καὶ ἡ τάξις καὶ ἡ πρὸς τὸν Θεὸν
οἰκείωσις ἑκάστῳ τηνικαῦτα γενήσεται."

Chapter 70

The blessed one spent many hours standing in this fashion, praising God unceasingly with certain mystical utterances. But as he contemplated the glory that enveloped him and the blessedness that will be given eternally to the saints, he began to think and say to himself, "Will I revert to my previous bodily form or am I going to stay like this?" As he was wondering about this, all of a sudden he realized that he was still carrying his bodily form around with him like a shadow or some immaterial substance. For when, as I have said, he felt himself, along with his body, becoming wholly light that was immaterial and without shape or form, he knew that his body was still joined to him, although it was somehow incorporeal and spiritual in some way. For he had the sense that it now had no weight or solidity, and he was amazed to see himself as though he were incorporeal when he still had his body. But then again the light, with the same voice as before, spoke within him and said, "After the resurrection in the age to come, this is how all the saints will be incorporeally clothed with spiritual bodies. These will either be lighter, more subtle, and floating higher in the air, or more solid, heavier, and sinking down toward the ground, and by this means each will have their station, rank, and intimacy with God established at that time."

71

Ταῦτα τοίνυν ἀκηκοὼς ὁ θεοπτικώτατος καὶ θεόληπτος Συμεών, ἰδών τε τὸ ἀνεκλάλητον φῶς τοῦ Θεοῦ καὶ εὐχαριστήσας τῷ δοξάσαντι Θεῷ τὸ γένος ἡμῶν καὶ κοινωνὸν τῆς αὐτοῦ θεότητός [cf. 2 Pt 1:4] τε καὶ βασιλείας ἀπεργασαμένῳ, ἐπανῆλθεν ὅλως αὖθις εἰς ἑαυτόν, καὶ πάλιν ἔνδον τοῦ κελλίου ἐν τῷ προτέρῳ τρόπῳ καὶ σχήματι εὑρέθη ἄνθρωπος ὅλος ὤν· "Πλὴν," ὅρκοις ἐπληροφόρει πρὸς οὓς ἐθάρρει καὶ ἀπεκάλυπτεν αὐτοῦ τὰ μυστήρια, "ὅτι ἐπὶ πολλὰς ἡμέρας τὴν κουφότητα ταύτην εἶχον τοῦ σώματος μήτε κόπου μήτε πείνης μήτε δίψης τὸ σύνολον αἰσθανόμενος."

2   Ἀλλὰ γὰρ ἐπεὶ τοῦ Πνεύματος διὰ τῶν τοιούτων ἐγίνετο μόνου, καὶ πεπληρωμένος ἦν τῶν ἐνθέων χαρισμάτων αὐτοῦ, εἰκότως καὶ αὐτὸς κεκαθαρμένος ὢν εἰς ἄκρον τὸν νοῦν, ὡς οἱ προφῆται πάλαι τὰς ὁράσεις ἔβλεπε καὶ τὰς ἀποκαλύψεις Κυρίου τὰς φρικτάς· οὕτω γὰρ καὶ ἀποστολικὴν τὴν διάνοιαν ἔχων ὡς ὑπὸ τοῦ θείου ἐνεργούμενός τε καὶ κινούμενος Πνεύματος, τὴν χάριν εἶχε τοῦ Λόγου ἐκχυνομένην διὰ τῶν χειλέων αὐτοῦ [cf. Ps 44(45):2] καὶ ἐπίσης ἐκείνοις¹⁴⁷ ἀγράμματος [cf. Act 4:13] ὢν ἐθεολόγησε καὶ τοῖς αὐτοῦ θεοπνεύστοις συγγράμμασι τοὺς πιστοὺς ἐκδιδάσκει τὴν τῆς εὐσεβείας ἀκρίβειαν. Οὕτως οὖν ἔχων καὶ τοιοῦτος τῷ πνεύματι ὢν ἐκτίθεται λόγους ἀσκητικοὺς κεφαλαιωδῶς περὶ ἀρετῶν καὶ τῶν ἀντικειμένων αὐταῖς κακιῶν, ἐξ ὧν αὐτὸς δι' ἐμπράκτου φιλοσοφίας ἔγνω καὶ

Chapter 71

When Symeon, that divinely inspired and most eminent seer of God, had heard these words and seen the ineffable light of God, and had given thanks to God who has glorified our race and enabled it to partake of His own divinity and kingdom, he returned completely to himself once more, and found himself back inside his cell in the same manner and form as before, entirely human. "Except that," as he swore to those in whom he confided and to whom he revealed his mystical experiences, "I retained that same lightness of body for many days and felt no weariness or hunger or thirst at all."

Since he came to be someone entirely of the Spirit in this way and was filled with Its divine gifts, his intellect was also correspondingly purified to the highest degree, and like the prophets of old he saw the visions and terrible revelations of the Lord. In this way too he acquired the same understanding as the apostles, and since he was inspired and moved by the divine Spirit, *the grace* of the Word *was poured out upon his lips.* Although like them he was *uneducated,* he became a theologian and, with his divinely inspired writings, taught orthodox religion to the faithful. As he had thus reached such a level of spirituality, he published his ascetic *Chapters* on the virtues and their opposing vices.[68] Based on his practical experience of the religious life and from divine knowl-

γνώσεως θείας, καὶ τοῖς ἀσκοῦσι τὸν ἐμφιλόσοφον βίον λογογραφεῖ τὴν ἀκρίβειαν, καὶ γίνεται τῷ Ἰσραηλιτικῷ τῶν μοναζόντων λαῷ *ποταμὸς Θεοῦ πεπληρωμένος ὑδάτων* [cf. Ps 64(65):9] τοῦ Πνεύματος.

72

Ἐπεὶ δὲ οὕτως ἡσυχάζων εἰργάζετο τὴν ἡσυχασταῖς ἁρμόζουσαν ἐργασίαν, καὶ οὕτως ὑψώθη διὰ τῆς τοῦ Πνεύματος χάριτος ὡς ἐξομοιωθῆναι διὰ βίου καὶ λόγου καὶ γνώσεως τοῖς πάλαι πατράσι καὶ θεολόγοις, ἐχρῆν δὲ κατ' ἐκείνους διὰ πυρὸς καὶ αὐτὸν διαβῆναι τῶν πειρασμῶν καὶ τὴν ὑπομονὴν αὐτοῦ δοκιμασθῆναι *ὡς τοῦ Ἰώβ* [cf. Job 1:6–2:6], ἐξαιτεῖται παρὰ τοῦ πειράζοντος [cf. Lk 22:31] καὶ αὐτῷ *παραδίδοται* [cf. Job 2:6]. Τὸ δὲ πῶς ἐντεῦθεν ὡς ἔχει τὰ τοῦ πράγματος διηγήσομαι.

2   Συμεὼν ὁ θεῖος ἐκεῖνος ἀνήρ, ᾧ ἦν ἐπώνυμον φερωνύμως ὁ Εὐλαβής, ὁ καὶ τοῦ θαυμαστοῦ τούτου Συμεὼν πατὴρ χρηματίσας ὁμοῦ καὶ διδάσκαλος, ἐπεὶ πρὸς *γῆρας ἦκεν ἤδη καλὸν* [cf. Gen 15:15] τεσσαράκοντα πέντε χρόνοις *νομίμως* τὸ τῆς συνειδήσεως *ἀθλήσας* [cf. 2 Tim 2:5]

edge, he wrote this exact guide for those who practice the ascetic life, and so became for the monks, who are the <new> people of Israel, *a river of God full of the water* of the Spirit.

6. Symeon's Conflict with Stephen of Alexina and the Ecclesiastical Authorities

Chapter 72

While living in this state of spiritual tranquillity, Symeon engaged in activity appropriate to those seeking such tranquillity [literally, "hesychasts"]. He was thus exalted by the grace of the Spirit so that he came to resemble the fathers and theologians of old in his way of life, his words, and his knowledge. But he too, like them, had to pass through the fire of the temptations and have his patience tested like Job. And so he *was demanded for trial* by the Tempter and was *handed over* to him. I will now narrate how this happened.

When that divine man Symeon, who was properly called Eulabes[69] and who was also our wondrous Symeon's spiritual father and teacher, had attained a *good old age* and had already *competed according to the rules* for forty-five years *in the testimony of his conscience,* he was judged worthy of the apos- 2

μαρτύριον [2 Cor 1:12], χάριτος ἀποστολικῆς ἠξιώθη ἰάσεις
καὶ θαύματα πεποιηκὼς καὶ βίβλον ὅλην πάσης ὠφελείας
οὖσαν πνευματικῆς ἀγράμματος [cf. Act 4:13] ὢν θείῳ
Πνεύματι συνεγράψατο. Ἔδει δὲ αὐτὸν καταπαῦσαι τῶν
μακρῶν ἐκείνων τῆς ἀσκήσεως πόνων, περὶ ὧν ὁ μαθεῖν
ζητῶν ἐκ τῶν κατὰ πλάτος γεγραμμένων αὐτῷ εἴσεται
ἀκριβῶς, νενοσηκὼς τὰ τῆς λύσεως πρὸς Κύριον ἐνεδήμησεν, ἐκδημήσας τοῦ πολυάθλου καὶ καρτερικοῦ αὐτοῦ σώματος [cf. 2 Cor 5:8]. Τοῦτον οὖν καὶ τὰ τούτου λαμπρὰ
κατορθώματα οἷα δὴ μαθητὴς ὁ μακάριος οὗτος εἰδὼς καὶ
τὸν[148] ἀποστολικὸν αὐτοῦ βίον ἀκριβῶς ἐπιστάμενος,
Θεοῦ ἔργα καὶ θεῖα χαρίσματα μὴ εἰδὼς κατορύττειν ἀλλ᾿
ἀνακηρύττειν καὶ ἐξυμνεῖν,[149] ὕμνους εἰς αὐτὸν καὶ ἐγκώμια ἐκ θείας ἀποκαλύψεως συνεγράψατο, καὶ ὅλον τὸν
βίον αὐτοῦ. Ἵνα δὲ καὶ πρὸς ζῆλον ἐγείρῃ τινὰς εἰς τὸ μι-
μήσασθαι τὸν ὑμνούμενον καὶ τῆς ἀρετῆς ἐργάτας γενέσθαι, τὴν μνήμην αὐτοῦ κατὰ τὴν τῶν ἀποστόλων παράδοσιν ἐτησίως μετὰ πάντων λαμπρῶς ἑώρταζε τῶν ἁγίων,
στήλην ἀρετῆς γεγραμμένην τὴν ἱστορίαν ἀναζωγραφή-
σας τῆς εἰκόνος αὐτοῦ.

73

Ἤκουσε ταῦτα καὶ Σέργιος ὁ πατριάρχης καὶ μετα-
πεμψάμενος τὸν ἅγιον πυνθάνεται περὶ τῶν ἀκουσθέντων

tolic grace of performing healings and miracles. By the power of the divine Spirit he also wrote a book full of spiritual help, even though he was *uneducated*. But it became necessary for him to rest from those long labors of asceticism (anyone who wants to learn about them may get an accurate understanding from his extensive writings), and after suffering a fatal illness, he *went to live with the Lord, leaving his home in* his sorely tried and long-suffering *body*. As his disciple, our blessed Symeon knew Symeon Eulabes's splendid accomplishments and understood his apostolic life very well. He was thus unable to conceal God's works and divine gifts, but rather, in order to proclaim and celebrate these in song, he wrote hymns to <his spiritual father> and encomia as a result of divine revelation, and a whole *Life* about him.[70] Also, so that he might make people eager to imitate the man he was praising and become workers of virtue, he celebrated Symeon Eulabes's memory magnificently every year along with all the saints according to the tradition of the apostles, and had a record of his image painted as a graphic memorial to his virtue.

Chapter 73

The patriarch Sergios[71] also heard about this. He summoned the saint and questioned him about what he had

αὐτῷ. Ὡς δὲ περὶ πάντων ἀνεδίδαξεν αὐτὸν ὁ μακάριος
καὶ ὅπως ἐκ θείας ἀποκαλύψεως ἄνωθεν ἐμπνευσθεὶς τοὺς
ὕμνους τῷ πατρὶ ἀνετάξατο καὶ τὸν βίον αὐτοῦ συνεγράψατο, ζητεῖ ταῦτα διελθεῖν καὶ αὐτοῖς ἐντυχεῖν τοῖς ὑπ᾽
αὐτοῦ γεγραμμένοις. Λαβὼν οὖν ἐπὶ χεῖρας τὰς βίβλους ὁ
πατριάρχης καὶ ἅπασαν τὴν πραγματείαν φιλοπόνως διελθὼν ἠγάσθη ἐπὶ τῷ πράγματι, καὶ πολλὰ προσεπαινέσας
καὶ τὸ βέβαιον τῆς αὐτοῦ πίστεως μεγάλως ἐγκωμιάσας
ἀπέλυσεν, ὑπομιμνήσκειν αὐτὸν[150] προτρεψάμενος κατὰ
τὸν καιρὸν τῆς τοῦ πατρὸς μνήμης, ὡς ἂν[151] καὶ αὐτὸς κη-
ροὺς καὶ μύρα παρέχῃ καὶ ἀφοσιῶται τὴν τιμὴν τῷ ἁγίῳ.
Ἐγένετο ταῦτα ἐπὶ χρόνοις ἑκκαίδεκα, καὶ Θεὸς μὲν ἐπὶ
τῇ μνήμῃ τοῦ θεράποντος αὐτοῦ ἐδοξάζετο, εὐφραίνοντο
δὲ οἱ λαοὶ ἐγκωμιαζομένου τοῦ δικαίου [cf. Prov 29:2], ἐτρέ-
φοντο πένητες, ἐφωταγωγοῦντο ναοί, ἀρετὴ ἐκηρύσσετο
καὶ πολλοὶ πρὸς μίμησιν διανίσταντο.

74

Τί οὖν ὁ Πονηρός; Ἡσύχασεν εἰς τέλος ταῦτα ὁρῶν,
ἢ ἐπελάθετο τῆς ἐμφύτου κακίας; Οὐμενοῦν[152] οὐδαμῶς!
Ἀλλ᾽ ἐξανίσταται καὶ τῷ παλαιῷ χρησάμενος ὅπλῳ τῷ
φθόνῳ, ὄγκον πειρασμῶν ἐπεγείρει κατὰ τοῦ Συμεὼν καὶ
παντοίας ἐπιφορὰς θλίψεων. Ἀλλ᾽ ἐστῶσιν ἀκούσατε τοῖς
ὠσί!

heard. When the blessed one told him about everything, and how he had been inspired by a divine revelation from above to compose these hymns to his spiritual father and write his *Life,* the patriarch demanded them so that he might go through them in detail and read what Symeon had written. When the patriarch received these texts, he went meticulously through all the material in detail. He was delighted by the whole corpus of work, however, and, after praising it highly and warmly congratulating Symeon on his resolute faith, dismissed him. He also urged him to remind him when it was the time for his spiritual father's commemoration so that he too might supply candles and perfumed oils and show his respect for the saint. This went on for sixteen years, and God was glorified by the celebration of His servant, *the people rejoiced when the righteous* man *was praised,* the poor were fed, churches illuminated, virtue proclaimed, and many people roused to imitation <of the saint>.

Chapter 74

But what did the Evil One do then? Did he also keep quiet[72] when he saw this, or forget his natural wickedness? Most certainly not! Rather he roused himself again and, making use of his old weapon envy, stirred up a mass of trials for Symeon and attacked him with all kinds of tribulations. Prick up your ears and listen!

2   Στέφανός τις ἐγένετο πρόεδρος ἐν τῇ μητροπόλει Νι-
κομηδέων, Στέφανος ὁ τῆς Ἀλεξίνης, ἀνὴρ λόγῳ καὶ γνώσει τῶν πόλλων διαφέρων καὶ δυνατὸς οὐ μόνον παρὰ
πατριάρχῃ καὶ βασιλεῖ, ἀλλὰ καὶ δοῦναι λύσεις παντὶ τῷ
πυνθανομένῳ περὶ καινῶν ζητημάτων εὐροίᾳ λόγου καὶ
γλώττης εὐστροφίᾳ, ὃς καὶ τὸν τῆς ἐπισκοπῆς παραιτησά-
μενος θρόνον λόγοις οἷς ἐκεῖνος καὶ Θεὸς οἶδεν ἀδήλοις,
συνῆν ἀεὶ τῷ πατριάρχῃ, καὶ μεγάλην ἐφέρετο παρὰ πᾶσι
τὴν φήμην τῆς γνώσεως. Ἐπεὶ δὲ καὶ ὁ μακάριος Συμεὼν
τὴν ἀληθινὴν γνῶσιν ἔχων τοῦ Πνεύματος παρὰ πᾶσι τῷ
τότε καιρῷ ἐπέραστος ἦν, καὶ ᾔδετο ὑπὸ πάντων ἡ τούτου
γνῶσις καὶ ἐθαυμάζετο, καὶ οὐ μόνον ὡς σοφὸς τῷ Πνεύματι, ἀλλὰ δὴ καὶ ὡς ἅγιος παρὰ παντὸς ἐτιμᾶτο ἀνθρώπου, ἦλθε ταῦτα—οὐδὲ γὰρ ἦν δυνατὸν πόλιν κρυβῆναι τοιαύτην ἐπ᾽ ὄρους κειμένην [Mt 5:14] σοφίας Θεοῦ—καὶ εἰς
ἀκοὰς τοῦ ῥηθέντος ἀνδρός.

3   Ὁ δὲ οἷα δὴ μεγάλα περὶ ἑαυτοῦ φρονῶν καὶ τῶν ἄλλων
ἁπάντων ὑπερφρονῶν, ὥσπερ εἰ τοῦ ἁγίου κατεμωκᾶτο
τῆς φήμης, καὶ τοὺς περὶ τῆς ἐκείνου γνώσεως λέγοντας
κατεμέμφετο, ἀμαθῆ τὸν ἅγιον ἀποκαλῶν καὶ πάντη
ἄγροικόν τε καὶ ἄναυδον καὶ μηδὲ γρῦξαι δυνάμενον ἐνώπιον σοφῶν τῶν εἰδότων ἔντεχνον κρίσιν ποιεῖσθαι τῶν
λόγων. Ὡς οὖν ταῦτα μὲν ἔλεγεν ὁ σοφώτατος σύγκελλος
καὶ κατὰ τοῦ ἁγίου ἐφρόνει, οἱ δὲ πεῖραν ἔχοντες ἐκείνου
βεβαίαν τὴν φήμην μᾶλλον ἐπλάτυνον ἀνὰ πᾶσαν τὴν
πόλιν καί· "Οὐκ ἔστι παρόμοιος τῷ Συμεώνῃ ἐν γνώσει
καὶ σοφίᾳ καὶ ἀρετῇ κατὰ ταύτην," ἐβόων, "τὴν γενεάν,"

A certain Stephen became metropolitan of Nikomedia, 2
Stephen of Alexina, a man superior to most in his speech
and knowledge. He not only had great influence with the
patriarch and emperor but was also able to provide solutions
with fluent speech and a supple tongue to anyone who asked
about novel issues.[73] He had resigned from his episcopacy
for undisclosed reasons, known only to himself and to God,
but was always with the patriarch and was held in great repute by everyone for his knowledge. However, the blessed
Symeon, who possessed the true knowledge of the Spirit,
was also much loved by everyone at that time, and his knowledge was known and admired by everybody. Indeed, he was
revered by everyone not only as a man who was wise in the
Spirit but also as a saint. As a result this came to Stephen's
notice, for such *a town standing on the hill* of God's wisdom
could not be hidden.

Stephen had a very high opinion of himself and looked 3
down on everybody else, and so he apparently used to mock
the saint's reputation and disparage those who spoke about
Symeon's knowledge, calling the saint ignorant and an utter
peasant, someone who was inarticulate and unable even to
grunt when faced with wise men who knew how to make
skillful arguments with words. But while that most wise *synkellos*[74] used to make these remarks and was contemptuous
of the saint, those who really knew Symeon spread his reputation ever more widely throughout the city, proclaiming, "There's no one in this generation equal to Symeon in
knowledge and wisdom and virtue." When the *synkellos*

βασκανίας κέντροις ἐβάλλετο ἀκούων ταῦτα ὁ σύγκελλος. Τὸν γὰρ φθόνον ἔχων τρεφόμενόν τε καὶ ὑποτυφόμε-
νον ἐν ἑαυτῷ, οὐ φορητὴν ἡγεῖτο ζημίαν εἰ Συμεὼν ἐν τῷ
τότε καιρῷ πλείονα ἕξει Στεφάνου τὴν φήμην τῆς γνώσεως παρὰ τὴν Κωνσταντίνου καὶ τὰ πρεσβεῖα τῆς τοῦ
λόγου σοφίας, καὶ μᾶλλον ὅτι καὶ λογογραφεῖν αὐτὸν
ἤκουε περὶ θείων καὶ ἀνθρωπίνων πραγμάτων καὶ θεολογίας ἅπτεσθαι, αὐτὸς ἐν λόγοις μόνοις καὶ φωνῇ διακένῳ
περιβομβῶν τὸν ἀέρα καὶ μόνην τέρπων τὴν ἀκοήν.

75

Ἀλλὰ ταῦτα μὲν οὕτως εἶχε, καὶ ὁ φθόνος ὑπετύφετο
μᾶλλον καὶ ὅσον οὔπω τὸν ἐμπρησμὸν κατεμήνυε. Βραχὺς
ὁ χρόνος, καὶ ὑπαντᾶται κατὰ τὸ ὑπερῷον τοῦ πατριαρχείου τῷ συγκέλλῳ ὁ ἅγιος, καί φησι πρὸς αὐτὸν φίλου
προσωπεῖον ὑποδυσάμενος· "Χαίροις, εὐλαβέστατε κῦρι
Συμεών, ὁ τὴν γνῶσιν μετὰ τῆς εὐλαβείας καὶ τὸν λόγον
περίφημος." Ὁ δὲ ἅγιος· "Ὁ Θεός, ᾧ ἐγὼ λειτουργῶ, δώῃ
σοι τὸν μισθὸν τῆς πρὸς ἡμᾶς σου φιλίας, εὐλογημένε μου
δέσποτα, ἀντιμετρῶν σοι τῷ ἀσπασμῷ τὴν εἰρήνην τοῦ
Πνεύματος." Καὶ ὁ σύγκελλος· "'Εκ πολλοῦ μοι," φησί,
"δι' ἐφέσεως ἦν ἀπολαῦσαι τῆς σῆς ὁμιλίας καὶ συγ-
καθεσθῆναί σοι καὶ περί τινων ἀναγκαίων κοινολογήσα-
σθαι, οἷα δὴ φίλῳ ἀνδρὶ καὶ ἀεὶ καταλαμπομένῳ καὶ περὶ

heard this, he was pricked with jealousy, and because he had nurtured and kept his envy smoldering within him, he regarded it as an unbearable slight if at that time Symeon should have a greater reputation for knowledge in Constantinople than he, Stephen, did and <be regarded as having> superiority in the wisdom of his speech. He was particularly upset because he heard that Symeon wrote about divine and human affairs and had a good grasp of theology, while he himself would only make the air hum with words and empty phrases that were nice to hear but nothing more.

Chapter 75

So this was how things stood, and the *synkellos*'s envy kept smoldering more and more and threatened an imminent conflagration. Before long the saint encountered the *synkellos* on the upper floor of the patriarchate. The latter feigned friendship and said to him, "Greetings, most pious Kyr Symeon, you who are famous for your knowledge and your ability with words as well as for your piety!" The saint replied, "May God, whom I serve, reward you for the friendship you show me, my blessed master, and repay you for your greeting with the peace of the Spirit." The *synkellos* said, "I've been hoping for a long time to have the pleasure of your conversation and to sit down and discuss some important matters with you as a friend and a person who is always enlightened and truly devotes himself to spiritual contem-

τὴν ὄντως θεωρίαν σχολάζοντι. Ἀλλ' ἐπεὶ τὰ πράγματα
σχολὴν καθαρὰν ἄγειν ἡμᾶς οὐκ ἐῶσι, τῆς ἐπιθυμίας ἀν-
εκοπτόμην, καὶ νῦν, ὡς ὁρᾷς, γέγονέ μοι πρόξενος τοῦ
καλοῦ ἡ παρ' ἐλπίδα πρὸς τὰ ἐνταῦθα ὑπαντή σου καὶ ἄφι-
ξις. Ἀλλὰ τὸν νοῦν ἐπιστήσας ἐφ' οἷς μέλλω πυνθάνεσθαί
σε, σοφώτατε, ὡς ἔχεις πρὸς τῆς Τριάδος αὐτῆς, λῦσόν μοι
τὸ θεώρημα· πῶς," εἰπέ, "χωρίζεις τὸν Υἱὸν ἀπὸ τοῦ Πατρός, ἐπινοίᾳ ἢ πράγματι;"

2   Τοῦτο προκατασκευάσας διὰ τῆς δεδολωμένης αὐτοῦ
πεύσεως, ὡς ἂν[153] εἴ τι τούτων εἴποι τοῦ ἑτέρου προκρίνας
τὸ ἕτερον, ἀμφικρήμνου τοῦ προβλήματος ὄντος, ὡς δῆθεν
ἀμαθὴς ὁ Συμεὼν ὀλισθήσῃ καὶ πολλὴν καθ' ἑαυτοῦ τὴν
κατάγνωσιν καὶ τὸν γέλωτα κινήσῃ ἐλεγχθεὶς ἐκ μιᾶς
προσβολῆς, καὶ τοῖς ἐπαινέταις κατάδηλος γένηται δῆθεν
ἡ ἀγνωσία αὐτοῦ.

76

Ὁ δὲ ἅγιος πρὸς τῇ πεύσει καὶ τὸ περίεργον τοῦ ἀνδρὸς
ἐκπλαγεὶς ἔφη· "Ὑμῖν ἐδόθη γνῶναι τὰ μυστήρια τοῦ Θεοῦ
[Lk 8:10; cf. Mt 13:11] τοῖς ἀρχιερεῦσι, ὦ σοφώτατε δέσποτα, καὶ ἀναπτύσσειν ταῦτα τοῖς ἐρωτῶσιν ὡς κεχρεωστη-
μένον ἐστὶν ὄφλημα· ἡμῖν δὲ τοῖς ταπεινοῖς καὶ οἷς οὐδὲν
ἕτερον διὰ παντὸς ἐφιλοσοφήθη τοῦ βίου ἢ μόνον τὸ ἑαυτοὺς ἐπιγνῶναι, τὸ ὑπέχειν τοῖς διδασκάλοις τὸ οὖς καὶ

plation. Unfortunately, business doesn't leave me any real time for leisure, so I've been thwarted in my desire. But now, you see, your arrival and this unexpected meeting with you here have provided me with a good opportunity. So turn your mind to what I'm going to ask you, and with all the great wisdom you have from the Holy Trinity, resolve this problem for me. How," he said, "do you distinguish the Son from the Father? By a conceptual distinction or a real distinction?"

The *synkellos* had prepared this in advance so that the ₂ problem would be surrounded by such pitfalls, due to the craftiness of his question, that if Symeon, who was supposedly ignorant, should make either response, choosing one over the other, he would slip up. <The *synkellos* thus intended that Symeon,> having been discredited at the very first attempt, would make himself the object of considerable contempt and laughter, and that his supposed ignorance would be revealed to his previous admirers.

Chapter 76

The saint, who was shocked by the man's meddlesome curiosity as well as his question, replied, "*It has been granted* to senior churchmen like you *to know the secrets of God,* most wise master, and disclosing them to those who ask is like a debt that you owe. But to humble people like me, who have spent all their lives thinking only about how to know themselves better, it has been granted to give ear to our teach-

τὴν σιωπὴν ἐπὶ τῶν σοφωτέρων ἀσπάζεσθαι. Χρὴ οὖν μᾶλλον σὲ μυσταγωγῆσαι ἡμᾶς τὴν περὶ τούτων γνῶσιν, καὶ πρὸς τούτῳ διδάξαι ταπεινοφρονεῖν καὶ τὰ οἰκεῖα μόνον θρηνεῖν ἁμαρτήματα, καὶ μὴ περιέργως τὰ βαθύτερα καὶ ὑψηλότερα ἡμῶν ἐρευνᾶν. Ἀλλ᾽ εἰ καὶ δοκιμὴν ζητεῖς τοῦ ἐν ἐμοὶ Πνεύματος καὶ μαθεῖν ἐθέλεις τίς ἡ δωρεὰ τοῦ Θεοῦ [John 4:10] ἢ τοῖς πτωχοῖς τῷ πνεύματι [Mt 5:3] δίδοται, ἐγὼ μέν, ὡς ὁρᾷς, μαθητής εἰμι ἁλιέων τὸν προφορικὸν οὐκ ἔχων λόγον, σοφώτατε.[154] Δυνατὸς δέ ἐστιν ὁ διδοὺς εὐχὴν τῷ εὐχομένῳ [1 Kings 2:9] καὶ λόγον ἐν ἀνοίξει τοῦ στόματος [Eph 6:19], προσθεῖναί μοι ὠτίον [Is 50:4], καὶ ἀνοῖξαι τὰ ὦτά μου [Is 50:5; cf. 1 Chr 17:25] τῆς ψυχῆς, καὶ ἃ δεῖ με ἀποκριθῆναι καὶ εἰπεῖν περὶ τούτου δοῦναι διὰ τῆς τοῦ Πνεύματος χάριτος [cf. Mt 10:19–20] αὐτομολοῦντι πρὸς τὸ κελλίον καὶ γεγραμμένως ἐκθέσθαι καὶ ἀποστεῖλαί σοι." Ὁ οὖν σύγκελλος τὸ "γεγραμμένως" ἀκούσας, καταμειδιῶν καὶ καταμωκώμενος τοῦ ἁγίου οὕτως ἔφη· "Καὶ ἐμοί ἐστιν ἐφετὸν πεπονημένον παρὰ σοῦ δέξασθαι τὸ θεώρημα."

77

Ὁ μὲν οὖν εἰς τὰ ἐνδότερα[155] τῶν ὑπερῴων ἐχώρησεν. Ὁ δὲ πρὸς τὸ ποίμνιον αὐτοῦ ὑποστρέψας τῇ καθαρᾷ καὶ ἀθολώτῳ καθοπλίζεται προσευχῇ καὶ ὑπὸ τοῦ πυρὸς τοῦ

ers and keep silence in the presence of those who are wiser. Thus it's rather you who should be initiating us into the knowledge of these matters, in addition to teaching us to be humble and lament only our own errors, and not inquire with unnecessary curiosity about matters that are beyond us in their profundity or their elevation. But if you seek proof of the Spirit that is in me and want to learn what is *the gift of God* that has been given to *the poor in spirit,* as you can see, *I am but a disciple of fishermen*[75] and I don't possess eloquent speech, most wise one. But He who *grants the prayer to the person who prays* and the *right word when he opens his mouth* has the power to *sharpen my hearing* and *open the ears* of my soul, and grant me through the grace of the Spirit what I need to respond and say about this. So I'll take myself off to my cell, and when I've set this down in writing I'll send it to you." When the *synkellos* heard "in writing," he smirked and said sneeringly to the saint, "I'll be delighted to receive the visionary doctrine[76] you manage to elaborate."

Chapter 77

The *synkellos* then went off into the inner chambers on the upper floor <of the patriarchate> while Symeon returned to his flock. There he armed himself with pure and untrou-

θείου τὴν καρδίαν πυρποληθεὶς ἅπτεται τοῦ προβλήματος, ἐκ προοιμίων τὴν γενομένην ἔλλαμψιν ἐν αὐτῷ πεζῷ τῷ λόγῳ καὶ μετὰ ταπεινοῦ φθέγματος ὑποφαίνων. Λεπτύνας οὖν τὴν ἔννοιαν τοῦ ῥητοῦ καὶ τῇ σαφηνείᾳ τοῦ λόγου διευκρινήσας καὶ διὰ στίχων ἀμέτρων κατὰ ποιητικὴν μέθοδον εἰς λόγον καθαρῶς συντάξας τὸ πόνημα, λέλυκέ τε καὶ διεσκέδασε τὰ δυσδιάλυτα τοῦ σοφοῦ ἅμματα δυνάμει Λόγου καὶ Πνεύματος καὶ νοημάτων πυκνότητι, ὡς λέων ἐμπεσὼν εἰς ἄγραν καὶ μόνῳ τῷ βρυχήματι αὐτήν τε διαρρήξας καὶ τοὺς ἀγρευτὰς φυγάδας ἀποτελέσας. Ἀλλὰ γὰρ καὶ αὐτὸς ὡς ἐν παραδρομῇ τοῦ σοφοῦ καθαψάμενος διὰ τῆς τῶν αἰνιγμάτων ἀναγωγῆς, καὶ τὸν λόγον μεταπηξάμενος τῷ τὴν γλῶτταν ἠκονημένῳ [cf. Ps 139(140):3] ἐξαποστέλλει συγκέλλῳ, αὐτὸς ἐντεῦθεν ἑαυτὸν ἑτοιμάσας εἰς πειρασμούς. Ἤδη γὰρ προέγνω τῷ Πνεύματι ὡς οὐκ ἠρεμήσει οὐδ' ὑπενέγκῃ τὴν ἧτταν καλῶς ἡττηθείς, εἰ μὴ καὶ κακοποιήσει δυστυχῶς ὑπὸ τοῦ φθόνου κρατούμενος, ἐπειδὴ κατὰ τὸ γεγραμμένον *παντὶ πρὸς τὸ ἀντιτεῖνον ἡ παράταξις*.

78

Δέχεται τοίνυν ὁ τεθηγμένην ἔχων τὴν γλῶτταν τὴν τοῦ προβλήματος λύσιν, ἐντυγχάνει τοῖς βαθυτάτοις τοῦ ἁγίου νοήμασιν, ὁρᾷ τοῦ λόγου τὸ μέγεθος ἐν λέξεσιν

bled prayer and, with his heart ablaze with divine fire, tackled the problem. To start with he produced a draft, in prose and using ordinary language, of the illumination within him. Then he refined the sense of his argument, carefully sorting out the clarity of his expression in the statement, and rewrote it as a work in free verse following the poetic method.[77] Thus Symeon loosened and undid the wise *synkellos*'s tangled knots by the power of the Word and the Spirit[78] and by the shrewdness of his thoughts, like a lion that has fallen into a hunter's net and, by its roaring alone, has broken out of it and sent the hunters fleeing. When he had copied the statement, Symeon sent it to the *sharp-tongued*[79] *synkellos,* but, as he also had attacked that wise one, in passing, as it were, through his mystical interpretation of his riddles, he prepared himself for trouble. For he already foresaw in the Spirit that the *synkellos* would not keep quiet nor, even though he had been well beaten, submit to the defeat without also doing some harm <in return>, being governed, as he unfortunately was, by envy. For, as it has been written, *everyone fights resistance.*[80]

Chapter 78

That sharp-tongued man received Symeon's solution to his problem. He read the profound thoughts of the saint, saw the great quality of his statement in the plain words of

ἁπλαῖς ἀφελείας, ὁρᾷ τὴν σαφήνειαν ἐν καθαρότητι λόγου, τῶν νοημάτων τὴν δύναμιν ἐν σφοδρότητι, τὸ ἐπιεικὲς
τῆς ἐντεύξεως ἐν γλυκύτητι, τὴν τῆς μεθόδου γοργότητα,
τὴν τοῦ ἤθους βαρύτητα, τὴν τοῦ ποιήματος δεινότητα ἐν
ἀμαθεῖ ἀνδρὶ καὶ ἀγεύστῳ τῆς θύραθεν γνώσεως, καὶ
ἐκπλήττεται τὴν διάνοιαν καὶ σὺν τῷ κεκροτημένῳ λόγῳ
καὶ αὐτὴν ἐγκόπτεται τὴν ἐνοῦσαν φωνήν. Ἀλλὰ τί τὸ
ἐντεῦθεν; βάλλεται τοῖς κέντροις τοῦ σοφωτάτου λόγου
τὴν καρδίαν ὁ σύγκελλος, ἐπειδὴ κατὰ τὸν Σολομῶντα
λόγοι σοφῶν ὡς τὰ βούκεντρα [Ecl 12:11]. Διεγείρεται θυμω-
θείς, καὶ ταῖς κατὰ τοῦ ἁγίου λοιδορίαις πρὸς ἄμυναν δια-
νίσταται. Καὶ πρῶτα μὲν ἔρευναν ποιεῖται τοῦ βίου αὐτοῦ,
εἴ πού τι καὶ ἐπιλήψιμον εὑρὼν εἰς βοήθειαν ἕξει τοῦτο τῆς
τυρευομένης κατ' αὐτοῦ συκοφαντίας. Εἶτα ὡς μηδὲν
εὗρεν ἐν τῷ ἀλήπτῳ, διεγείρει τινὰς τῶν ἀπὸ τῆς ἐκκλησίας, οἱ δὲ τῶν ἀπὸ τῆς μάνδρας ἐκείνου, καὶ καταβοᾶν
αὐτοῦ ἐπισκήπτει διὰ τὴν πρὸς τὸν πατέρα τιμὴν καὶ
πανήγυριν. Οἱ μὲν οὖν ἐβόων καὶ ἔλεγον *ἀνομίαν κατὰ τοῦ
δικαίου* [Ps 30(31):18], *ὁ δὲ εἰς οὐρανὸν ἔθετο τὸ στόμα αὐτοῦ
καὶ ἡ γλῶσσα αὐτοῦ διῆλθεν ἐπὶ τῶν ἀκοῶν τοῦ ἀρχιερέως
καὶ ἀδικίαν εἰς ὕψος τῆς ἁγίας συνόδου ἐλάλησεν* [Ps
72(73):8–9].

its simple style, saw the clarity in its pure wording, the force of the ideas in its vehemence, the appropriateness of the discourse in its pleasant style, the vigor of its method, the gravity of its character, and the extraordinary poetic skill of a man without learning and with no experience of secular knowledge. When he did so he was totally shocked and he actually lost the use of his voice along with its usual chatter. But then what? The *synkellos* was struck through the heart by the barbs of Symeon's most wise statement, for according to Solomon *the sayings of the wise are like goads.* He worked himself into a fury and strove to get his revenge by abusing the saint. First he conducted an investigation of Symeon's life to see if he could find something reprehensible to help him in the calumny he was concocting against him. Then, as he found nothing in that irreproachable life, he stirred up some members of the church, who were actually from Symeon's monastery, and ordered them to denounce him over his honoring and celebration of his spiritual father. So these people were yelling and speaking *impiously against the righteous man,* while the *synkellos* himself *set his mouth against heaven and his tongue strutted into* the hearing of the patriarch and *spoke unjustly* about Symeon all the way *up to* the holy synod.

79

Ἐπεὶ δὲ[156] ἄνωθεν εἴρηται οὐκ ἐν ἀγνοίᾳ τοῦ γινομένου ὁ ἀρχιερεὺς ἦν καὶ οἱ λοιποὶ τῶν ἐπισκόπων, ἀπεσείοντο μὲν κατ' ἀρχὰς τὴν διαβολήν, εἰδότες φθόνῳ βληθέντα τὸν σύγκελλον, καὶ "Τί τοῦτο," ἔλεγον, "ἀπᾷδον τῇ καθολικῇ ἐκκλησίᾳ ἢ τοῖς κανόσιν ἐστίν, ὅποτε οὐδὲ βλάβη τις, ἀλλὰ τοὐναντίον ὠφέλεια[157] ψυχαῖς προξενεῖται, ἀρετῆς ἐγκωμιαζομένης ἀναφανδόν;" Ὁ δὲ εὐφυὴς ἐς τὰ μάλιστα ὢν πρὸς πειρασμὸν διεγεῖραι, διορύττων οὐκ ἐνεδίδου τοῦ ἀρχιερέως ὁσημέραι τὰς ἀκοάς. Ὁ γοῦν πατριάρχης καὶ οἱ τῆς ἁγίας συνόδου ἀρχιερεῖς τὰς ἀκοὰς ἔβυον ἐπὶ δυσὶν ἐνιαυτοῖς τῇ βασκάνῳ φωνῇ τόπον μὴ διδόντες εἰσόδου. Δι' αἰσχύνης γὰρ εἶχον αὐτοὶ ἑαυτοὺς καταμέμφεσθαι, ἐπεὶ ὁ μὲν μύροις καὶ κηροῖς ἐτησίως τῷ ἁγίῳ ἀπένειμε τὴν τιμήν, τῶν δὲ αὐτόμολοι οἱ πλείους[158] ἐν τῇ τοῦ πατρὸς ἑορτῇ παρεγίνοντο, καὶ οὕτω τιθέναι τὸ φῶς σκότος αἰσχύνοντο *καὶ τὸ σκότος φῶς καὶ εἰπεῖν τὸ πικρὸν τῆς τοῦ συγκέλλου γλώττης γλυκύ, τὸ δὲ γλυκὺ τῆς τοῦ Συμεὼν ἀληθείας πικρόν* [cf. Is 5:20]. Τοίνυν καὶ ὡς εἶχεν οὕτω ταῦτα, μάχη τις ἦν μέσον ἀληθείας καὶ ψεύδους, τῆς μὲν συνηγορούσης τῷ δικαίῳ καὶ δυνατῶς ἀπορραπιζούσης τὴν τοῦ ψεύδους παράνοιαν, τοῦ δὲ τῇ ἀδικίᾳ συναιρομένου καὶ τῷ καλῷ ὑπερβολῇ σκαιότητος ἀντιπίπτοντος.

Chapter 79

But since the patriarch and the rest of the bishops were aware of what was happening (as has been mentioned above), at first they dismissed the slander, as they knew that the *synkellos* had been attacked by envy. "How," they said, "is this at variance with the universal church or its canons, since the praise of virtue in public causes no harm but, quite the contrary, offers people spiritual help?" But the *synkellos,* who had a natural genius for stirring up trouble, did not give up worming his way into the ears of the patriarch every day. In any case, the patriarch and the senior clergy of the holy synod plugged their ears for two years and allowed his jealous voice no point of entry. For they were ashamed to criticize themselves since the patriarch had honored the saint every year with perfumed oils and candles, and most of the bishops had of their own accord attended the celebration of the father's feast day. Thus they were ashamed *to turn the light into darkness and the darkness into light* and to call *the bitterness* of the *synkellos's* tongue *sweet, but the sweetness* of Symeon's truth *bitter.* So, while matters were like this, a struggle ensued between truth and falsehood, the former advocating justice[81] and forcefully beating back the madness of falsehood, the latter supporting injustice and resisting the good with an excess of perversity.

80

Εἰς τί οὖν καταλήγει τὰ τῆς μάχης αὐτοῖς; Νικᾷ τὸ κακόν, ἐνίοτε γὰρ καὶ πρὸς καιρὸν συγχωρούμενον καὶ κατευμεγεθεῖ τοῦ καλοῦ. Καὶ ὅρα πῶς νικᾷ τὴν Ἰωάννου δικαιοσύνην ἡ τῆς Ἡρωδιάδος κακία· κατορχεῖται ταύτης πρὸς τὸ παρὸν καὶ καυχᾶται τὰ νικητήρια [Mk 6:17–29; cf. Mt 14:6–11]· οὕτω τοιγαροῦν καὶ ὁ φθόνος ὧδε τῆς ἀληθείας καταψευσάμενος αἴρει τὸ νῖκος τοῦ δικαίου κατακαυχησάμενος [cf. Ja 3:14] καὶ ὑπερφρονήσας αὐτοῦ· τῷ συνεχεῖ γὰρ ὁ σύγκελλος τῆς διαβολῆς δι' ὄχλου τῷ πατριάρχῃ καὶ τοῖς ἀρχιερεῦσι γινόμενος—ὦ τῆς ἀδικίας, ὦ τῶν ἐνεδρῶν τοῦ Σατανᾶ!—σαλεύει τὰς τούτων ψυχάς, ἀνθρώπων πάντως καὶ αὐτῶν ὄντων, καὶ δοῦναί τινα κατηγορίας ἀφορμὴν αὐτῷ ἐπισκήπτουσι κατὰ τοῦ ἁγίου, ὡς ἂν[159] καὶ ἡ κατ' αὐτοῦ σπουδαζομένη ψῆφος μὴ ἄνευ προφάσεως γένηται. Οὕτω καὶ πέτρας οἶδα κοιλαίνεσθαι τὸ στερρὸν καὶ ἀντίτυπον ἐνδελεχούσης ρανίδος, καὶ ψυχῆς τὸ σταθερόν τε καὶ ἔμμονον ἐπιμενούσης τινὸς καὶ διορυττούσης κακίας.

Chapter 80

How, then, did this struggle turn out for them? Evil triumphed, since occasionally and for a time it is allowed to overcome good. Look how Herodias's wickedness conquered John [the Baptist]'s righteousness, for she danced in triumph over it and boasted of victory for a while.[82] So here too envy falsified the truth and secured victory over justice, boasting over it and despising it. For the *synkellos* kept pestering the patriarch and the senior clergy with his persistent slander and—oh, what injustice, what Satanic treachery!— he shook their spiritual resolve, for even they were only human, and they pressed him to provide them with some pretext for bringing an allegation against the saint, so that the sentence they sought against him might not be unfounded. Thus, as even the hardness and resilience of stone can be hollowed out by a persistent drip, so the steadfastness and constancy of a soul <can also be undermined> by the tenacity of an evil that keeps burrowing away.

81

Ἐπειδὴ γὰρ ἐτησίως τοῦ πνευματικοῦ πατρὸς τὴν μνήμην πανηγυρικῶς ἑώρταζεν οἷα δὴ τούτου μαθητὴς ὁ ἐμὸς
Συμεών, ἐκεῖνος δὲ προνεκρωθεὶς ἐξ ἄκρας ἀπαθείας τὴν
σάρκα, ἔτι περιὼν τέλεον τὰς ἐμφύτους ἀπεμαράνθη κινήσεις αὐτῆς καὶ οἷα νεκρὸς πρὸς νεκρὸν αἴσθησιν ἔχων ἐν
τοῖς αὐτῷ¹⁶⁰ πλησιάζουσι σώμασιν, ὑπεκρίνετο τὴν ἐμπά-
θειαν, τοῦτο μὲν συσκιάζειν βουλόμενος τὸν τῆς ἀπαθείας
αὐτοῦ θησαυρόν (ἔφευγε γὰρ ὡς ὄφιν δάκνοντα¹⁶¹ πτέρναν
[cf. Gen 49:17; 3:15] τὴν δόξαν καὶ τοὺς τῶν ἀνθρώπων
ἐπαίνους), τοῦτο δὲ καί τινας εἰ οἷόν τε καὶ πάντας τοὺς
κάτω κειμένους τῷ δελεάματι τούτῳ λανθανόντως τοῦ βυ-
θοῦ τῆς ἀπωλείας ἀνελκύσαι καὶ τοῦ θανάτου λυτρώσα-
σθαι, δράσσεται τῆς θαυμαστῆς ἀλείας ἐκείνου τὴν μέθοδον εἰς ἀφορμὴν εὐπροσώπου κατηγορίας ὁ σύγκελλος
καὶ προβάλλεται ταύτην ἐπὶ συνόδου λέγων· "Ὡς ἁμαρ-
τωλὸν ὄντα τὸν αὐτοῦ πνευματικὸν πατέρα μετὰ τῶν ἁγίων οἷάπερ ἅγιον ἀνυμνεῖ καὶ τὴν εἰκόνα αὐτοῦ ἀνιστορή-
σας προσκυνεῖ."¹⁶² Αὕτη ἡ ἐφευρεθεῖσα τῷ σοφῷ συγκέλλῳ
κατηγορία κατὰ τοῦ μηδὲν μηδαμῶς ἠδικηκότος αὐτόν
ποτε Συμεών· αὕτη ἡ τῆς τοῦ μακαρίου τούτου κατακρίσεως ἀφορμή, ἴσην ἔχουσα μετὰ τῆς κατηγορίας Χριστοῦ
τὴν κατάγνωσιν, φάγος γὰρ κἀκεῖνος καὶ οἰνοπότης, φίλος
τελωνῶν καὶ ἁμαρτωλῶν [Mt 11:19] παρὰ τῶν θεοκτόνων
τηνικαῦτα κατηγορεῖτο, καὶ ὡς δαιμονῶν ἠτιμάζετο, ἐπει-

Chapter 81

My Symeon, since he was Symeon Eulabes's disciple, thus used to celebrate the memory of his spiritual father every year with a festival. Symeon Eulabes had mortified his flesh through his extreme dispassion and, while still alive, had caused its natural emotions to wither completely away so that he had the same <absence of> feelings toward the bodies of people who came into close physical contact with him as a corpse would have for another corpse.[83] He used to pretend to have passionate feelings, however, doing so on the one hand because he wanted to conceal the treasure of his dispassion (for he used to flee the glory and praise of men as if it were a *serpent biting the heel*) and, on the other, so that by means of this bait he might surreptitiously drag back from the pit of destruction and deliver from death some, and if possible all, of those who lay buried <in sin>. But the *synkellos* seized upon Symeon Eulabes's wonderful method of fishing as the pretext for a convincing allegation, and he laid it before the synod. "Although his spiritual father was a sinner," he said, "Symeon sings his praises as though he were a saint among the saints and venerates the icon of him that he has had painted." This was the allegation devised by the wise *synkellos* against Symeon, who had never wronged him at all. This was the pretext for that blessed man's condemnation, an allegation equal to that used for the condemnation of Christ; for He was then accused by the God killers as *a glutton and a drinker, a friend of tax gatherers and sinners,* and He was disparaged as a demoniac since He said that God was

δὴ Πατέρα ἴδιον ἔλεγε καὶ ἐτίμα τὸν Θεόν, καθὼς πρὸς αὐτοὺς ἀπεκρίνετο· *"Ἐγὼ δαιμόνιον οὐκ ἔχω, ἀλλ' ὅτι τιμῶ τὸν Πατέρα μου, ὑμεῖς ἀτιμάζετέ με* [John 8:49]."

82

Ἄγεται οὖν ὁ μακάριος Συμεὼν λόγους ἀποδώσων ἀνευθύνου εὐθύνης μέσον συνόδου ἁγίας, καὶ εἰσάγεται ὁ μηδένα μηδαμῶς ἀδικήσας κατάκριτος, καί φησιν ὁ πατριάρχης· "Τίς ἡ τοσαύτη σου, κῦρι Συμεών, περὶ τὴν τιμὴν τοῦ πατρὸς[163] φιλοτιμία, ὡς καὶ πᾶσαν τὴν πόλιν ἐν ταῖς πανηγύρεσιν ἐκείνου συντρέχειν καὶ τὴν ὑπερβολὴν τῆς τιμῆς ἐκπλήττεσθαι, καὶ ταῦτα κατηγορουμένου, ὡς ὁρᾷς, παρὰ τοῦ θεοφιλεστάτου συγκέλλου πικρῶς καὶ οὐκ ἀγαθὰς ὑπολήψεις ἔχοντος περὶ αὐτοῦ. Εἰ γὰρ καὶ αὐτὸς ἐγὼ ἐπαινῶν ἀποδέχομαι τοῦτο, ἀλλ' οὖν ἐπειδὴ πολλάκις δι' ὄχλου ἡμῖν καὶ τῇ συνόδῳ ὁ σύγκελλος γέγονε καί τινα λέγει τοῦ κεκοιμημένου καταβοῶν, ἔασαι τὴν πολλὴν περὶ τὴν[164] φιλοτιμίαν σπουδήν,[165] καὶ μετὰ μόνων τῶν ὑπὸ σὲ μοναχῶν τὰ τῆς μνήμης ἐκείνου ποιεῖν σε βούλομαι· οὕτω γὰρ πάντως καὶ ὁ κατήγορός σου τῆς πολλῆς κατὰ σοῦ λωφήσει ποτὲ μανίας καὶ ἡμεῖς τῆς αὐτοῦ ἀπαλλαγῶμεν ὀχλήσεως." Ὁ δὲ μακάριος ὑπολαβὼν ἔφη· "Περὶ μὲν τῆς εἰς τὸν πνευματικόν μου πατέρα πίστεώς τε καὶ πανηγύρεως ὅσα ἔξεστι λέγειν εὖ οἶδ' ὅτι καὶ αὐτὸς ἐπίστασαι

His own Father and honored Him, as His reply to them <indicates>, "*I do not have a demon, but because I honor my Father, you dishonor me.*"

Chapter 82

So the blessed Symeon was brought before the holy synod to account for something for which he was quite unaccountable and, although he had done nothing wrong at all, was brought in like a condemned man. The patriarch said, "Why are you so ostentatious about honoring your spiritual father, Kyr Symeon, so that the whole city flocks to his festival and everyone is astonished at the extravagance of the honor shown him, especially when, as you see, this is harshly criticized by the most God-loving *synkellos,* who does not hold a good opinion of him? Even though I support this veneration myself and approve of it, because the *synkellos* has so often been pestering me and the synod and raises concerns about the deceased man, I want you to desist from so much zeal for ostentation and celebrate your father's memory only with your own monks. In that way, at all events, your accuser will finally get over his rage against you and we'll no longer be bothered by him." But the blessed one replied, "As far as the faith in my spiritual father and his festival goes, I'm sure, all holy master, that you know better than me, your servant,

μᾶλλον ἐμοῦ τοῦ σοῦ οἰκέτου, πανίερε δέσποτα· περὶ δὲ
τῶν κατ' ἐκείνου παρὰ τοῦ θεοφιλεστάτου συγκέλλου
κατηγοριῶν τότε αὐτὸν ἀπολογίας ἀξιώσω, ὅταν ἃ λέγῃ
κατηγορῶν ἀποδείξῃ."

2   Καὶ ὁ πατριάρχης· "Εὐστόχως," φησί, "καὶ νομίμως ἀπελογήσω,[166] ἀλλ' ἔχεις τό γε νῦν ἔχον ἀποδεῖξαι σύ, ὡς δε-
δογμένον τοῖς πατράσι καὶ ἀποστόλοις ποιεῖς οὕτω τὴν
τοῦ σοῦ πατρὸς μνήμην ἴσα καὶ τῶν παλαιῶν ἁγίων ἑορτάζων, ἵνα καὶ σεαυτὸν ἀπὸ τῆς ἀκριβείας τῶν ἱερῶν νόμων νομίμως ποιοῦντα συστήσῃς;" Καὶ ὁ ἅγιος· "Εἰ μὴ τὰς
ἀποδείξεις ἔχω δοῦναι, ὥσπερ ὁ ἐμὸς ἔφη[167] δεσπότης, ἀπὸ
πάσης τῆς θείας γραφῆς ἐπὶ τοῦτό με παρορμώσας,[168] ἔστω
καὶ ὁ ἐμὸς ἀληθεύων κατήγορος ἐφ' οἷς με κατηγορεῖ καὶ
πιστὸς εἰς τὸ ἀκουσθῆναι, κἀγὼ παντὸς ἐπιτιμίου ὑπεύθυνος." Καὶ ὁ πατριάρχης· "Ὡς ἔχεις ἤδη λέξον ἐξαυτῆς τὰ
ἀπὸ τῶν θείων συνιστῶντά σε νόμων, καὶ ἡμεῖς ἑστώσαις
ἀκοαῖς ἀκούσομεν."

83

Ἀρξάμενος τοίνυν τοῦ λέγειν ὁ τὰ θεῖα σοφὸς Συμεὼν
ὧδέ πως ἔφη πεπαρρησιασμένῃ ψυχῇ· "Τίς οὐκ οἶδεν, ὦ
σύνοδος ἱερά, τὰς τῷ Εὐαγγελίῳ[169] γεγραμμένας φωνὰς
τοῦ Χριστοῦ διαρρήδην οὕτω βοώσας· ὁ δεχόμενος ὑμᾶς
ἐμὲ δέχεται [Mt 10:40] καὶ ὁ ἀθετῶν ὑμᾶς ἐμὲ ἀθετεῖ, ὁ δὲ

what can be said about it. But concerning the allegations made against him by the most God-loving *synkellos,* I will only consent to offer a defense at such time as he may prove what he says in his allegation."

"You've spoken pertinently and properly in your defense," 2 said the patriarch, "but can you prove here and now that when you celebrate your father's memory in the same way as the long-established saints, you are acting in accordance with the teachings of the fathers and apostles, and thus demonstrate that you are yourself acting lawfully in strict accordance with the holy laws?" "If, as you my master have requested," replied the saint, "I can't provide from the whole of holy scripture these proofs that you're pressing me for, then let my accuser indeed be proved true and credible in his allegations against me, and may I be liable to every penalty." Then the patriarch said, "Tell us whatever you can right now that supports you from divine law. We'll be listening attentively."

Chapter 83

When Symeon, that wise man in divine matters, began to speak, he said something like this, with confidence from <the depths of> his soul. "Who does not know, O holy synod, Christ's words recorded in the gospels that proclaim explicitly, *He who receives you receives me,* and *he who rejects*

ἐμὲ ἀθετῶν ἀθετεῖ τὸν ἀποστείλαντά με [Lk 10:16]; Καὶ πά-
λιν· ὁ δεχόμενος ἅγιον εἰς ὄνομα ἁγίου μισθὸν ἁγίου λήψεται, καὶ ὁ δεχόμενος προφήτην εἰς ὄνομα προφήτου μισθὸν
προφήτου λήψεται [Mt 10:41].

2   "Τί δέ φασι καὶ οἱ αὐτόπται τοῦ Λόγου ἐν ταῖς αὐτῶν
διατάξεσι; Οὐχὶ τὸν λαλοῦντά σοι, εἶπον, τὸν λόγον τοῦ
Θεοῦ δοξάσεις, μνησθήσῃ δὲ αὐτοῦ ἡμέρας καὶ νυκτός, τιμή-
σεις δὲ αὐτὸν ὡς τοῦ εὖ εἶναί σοι πρόξενον γενόμενον; Ὅπου
γὰρ ἡ τοῦ Θεοῦ διδασκαλία ἐκεῖ καὶ ὁ Θεὸς πάρεστι. Καὶ
αὖθις· εἰ γὰρ περὶ τῶν κατὰ σάρκα γονέων φησὶ τὸ ὅσιον
λόγιον· 'τίμα τὸν πατέρα σου[170] καὶ τὴν μητέρα σου, ἵνα εὖ σοι
γένηται' [Ex 20:12], καί· 'ὁ κακολογῶν πατέρα ἢ μητέρα
τελευτάτω' [cf. Ex 21:16], πόσῳ μᾶλλον ἡμᾶς περὶ τῶν πνευ-
ματικῶν γονέων ἡμῶν ὁ Λόγος παραινέσει τιμᾶν αὐτοὺς καὶ
στέργειν ὡς εὐεργέτας καὶ πρεσβευτὰς πρὸς Θεόν; Τοὺς δι᾽
ὕδατος ἡμᾶς ἀναγεννήσαντας [cf. John 3:5], τοὺς τῷ Ἁγίῳ
Πνεύματι πληρώσαντας, τοὺς τῷ Λόγῳ γαλακτοτροφήσαν-
τας, τοὺς ἐν τῇ διδασκαλίᾳ ἀναθρεψαμένους, τοὺς ἐν ταῖς
νουθεσίαις στηρίξαντας, τοὺς τοῦ σωτηρίου σώματος καὶ τοῦ
τιμίου αἵματος ἀξιώσαντας, τοὺς τῶν ἁμαρτιῶν λύσαντας καὶ
τῆς ἁγίας καὶ ἱερᾶς εὐχαριστίας μετόχους ποιήσαντας[171] καὶ
τῆς ἐπαγγελίας τοῦ Θεοῦ κοινωνοὺς καὶ συγκληρονόμους
θεμένους ἡμᾶς. Τούτους εὐλαβούμενοι τιμᾶτε παντοίαις
τιμαῖς, οὗτοι γὰρ παρὰ Θεοῦ ζωῆς καὶ θανάτου ἐξουσίαν
εἰλήφασι.

you rejects me and he who rejects me rejects Him who sent me? And again, he who receives a saint as a saint shall receive a saint's reward, and *he who receives a prophet as a prophet will receive a prophet's reward.*

"And what do the <apostles> who actually saw the Word 2 for themselves say in their *Constitutions?* Did they not say this? *You shall glorify the person who speaks the word of God to you, and shall remember him night and day, and honor him [. . .] as someone who has become the source of your well-being. For where the teaching of God is, there also God is present.*[84] And again, *For if the holy Bible says about our parents in the flesh, 'Honor your father and your mother so that it may go well for you,' and 'Whoever curses his father or his mother, let him die,' how much more does the Word exhort us to honor our spiritual parents, and to love them as benefactors and ambassadors before God? For they have regenerated us through water, and filled us with the Holy Spirit, they have nursed us with the milk of the Word, they have fed us with teaching, they have steadied us with their admonitions, they have deemed us worthy of the saving body and precious blood, they have released us from our sins, they have made us sharers in the holy and sacred Eucharist, and rendered us partakers and fellow heirs of the promise of God. Revering them, honor them with every kind of honor, for they have received from God the power of life and death [. . .].*[85]

84

"Τί δὲ ὁ τὴν γλῶτταν χρυσοῦς Ἰωάννης ἐγκωμιάζων τὸν Φιλογόνιον; Εἰ ʽὁ κακολογῶν,ʼ φησί, ʽπατέρα ἢ μητέρα θανάτῳ τελευτᾷʼ [cf. Ex 21:16], εὔδηλον ὅτι ὁ εὐλογῶν ζωῆς ἀπολαύσεται, καὶ εἰ τοὺς φυσικοὺς γονεῖς τοσαύτης παρʼ ἡμῶν ἀπολαύειν εὐνοίας χρή, πολλῷ μᾶλλον τοὺς πνευματικούς, καὶ μάλιστα ὅταν τοὺς μὲν κατοιχομένους[172] ὁ ἔπαινος μηδὲν ποιῇ λαμπροτέρους, τοὺς δὲ συνιόντας[173] ἡμᾶς καὶ τοὺς λέγοντας καὶ τοὺς ἀκούοντας βελτίους ἐργάζηται. Ὁ μὲν γὰρ εἰς τὸν οὐρανὸν ἀναβὰς οὐδὲν ἂν δέοιτο τῆς ἀνθρωπίνης εὐφημίας πρὸς μείζονα καὶ μακαριωτέραν λῆξιν ἀπελθών, ἡμεῖς δὲ οἱ τέως ἐνταῦθα στρεφόμενοι καὶ πολλῆς πανταχόθεν παρακλήσεως χρῄζοντες τῶν ἐγκωμίων δεόμεθα τῶν ἐκείνου, ἵνα εἰς τὸν αὐτὸν ζῆλον διαναστῶμεν. Διὰ τοῦτο καί τις σοφὸς παραινεῖ λέγων· ʽμνήμη δικαίου μετʼ ἐγκωμίουʼ [cf. Prov 10:7], οὐχ ὡς τῶν ἀπελθόντων ἀλλʼ ὡς τῶν ἐγκωμιαζόντων ταύτῃ τὰ μέγιστα ὠφελουμένων.

2 "Ὅτι δὲ τὸ οὕτως γινόμενον παρʼ ἡμῶν εὐαπόδεκτόν ἐστι τῷ Θεῷ καὶ οὕτω γίνεσθαι ἡ τοῦ Πνεύματος ἄνωθεν ᾠκονόμησε χάρις, μαρτυρεῖ μοι τῷ λόγῳ Μωσῆς τε ὁ θεόπτης τοὺς τῶν παλαιῶν βίους, οὐ μόνον δὲ ἀλλὰ καὶ τὸν ἑαυτοῦ βίον ἀναγραψάμενος, Ἔσδρας τε καὶ ὁ σοφώτατος Σολομῶν τὸν τοῦ Ἰὼβ ἀναγραψάμενος βίον καὶ αὐτὸς ὁ τὸ στόμα χρυσοῦς τοὺς ἁγίους ἐγκωμιάζων. Φησὶ γάρ· τοὺς τῶν ἁγίων βίους καὶ τὴν πολιτείαν διὰ τοῦτο ἀναγρά-

Chapter 84

"And what does John Chrysostom say in his eulogy of Philogonios? *If 'whoever curses his father or his mother is put to death,' it is clear that whoever praises them will have the benefit of life. Thus if our natural parents ought to enjoy such affection from us, how much more should our spiritual parents do so, especially when our praise does not make those who have passed away any more splendid, but does make us better, who have gathered together, and who speak and hear it? For the person who has ascended into heaven has no need of human repute, having departed to a better and more blessed state, but we who, for the time being, are still living here and require much consolation in every way, we need the eulogies of that person, so that we may rouse ourselves to the same zeal. For this reason too, a wise man exhorts us, saying, 'The memory of a righteous man comes with a eulogy,' not because those who have departed benefit from this but because those who do the eulogizing benefit very greatly.*[86]

"In fact Moses, the man who saw God, bears witness to me that our doing this is acceptable to God and thus that the grace of the Holy Spirit from above has made it happen, for he recorded the lives of men from former times, as well as his own life. So does Esdras, and the most wise Solomon who recorded the life of Job, and also [John] Chrysostom himself in eulogizing the saints. For he says, *For this reason the grace of God has bequeathed to us in writing the lives of the*

πτους ἡμῖν καταλέλοιπεν ἡ τοῦ Θεοῦ χάρις, ἵνα μαθόντες, ὡς τῆς αὐτῆς ὄντες ἡμῖν φύσεως ἅπαντα τὰ τῆς ἀρετῆς κατώρθωσαν, διαναστῶμεν περὶ τὴν ταύτης ἐργασίαν καὶ σφοδρὸν τὸν ἔρωτα τῆς πρὸς αὐτοὺς ἀγάπης ἀνάψωμεν. Πῶς οὖν τοῦτο γενήσεται; Ἂν συνεχῶς ἐχώμεθα τῶν ἀνδρῶν ἐκείνων καὶ ἐν διανοίᾳ αὐτοὺς περιφέροντες τῆς αὐτῆς ἐκείνοις ἐχώμεθα πολιτείας· ἐν τούτῳ γὰρ πλέον ἢ πᾶσιν ὁμοῦ τοῖς ἄλλοις ὁ Θεὸς δοξασθήσεται. Εἰ γὰρ ὑρανοὶ διηγοῦνται δόξαν Θεοῦ' [Ps 18(19):1] οὐ φωνὴν ἀφιέντες ἀλλ᾽ ἑτέρους διὰ τῆς ὄψεως εἰς τοῦτο παρασκευάζοντες, πολλῷ μᾶλλον οἱ παρεχόμενοι βίον θαυμαστόν, κἂν σιγῶσι, τὸν Θεὸν δοξάζουσι, ἑτέρων δι᾽ αὐτοὺς τὸν Θεὸν δοξαζόντων.

85

"Ὁρᾶτε ὅπως δοξάζεται Θεὸς διὰ τῆς εἰς τὸν ἐμὸν πατέρα τιμῆς, ὦ δεσπόται, ἣν ἀπονέμομεν ἡμεῖς ἐτησίως αὐτῷ. Μάθετε ἀκριβῶς ὅτι οὐ μόνον εἰς δόξαν Θεοῦ ἐστι τὸ γινόμενον, ἀλλὰ καὶ ὠφέλιμόν ἐστι σφόδρα τοῖς λαοῖς· καὶ τοῦτο δῆλον ἐξ ὧν φησιν ὁ σοφός· ἐγκωμιαζομένου δικαίου εὐφρανθήσονται λαοί [cf. Prov 29:2], ὅπερ ὁ μέγας ἑρμηνεύων Βασίλειος Γόρδιον ἐγκωμιάζων τὸν μάρτυρα οὕτω φησίν· εὐφραίνονται οἱ λαοὶ εὐφροσύνην πνευματικὴν ἐπὶ μόνῃ τῇ ὑπομνήσει τῶν τοῖς δικαίοις κατωρθωμένων εἰς

saints and their conduct, so that when we learn that they accomplished every kind of virtue while being of the same nature as we are, we may rouse ourselves to do this and may kindle in ourselves a fierce desire to show our love for them. So how will this happen? If we devote ourselves constantly to those men and bear them in mind, we may lead the same sort of life as them. For God will be glorified in this way more than by all the others put together. For if 'the heavens are telling the glory of God' and they do so without a sound, making others do this through their appearance, *then those who have led a wondrous life glorify God all the more, even if they are silent, when others glorify God because of them.*[87]

Chapter 85

"So you can see, my masters, how God is glorified by the honor that we render annually to my father. And you should also surely learn that this not only renders glory to God but is also most beneficial to the people. This is clear from the words of the wise [Solomon], who says, *When the righteous man is eulogized the people will rejoice,* a statement which Basil the Great explains as follows while eulogizing the martyr Gordios:[88] *The people rejoice with spiritual joy simply at the recollection of what the righteous accomplished, and they are thus en-*

ζῆλον καὶ μίμησιν τῶν ἀγαθῶν ἀφ᾽ ὧν ἀκούουσιν ἐναγόμενοι. Ἡ γὰρ τῶν εὐπολιτεύτων ἱστορία οἷόν τι φῶς τοῖς σωζομένοις πρὸς τὴν τοῦ βίου ὁδὸν ἐμποιεῖ. Τοῖς μὲν γὰρ ἄλλοις ἀνθρώποις ἐκ τῆς τῶν λόγων αὐξήσεως συνίσταται τὰ ἐγκώμια, τοῖς δικαίοις δὲ ἀρκεῖ τῶν πεπραγμένων αὐτοῖς ἡ ἀλήθεια πρὸς τὸ δεῖξαι αὐτῶν τὸ ὑπερβάλλον τῆς ἀρετῆς, ὥστε ὅταν διηγώμεθα τοὺς βίους τῶν διαπρεψάντων ἐν εὐσεβείᾳ, δοξάζομεν πρῶτον τὸν Δεσπότην διὰ τῶν δούλων, ἐγκωμιάζομεν τοὺς δικαίους διὰ τῆς μαρτυρίας ὧν ἴσμεν, εὐφραίνομεν δὲ τοὺς λαοὺς διὰ τῆς ἀκοῆς τῶν καλῶν. Ὥσπερ γὰρ τῷ πυρὶ αὐτομάτως ἕπεται τὸ φωτίζειν καὶ τῷ μύρῳ τὸ εὐωδεῖν,[174] οὕτω καὶ ταῖς ἀγαθαῖς πράξεσιν ἀναγκαίως ἕπεται τὸ ὠφέλιμον.

86

"Ἵνα δὲ καθ᾽ ὑπερβολὴν λέγων δείξω ὑμῖν ὅτι οὐδὲ συμφέρον ἐστὶ τῷ βίῳ μὴ τιμᾶσθαι τοὺς ἐν πολλοῖς κατορθώμασι διηνυκότας τὸν βίον, καθὰ δὴ καὶ αὐτὸς ἐγὼ ποιῶ σήμερον, αὐτὸν τὸν ἐν θεολογίᾳ βεβοημένον Γρηγόριον εἰς μαρτυρίαν παραγαγὼν καταπαύσω τὸν λόγον. Τί οὖν ἐν τοῖς ἐγκωμίοις Ἀθανασίου φησίν; οὐδὲ γὰρ ὅσιον οὐδὲ ἀσφαλὲς ἀσεβῶν μὲν βίους τιμᾶσθαι ταῖς μνήμαις, τῶν δὲ ἐν εὐσεβείᾳ διενεγκόντων σιωπῇ παραπέμπεσθαι. Εἰ τοίνυν ὡς παρ᾽ ἐμοῦ ἀκηκόατε σήμερον, ὦ ἱερὰ σύνοδος, οὕτω

*couraged to emulate and imitate the good deeds about which they
hear. For the story of people who live good lives creates a kind of
light in those who have been chosen for salvation, <leading them>
toward the path of life. For the eulogies of other men are composed
of exaggerated words, but in the case of the righteous the truth of
their actual deeds suffices to show the excellence of their virtue. As
a result, when we narrate the lives of those who have been distinguished by their piety, we first glorify the Master through His servants, then we eulogize the righteous through the evidence of what
we know, and finally we make the people rejoice by hearing about
good things. For just as illumination results automatically from fire
and sweet fragrance from perfume, thus also benefit necessarily results from good deeds.*[89]

Chapter 86

"In order to emphasize my point, I will show you that
failure to honor, as I myself do today, those who have lived
good lives in all sorts of ways is of no benefit to the quality of
our lives. I will introduce the renowned theologian Gregory
as a witness, and then will conclude my statement. What
then does he say in his eulogy of Athanasios?[90] *It is neither
devout nor safe for those who have spent their lives in piety to be
dismissed in silence, when the lives of impious men are honored
with memorials.*[91] If then, as you, holy synod, have heard from

κελεύει τὸ Εὐαγγέλιον, οὕτω τοῦ λόγου οἱ αὐτόπται διδά-
σκουσι καὶ οἱ πατέρες ἡμῶν διηγήσαντο ἡμῖν οὕτω ποιεῖν
ὥσπερ ἐγὼ τοὺς πιστοὺς προτρεπόμενοι, τίνος ἄλλου τῶν
ἄλλων ἁπάντων ἀνθρώπων ἄρα ἐπ' ἀνατροπῇ τῶν εἰρημένων διδάσκοντος ἀκουσόμεθα; εἰ δὲ καὶ βαθύτερόν τι τούτων ὁ ἐμὸς κατήγορός ἐστιν εἰδὼς ὃ ἐμέ τε ἴσως καὶ τοὺς
πατέρας καὶ[175] ἀποστόλους διέλαθε, προτεινέσθω τοῦτο μέσον ὑμῶν τῶν ἁγίων, κἀγὼ σιωπῶν ἀκούσομαι, οὐ μὴν
ἀλλὰ καὶ πεισθήσομαι καὶ τὸ δοκοῦν τοῖς ἱεροῖς νόμοις
εὐθύμῳ ψυχῇ διαπράξομαι, εἰ τὸ πιθανὸν ἀπὸ τῆς θείας
γραφῆς ἐπιφέρεται."

87

Ὡς δὲ ὁ κατήγορος σύγκελλος κατήγορος πικρὸς μόνος ἦν[176] τοῦ δικαίου μὴ ἔχων εἰπεῖν ἢ χρήσεις τῶν θείων
γραφῶν ἢ εὐπρόσωπον ἀφορμήν, δι' ὧν ἀνασκευάζειν
ἔμελλε τὰ ὑπὸ τοῦ ἁγίου ῥηθέντα, ἔσχε δὲ καὶ τὴν ἐντροπὴν
ἀπάρτι πᾶσαν τῶν συνεδριαζόντων[177] νεύουσαν εἰς αὑτόν,
κωφοῖς ᾄδειν ἐῴκει ὁ Συμεὼν καὶ πρὸς ἀέρα ποιεῖσθαι
τοὺς λόγους, ὅθεν καὶ ὡς ἐν στάσει διαμαχομένη τοῖς λόγοις καταντήσασα[178] ἡ ἐξέτασις λύεται. Ἐπεὶ δὲ φιλόνεικον
ὁ φθόνος κακόν, καὶ οὔτε νικώμενος ἡττᾶσθαι φιλεῖ, οὔτε
νικῶν ἠρεμεῖ, εἴχετο σπουδαίως τῆς μάχης ὁ ὑπ' αὐτοῦ
ἐνεργούμενος. Ἔνθεν τοι καὶ ἐν ὅλοις ἓξ ἔτεσιν εἷλκέ τε

me today, the Gospel thus commands us, the <apostles> who actually saw the Word for themselves teach us, and our fathers have told us to act in encouraging the faithful just as I have, why should we listen to anyone else at all who teaches the opposite of these declarations? But if my accuser knows something more profound than this that perhaps has escaped me, as well as the fathers and apostles, let him present it to your holinesses. I will listen in silence, and indeed, if he can offer a persuasive argument from holy scripture, I will be convinced and will carry out what is established by holy law with a cheerful spirit."

Chapter 87

As the *synkellos* was only an embittered accuser of the righteous Symeon, he was unable to adduce passages from the holy scriptures or a plausible pretext with which he might refute the saint's words. By this time, however, he had gained the complete respect of his fellow councilors and Symeon thus seemed to be singing to the deaf and speaking to thin air. So the inquiry descended into verbal disagreement and broke up. But since envy is a contentious evil that neither gives up when conquered nor stays quiet when conquering, the *synkellos,* who was motivated by it, was eager for battle. And so, mark you, this wise man, this senior cleric,

εἰς κρίσεις τὸν δίκαιον αἰδῶ πᾶσαν ἀποσεισάμενος,[179] καὶ
κρίματι θανάτου παραδοῦναι αὐτὸν ἔσπευδεν—ὦ τῆς ἀνοχῆς σου, Χριστὲ Βασιλεῦ!—ὁ σοφός, ὁ ἀρχιερεύσας, ὁ μονάζων, ὁ καὶ φῶς γνώσεως τοῖς ἄλλοις εἶναι δοκῶν καὶ τὸ
ἅλας τοῦ Πνεύματος [cf. Mt 5:13; Mk 9:49–50; Lk 14:34–35]
οἰόμενος ἐπιφέρεσθαι.

2   Ἀλλὰ γὰρ ἐπειδὴ πάντας ἐξήγειρε σχεδὸν τοὺς ἀρχιερεῖς κατὰ τοῦ δικαίου, καὶ αὐτὸν ὡς οὐκ ὤφελε τὸν πατριάρχην ἐχθρὸν αὐτοῦ ἀπειργάσατο, ἦσαν δέ τινες καὶ τῶν
ἀπὸ τῆς αὐλῆς τοῦ Συμεὼν διάβολοι τὴν τοῦ Ἰούδα μανίαν καὶ αὐτοὶ κατὰ τοῦ διδασκάλου νοσοῦντες, αὐτῷ τε
τῷ πατριάρχῃ καὶ τῷ συγκέλλῳ θαρρήσαντες, κλέπτουσιν
ἐν μιᾷ τῶν νυκτῶν τὴν τοῦ ἁγίου πατρὸς αὐτοῦ Συμεὼν
εἰκόνα, δι' ὃν καὶ ὁ πολὺς πόλεμος τοῦ συγκέλλου, καὶ
ἀναβιβάζουσιν εἰς τὸ πατριαρχεῖον αὐτήν, ἣν οἱ ὁρῶντες
μετὰ πολλῶν ἁγίων συνεικονισμένην καὶ αὐτοῦ τοῦ Χριστοῦ, οἱ μέν, ὅσοι τῆς μοίρας ἦσαν τοῦ κατηγόρου, ἐβλα-
σφήμουν τὸν ἅγιον ψευδῆ κατηγοροῦντες, οἱ δέ, ὅσοι τῆς
ἀληθοῦς γνώσεως μετεῖχον ποσῶς, τῶν δραματουργῶν
κατεστέναζον, καὶ τὴν ὕβριν ἔφριττον τοῦ εἰπόντος Χρι-
στοῦ· ὁ δεχόμενος ὑμᾶς ἐμὲ δέχεται [Mt 10:40], καί, ἐφ' ὅσον
ἐποιήσατε ἑνὶ τούτων τῶν ἀδελφῶν μου ἐμοὶ ἐποιήσατε [Mt
25:40], ὡς εἰδότες ἐνδεδυμένους Χριστὸν [cf. Gal 3:27]
τοὺς ἁγίους αὐτοῦ.

this monk, this person who pretended to be a light of knowledge to others and supposed that he was endowed with the salt of the Spirit, abandoned any self-respect and dragged the righteous Symeon through the courts for six whole years. He even tried to have him sentenced to death—oh, your forbearance, Christ the King!

For the *synkellos* stirred up nearly all the senior clergy 2 against the righteous man, and made the patriarch himself, as he ought not to have been, into Symeon's enemy. There were also some slanderers among the monks of Symeon's fold who were infected with the madness of Judas against their teacher. One night, encouraged by the patriarch himself and his *synkellos,* these men stole the image of Symeon's holy father Symeon [Eulabes], which was the cause of the *synkellos*'s great war, and brought it to the patriarchate. When they saw this image depicting Symeon Eulabes alongside <the icons> of many saints and Christ himself,[92] some people, who were of the accusers' party, blasphemed the saint,[93] alleging that he was a fraud, but others, who to some extent partook of the true knowledge, grieved for those who had staged this, and shuddered at their presumption, since Christ says, *He who receives you receives me,* and *anything you did for one of my brothers, you did for me,* for they knew that Christ's saints have put Him on as a garment.

88

Οὕτως οὖν παρὰ μὲν τῶν βλασφημούμενος, παρὰ δὲ τῶν ἐπαινούμενός τε καὶ συνηγορούμενος ὁ χαρακτὴρ τῆς εἰκόνος τοῦ ἁγίου εἰσάγεται παρὰ τοῦ κατηγόρου ἐπὶ συνόδου· ἐμφανισθέντος δὲ πᾶσι τοῦ χαρακτῆρος, ἀλλὰ καὶ αὐτῷ τῷ πατριάρχῃ, ἄγεται πάλιν ὁ δίκαιος καὶ περὶ ταύτης λόγους εἰσπράττεται καί φησιν· "Ἐγὼ μέν, ὥς γε λελογισμένως ἐμαυτὸν ἐξετάζω, οὐδὲν ἀσύνηθες ἢ ξένον τῇ παραδόσει τῶν πατέρων καὶ ἀποστόλων πεποίηκα, ἀλλὰ καθὼς παρέθεντο ἡμῖν ἐξ ἀρχῆς οἱ κατὰ διαδοχὴν τὰ ἔθιμα καὶ τοὺς τύπους παραλαβόντες τῆς τῶν πιστῶν ἐκκλησίας πατέρες ἡμῶν, ἵνα τῶν πατέρων ἡμῶν τῶν ἁγίων ἱστορῶμεν τοὺς χαρακτῆρας καὶ τιμῶμεν καὶ ἀσπαζώμεθα, ὡς πρὸς τὸ πρωτότυπον τῆς τιμῆς διαβαινούσης αὐτὸν τὸν Χριστόν, οὗ καὶ τὴν εἰκόνα φοροῦμεν, εἰ καὶ τὴν ἡμετέραν αὐτὸς οὐκ ἀπηξίωσεν ἀναδέξασθαι, γέγραφα ταύτην τὴν εἰκόνα ὡς δούλου Χριστοῦ καὶ τὰ μέλη φοροῦντος αὐτοῦ καὶ γεγονότος *συμμόρφου τῆς εἰκόνος αὐτοῦ* [cf. Rom 8:29], ἣν καὶ σεβόμενος ἀσπάζομαι προσκυνῶν τὸν Χριστὸν ἐν τῷ ἁγίῳ τούτῳ καὶ αὐτὸν ἐν τῷ Χριστῷ καὶ Θεῷ, ἐπειδὴ αὐτὸς ἐν τῷ Χριστῷ διὰ Πνεύματος καὶ ὁ Χριστὸς ἐν τῷ Θεῷ καὶ Πατρὶ καὶ ὁ Πατὴρ ἐν τῷ Χριστῷ καὶ Θεῷ κατὰ τὸ ὅσιον λόγιον· *ἐν ἐκείνῃ*, φησί, *τῇ ἡμέρᾳ γνώσεσθε ὑμεῖς, ὅτι ἐγὼ ἐν τῷ Πατρί μου καὶ ὑμεῖς ἐν ἐμοὶ κἀγὼ ἐν ὑμῖν* [John 8:20].

Chapter 88

Thus the picture of the saint's image, blasphemed by some but praised and defended by others, was brought into the synod by Symeon's accuser. When the picture had been exhibited to everyone, including the patriarch himself, the righteous Symeon was brought there again and was asked for an explanation of it. He said, "I've examined myself carefully <and come to the conclusion that> I've done nothing unusual or alien to the tradition of the fathers and the apostles. Our fathers, who have received in succession the customs and rules of the church of the faithful, have recommended to us from the beginning that we should portray pictures of our holy fathers and should honor and venerate them, since the honor extends to their prototype Christ Himself[94] whose image we also bear, given that He did not think it unworthy to take our own human image upon Himself. I have thus had this image painted as that of a servant of Christ, bearing His limbs and being a man *conformed to His image,* and I also venerate it, revering and worshiping Christ in this saint and him in Christ and God, since he is in Christ through the Spirit, and Christ is in God and the Father, and the Father in Christ and God according to the holy text that says, *On that day you will know that I am in my Father, and you in me, and I in you.*

89

"Ἀλλὰ γὰρ καὶ ὁ Δαμασκηνὸς πατὴρ[180] Ἰωάννης οὕτω προτρεπόμενος ποιεῖν πᾶσι πιστοῖς ὧδέ φησι· *τοὺς προστάτας παντὸς τοῦ γένους ἡμῶν, τοὺς τῷ Θεῷ ὑπὲρ ἡμῶν τὰς ἐντεύξεις ποιουμένους τιμητέον, ναοὺς ἐγείροντας τῷ Θεῷ ἐπὶ τῷ τούτων ὀνόματι, καρποφορίας προσάγοντας, τὰς τούτων μνήμας γεραίροντας, καὶ ἐν αὐταῖς εὐφραινομένους πνευματικῶς, ἵνα οἰκεία τῶν συγκαλούντων ἡ εὐφροσύνη γένηται.* Καὶ μετ' ὀλίγον· 'ἐν ψαλμοῖς καὶ ὕμνοις καὶ ᾠδαῖς πνευματικαῖς' [Eph 5:19] *καὶ κατανύξει καὶ τῶν δεομένων ἐλέῳ τοὺς ἁγίους πιστοὶ θεραπεύσωμεν, οἷς μάλιστα καὶ Θεὸς θεραπεύεται, στήλας αὐτοῖς ἐγείρωμεν ὁρωμένας τε εἰκόνας καὶ αὐτοὶ ἔμψυχοι στῆλαι καὶ εἰκόνες αὐτῶν τῇ τῶν ἀρετῶν μιμήσει γενώμεθα.*

2   "Εἰ τοίνυν καταψεύδομαι ταῦτα λέγων τοῦ σωτηρίου κηρύγματος, καταψεύδομαι μετὰ τῆς ἀληθείας καὶ τῆς πίστεως, καὶ πρᾶγμα εἰργασάμην ἀσύνηθες, ὃ οὐδεὶς ἐν τῇ τῶν πιστῶν ἐκκλησίᾳ μέχρι τοῦ παρόντος πεποίηκεν, ἁγίου ἀνδρὸς ἢ καὶ κοινοῦ ἱστορήσας εἰκόνα· εἰ δὲ τοῦτο μὲν πανταχοῦ παρὰ παντὸς πιστοῦ κατὰ πᾶσαν γίνεται ἐκκλησίαν, ἐγὼ δὲ μόνος σήμερον παρὰ τοῦ σοφοῦ συγκέλλου λόγους ὡς παρανομήσας ἐν τούτῳ εἰσπράττομαι, καὶ ὡς ὑπεύθυνος κρίνομαι καὶ τιμωρίας[181] καὶ ποινὰς ὑποστῆναι κινδυνεύω, ποῦ τὸ δίκαιον εἴπατε; Ἐγὼ γὰρ οὐ μόνον ὡς ὁρᾶτε ἱστόρησα, ἀλλὰ καὶ τὸ παρ' ἐμοῦ ἀνανεωθὲν μοναστήριον πίστει καὶ πόθῳ κατὰ παντὸς τοίχου

Chapter 89

"The father John of Damascus also urges all the faithful to do this when he says, *We should honor the leaders of our whole race, who make entreaties to God on our behalf, by erecting churches to God in their name, bringing offerings, revering their memory, and rejoicing spiritually in them, so that we may appropriate as our own the joy of those who invite us to join them in doing so.* And a little later, *Let us, the faithful, venerate the saints 'with psalms and hymns and spiritual songs,' with compunction, and with compassion for the needy, for it is by these things especially that God is also venerated. Let us erect visible memorials and images for them, and let us ourselves become their living memorials and images by imitation of their virtues.*[95]

"If, then, in saying these words, I am misrepresenting the   2 message of salvation, I am misrepresenting it in the same way that the truth and the faith do. And by having had an image of a holy man or even an ordinary one painted, I have also <apparently> managed to do something unusual, something that no one else in the church of the faithful has done until now! But if this is <actually> what happens everywhere and is done by every faithful person throughout the entire church, yet I alone today, due to the wise *synkellos*'s words, am being called to account for it as though I have broken the law, and as though I am liable and am in danger of incurring a punishment and penalties, where, tell me, is the justice in that? Anyway, I have not had painted only the image that you see, but with faith and affection I have had this picture, along with Christ, painted on every wall of the monas-

σὺν τῷ Χριστῷ τὸν χαρακτῆρα τοῦτον ἱστόρησα στήλην ἀρετῆς ἀνεγείρας καὶ ἄλλοις πράγματος ἀγαθοῦ ὑπογραμμὸν προθεὶς καὶ ἀρχέτυπον."

90

Tαῦτ᾽ εἰπὼν[182] καὶ πάντων ἐπ᾽ ὄψεσι προσκυνήσας τὴν τιμίαν εἰκόνα τοῦ πατρὸς αὐτοῦ, ἠσπάσατο αὐτὴν ἐπὶ[183] λέξεσιν οὕτως εἰπών· "Ἅγιε Συμεών, ὁ τῆς τοῦ Κυρίου μου Ἰησοῦ Χριστοῦ εἰκόνος διὰ τῆς τοῦ Ἁγίου Πνεύματος κοινωνίας γενόμενος σύμμορφος [cf. Rom 8:29; 2 Cor 13:13], ὁ δοξάσας αὐτὸν ἐν τοῖς μέλεσί [cf. 1 Cor 12:26] σου τῇ νεκρώσει τῶν ἡδονῶν, ὁ τὸ ἔνδυμα τῆς ἀπαθείας φαιδρὸν ἐνδυσάμενος [cf. Mt 28:3] τῇ χρονίῳ ἀσκήσει, ὁ τοῖς ἰδίοις ἀπολουσάμενος δάκρυσιν ἐξισωθεῖσι τῷ πλήθει τῇ πηγῇ τοῦ βαπτίσματος, ὁ φέρων ἐν ἑαυτῷ τὸν Χριστόν, ὃν ἐπόθησας, καὶ ὑφ᾽ οὗ πολλὰ ἠγαπήθης, καὶ παρ᾽ οὗ τοῖς θαύμασιν ἐδοξάσθης, ὁ ἐκ τῆς ἄνωθεν ἐνεχθείσης μοι φωνῆς τὴν ἴσην μαρτυρηθεὶς τῶν ἀποστόλων ἁγιωσύνην, πρόστηθί μου τοῦ ταπεινοῦ καὶ διὰ σὲ σήμερον, ὡς ὁρᾷς, κρινομένου, καὶ δύναμιν παρασχεθῆναί μοι πρέσβευε, ἵνα τοὺς ὑπὲρ σοῦ καὶ τῆς σῆς εἰκόνος ἢ μᾶλλον εἰπεῖν τοῦ Χριστοῦ, ἐπειδὴ πάντα πλὴν ἁμαρτίας ἠμπέσχετο[184] τὰ ἡμέτερα καὶ οἰκειοῦται τὰ εἰς ἡμᾶς Θεὸς ὤν, γενναίως

tery that I have restored. In doing so I have erected a memorial of virtue and set before others an example and model of good conduct."

Chapter 90

When Symeon had said this, he prostrated himself before the venerable image of his spiritual father in full view of everyone and kissed it, while saying these words: "Holy Symeon, you have come to be *conformed to the image* of my Lord Jesus Christ through *the fellowship of the Holy Spirit,* you have glorified Him in your limbs through mortification of the pleasures, you have been dressed in the bright *garment* of dispassion as a result of your long practice of asceticism, you have been washed clean by your own tears that equal in their abundance the baptismal spring, you bear within you the Christ whom you desired and by whom you have been much loved and through whom you have been glorified by your miracles, you have been attested by the voice which came to me from above as possessing holiness equal to that of the apostles. Now, holy Symeon, help me, wretch that I am, for today, as you see, I am being judged on account of you. Intercede for me, so that I may receive the strength to bear nobly the reproaches and jeers with which I am being insulted on account of you and your image (or, rather, on account of Christ, since He took upon Himself everything that is ours, except sin, and, being God, made everything

ὑποφέρω προπηλακισμούς τε καὶ τωθασμοὺς παροινούμε-
νος, ὡς ἂν¹⁸⁵ καὶ τῆς αὐτῆς σοι δόξης συγκοινωνὸς¹⁸⁶ γέ-
νοιμι, ἧς καὶ ἐν σαρκὶ ζῶν ἔτι ἀπήλαυσας, ὡς ἐμοὶ ἐδείχθης
ἐκ δεξιῶν τοῦ Θεοῦ παριστάμενος, καὶ νῦν ἀπολαύεις μετὰ
πάντων τῶν¹⁸⁷ ἁγίων τρανότερον."

91

Οὕτως εὐξάμενος στραφεὶς ἱλαρῶς πως πρὸς τὸν κατ-
ήγορον ἔβλεψε καί φησιν· "Εὖγέ σοι, ὦ καλὲ δέσποτά μου
καὶ σύγκελλε, τῶν ἀγώνων καὶ τῆς ὑπὲρ τοῦ δικαίου ἐνστάσεως, ὅπως τἄλλα λελοιπὼς πάντα καὶ τῆς οἰκείας ἐπι-
μελούμενος συνειδήσεως τῶν ἀποστολικῶν ἀντέχῃ σπουδαίως κανόνων καὶ διατάξεων, καὶ οὐ λύεις μίαν καὶ τὴν
ἐλαχίστην τοῦ Χριστοῦ ἐντολήν. Ἀλλὰ τί βραδύνομεν καὶ
τί ἔτι τὴν καθ᾽ ἡμῶν ἀναβάλλῃ ψῆφον; Πάντα σά, οἱ θρό-
νοι, αἱ ἐξουσίαι [cf. 1 Col 1:16], οἱ ὑπηρέται, αἱ ἀκοαί, αὐτὸ
τοῦτο τὸ βούλεσθαι. Χρῶ τοῖς σοῖς! Ἕτοιμοι τοῦ παθεῖν
ἡμεῖς πάντα, ὅσα σου τῷ φθόνῳ προκατεσκεύασται!" Ὡς
δὲ ταῦτα μὲν ὁ ἅγιος ἔλεγεν, ἐκεῖνος δὲ τῷ φθόνῳ ἐπρίετο
καὶ οὐκ εἶχεν ὅ τι καὶ πράξοι ἔτι τὴν σύνοδον ἀναβαλλο-
μένην ὁρῶν καὶ εὐλαβουμένην τὸ Εὐαγγέλιον καὶ τὸν
τοῦτο καθαρῶς ἐν γνώσει δίκαιον ἱερουργοῦντα, ὃ τέως
ἴσχυσε χωρεῖ κατὰ τῆς εἰκόνος καὶ τὸν πατριάρχην ἀναπεί-
θει καὶ τοὺς ἀρχιερεῖς τῆς ἁγίας συνόδου ξέσαι κἂν τὴν

within us His own). Do this also in order that I may partake in that same glory which you enjoyed while still living in the flesh, as when you were shown to me standing at the right hand of God, and which glory you now enjoy more clearly with all the saints."

Chapter 91

When Symeon had prayed in this way, he turned around and looked almost cheerfully at his accuser. "Congratulations, my good master and *synkellos,*" he said, "on all your hard work and exertion in the cause of righteousness. In doing so, you've forsaken everything else to take care of your own conscience and have zealously upheld the apostolic canons and regulations, without breaking even the least single commandment of Christ. But why are we waiting? Why are you still putting off the verdict against me? Everything belongs to you: *thrones, authorities,*[96] servants, people who listen to you, whatever you want. Use what is yours! I'm ready to suffer whatever you've prepared in your envy!" When the saint said this, the *synkellos* was consumed by his envy but did not know what to do, for he saw the synod still delaying out of respect for the Gospel and that righteous man who ministered it so purely and knowledgeably. But at this point the *synkellos* did what he could to attack the image and convinced the patriarch and clergy of the holy synod to scrape

ἐπιγραφὴν τῆς ἁγίας εἰκόνος τὴν ἔχουσαν· "ὁ ἅγιος." Ὁ καὶ πεποιηκότες λῆξιν μικρὰν παρέχουσιν αὐτοῦ τῷ θυμῷ, καὶ οὕτως πάλιν λύεται τὸ κριτήριον ἀντιδοθείσης τῆς εἰκόνος τῷ Συμεώνῃ.

92

Τί οὖν; Σεσιώπηκε τοῦ λοιποῦ ὁ τὴν βασκανίαν ἐφάπαξ δεξάμενος; Οὐδαμῶς. Τὰ κέντρα γὰρ τῆς ἀληθινῆς σοφίας τοῦ Συμεὼν κατακεντοῦντα τὴν καρδίαν αὐτοῦ οὐκ ἐδίδου ὅλως αὐτῷ ἠρεμεῖν. Ὅθεν καὶ τὸν πατριάρχην—ὢ πῶς ἐκτραγῳδήσω τὸ τηνικαῦτα γεγονὸς ἄτοπον ἐν τῇ πόλει; —ταῖς κατὰ τῶν ἁγίων τούτων συκοφαντίαις ἀναταράξας—φεῦ τῆς κακίας, ἐς ὅσα καὶ κατὰ ποίων πραγμάτων χωρεῖ!—ἐξαποστεῖλαι ὡς οὐκ ὤφελε πείθει καὶ καθελεῖν πάσας τὰς ἁγίας εἰκόνας τοῦ μεγάλου πατρὸς ἐκείνου, ἔνθα καὶ ὅπου ἱστορημέναι ἐγράφησαν. Ὄντως γὰρ ἅπτεται καὶ τῶν ἀρίστων ὁ μῶμος.

2   Πῶς οὖν οὐκ ἐμνήσθη ὁ ἐπὶ σοφίᾳ βεβοημένος ἐκεῖνος ἀνὴρ τοῦ θείου πατρὸς Ἰωάννου τοῦ Δαμασκηνοῦ οὕτω περὶ τῶν ἁγίων ἀποφαινομένου εἰκόνων καὶ λέγοντος· γινωσκέτω οὖν πᾶς ἄνθρωπος, ὡς ὁ τὴν εἰκόνα τὴν πρὸς δόξαν καὶ ὑπόμνησιν τοῦ Χριστοῦ ἢ τῆς τούτου μητρὸς Θεοτόκου ἤ τινος τῶν ἁγίων καὶ πρὸς αἰσχύνην τοῦ Διαβόλου καὶ τῆς ἥττης αὐτοῦ καὶ τῶν δαιμόνων αὐτοῦ ἐκ θείου πόθου καὶ

off at least the inscription on the holy image which contained the word "saint." By doing so they placated his anger a little, and thus once again the tribunal was adjourned and the icon returned to Symeon.

Chapter 92

What then? Did the *synkellos* who was once and for all consumed with jealousy now keep quiet? Certainly not. For the goads of Symeon's true wisdom that were piercing his heart gave him no respite at all. And so he stirred up the patriarch—how can I tell the sorry tale of the outrage that then occurred in the city?—with his slander against these holy men—alas for evil, that goes to such lengths in such matters!—and persuaded him, as he ought not to have done, to send men out to destroy all the holy images of Symeon's eminent father, wherever they had been painted. For truly *blame attaches even to the best of men.*[97]

But how then did the *synkellos,* who was so renowned for   2 his wisdom, not recall the words of our divine father John of Damascus concerning the holy images? For he said: *Everybody should understand this. A person who tries to destroy an image that has been created with divine affection and fervor and that has as its purpose the glory and remembrance of Christ or His mother the Theotokos or any of the saints, as well as the shaming of the Devil and the defeat of him and his demons, and who does not*

ζήλου γενομένην καταλύειν ἐπιχειρῶν καὶ μὴ προσκυνῶν καὶ τιμῶν καὶ ἀσπαζόμενος ὡς εἰκόνα τιμίαν καὶ οὐχ ὡς Θεόν,[188] ἐχθρός ἐστι τοῦ Χριστοῦ καὶ τῆς ἁγίας Θεοτόκου καὶ τῶν ἁγίων καὶ ἐκδικητὴς τοῦ[189] Διαβόλου καὶ τῶν δαιμόνων αὐτοῦ, ἔργῳ ἐπιδεικνύμενος τὴν λύπην ὅτι ὁ Θεὸς καὶ οἱ ἅγιοι αὐτοῦ τιμῶνται καὶ δοξάζονται· ἡ γὰρ εἰκὼν θρίαμβός ἐστι καὶ φανέρωσις καὶ στηλογραφία εἰς μνήμην μὲν τῶν ἀριστευσάντων καὶ διαπρεψάντων, εἰς αἰσχύνην δὲ τῶν ἡττηθέντων καὶ καταβληθέντων ὑπὸ τοῦ Πονηροῦ.

93

Τί τοίνυν γίνεται; Εὐθὺς οἱ τὸ δεινὸν τοῦτο τολμήσαντες ἀποστέλλονται καὶ τὰς μὲν τῶν τοῦ ὁσίου ἀνδρὸς εἰκόνων—ὦ πῶς ἀδακρυτὶ τὸ τολμηθὲν τότε τοῖς ἀκούουσι διηγήσομαι; Ἀξίνῃ καθεῖλον φονώσῃ χειρί, ποτὲ μὲν κατὰ τῆς κεφαλῆς τὴν εἰκόνα παίοντες ἀσχέτῳ θυμῷ, ποτὲ δὲ κατὰ τῶν στέρνων, ἄλλοτε κατὰ τῆς γαστρός, ἐνίοτε δὲ κατὰ τῶν μηρῶν, καὶ οὐ πρότερον τοῦ παίειν ὑφῆκαν, ἕως οὗ εἰς κόνιν ταύτας ἐλέπτυναν· τὰς δὲ ἀσβόλῃ καὶ τιτάνῳ προσεπιχρίσαντες ἐξηφάνισαν, ὀλοφυρομένων περιπαθῶς τῶν ὁρώντων μοναχῶν τε καὶ λαϊκῶν τὰ πραττόμενα παρὰ Χριστιανῶν ἐν μέσῳ τῆς τῶν πιστῶν ἐκκλησίας, ἃ πάλαι

*venerate and honor and kiss this image (but only as a venerable im-
age and not as God), that person is an enemy of Christ and of the
holy Theotokos and of the saints, and is a champion of the Devil
and his demons, because he demonstrates by his action his distress
that God and His saints are being honored and glorified. For the
image is a triumph and manifestation and monument to the memory of those who are bravest and most eminent, just as it is to the
shame of those defeated and struck down* by the Evil One.[98]

Chapter 93

What happened next? Men audacious enough to per-
form such a terrible deed were dispatched—oh, how can I
refrain from tears as I tell my listeners what they dared do
then? For they destroyed some images of the blessed man
with an ax in their murderous hands, now striking the head
of the image in their uncontrollable anger, now the chest,
now again the stomach and the thighs, and they did not stop
until they had reduced them to dust. Others they obliter-
ated by smearing them with soot and lime plaster, while the
monks and laypeople lamented with great emotion as they
watched what was being done by Christians in the midst of
the church of the faithful (this was also what happened in

παρὰ τοῦ Κοπρωνύμου ἐπὶ καταστροφῇ τῶν θείων ἐκκλησιῶν γεγόνασι, καὶ τοὺς δραματουργοὺς τῶν τοιούτων μὴ
δυναμένων ἀμύνασθαι διὰ τὴν ὁμωνυμίαν τῆς πίστεως.

2   Καὶ τὰ μὲν τῆς σκηνῆς ὡς ἔν τισι τῶν ἐκκλησιῶν καὶ
ἱερῶν καταπετασμάτων καλλωπισμοῦ ἕνεκα γράφεται, πα-
λαῖστραί φημι καὶ κυνηγέσια καὶ ὀρχῆστραι, κυνῶν τε[190]
γένη καὶ πιθήκων καὶ ἑρπετῶν θηρίων τε καὶ πετεινῶν
ἀγέλαι καὶ ἵππων, τέρψις ἐλογίσθη καὶ κόσμος αὐτοῖς·
ἀνθρώπου δὲ μορφαὶ καὶ εἰκόνες, οὗ τὴν *μορφὴν* ὁ Πλα-
στουργὸς πεφιληκὼς ἐμορφώθη [cf. Phlp 2:7] καὶ μεθ᾽ ἧς
γράφεται ἄνθρωπος τέλειος καὶ Θεὸς τέλειος ἐν μιᾷ γνω-
ριζόμενος ὑποστάσει, ὡς εἴδωλον καθῃρέθη ἐκ μέσου τῆς
ἐκκλησίας, καὶ οὐδεὶς ἐγένετο λόγος τοῦ σκανδάλου τούτοις ἢ τῶν σκανδαλισθέντων ἀνθρώπων.

3   Ὡς ἀπόλοιτο ἡ κακία καὶ ὁ ταύτης αἴτιος φθόνος δι᾽ οὗ
πάντων ἁγίων αἱ μυριάδες ἔργον θανάτου βιαίου γεγόνασι. Οὕτω φθονηθεὶς ὁ χρυσοῦς τὴν γλῶτταν Ἰωάννης
τῷ Αἰγυπτίῳ Θεοφίλῳ ἔργον τοῦ φθόνου αὐτοῦ ὁ[191] οὐράνιος ἄνθρωπος γέγονεν· οὕτω καὶ τῷ σοφῷ Στεφάνῳ τῆς
Ἀλεξίνης ὁ ἐμὸς Συμεὼν τὸ *σκεῦος τῆς ἐκλογῆς* [Act 9:15],
τὸ πολύφωνον ὄργανον τοῦ Πνεύματος, φθονηθεὶς τὰ ἴσα
δεινὰ τῷ ῥηθέντι ἁγίῳ παρ᾽ ἐκείνου ὑπέμεινε.

the old days with the destruction of the holy churches by Kopronymos),[99] but could not defend them against the perpetrators of these deeds because they also identified themselves as faithful Christians.

These people consider the theatrical images that are portrayed as decoration in some churches and on sacred curtains to be a delight and an ornament—by these I mean images of wrestling bouts, hunts, and dances, and various kinds of dogs and monkeys and creatures that crawl and fly, and herds of horses. But as for human forms and images, the human *form* which the Creator assumed out of love and with which He is portrayed as perfect man and perfect God recognizable in one person, that form was torn out of the church as though it were an idol, and these people gave no thought to the scandal <of their actions> or to those who were scandalized.

I pray that evil, and the envy that causes it, may be destroyed, for it is because of this envy that all those thousands of saints have suffered a violent death. Thus even that heavenly man the golden-tongued John [Chrysostom] became a victim of envy when he was envied by the Egyptian Theophilos.[100] Thus also my Symeon, the *chosen vessel,* the resounding instrument of the Spirit,[101] endured a terrible fate equal to that of the previously mentioned saint [Chrysostom] because he was envied by the wise Stephen of Alexina.

94

Ἀλλὰ γὰρ ἐπειδὴ τὴν φλόγα τοῦ φθόνου ἔτι πλέον ὑποτυφομένην ἑώρα ὁ τὰ θεῖα πολὺς Συμεών, καὶ ὅτι οὐκ ἠρεμήσει, ἐὰν μὴ[192] κακοποιήσῃ ὁ τοῖς λόγοις δυνατὸς καὶ ἀντιπαραταττόμενος αὐτῷ τε καὶ τῇ ἀληθείᾳ, δεῖν ἔγνω ὑπὲρ ὧν ἐγκαλεῖται ἐγγράφως ἀπολογήσασθαι. Ἔνθεν τοι καὶ τὸν πρῶτον ἀπόλογον σχεδιάσας αὐτοῦ ἐν καιρῷ παλινδικίας φρονίμως ἐταμιεύσατο, ὅλον ἑαυτὸν ὑπὲρ τοῦ καλοῦ ἑτοιμάσας εἰς θάνατον. Βραχὺς ὁ ἐν μέσῳ καιρός, καὶ πάλιν ὁ ἐμὸς Συμεὼν ἄγεται ἀπὸ τοῦ ἀσκητηρίου ἐπὶ τὸ κριτήριον. Ἡ τῶν λόγων μάχη αὖθις συγκροτεῖται παραπλησία. Ἡ πάλη τῶν ἀμφοτέρων ταῖς προλαβούσαις ὁμοία· ἢ παύσασθαι πάντη τῶν τοῦ πατρὸς ἐγκωμίων καὶ τῶν φαιδρῶν πανηγύρεων ἢ ἐκ μέσου γενέσθαι μὴ μόνον τῆς παρ' αὐτοῦ κτισθείσης μονῆς, ἀλλὰ καὶ πάσης τῆς μεγάλης ταύτης[193] καὶ περιφανοῦς πόλεως. Εἶχεν οὖν οὕτω τὰ τῆς ὑποθέσεως καὶ ὁ ἀπόλογος δίδοται παρὰ τοῦ ἁγίου τῷ πατριάρχῃ. Ὡς δὲ μέσον τῆς ἁγίας συνόδου ἐφ' ἱκανὰς τὰς ὥρας ἀνεγινώσκετο, καὶ τῇ δυνάμει τῶν νοημάτων, εὐμεγέθει τοῦ λόγου, αὐτῇ τε τῇ τῶν χρήσεων εὐαρμοστίᾳ σὺν ἀκμῇ καὶ σφοδρότητι ἐν ἀξιωματικῇ τοῦ λόγου ἰδέᾳ καὶ τῇ λαμπρότητι τῆς ἀληθείας[194] τῶν ἀκρωμένων κατεβρόντησε τὴν διάνοιαν, οὐκ ἔχοντες ἐκεῖνοι ὅπως παραλογισμοῖς τὴν τοῦ λόγου πυκνότητα παραλύσωσιν, ἀνέστησάν τε τῶν θρόνων ἀφασίᾳ πεδηθέντες τὰς γλώττας καὶ ἐρήμην τῷ δικαίῳ καταψηφίζονται καὶ ἐξορίαν καταδικάζουσι.

Chapter 94

Since, however, the most godly Symeon saw the flame of envy smoldering still more intensely and knew that his persuasive opponent would not keep quiet until he could harm him and the truth, he realized that he had to defend himself with regard to the accusations against him. He thus hurriedly drafted his first response and prudently kept it in reserve for the occasion of a new trial, while being quite prepared for death in the cause of good. Not long afterward my Symeon was again taken from his monastery to the tribunal. The same battle of words was joined once more, and both sides engaged in a struggle similar to the previous one. Either Symeon was to desist completely from his eulogies of his father [Symeon Eulabes] and his festal celebrations, or be removed, not only from the monastery that he had founded, but also from this great and famous city altogether. This was the proposal when the saint delivered his response to the patriarch. His defense was read aloud for quite some time in the midst of the holy synod, and by the force of its ideas, the grandeur of its statement, the aptness of its examples, the great vehemence yet dignity in the form of its actual wording, and the brilliance of its truth, it thundered in the minds of those who heard it. Since they were unable to undermine the force of Symeon's statement with fallacious arguments, they rose from their seats, tongue-tied in their speechlessness and, passing sentence on the just man by default, condemned him to banishment.

95

Τοιοῦτον, ὦ φίλοι, τὸ τοῦ σοφοῦ συγκέλλου καὶ μονα-χοῦ καὶ ἱερέως σοφὸν ἀποτέλεσμα, καὶ ἐς τοσοῦτον ἀνέβη ὕψος λαμπρότατον ἡ βεβοημένη γνῶσις αὐτοῦ μετὰ τῆς εἰς τὸν πλησίον ἀγάπης! Οἴμοι ὅτι ὡμοιώθημεν λαῷ οἱ τῆς ἱερᾶς τάξεως *μὴ ἔχοντι γνῶσιν* [cf. Hos 4:6] κατὰ τὸν εἰρη-κότα, καὶ ἐδόθη ἡμῖν *μήτρα δυστυχῶς ἀτεκνοῦσα καὶ μα-στοὶ ξηροί* [cf. Hos 9:14].

2   Ἐπεὶ δὲ τὴν Προποντίδα τῆς πρὸς ἡμᾶς Χρυσοπόλεως διαπεράσαντες τὸν μακάριον ἐπί τι πολίχνιον οἱ ἀπάγον-τες αὐτὸν προσώκειλαν τὸ πλοιάριον, ὃ Παλουκιτῶν ὀνο-μάζεται, ἄσκευον πάντη χειμῶνος ὥρᾳ, καὶ ἐν ἐρήμῳ τόπῳ, ἐν ᾧ καὶ τοῦ κατακρίτου δελφῖνος ἵσταται κίων, τὸν ἅγιον ἔστησαν μονώτατον αὐτὸν καταλείψαντες καὶ μηδὲ τῆς ἐφημέρου *τροφῆς* [cf. Ja 2:15] οἱ ἀσυμπαθεῖς ἀξιώσαν-τες. Ὁ οὖν μακαριώτατος Συμεὼν ὡς τὴν τοῦ συγκέλλου μανίαν εἶδε νικήσασαν καὶ τὸν φθόνον αὐτοῦ τὸν βεβου-λευμένον διαπεράναντα,[195] ηὐχαρίστει[196] μὴ σκυθρωπάσας τῷ κατ' αὐτὸν οὕτω γενέσθαι συγκεχωρηκότι Θεῷ. Τοι-γαροῦν καὶ ἐπὶ τοῦ τραχυτάτου βουνοῦ ἐκείνου ἀναστρε-φόμενος εὐθύμῳ πως ἔψαλλε τῇ ψυχῇ λέγων· *φωνῇ μου*

7. *Symeon's Exile and the Struggle to Clear His Name*

Chapter 95

This, my friends, was what that wise *synkellos,* that monk and priest, accomplished in his wisdom, this the most glorious height to which his acclaimed knowledge ascended, along with his love for his neighbor! Alas that we of priestly rank *have become like a people without knowledge,* as it has been said, and we have unfortunately been given *a childless womb with dry breasts.*

Those who were transporting the blessed Symeon crossed   2
the Bosporus between Constantinople and Chrysopolis and beached the boat at a small settlement called Paloukiton.[102] There were no amenities there in the winter, and those cruel men stopped in a deserted spot, where a column of the condemned dolphin stands,[103] and left the saint there, completely alone. They were not even sufficiently considerate to give him *enough food for the day.* But when the most blessed Symeon saw that the *synkellos*'s madness had triumphed and his envy of him had achieved what the latter wanted, he gave thanks, without recrimination, to God, who had allowed this to happen to him. So while he was wandering about on that rugged mountain, he chanted with a cheerful soul the words of the psalm, *I cried with my voice to the Lord, with my*

πρὸς Κύριον ἐκέκραξα, φωνῇ μου πρὸς Κύριον ἐδεήθην·
ἐκχεῶ[197] ἐνώπιον αὐτοῦ τὴν δέησίν μου· τὴν θλῖψίν μου ἐνώπιον αὐτοῦ ἀπαγγελῶ· ἐν ὁδῷ ταύτῃ ᾗ ἐπορευόμην, ἔκρυψαν
παγίδα μοι· κατενόουν εἰς τὰ δεξιὰ καὶ ἐπέβλεπον[198] καὶ οὐκ
ἦν ὁ ἐπιγινώσκων με [cf. Ps 141(142):1–4]. Καὶ πάλιν· Ἰδοὺ
ὁ Θεός μου, Σωτήρ μου Κύριος καὶ πεποιθὼς ἔσομαι ἐπ'
αὐτῷ καὶ σωθήσομαι ὑπ' αὐτοῦ καὶ οὐ φοβηθήσομαι, διότι
ἡ δόξα μου καὶ ἡ αἴνεσίς μου Κύριος καὶ ἐγένετό μοι Σωτήρ
[Is 12:2].

96

Κατελθὼν τοίνυν εἰς τὴν τοῦ βουνοῦ ὑπώρειαν καὶ
εὐκτήριον ἐκεῖσε τῆς ἁγίας ἐπονομαζόμενον Μαρίνης
ἐρείπιον εὑρών, εἰσῆλθεν ἐν αὐτῷ καὶ τὰς τῆς ἐνάτης ὥρας
εὐχὰς ἀπέδωκε τῷ Θεῷ. Εἶτα μικρᾶς μετασχὼν ἀναπαύσεως δεξιοῦται τὸν φίλον σύγκελλον οἷα δὴ Χριστοῦ μαθητὴς τοῖσδε τοῖς γράμμασι.

2 "Τῷ πανιέρῳ καὶ ἁγίῳ δεσπότῃ μου τῷ ἐνδοξοτάτῳ
συγκέλλῳ, ὁ διὰ σοῦ ἐξόριστος καὶ δεδιωγμένος Συμεὼν
ὁ σός. Ἰδού, πανίερε δέσποτα, τῶν κατὰ Θεόν σου ἀγώνων
καὶ λόγων τὰ σπέρματα οἷα πεποιήκασι τὰ γεώργια, οἵαν
μοι δόξαν καὶ χαρὰν προεξένησαν, ὅσων μοι στεφάνων γε-
γόνασιν αἴτια, ὅσης με τῆς εὐφροσύνης ἐνέπλησαν![199] Εἰς
ὕψος τε πνευματικῆς ἀνήγαγον γνώσεως καὶ ἐπὶ πέτραν

voice I made supplication to the Lord. I pour out my complaint before Him. I tell my trouble before Him. In the path where I was walking they hid a trap for me. I looked to my right hand and I saw no one who recognized me. And again, *Behold, God is my Savior and my* Lord. *I will be confident in Him* and I will be saved by Him *and I will not be afraid, for the Lord is my glory and my praise, and He has become my* Savior.

Chapter 96

Symeon went down to the foot of the mountain and there found a ruined chapel dedicated to Saint Marina.[104] Going inside, he offered to God the prayers of the ninth hour.[105] Then, when he had taken a little rest, like a true disciple of Christ, he greeted his friend the *synkellos* with this letter:

"To my holy master, the most reverend and illustrious *synkellos,* from your Symeon who is in exile and being persecuted because of you. Behold, most reverend master, what grain the fields of your efforts and your words on God's behalf have yielded! See what glory and joy they have granted me, what crowns they have caused me to win, with what happiness they have filled me! For they have led me up to the summit of spiritual knowledge and have planted *the feet* 2

τοὺς πόδας μου [Ps 39(40):2] τοῦ νοὸς καλῶς προσερείσαντο καὶ αὐτήν με τὴν πέτραν ἐνδύσασθαι παρεσκεύασαν [cf. 1 Cor 10:4; Gal 3:27], ἐξ ἧς ἔχω τὸ ὕδωρ τὸ ζῶν [cf. John 4:10–14; Ex 17:6] ἐνυποστάτως βλύζον ἐν ἐμοί, κινούμενον καὶ λαλοῦν καὶ γράφειν μὲν πρὸς σὲ προτρεπόμενον, πάσης δὲ²⁰⁰ θυμηδίας ἐμπιπλῶν, καὶ μὴ ἐῶν ὅλως με τῶν θανατηφόρων πειρασμῶν ἐπαισθάνεσθαι, ἀλλ᾽ ὡς τοὺς τρεῖς παῖδας ἀφλέκτους ἐν τῇ καμίνῳ ἐφύλαξεν [Dn 3:12–27], οὕτω κἀμὲ ὡς ἐν σκηνῇ αὐτοῦ κρύπτον [cf. Ps 26(27):5], ἄλυπον διατηρεῖ καὶ ἀπήμαντον. Ὑπὲρ ὧν καὶ εὐχαριστῶ σοι, εὐχαριστεῖν τε καὶ ὑπερεύχεσθαι²⁰¹ οὐδέποτε παύσομαι. Λοιπὸν εἴ τινα καὶ ἕτερα ἔχεις εἰς προσθήκην εὐφροσύνης καὶ δόξης τῶν ἀγαπώντων σε, μὴ ἀποκνήσῃς ποιήσασθαι, ὅπως ὁ μισθός σοι πολλαπλασιασθῇ καὶ ἡ ἀντάμειψις παρὰ Θεοῦ τοῦ ταῦτα νομοθετήσαντος δαψιλεστέρα σοι γένηται. Ἔρρωσο."

97

Ταύτην δεξάμενος τὴν ἐπιστολὴν ὁ μεγάλα ἐπὶ σοφίᾳ φυσῶν [cf. 1 Cor 8:1] σύγκελλος καὶ τὸ ὕφος²⁰² αὐτῆς ἀναγνοὺς καὶ τὰ πλείω μὴ ἐπιγνούς, βάλλεται πλέον τοῖς κέντροις τοῦ λόγου ἢ ὡς ἐδόκει τοῖς κακοῖς τὸν ἅγιον ἔβαλλε, καὶ ἀντιπνέει λόγοις μὲν οὐδαμῶς, οὐ γὰρ οἷός τε ἦν, τοῖς δὲ πράγμασι. Αὐτίκα γοῦν καὶ μακρόθεν ὄντα

of my intellect firmly *on the rock,* and have even caused me to be clothed in this rock [Christ] itself, from which I have *the living water* actually gushing forth in me, moving and speaking and encouraging me to write to you. This fills me with every delight and renders me completely unaware of the deadly trials <around me>. Like the three boys whom it kept from being burned in the furnace, it has thus also *hidden me in its shelter* and preserves me free from grief and misery. For this I thank you and will never cease from thanking you and praying for you. So if you can do anything else to increase the happiness and glory of those who love you, please do not hesitate to do it, so that your reward may be multiplied and your recompense from God, who has set out the laws concerning these things, may be more abundant. Farewell."

Chapter 97

When the *synkellos,* who was so very conceited in his wisdom, received this letter, he read the actual text but did not understand its deeper significance. As he did so he was struck more sharply by Symeon's pointed words than he himself, it seems, had struck the saint with all his evil deeds. Unable to respond in any way with words, he turned to actions instead. Immediately, even though Symeon was far

τοξεύειν ἐπιχειρεῖ τὸν ἀήττητον οὐχ ὡς σοφὸς λογικαῖς τισιν ἀντιθέσεσιν, οὐδὲ γὰρ εἶχε τὸν λόγον ἐλεύθερον ἅτε μὴ ὑπὸ ἀγάπης κινούμενος, ἀλλ' ὡς τὰ πάντα δεινὸς καὶ τὴν πονηρίαν πολὺς καταλαλιαῖς δολίαις καί τισιν ἐπιβούλοις καὶ ἀνελευθέροις τεχνάσμασι.

2 Τοίνυν καὶ τῷ πατριάρχῃ ὡς εἶχεν εὐθὺς κατὰ τοῦ Συμεὼν ἐντυχὼν καὶ ἐπιψιθυρίσας αὐτῷ εἰς τὸ οὖς καὶ ταῖς διαβολαῖς τοὺς ἄνθρακας τοῦ θυμοῦ δυνατῶς ἐμφυσήσας, ἀνάπτει πάλιν αὐτοὺς καὶ φλόγα μεγίστην ἐγείρει αὖθις τῷ Συμεὼν πειρασμῶν. Ὡς γὰρ τὸ φιλότιμον ἀκριβῶς ᾔδει τοῦ γενναίου ἐν ταῖς τοῦ πατρὸς ἑορταῖς καὶ τὴν εἰς τοὺς πένητας ἀφθονωτάτην τῶν χρημάτων διάδοσιν, ὑπονοεῖ καθ' ἑαυτὸν ὁ κατὰ τὸν Μίδαν ἐκεῖνον τὰ πάντα βλέπων χρυσὸν χρυσοῦ θησαυροὺς κατορωρυγμένους ἔχειν τὸν ἄνδρα ὑφ' ἣν τοὺς ἀσκητικοὺς ἀγῶνας καὶ[203] ἱδρῶτας κατεβάλλετο κέλλαν· καὶ αὖθις πείθει τὸν πατριάρχην ἐξαποστεῖλαι καὶ τοὺς θησαυροὺς ἀνερευνῆσαι τοὺς μηνυθέντας αὐτῷ τοῦ ἁγίου. Οὐ μόνον δέ, ἀλλὰ σὺν αὐτοῖς καὶ τὴν ἅπασαν δημεῦσαι τὴν ἐνοῦσαν αὐτῷ εὐπορίαν, βίβλων λέγω καὶ χρειῶν ἄλλων καὶ σκεπασμάτων τοῦ σώματος.

98

Ὁρᾶτε οἷα ὁ φθόνος καὶ τὸ κατὰ τοῦ πλησίον μῖσος ἐργάζεται; Τυφλώττει γὰρ ἀληθῶς καὶ τὰ μὴ ὄντα ὡς ὄντα

away, he tried to target that invincible man, not using rational counterarguments as a truly wise man would (for his reason was not free because he was not acting out of love), but rather employing the crafty slanders and treacherous and mean tricks of an extremely wicked person who was capable of anything.

As soon as he could, the *synkellos* thus met with the patriarch concerning Symeon. He whispered maliciously in his ear and fanned the coals of his anger with his false accusations until he ignited them again and stirred up a fresh firestorm of troubles for Symeon. Precisely because he had witnessed the noble Symeon's munificent celebration of his spiritual father's feast days and his extremely generous distribution of money to the poor, he imagined (since he himself, like Midas, saw gold everywhere) that Symeon had stacks of gold buried under the cell in which he used to shed[106] the sweat of his ascetic labors. He thus persuaded the patriarch to send out his men again to search for the saint's treasure, which he had told him about, and to seize as well, along with the gold, all Symeon's possessions—I mean his books and other necessities and even his clothing.

Chapter 98

D o you see what envy and hatred of one's neighbor does? For it is truly blind and imagines that things which do not

φαντάζεται καὶ καθ᾽ ὧν οὐκ ἔστιν ὑπόστασις ὡς ἐνυποστά-
τοις αὐτοῖς χρῆται καὶ διαμάχεται. Διερευνᾶται οὖν ἡ τοῦ
μακαρίου κέλλα, ἡ τὸν θησαυρὸν ἐσχηκυῖά ποτε τῶν χαρισμάτων τοῦ Πνεύματος ἔνοικον, περὶ θησαυρῶν χρυσί-
ων κατορυχθέντων τοῦ τὰ πάντα βδελυξαμένου καὶ ῥίψαν-
τος καὶ μηδὲν πλὴν τοῦ τριχίνου καὶ τῆς ἀμπεχόνης τῶν
σκεπασμάτων κτησαμένου τοῦ σώματος, ᾧ καὶ τὸ ἐφόλκι-
ον εἰς βάρος ἦν τῆς σαρκὸς καὶ αὐτὸ ἐκτεταριχευμένον
ὑπὸ τῆς ἄγαν ἀσκήσεως. Διερευνᾶται δὲ σκαφείοις τισὶ καὶ
μηχανήμασιν ἀνασκαλευομένου τοῦ ἐδάφους, διορυττο-
μένων τῶν τοίχων, ἀνακαλυπτομένης τῆς στέγης καὶ αὐτοῦ τοῦ χοὸς εἰς ἀέρα λικμιζομένου. Ὡς δὲ πολλὰ δι᾽ ὅλης
ἡμέρας ἡ ἄψυχος ἀπαιτουμένη κέλλα καὶ ἴσην²⁰⁴ τῷ οἰκο-
δεσπότῃ αὐτῆς ὑποστᾶσα τὴν τιμωρίαν, οὐδὲν ὧν ἀπῃτεῖτο
καὶ ὧν ἐπόθουν οἱ ἐρευνῶντες τυχεῖν καταστιχθεῖσα ἀπέδωκε, δημεύεται τὰς ἀποκειμένας ἐν αὐτῇ βίβλους καὶ
τὴν μικρὰν ἐκείνου παραμυθίαν τοῦ σώματος, ὅση περὶ
τὸν χιτῶνα καὶ τὰ σκεπάσματα ἦν τοῦ ἀνδρὸς διὰ τὴν
ἐνοῦσαν ἀσθένειαν.

2 Μαθὼν οὖν δέχεται μετὰ χαρᾶς οἷα δὴ ἀποστολικὸς
τὴν διάνοιαν ὁ Συμεὼν καὶ τὴν ἁρπαγὴν τῶν ὑπαρχόντων
αὐτοῦ, μεγάλα τῶν κατασοφισαμένων αὐτοῦ καταγνοὺς
καὶ τῆς εὐηθείας καταγελάσας αὐτῶν, ὅτι δὴ καὶ χρυσοῦ
θησαυροὺς ἐνόμισαν εὑρεῖν παρ᾽ ᾧ²⁰⁵ ἡ κατὰ Χριστὸν πενία πλοῦτος ἦν διὰ βίου παντὸς καὶ ἡ ἔνδεια τράπεζα
πολυτελὴς καὶ τῶν ἁβροδιαιτοτέρων ἀφθονωτέρα.

actually exist do exist, and treats things that are unreal as though they were real and fights with them. So the blessed Symeon's cell, which once had the treasure of the graces of the Spirit dwelling in it, was searched for the buried stacks of gold <supposedly belonging> to this man who loathed all material possessions and threw them away and owned nothing except for the hair shirt and the mantle[107] that he had to cover his body (which was itself so withered by his great asceticism that even the appendage of his flesh was a burden to it). So his cell was searched with shovels and various implements. The floor was excavated, holes were dug in the walls, the roof was opened up, and even the soil itself was winnowed in the open air. The inanimate cell was thoroughly examined all day long and underwent a punishment equal to that of its owner. But despite being badly scarred, it yielded none of those things for which it had been examined and that its searchers were eager to find. But the books that were kept in it were seized, along with what little comfort Symeon had for his body, namely the tunic and clothing which he needed in his frailty.

When Symeon learned of this he accepted even the sei- 2 zure of his belongings with joy, as someone who indeed thought like one of the apostles, but he had enormous contempt for those who falsely accused him, and he laughed at their foolishness for having actually thought they would find stacks of gold in the possession of a man for whom the poverty of Christ had been wealth during his whole life, and for whom deprivation had been a well-set table, more sumptuous even than that of those who live a life of luxury.

99

Ἀλλ' ὁ μὲν ἔδρα οἶα δὴ σοφὸς τὴν κακίαν ἐκεῖνα δι' ὧν ἐδόκει δριμύτερον²⁰⁶ τοῦ ἁγίου καθάπτεσθαι· ὁ δὲ αὖθις ἐπέστελλε καὶ πλέον ἐκεῖνος ἢ οὗτος τὰς πληγὰς κατὰ καρδίας ἐδέχετο, καί φησιν ἐπιστείλας αὐτῷ·

2 "Καλούς μοι στεφάνους ὁ καλὸς Στέφανος καὶ δεσπότης μου ἐπὶ τοῖς ἐμοῖς στεφάνοις πάλιν προσέθετο. Ἀλλὰ τί σοι ἀνταποδώσομεν ὑπὲρ ὧν ἡμᾶς τοὺς ταπεινοὺς ἀγαθῇ κινούμενος διαθέσει πεποίηκας καὶ ποιεῖς καὶ οἶδ' ὅτι πάλιν ποιήσεις, εὐεργετῶν καθ' ἑκάστην ἡμᾶς ἐπὶ χρόνοις²⁰⁷ ἤδη ἑπτά; Τί οὖν σοι ἀπολογησόμεθα τῷ περὶ τὰ τοιαῦτα σπουδαίῳ καὶ φιλοτιμώτερον εἰδότι δεξιοῦσθαι τοῖς γλυκέσι σου φαρμάκοις τοὺς φίλους; Ἀλλὰ δεόμεθά σου μὴ στῆς τῆς προθέσεως, μὴ καταπαύσῃς ἀπὸ τῶν ἔργων σου, πρόσθες εἰ δοκεῖ τούτοις τὰ ἔτι γλυκυτέρους τῇ ἐπιτάσει ποιοῦντα τοὺς πόνους μοι. Ηὔξησάς μοι τὸ φῶς, τὴν χαράν, τὴν ἡδύτητα, ἃ καὶ βλύζει παραδόξως ἐν ἐμοὶ διὰ τῆς εἰρήνης τῶν λογισμῶν τὴν ἄρρητον εὐφροσύνην τοῦ Πνεύματος, ἃ καὶ αὐξήσαις ἔτι πάντως καὶ ἔτι ποιῶν τὰ οἰκεῖα καὶ τῷ φιλουμένῳ τάχιον ἑνώσαις ἡμᾶς Θεῷ, ὑπὲρ οὗ φέρω πάντα προθύμως καὶ δι' ὃν ὡς²⁰⁸ ὁρᾷς τὴν ἄλυσιν ταύτην παρὰ σοῦ τῆς ἐξορίας περίκειμαι. Ἔρρωσο. Τῷ πανιέρῳ καὶ ἁγίῳ δεσπότῃ μου ὁ διὰ σοῦ ἐξόριστος καὶ τῶν προσόντων γυμνὸς γεγονὼς Συμεὼν ὁ σός."

Chapter 99

T hus, as someone who was well versed in evil, the *synkellos* did what he imagined would hurt the saint most keenly. But Symeon again sent him a message, and as a result, it was the <*synkellos*> who received more severe blows to the heart than the <holy one>. This was his message to him:

"My good master Stephen[108] has once again added more 2 noble crowns to the crowns of victory that I already have. How can I repay you for all that you, in your goodness, have done for me, your humble servant, and for all that you continue to do, and that I know that you will do again? For you have been my benefactor every day for seven years already. How can I make amends to you when you are so zealous in these matters and know how to endow your friends so munificently with your sweet remedies?[109] But, I beg you, do not halt your plans, do not give up your work! Add to them, if you will, things that, by their intensity, will make my sufferings even sweeter. For you have increased for me the light, the joy, the sweetness, everything that gushes forth in me in such a marvelous way in the peace of my thoughts through the ineffable gladness of the Spirit. Please go on increasing these by all means, and, continuing to do what you do, unite me more swiftly with my beloved God, on whose behalf I willingly bear everything and because of whom, as you see, I am enveloped by you in the chains of exile. Farewell. To my most reverend and holy master, your Symeon, who, because of you, is an exile, stripped of all his possessions."

100

Ἐπεὶ δὲ τὸ εἰρημένον εὐκτήριον καὶ ὁ τόπος ἐν ᾧ ἵστατο ἑνὸς ἦν τῶν ἐν τέλει ἀνδρῶν Χριστοφόρου ἐκείνου ᾧ
Φαγούρα ἦν τὸ²⁰⁹ ἐπώνυμον, κατάδηλος γίνεται καὶ αὐτῷ
μαθητῇ ὄντι ἡ ἐξορία τοῦ ἁγίου καὶ ἡ πρὸς τὸ εὐκτήριον
αὐτοῦ κατασκήνωσις. Ἐξαυτῆς οὖν τὴν Προποντίδα ὁ
ἀνὴρ διαπλεύσας καὶ ἕως τοῦ τόπου γενόμενος, ὡς εἶδε
τὸν μακάριον μεθ' ἑνὸς μαθητοῦ ἐκεῖσε καθήμενον, μηδὲν
τῶν εἰς παραμυθίαν τοῦ σώματος ἔχοντα, δακρύων πλη-
ρωθεὶς πίπτει πρηνὴς ἐπὶ τοὺς ὡραίους πόδας [Rom 10:15;
cf. Is 52:7] ἐκείνου καὶ περιπαθῶς τὴν τοῦ διδασκάλου
συμφορὰν ἀνακλαίεται.

2   Ἐπειδὴ δὲ καὶ τὴν αἰτίαν μεμαθήκει τῆς ἐξορίας αὐτοῦ,
πολλὰ καταγνοὺς τῶν περὶ τὸν διώκτην,²¹⁰ ὡς δεδιωγμέ-
νον αὐτὸν καὶ πᾶν πονηρὸν ῥῆμα ἀκηκοότα ἕνεκεν τῆς
ἐντολῆς τοῦ Θεοῦ [cf. Mt 5:11] ἐμακάριζε. Ἐδυσώπησε δὲ
λόγοις τὸν ἅγιον τὰ κατὰ χρείαν τοῦ σώματος κομίζεσθαι
ὑπ' αὐτοῦ καὶ μὴ ἐνδεῶς ἔχειν τῶν ἀναγκαίων. Ὁ δὲ ἅγιος·
"Τί δὲ δεῖ," φησί, "καὶ πλέον ἡμῖν, ὦ τέκνον, τῆς ἐφημέρου
τροφῆς [cf. Ja 2:15], ἣν ἄρτος καὶ ἅλας²¹¹ μετὰ ὕδατος ἀφθο-
νωτέραν ἡμῖν ἀπεργάζονται τῶν πολυτελῶν τοῖς ἐδέ-
σμασιν; ἀλλ' εἴ τί σοι μᾶλλον διὰ φροντίδος ἐστὶν ἡμᾶς
τοὺς γεγεννηκότας σε διὰ Πνεύματος θεραπεῦσαι, ἐπιδώ-
σεις μᾶλλον ἡμῖν τοῖς ἀστέγοις τοῦτο δὴ τὸ εὐκτήριον
κατὰ δωρεὰν καὶ εἴ που Θεὸς ἐπὶ τὴν θλῖψιν ἡμῶν ἐπίδοι,
καὶ ἐπιβλέπων ἐπιβλέψειε καὶ παραμυθίας τινὸς ἀξιώσειε

Chapter 100

The aforementioned chapel and the land on which it stood belonged to a highly placed man called Christopher, who had the surname Phagouras. Since he was also a disciple of Symeon, the saint's exile and the fact that he was camping out at the chapel became known to him. He immediately sailed across the Bosporus, and when he reached the place and saw the blessed one sitting there with a single disciple and with no physical comforts at all, his eyes filled with tears and he prostrated himself at Symeon's *beautiful feet,* emotionally bewailing his teacher's misfortune.

When Christopher learned the cause of his exile, he bitterly condemned the actions of Symeon's persecutor, while blessing Symeon himself for being persecuted and being forced to hear *all kinds of evil uttered* about him for following God's commandment. He begged the saint to let him provide for his physical needs so that he would not lack the necessities. But the saint replied, "What more do I need, my child, than *enough food for the day* with which bread and salt and water supply me more abundantly than luxurious foods? But if you are concerned and want to look after me, your spiritual father who has begotten you through the Spirit, you may instead grant this chapel to me as a gift because I am homeless. And if ever God should look at my tribulation, and, seeing it, may see fit to consider me worthy of

τοὺς δεδιωγμένους ἡμᾶς χάριν τῆς αὐτοῦ ἐντολῆς, μονὴν μοναστῶν καὶ οἶκον σωζομένων αὐτὸ ἀποκαταστήσομεν, καὶ σοὶ μὲν ἔσται εἰς μισθὸν τὸ πρᾶγμα καὶ καταλλαγὴν πρὸς Θεόν, ἡμῖν δὲ εἰς προσευχῆς ἐργαστήριον καὶ ἐργασίαν τῶν ἐντολῶν τοῦ Χριστοῦ." Ἤκουσεν ὁ ἀνὴρ καὶ ἐπὶ τῷ ῥήματι κατὰ πολὺ εὐφρανθεὶς δωρεῖται τὸ εὐκτήριον τῷ ἁγίῳ καὶ ἀφιεροῖ ἐξαυτῆς αὐτὸ τῷ Θεῷ.

IOI

Ἀλλὰ περὶ μὲν τῆς οἰκοδομῆς τοῦ μοναστηρίου ὁ λόγος ἀναμεινάτω, ἐχέσθω δὲ τῆς διηγήσεως ἔτι τῶν τοῦ πατρὸς παθημάτων καὶ διηγείσθω πάντα ὡς πέπρακται. Ἐπεὶ οὖν ἡ φήμη τοῦ ἀνδρὸς εἰς ὅσους ἔφθανεν, ὡς ἀστραπή τις αὐτοὺς περιήστραπτε,²¹² καὶ πολλοὺς ἔπειθε φοιτᾶν πρὸς αὐτόν, εἶχε δὲ ἄλλους μὲν ἄλλη, ἑτέρους δὲ ἑτέρα ὑπόληψις περὶ τῆς ὑπερορίας αὐτοῦ, δεῖν ἔγνω πρόνοιαν καὶ τῶν σκανδαλιζομένων [cf. Mt 13:21; Mk 4:17; Lk 8:13] ποιήσασθαι ὡς ἀποστολικὸς τὴν διάνοιαν. Διὸ καὶ τοῖς προσφοιτῶσιν ἐκδιηγούμενος τὰ ὑπὸ τῶν κατηγόρων αὐτοῦ εἰς αὐτὸν πεπραγμένα, οὓς μὲν εἰς δάκρυα συμπαθείας ἐκίνει ὁρῶντας τὸ γῆρας αὐτοῦ καὶ τὴν γύμνωσιν, οἱ δὲ ὅσοις ἦν γνῶσις θεία καὶ λόγος ἐλεύθερος ἐμακάριζον αὐτὸν λέγοντες· "Μακάριος εἶ, πάτερ, ὅτι διωγμὸν ὑπέμεινας καὶ ὀνειδισμοὺς [cf. Mt 5:10–11] διὰ δικαιοσύνην κατὰ

some consolation because I am being persecuted for following His commandments, I will restore it as a monastery for monks and a home for those seeking salvation. For you this will be a transaction that is both rewarding and brings reconciliation with God, while for me it will provide a workshop for prayer and for carrying out the commandments of Christ." Christopher was very happy when he heard this and immediately presented the chapel to the saint and dedicated it to God.

Chapter 101

An account of the monastery's construction will have to wait, however, because I want my narrative to stay on the subject of the father's sufferings and tell everything as it happened. Because Symeon's reputation dazzled everyone who heard about it like a flash of lightning,[110] it convinced many people to go and visit him. But since some people had one theory about his banishment and others another, he realized (having a truly apostolic mind) that he had to take some thought for those who were being caused to have doubts about him. He thus explained to his visitors what his accusers had done to him. He moved some of them to tears of sympathy when they saw his advanced age and <the extent of> his privation, but those who possessed divine knowledge and were able to speak freely blessed him, saying, "You are blessed, father, because you have endured persecution and reproach for the sake of righteousness, accord-

τὸν οὕτω κεκραγότα ἀπόστολον· εἰ ὀνειδίζεσθε ἐν ὀνόματι
Χριστοῦ, μακάριοι ὅτι τὸ τῆς δόξης καὶ δυνάμεως καὶ τὸ τοῦ
Θεοῦ Πνεῦμα ἐφ' ὑμᾶς ἀναπέπαυται. Μὴ γάρ τις ὑμῶν πασχέτω ὡς φονεύς, ἢ[213] κλέπτης ἢ κακοποιός· εἰ δὲ ὡς Χριστιανός,
μὴ αἰσχυνέσθω, δοξαζέτω δὲ τὸν Θεὸν ἐν τῷ ὀνόματι τούτῳ,
ὅτι καιρὸς τοῦ ἄρξασθαι τὸ κρῖμα ἀπὸ τοῦ οἴκου τοῦ Θεοῦ [1
Pt 4:14–16]." Ταῦτα λέγοντες ὑπέστρεφον πεπληροφορη-
μένοι εἰς τὸν ἠκριβωμένον βίον καὶ λόγον αὐτοῦ.

102

Ἀλλὰ γὰρ ἵνα μὴ μόνον τοῖς προσφοιτῶσι, τοῖς μακρὰν
δὲ μᾶλλον οὖσιν αὐτοῦ τοῖς νῦν τε καὶ τοῖς μετέπειτα
ἐρχομένοις ἀνθρώποις ἑαυτὸν ἀποδείξῃ ἀθῷον πάσης
κατακρίσεως καὶ τὴν αἰτίαν πᾶσαν ἀπογυμνώσῃ τῆς ὑπερορίας αὐτοῦ, ἐκτίθεται τὸν καθ' ἑαυτοῦ[214] λίβελλον καὶ
τῷ πατριάρχῃ ἐπιστέλλει Σεργίῳ ἐν ἁπλαῖς λέξεσιν ἀφελείας καὶ ἐν τούτοις τήν τε πίστιν αὐτοῦ καὶ τὴν παρρησίαν δημοσιεύει τρανῶς. Ταῦτα οὖν γεγραφὼς ἀποστέλλει
Γενεσίῳ τῷ πατρικίῳ καὶ τοῖς λοιποῖς ἄρχουσιν, οἷς ἦν
εὐσεβείας διδάσκαλος, τοῦ προσκομίσαι τῷ πατριάρχῃ καὶ
τοῖς ἀρχιερεῦσι τῆς ἐκκλησίας. Τοίνυν καὶ ἀνελθόντες οἱ
περίβλεπτοι τῶν ἀρχόντων πρῶτα μὲν ὑπαντῶσι καὶ λόγοις συμπλέκονται[215] τῷ πατριάρχῃ περὶ τῆς τοῦ ἁγίου
ὑπερορίας καὶ δέους πληροῦσιν αὐτοῦ τὴν ψυχὴν τὸ παρά-
νομον ἐξελέγχοντες, εἶτα τὸν λίβελλον καὶ τὴν ἐπιστολὴν

ing to the apostle who has proclaimed: *If you are reproached for the name of Christ, you are blessed, because then that glorious and powerful Spirit, which is the Spirit of God, is resting upon you. If you suffer, let it not be for murder, or theft or wrongdoing. But if anyone does so as a Christian, let him not be ashamed, but let him glorify God under that name. For the time has come for judgment to begin with the household of God.*" When they had said this they returned, fully assured of the correctness of Symeon's life and thought.

Chapter 102

To demonstrate his complete innocence of every charge and to reveal the full reason for his banishment, not only to his visitors but also to people who were far away both at the time and in the future, Symeon put together a brief written apologia concerning himself and wrote a letter to the patriarch Sergios in plain and simple terms, making quite clear in these documents both his faith and his willingness to speak his mind. When he had written them, he sent them to the patrician Genesios[111] and to those other members of the ruling elite whose spiritual teacher he was, so that they would bring them to the attention of the patriarch and the senior clergy of the church. The most eminent among these elite and powerful men first went up and met with the patriarch. They exchanged words with him about the saint's banishment, and in doing so they thoroughly frightened him by proving its illegality. They then handed him Symeon's apolo-

αὐτῷ ἐγχειρίζουσιν. Ὁ δὲ πρὸς τοὺς παραγενομένους πολλοὺς ὄντας καὶ περιφανεῖς ἀπιδὼν καὶ τὸ περίβλεπτον αὐτῶν αἰδεσθείς, δείσας μὴ καὶ μέχρι βασιλέως τὰ τοῦ δράματος ἔλθη καὶ εἰς μεγάλην αὐτοῦ κατάγνωσιν ἀποβῇ, κελεύει ἐπὶ συνόδου ταῦτα ἀναγνωσθῆναι. Ὡς δὲ ἀνεγινώσκοντο καὶ οἱ μητροπολῖται προσεχῶς ἤκουον, πολλοὶ μὲν ἐκ τούτων τοῦ δραματουργοῦ κατεστέναζον τῶν τοιούτων²¹⁶ συγκέλλου, πολλοὶ δὲ καὶ ὑπερελάλουν τοῦ φρονήματος τοῦ ἁγίου καὶ τῆς καθαρᾶς πολιτείας αὐτοῦ.

103

Ἀλλὰ τῶν γραφέντων τελείωσε²¹⁷ τῆς ἀναγνώσεως, φησὶν ὁ πατριάρχης τοῖς ἄρχουσι καὶ μαθηταῖς τοῦ ἁγίου· "Ἐγὼ μέν, ἐνδοξότατοι, οὐδεμίαν ἔλαβον πώποτε πονηρὰν ὑπόληψιν κατὰ τοῦ κυροῦ Συμεών, ἀλλὰ καὶ ἀναγνοὺς καταρχὰς τὰ εἰς τὸν πατέρα τούτου ὑπ᾽ αὐτοῦ γεγραμμένα, ἥσθην ἐπ᾽ αὐτοῖς τὸν ἐκείνου βίον εἰδώς, καὶ ψάλλειν ἐπέτρεψα ἐπ᾽ ἐκκλησίας αὐτὰ ὑπερεπαινέσας τὴν πίστιν αὐτοῦ. Ἀλλ᾽ οὐκ οἶδ᾽ ὅθεν καὶ τίς γέγονεν ἀναμεταξὺ ἐκείνου καὶ τοῦ συγκέλλου διαφορά, καὶ μυρίας κατ᾽ αὐτοῦ καὶ τοῦ πατρὸς αὐτοῦ τὰς κατηγορίας ἐξήγειρεν οὐδὲν πλέον ἐχούσας ἢ μόνον διαβολάς. Ἃ δὲ πέπονθε παρ᾽ ἡμῶν, οὐχ ὡς παρασφαλεὶς ἐν τοῖς τῆς ἐκκλησίας δόγμασι, δι᾽ ὧν ἡ ὀρθὴ καὶ ἀμώμητος πίστις ὠχύρωται, πέπονθεν,

gia and letter. When the patriarch saw how many distinguished people had come, he was intimidated by their eminence, and was afraid that news of the affair would reach the emperor and result in his own serious condemnation. So he gave orders for Symeon's statements to be read to the synod. The metropolitans listened attentively as these were read out. Many lamented the role of the *synkellos* in engineering such an affair, and many also spoke up for the saint's views and his pure way of life.

Chapter 103

When he had finished the reading of Symeon's writings, the patriarch spoke to the saint's powerful <supporters> and disciples. "Most illustrious gentlemen," he said, "I have never had any doubts about Kyr Symeon. Right from the start when I read what he had written about his spiritual father, I approved of it because I was familiar with Symeon Eulabes's life. I thus permitted them to sing Symeon's hymns in church and I praised his faith <in his spiritual father> very highly. But I do not know why or for what reason the disagreement occurred between him and the *synkellos* that has stirred up all these thousands of accusations against him and his spiritual father, accusations that are nothing but slander. Whatever he has suffered on my orders he has not suffered because he erred in the dogmas of the church, by which the correct and spotless faith is made strong. Rather, I removed

ἀλλ' ἐπειδὴ ἐκεῖνος μὲν τοῦ ἰδίου ἀμεταθέτως εἶχε σκοποῦ, καὶ τιμῶν τὸν πατέρα τοῦ λαμπρῶς ἑορτάζειν οὐκ ἐπαύετο, οἱ κατήγοροι δὲ αὐτοῦ ἐταράσσοντο καὶ δι' ὄχλου καθ' ἑκάστην ἡμῖν ἐγίνοντο, διὰ τοῦτο τῆς μονῆς αὐτοῦ καὶ τῆς πόλεως αὐτὸν παρεκίνησα. Νῦν δέ, εἰ βούλεται καὶ τοῖς ἐμοῖς εἴξει λόγοις, κύριος αὖθις καὶ τῆς ἰδίας μονῆς γενήσεται, καὶ ἀρχιερέα τοῦτον ἐν μιᾷ τῶν ὑψηλῶν μητροπόλεων συνευδοκούσης πάσης τῆς ἱερᾶς συνόδου χειροτονήσω, καὶ τὰ κακῶς ἐκβεβηκότα διορθώσεως τεύξονται τῆς προσηκούσης, καὶ ὑμῶν²¹⁸ ἡ εἰς αὐτὸν πίστις ἄσβεστος διαφυλαχθήσεται."

104

Εἶπε καὶ ἀποστείλας εἰσάγει τὸν ἅγιον ἀπὸ τῆς ἐξορίας. Λαληθείσης τοίνυν τῆς εἰσόδου πανταχοῦ τοῦ ἁγίου, ἐπισυνάγονται πάντες ὡς εἰς μεγάλην ἑορτὴν λαϊκοί τε καὶ μοναχοί, ἱερεῖς καὶ λευῖται, καὶ ὅσοι περὶ τὴν σύγκλητον ἄνδρες περιφανεῖς, οἷς ἦν γνωστὸς ὁ μακάριος ἐκ τῆς ἀρετῆς, καὶ ὧν διδάσκαλος καὶ πατὴρ ἐχρημάτιζε, καὶ συνανέρχονται αὐτῷ πρὸς τὸν πατριάρχην.

2 Ὡς δὲ δήλη γέγονεν ἡ τοῦ πατρὸς ἄνοδος, ἐξέρχεται ὁ πατριάρχης ἐν τῷ μικρῷ σεκρέτῳ καὶ ὑπαντᾶται μετὰ τῶν ἐν τέλει τούτῳ ὁ ἅγιος. Ὁ δέ· "Τί σοί," φησίν, "ἔδοξεν, εὐλαβέστατε κῦρι Συμεών, ἑαυτὸν μὲν εἰς ταραχὰς ἐμβαλεῖν, ἡμᾶς δὲ ἐκταράξαι, τοὺς δὲ φιλοῦντάς σε τούτους

238

him from his monastery and from the city because he held unwaveringly to his own personal objective and would not stop holding such extravagant celebrations in honor of his spiritual father, even though his accusers were agitating over this and causing trouble for me every day. But now, if he is willing to heed my words, he may become master of his own monastery again and I will consecrate him bishop in one of the great metropolitan cities, if the entire holy synod agrees. That way, proper amends will be made for what has turned out so badly and your unshakeable faith in him will be preserved intact."

Chapter 104

When he had said this, the patriarch sent out for the saint and brought him back from his exile. The saint's return had been discussed everywhere, and so everyone, monks and laymen, priests and deacons, and all those eminent senators who knew that blessed man's virtue and whose teacher and spiritual father he was, gathered as though for a great feast, and accompanied him to the patriarch.

When the father's arrival was announced, the patriarch 2 came out into the small council chamber[112] and the saint met with him there, along with his dignitaries. "What were you thinking of, most pious Kyr Symeon," he said, "getting yourself involved in all this uproar, disturbing me, distressing

μαθητὰς λυπῆσαι, καὶ τοιαῦτα παθεῖν, ἃ τυχὸν ἔδει κατα-
κρίτῳ ἐπενεχθῆναί τινι, μή τί γε τοιούτῳ τὴν γνῶσιν καὶ
τὴν ἀρετὴν οἷος σύ; Ἐγὼ γάρ, μάρτυς ἡ ἔφορος²¹⁹ Δίκη,
μεγάλην καὶ ἀγαθὴν εἶχον τὴν ὑπόληψιν περὶ σοῦ, καὶ
ἄλλα τινὰ ἔστρεφον καθ᾽ ἑαυτὸν ὑπὲρ σοῦ, ἃ καὶ εἰς πέρας
ἄξω εἴ γε τοῖς ἐμοῖς λόγοις πειθαρχήσεις καὶ τῆς πολλῆς
ἐνδώσεις ἐνστάσεως. Ἀλλὰ θέλησον τέως κἂν ἐν τούτῳ
ἡμῶν ἐπακοῦσαι, καὶ πάλιν πρὸς τὴν μάνδραν σου, ἐν ᾗ
πόνους κατεβάλου πολλούς, ἐπίστρεψον, καὶ περὶ τοῦ ἑορτάζειν τὰ τῆς τοῦ πατρός σου μεταστάσεως οὐδὲ ἡμεῖς
εἴργομεν· πλὴν τοῦτο παραινοῦμεν ὑφεῖναι μικρὸν τῆς
φαιδρότητος καὶ τῶν πολυημέρων σου πανηγύρεων, καὶ
μετὰ μόνων τῶν ὑπὸ σὲ μοναχῶν καὶ τῶν ἄλλοθεν κατὰ
φιλίαν²²⁰ ἐρχομένων ἑορτάζειν, μέχρις ἂν οἱ φθόνῳ κατὰ
σοῦ κινούμενοι ἢ παύσωνται ἢ ἐκ τοῦ βίου καὶ τῆς παρούσης ζωῆς γένωνται, καὶ τηνικαῦτα ἔσῃ ποιῶν ὡς ἀρεστὸν
σοί τε δοκεῖ καὶ Θεῷ."

105

Ὁ δὲ ἅγιος ὑπολαβὼν ἔφη· "Περὶ μὲν τῆς ταραχῆς καὶ
τοῦ σκανδάλου ὧν εἴρηκας, ὁ ἐμὸς δεσπότης,²²¹ οὐκ ἐγὼ
αἴτιος ἀλλ᾽ ὁ συνετὸς σύγκελλος καὶ κατενώπιον αὐτοῦ ἐπι-
στήμων [cf. Is 5:21], ᾧ καὶ δωρεὰν ἐφθονήθην ἐγὼ [cf. Ps
68 (69):4] δι᾽ οὐδὲν ἕτερον ἢ διὰ περιττὰς καὶ ματαίας

your friends and disciples here, and suffering a fate appropriate perhaps for a condemned criminal but not a knowledgeable and virtuous person like yourself? Now I, and <all->seeing Justice is my witness, have always had a strong and favorable opinion of you and I've been considering other opportunities for you, which I'll bring to pass if you're convinced[113] by my words and give up your stubborn resistance. But for the time being, please agree to obey me in this at least: return to your monastic fold, where you have expended so much effort, and I will not prevent you from celebrating the anniversary of your spiritual father's death. But I do ask that you scale back a little on the splendor and the number of days of festivities, and celebrate only with your own monks and those who come from elsewhere as friends, until those who are inspired by envy against you either desist or depart from life and this present existence. Then you will be able to do whatever may please you and God."

Chapter 105

The saint replied, "I am not responsible for the uproar and the scandal of which you have spoken, my master," he said, "but rather your clever *synkellos* who is *wise in his own opinion*. I have been envied by him without cause over nothing but ridiculous and frivolous issues. He has taken plea-

ζητήσεις, αἷς ἐκείνῳ φίλον ἐμματαιάζειν καὶ μεθ' ὧν ἐπ-
απορεῖν δοκεῖ καὶ πειράζειν τὴν τῶν ἄλλων γνῶσιν καὶ
σύνεσιν, ἵνα μηδεὶς ἐκείνου τὸ πλέον ἔχειν δοκῇ, ἀλλ' ἵνα
πάντες ἡττῶνται τῆς ἐκείνου σοφίας καὶ γνώσεως. Ὃς καὶ
τὸ κρῖμα τῆς ταραχῆς ταύτης βαστάσει δικαίως καθά φησιν ὁ ἀπόστολος οὕτω λέγων·[222] ὁ ταράσσων ὑμᾶς ἐκεῖνος
βαστάσει καὶ[223] τὸ κρῖμα, ὅστις ἂν ᾖ [Gal 5:10].

2   "Περὶ δὲ ὧν ἔπαθον καὶ ὑπέστην, ἴσως δὲ καὶ ὑποστή-
σομαι, χάριν ὁμολογῶ τῷ Θεῷ μου καὶ σοὶ τῷ[224] δεσπότῃ
μου, ὅτι οὐχ ὡς μοιχὸς ἢ κακοποιός, ἀλλ' ὡς δοῦλος Χριστοῦ καὶ τῶν ἀποστολικῶν κανόνων καὶ διατάξεων ἀντ-
εχόμενος ἔπαθον καὶ ἔτι πείσομαι τάχα, καθά με Πέτρος ὁ
κορυφαῖος τῶν ἀποστόλων διδάσκει οὕτω λέγων· μὴ γάρ
τις ὑμῶν πασχέτω ὡς φονεὺς ἢ ὡς κλέπτης ἢ ὡς κακοποιός,
εἰ δὲ ὡς Χριστιανὸς μὴ αἰσχυνέσθω [cf. 1 Pt 4:15–16]. Διὸ οὐ
μόνον οὐκ αἰσχύνομαι ἐφ' οἷς ὑφίσταμαι διὰ τὴν κελεύου-
σαν ἐντολὴν τοῦ Θεοῦ μὴ ἀθετεῖν τοὺς πατέρας ἡμῶν [cf.
Ex 20.12; Dt 5:16; Mt 15:4; Mk 10:19; Eph 6:2], ἀλλὰ χαίρω
καὶ μακάριον ἥγημαι ἐμαυτόν, ὅτι καὶ αὐτὸς ὁ ταπεινὸς
ἐγὼ κατηξιώθην ὑπὲρ μιᾶς ἐντολῆς τοῦ Θεοῦ μου λόγους
εἰσπραχθῆναι καὶ ὑπὲρ δικαιοσύνης κατακριθῆναι καὶ
ὑπερορίαν ὑποστῆναι κατὰ τοὺς παλαιοὺς πατέρας ἡμῶν.

sure in gossiping idly about these matters, intending to raise doubts and using them to try the knowledge and intelligence of others. <He has done this> so that no one else might seem to have more <knowledge and intelligence> than him, and to prove everyone else inferior to his wisdom and knowledge. And so it is he who should rightly bear judgment for this uproar, as the apostle states when he says, The person *who is troubling you will bear his judgment, whoever he may be.*

"As for what I have suffered and endured, and perhaps 2 will endure again, I offer thanks to my God and to you my master that I have suffered, and will possibly still suffer in the future, not as an adulterer or a wrongdoer, but as a servant of Christ and an upholder of the apostolic canons and constitutions, just as Peter, the chief of the apostles, teaches when he says, *If any of you suffer, let it not be for murder, or theft or wrongdoing. But if anyone does so as a Christian, let him not be ashamed.* For this reason, I am not only unashamed of what I am enduring on account of God's commandment that orders us not to dishonor our fathers, but I rejoice and consider myself blessed that I too, wretch though I am, have been considered worthy to be called to account for one of God's commandments, to have been condemned for my righteousness, and to have endured exile like our fathers of old.[114]

106

"Περὶ δὲ τῆς εἰς ἐμέ σου παλαιᾶς διαθέσεως καὶ αὐτὸς ἐγὼ μάρτυς, οὐ μόνον δέ, ἀλλὰ καὶ αὐτὴ ἡ μέσον πολιτευομένη ἡμῶν Ἀλήθεια, ὅτι καὶ τετίμηκας ἡμᾶς παρὰ τὴν ἀξίαν πολλάκις, καὶ διὰ τιμῆς εἶχες ἀεὶ τὰ ἡμέτερα, καὶ τὴν πρὸς τὸν πατέρα πίστιν ἡμῶν ἐκθειάζων ὑπερεπήνεις, θαυμάζων τὰ τελούμενα παρ' ἡμῶν, καὶ ὁμολογῶν²²⁵ τὰ τῆς σῆς, δέσποτά μου, πρὸς ἡμᾶς διαθέσεως. Ἀλλ' ὁ τοῦ Σατανᾶ φθόνος, οὐκ οἶδ' ὅπως εἰπεῖν, ὡς οὐκ ὤφελεν ἔστρεψέ σου τὰ σπλάγχνα καὶ τὸ γλυκὺ πικρὸν ἀπειργάσατο καὶ τὸ φῶς ἔθετο σκότος [cf. Is 5:20] οὐ μόνον ἡμῖν, ἀλλὰ καὶ ἐφ' ὅσην ἦλθε τὴν γῆν τὰ δραματουργηθέντα καθ' ἡμῶν τοῖς ἀκούσασιν.

2   "Ὅτι δὲ καὶ ἄλλα τινὰ ὡς ἔφης ἐλογίζου ὑπὲρ ἡμῶν, καὶ καθ' ἑαυτὸν²²⁶ ἔστρεφες, καὶ ἔτι ἐννοῇ καὶ πληρώσειν αὐτὰ ὑπισχνῇ, εἰ πειθαρχήσομεν τοῖς ὑπὸ σοῦ λεγομένοις, εἰ μὲν περὶ τῶν προσκαίρων εἰσὶν ἀγαθῶν καὶ τῆς παρούσης τῶν ἀνθρώπων δόξης τε καὶ τιμῆς, λόγος τούτων οὐδείς μοι τῷ δούλῳ σου τοῦτο πεφιλοσοφηκότι πάλαι, τὸ τὴν μὲν ἀτιμίαν τῶν ἀνθρώπων ὡς πρόξενον οὐρανίου δόξης ἡγεῖσθαι, τὴν δὲ δόξαν αὐτῶν ὡς ὕβριν καὶ λοιδορίαν ὑφίστασθαι· εἰ δὲ περί τινων θεοφιλῶν καὶ τῶν εἰς ψυχὴν φερόντων τὸ κέρδος, ἕξεις με πάντως τοῖς σοῖς προστάγμασι προθύμως ὑποτατόμενον. Καὶ τίς γὰρ οὐκ ἐπαινέσει τοῦτο, ὁπηνίκα ἃ Χριστὸς καὶ οἱ τούτου μαθηταὶ εἶπον καὶ ἐνετείλαντο διδάσκεις τηρεῖν ὁ δεσπότης μου,

Chapter 106

"As regards your earlier attitude toward me, I myself am a witness (and not only I but also the Truth that governs in our midst) that you, my master, have honored me more than I deserve on many occasions, have always respected what I do, and, out of reverence, have praised my faith in my father very highly, admiring what I have accomplished and admitting your favorable attitude toward me. But Satan's envy (I don't really know how else to say this) unfortunately altered your feelings, making *the sweet* appear *bitter* and turning *the light to darkness,* not only for me <here> but also for all those who heard the stories fabricated about me wherever they spread on earth.

"<On another matter,> you said that you were consid- 2 ering and thinking about other opportunities for me, and that you still have these in mind and promise to bring them about if I'm convinced by your words. If these opportunities involve things that are of only transient value and ephemeral human glory and honor, then they are of no account to me, your servant; for I have long since adopted the view that I should consider that which is without honor among men as a source of heavenly glory, but should take their glory as a rebuke and a reproach. If, however, these opportunities involve things that are dear to God and bring benefit to the soul, you will definitely find me eager to obey your orders. For who would not agree to do so whenever, my master, you instruct people to observe the teachings and commandments of Christ and His disciples, in accordance with what

LIFE OF SAINT SYMEON

κατὰ τὸν εἰρηκότα Υἱὸν τοῦ Θεοῦ, διδάσκοντες αὐτοὺς τηρεῖν πάντα ὅσα ἐνετειλάμην ὑμῖν [Mt 28:20];

3   "Θέλησον οὖν κατὰ τὸ θεῖον λόγιον διδάσκειν τοῖς προ-
λαβοῦσιν ἁγίοις πατράσιν ἑπόμενος, καὶ ὡς ὁμότροπόν σε
τῶν ἀποστόλων δεξόμεθα, καὶ γῆ καὶ σπόδος [Gen 18:27;
Sir 10:9, 17:32] ὑπὸ τοὺς ἁγίους σου πόδας γενοίμεθα, καὶ
τὸ πατεῖσθαι ὑπὸ σοῦ, καθὰ προέγραψα, ἁγιασμὸν ἡγησό-
μεθα· οὐ μόνον δέ, ἀλλὰ καὶ τὰς ἐντολάς σου μέχρι θανάτου φυλάξομεν, καὶ σὺ ὑπεραγαπήσεις²²⁷ ἡμᾶς ὡς δούλους
καὶ εὐγνώμονας μαθητὰς τοῦ Χριστοῦ καὶ ὡς καλῶς λέγοντας ὑπερεπαινέσεις ἡμᾶς.

107

"Εἰ δὲ μὴ διδάσκειν οὕτως ἐθέλεις, ἵνα καὶ τοῖς σοῖς ὡς
εἴρηται πειθαρχῶμεν προστάγμασιν, ἀλλὰ μεθ' ὑποσχέ-
σεών τινων, δι' ὧν φανήσομαι τοῖς ἀνθρώποις ἐν βίῳ περί-
δοξος, καὶ σύνεδρος ἔσομαί σοί τε καὶ πᾶσι τοῖς ἀρχιερεῦσι
τῆς ἐκκλησίας, προβιβάζεις²²⁸ ἡμᾶς ἀθετῆσαι τὸν πατέρα
ἡμῶν τὸν ἅγιον, τὸν φωτίσαντα ἡμᾶς καὶ νῦν ὑπὲρ ἡμῶν
πρεσβεύοντα καὶ προϊστάμενον ἡμῶν ἐν ταῖς τοῦ βίου ἀεὶ
περιστάσεσιν ὡς φιλοστοργότατος πατήρ, καὶ διὰ τούτου
προσκροῦσαι σπουδάζεις ἡμᾶς τῷ εἰπόντι Χριστῷ, ὁ ἀθετῶν
ὑμᾶς ἐμὲ ἀθετεῖ [Lk 10:16], οὐδὲν ἕτερον ἀλλ' ἢ μετὰ τῶν
μαθητῶν τοῦ Χριστοῦ καὶ ἡμεῖς εἴπωμεν,²²⁹ πειθαρχεῖν δεῖ

246

the Son of God said, *teaching them to observe all that I have commanded you?*

"So, demonstrate your willingness to teach in accordance 3 with the divine scripture, following the holy fathers who have gone before,[115] and I will accept you as someone equal to the apostles, and will become *dust and ashes* beneath your holy feet, and, just as I have written, will consider it sanctification to be trampled upon by you. Not only that, but I will also keep your commandments until the day I die, and you will love me dearly as a servant and grateful disciple of Christ and will praise me highly for saying what is right.

Chapter 107

"But if you are not willing to teach in such a way that I am convinced by your injunctions, as I've said, but rather are pressuring me to reject my father the saint (who enlightened me and now, as a most loving father, always acts as my intercessor and defender at moments of crisis in my life) with all sorts of promises as a consequence of which I will appear illustrious to people in this life and will sit on the synod with you and all the bishops of the church, and if for this reason you are encouraging me to offend Christ, who says, *He who rejects you rejects me,* then I have nothing more to say except, in common with the disciples of Christ, *We must obey God*

Θεῷ μᾶλλον ἢ ἀνθρώποις [Act 5:29]. Εἰ γὰρ ἀνθρώποις
τοῦτο ποιῶν ἀρέσκειν ἔσπευδον, Χριστοῦ δοῦλος οὐκ ἂν
ἤμην [Gal 1:10].

2   "Ἐγὼ γὰρ ἴσθι ἀπό γε τοῦ παρόντος οὐ προκρίνω τῆς
διὰ δικαιοσύνην Θεοῦ γενομένης μοι ὑπερορίας μοναστήριον ἢ πλοῦτον ἢ δόξαν ἢ ἕτερόν τι τῶν σπουδαζομένων
ἀνθρώποις ἐν βίῳ. Οὐδὲν γάρ με τούτων, ἀλλ᾽ οὐδὲ θάνατος, οὐδὲ ζωὴ χωρίσει ἀπὸ τῆς τοῦ Χριστοῦ μου ἀγάπης [cf.
Rom 8:38–39] καὶ αὐτοῦ τοῦ πνευματικοῦ μου πατρός· ἀφ᾽
οὗ γὰρ τὴν φροντίδα πᾶσαν τῆς ἡγουμενείας τῷ μαθητῇ
μου κατεπίστευσα Ἀρσενίῳ καὶ προΐστασθαι ἀντ᾽ ἐμοῦ κέ-
κρικα τῶν αὐτοῦ ἀδελφῶν, ὅλως ἐγὼ καὶ ὢν ἐκεῖσε τῶν
πραγμάτων καὶ πόνων μου ἔξω γέγονα καὶ ὡς μὴ ὢν ἤμην
ἐν μέσῳ αὐτῶν ἀπρόϊτος καθεζόμενος. Καὶ ἐπειδὴ²³⁰ διὰ
δικαιοσύνην καὶ φυλακὴν ἐντολῆς Θεοῦ ζῶντος ἐξωρί-
σθην ἐκεῖθεν, οὐκέτι ἄλλο ἀνθυποστρέψω ἐκεῖσε ἕως ἐν
ζῶσίν εἰμι, ἀλλὰ συναποθανοῦμαι [cf. 2 Tim 2:11] τῇ ἐντολῇ
τοῦ Χριστοῦ μου μὴ ἀθετήσας αὐτόν [cf. Lk 10:16], καὶ εὖ
οἶδα ὅτι οὐκ ἐκπέσω τῶν αὐτοῦ θεοπνεύστων μακαρισμῶν.
Ἔφη γάρ· μακάριοί ἐστε, ὅταν ὀνειδίσωσιν ὑμᾶς καὶ διώξωσι
καὶ εἴπωσι πᾶν πονηρὸν ῥῆμα καθ᾽ ὑμῶν ψευδόμενοι ἕνεκεν
ἐμοῦ [Mt 5:11]."

rather than men. For if I were eager to please men by doing this, *I should not be a servant of Christ.*

"So, from now on, you should understand that I will not 2
choose a monastery, or wealth, or glory, or anything else that is eagerly sought by people in life, over the exile I have suffered for God's righteousness. For none of these things, *not even death nor life, will separate me from the love of my Christ* and my spiritual father. From the moment I entrusted all the concerns of being the superior to my disciple Arsenios and decided to choose him as leader of his brothers in my place, although I was still there, I separated myself completely from my <former> affairs and labors, and I stayed withdrawn in the midst of them as though I were not really there. But now, since I have been expelled from that place for righteousness and keeping the commandment of the living God, I will never return again as long as I live. I will instead *die with* my Christ at His command, without rejecting Him, and I thus know for sure that I will not be excluded from His divinely inspired blessings. For He said, *Blessed are you when they insult you and persecute you and say falsely all kinds of evil things about you for my sake.*"

108

Τ αῦτα τοίνυν ὁ πατριάρχης παρ' ἐλπίδα πᾶσαν ὡς ἤκουσεν, "Ὄντως," ἔφη, "Στουδίτης εἶ φιλοπάτωρ, κῦρι Συμεών, καὶ τὴν ἐκείνων ἔνστασιν καὶ αὐτὸς φέρεις ἐπαινουμένην τάχα καὶ νομίμως ἔχουσαν." Διὸ καὶ σύντομον
ἀπεφήνατο τὴν αὐτοῦ κρίσιν οὕτως εἰπών· "Ἐγὼ μὲν ἔλε-
γον· τῆς πολλῆς σε περὶ τὸ πρᾶγμα ἐνστάσεως περικόψο-
μαι ποσῶς. Ἐπεὶ δὲ ὁ αὐτὸς εἶ ἔτι καὶ οὐδαμῶς ἠλλοίωσαι,
ἀλλὰ ἀμεταθέτως ἔχεις τῆς πρὸς ἐκεῖνον τὸν πνευματικόν
σου πατέρα τιμῆς τε καὶ πίστεως, τοῦτο μὲν ἐμοί τε καὶ
πᾶσιν ἐπαινετὸν δοκεῖ καὶ νόμιμον. Σὺ δὲ πάντως τοῖς λόγοις τοῖς ἡμετέροις ἐδείχθης[231] μὴ πειθαρχῶν. Τοῦ λοιποῦ
οὖν ἔσο ἔνθα καὶ βούλει, τοῖς σοῖς δηλαδὴ μαθηταῖς συν-
αναστρεφόμενος καὶ τὰ κατὰ βούλησιν ποιῶν καὶ μὴ πρὸς
ἡμῶν κωλυόμενος, εἴτε ἐν τοῖς ἔξω, εἴτε ἐν ταύτῃ τῇ πόλει
πανηγυρίζων εἰ καὶ τοῖς φίλοις συνευφραινόμενος." Οὕτως
εἰπὼν ἀπέλυσεν αὐτοὺς ἐν εἰρήνῃ.

109

Ὁ οὖν μακάριος Συμεών, ὁ καὶ δίχα διωγμοῦ ἐθελού-
σιος μάρτυς ἀναδειχθεὶς ἔν τε τῷ τῆς συνειδήσεως μαρτυ-
ρίῳ καὶ ἐν τῇ ὑπομονῇ τῶν διὰ τὴν ἐντολὴν τοῦ Θεοῦ

Chapter 108

As soon as the patriarch heard this response, which was contrary to all his expectations, he said, "You really are a Stoudite,[116] Kyr Symeon, for you love your spiritual father and also demonstrate the same resistance as them, something that is probably praiseworthy and quite proper." And so he pronounced his judgment on Symeon, briefly as follows. "I said that I would curtail your stubborn resistance in this matter to an extent, but since you are still the same and have not changed at all, but maintain unshakably your honor for, and faith in, that spiritual father of yours, this seems praiseworthy and proper to me and everyone else. You have shown that you are not convinced at all by my words. In future, then, you can stay wherever you want, that is to say, living with your disciples and doing as you will. And I will not prevent you from celebrating <your spiritual father> and rejoicing with your friends whether outside the city or within it." Having said this, he dismissed them in peace.

Chapter 109

The blessed Symeon had thus shown himself to be a willing martyr, even without persecution, both in the martyrdom of his conscience and in his endurance of the trials which befell him on account of God's commandment. He

ἐπελθόντων αὐτῷ πειρασμῶν, τοῖς φίλοις αὐτοῦ τέκνοις
τοῖς δηλωθεῖσιν ἄρχουσι τοῦ πατριαρχείου χαίρων συνεξελ-
θών, μετὰ πάντων ἐκείνων ξενίζεται ἐν τῷ οἴκῳ τοῦ θαυμαστοῦ Χριστοφόρου, ᾧ ἦν ἡ Φαγούρα τὸ ἐπώνυμον,
κἀκεῖσε ἡμέρας πεποιηκὼς οὐκ ὀλίγας, αὐτῷ τε πρῶτον
καὶ τοῖς αὐτοῦ δυσὶν ἀδελφοῖς μεταδοὺς τῆς ὠφελείας
ἀφθόνως, ἔπειτα δὲ καὶ πολλοῖς ἄλλοις τῆς διδασκαλίας
τῶν αὐτοῦ μελιρρύτων λόγων τὴν μέθεξιν δαψιλῆ χαρισά-
μενος, ἱερεῦσι, λευΐταις, ἄρχουσιν, ἰδιώταις, ἀνδράσι τε καὶ
γυναιξί, παισί τε καὶ γέρουσι, καὶ ὅσοις δηλαδὴ ὁ ἀνὴρ
καταφανὴς ἦν καὶ ἐπέραστος, διαπερᾷ πρὸς τὴν φίλην
αὐτοῦ ἐρημίαν ἡσυχίας ἐκεῖσε ποθῶν κατασκευάσαι κελλίον. Ὁ δὲ διδοὺς νεοσσοῖς ἀετῶν νοσσιὰν [cf. Dt 32:11] καὶ
ἄρτον εἰς βρῶσιν ἀνθρώποις Θεὸς ὕει δίκην ὑετοῦ [cf. Is
55:10; 2 Cor 9:10] καὶ τῷ μακαρίῳ τούτῳ τὰ χρήματα, καὶ
ἀνοίγει αὐτῷ τοὺς²³² θησαυροὺς τῶν ἀρχόντων, καὶ πάντες ὁμοῦ χορηγοῦσι συγγενεῖς φίλοι τέκνα χρυσοῦ ποσό-
τητα ἱκανήν, ἣν δεξάμενος ὁ μακάριος ἅπτεται Θεῷ θαρρήσας, ᾧ καὶ ὑπὲρ τούτου προσηύξατο,²³³ τοῦ ἔργου καὶ
τῆς ἀνοικοδομῆς τοῦ μοναστηρίου.

left the patriarchate rejoicing, along with his beloved children, the members of the ruling elite who have been mentioned, and was entertained with all of them in the house of the wondrous Christopher Phagouras. He spent a good many days there, first giving his spiritual assistance liberally to Christopher and his two brothers and then also providing many others with an abundant share of the honeyed words of his teaching: priests, deacons, members of the ruling elite, ordinary people, men and women, children and old people, that is to say, everyone by whom he was known and loved. Afterward he crossed over to the solitude that was so dear to him as he wanted to build a cell there <in which to practice> spiritual tranquillity.[117] And God, who gives a nest to the nestlings of eagles and *bread* to people *for food,* rained down a shower of resources upon the blessed one and opened the treasuries of the ruling elites to him, for everyone together, relatives, friends, and children, provided a great quantity of gold. When the blessed Symeon received this, he placed his trust in God, prayed to Him about the <project>, and so set to work on the construction of the monastery.

IIO

Ἀλλὰ τίς ἱκανὸς τοὺς ἀναφυέντας πάλιν ἐκεῖθεν αὐτῷ πειρασμοὺς ἀπό τε δαιμόνων καὶ τῶν πλησιοχώρων ἐκδιηγήσασθαι; Οἱ μὲν γὰρ ἀφανῶς ὅσαι ὧραι, οἱ δὲ φανερῶς τοὺς ὀδόντας ἔβρυχον [Act 7:54] κατ᾽ αὐτοῦ, λίθοις ἔβαλλον, ὕβρεσιν ἔπλυνον, ἀπειλαῖς καὶ φόβοις ἐξεδειμάτουν αὐτόν· τί οὐκ ἐποίουν πρὸς τὸ ἀναχαιτίσαι αὐτὸν τῆς τοῦ φροντιστηρίου οἰκοδομῆς; Ἀλλ᾽ ὁ τὴν πέτραν ἐνδεδυμένος [cf. Gal 3:27; 1 Cor 10:4] Συμεών, ἐπ᾽ αὐτὴν ἐρηρεισμένας ἔχων ἀεὶ τὰς βάσεις τῆς διανοίας αὐτοῦ [cf. Ps 39(40):2], ταῖς τῶν πειρασμῶν προσβολαῖς τε καὶ ἀντιπνοίαις ἀκατάσειστος καὶ ἀκράδαντος ἔμεινεν. Οἱ μὲν γὰρ πρόσοικοι φθόνῳ βαλλόμενοι ταῖς ἀπειλαῖς φανερῶς διεκώλυον, καὶ ταῖς βολαῖς τῶν λίθων αὐτὸν ἐξεδίωκον, οἱ δὲ πάλαι ἐκπολεμωθέντες αὐτῷ δαίμονες τὰς οἰκοδομὰς κατέσειον αὐτοῦ ἀφανῶς καὶ κόπους αὖθις παρεῖχον αὐτῷ. Καὶ τί[234] πολλὰ λέγω; Θάλασσα κακῶν ἐπὶ ἀγρίοις κύμασιν αὐτῷ καθ᾽ ἑκάστην ἠγείρετο ἡ τῶν πειρασμῶν τρικυμία ἐκ δαιμόνων καὶ ἀνθρώπων ὁμοῦ.

2   Πλὴν ὅμως διὰ πολλῶν πόνων πρὸς αὐτοῦ τελειοῦται,

8. Symeon's Life at Saint Marina
and the Miracles He Performed There

Chapter 110

But who could possibly relate the trials that, once again from that time on, were produced for him by the demons and his neighbors? The former acted invisibly at all hours, the latter visibly, *grinding their teeth* against him, throwing stones, abusing him with insults, scaring him with threats, and giving him frights. Indeed, what did they not do to thwart his construction of the monastery? But Symeon, who was clothed in the rock [Christ] and always had the foundation of his thought firmly based on this, remained unshaken and unmoved by the onslaughts and fierce gales of these trials. His neighbors, motivated by envy, hindered him openly with threats and tried to chase him away by throwing stones, while the demons, who had fought against him in the past, shook his buildings without being seen and caused trouble for him again. But need I say more? A sea of ills, full of tempestuous waves, was raised up against him every day, a veritable tidal wave of trials from demons and men alike.

Nevertheless, as a result of much hard work, he com- 2

ὡς νῦν ὁρᾶται, τὸ βραχύτατον τοῦτο ποίμνιον, παράδεισον ἐν αὐτῷ καὶ ἀμπελῶνα φυτεύσαντος εἰς παραμυθίαν τῶν μελλόντων προσκαρτερεῖν ἐν αὐτῷ μοναχῶν. Ἦν οὖν ὁ Συμεὼν πάλιν συγκροτῶν ἄλλο ποίμνιον καὶ φιλοτιμότερον ἑορτάζων τὴν τοῦ πατρὸς ἑορτὴν ἢ πρότερον· συνήρχετο γὰρ σχεδὸν ἐν τῷ ναῷ τῆς Θεοτόκου τῶν Εὐγενίου, ἔνθα καὶ μετόχιον ἐξωνήσατο, ὁ τῆς μεγάλης τοῦ Θεοῦ ἐκκλησίας κλῆρος, τῷ λαοσυνάκτῃ ἑπόμενος, καὶ πολλοὶ ἔκ τε μοναζόντων καὶ λαϊκῶν, καὶ ἐν ἡμέραις ὅλαις ὀκτὼ τὰ τῆς ἑορτῆς ἐτελεῖτο, καὶ οὐδεὶς ἦν ὁ κωλύων ἢ κατηγορῶν ὡς τὸ πρότερον.

III

Ἀλλὰ γὰρ ἐπεὶ κατέπαυσεν ἀπὸ πάντων τῶν ἔργων αὐτοῦ [cf. Gen 2:2–3], ἅπτεται πάλιν τῆς φίλης ἡσυχίας, ἧς οὐκ ἐχωρίσθη ποτὲ κἂν πολλαῖς ταραχαῖς πραγμάτων ὡμίλησε, καὶ ὅλως τῶν συνήθων θεωριῶν καὶ ἐλλάμψεων ἐν τῷ πνεύματι γίνεται. Ἐντεῦθεν τὴν ὕλην καὶ τὸ πάχος τοῦ σώματος διασχὼν ἐκδημεῖ τούτου, καὶ οὗ μηδαμῶς ἐχωρίσθη Θεοῦ, ἑνοῦται τούτῳ διὰ λόγου καὶ πνεύματος τελεώτερον,[235] καὶ γλῶσσα πυρὸς ἡ τούτου γίνεται γλῶττα [Act 2:3; cf. Ja 3:5–6], καὶ θεολογεῖ τῶν θείων ὕμνων τοὺς ἔρωτας, καὶ ἄκων δημοσιεύει τῇ βιαίᾳ πνοῇ [Ps 47(48):7; Is 11:15] τοῦ πνεύματος ἅ τε εἶδεν ἐν ἀποκαλύψει Θεοῦ καὶ ἃ

pleted this tiny monastery, as may be seen today, and he planted a garden and vineyard in it to provision the monks who were going to live in it. So Symeon was <busy> again, assembling another flock and celebrating his spiritual father's feast day even more munificently than before. For the clergy of the Great Church of God [Hagia Sophia], led by the *laosynaktes*,[118] along with many monks and laypeople, gathered nearby in the church of the Theotokos at Ta Eugeniou, where Symeon had purchased a *metochion*,[119] and the celebration of the festival went on for eight whole days, and now there was no one trying to stop it or find fault with it as in the past.

Chapter III

When Symeon *rested from all his work,* however, he took up again his beloved spiritual tranquillity, from which he had never really been separated even though he was preoccupied with many troublesome matters, and he gave himself completely to his usual spiritual visions and enlightenment. Distancing himself in this manner from the matter and the solidity of his body, he passed beyond it. Never having been separated from God, he now became more perfectly united with Him, in both word and spirit.[120] His tongue became a *tongue of fire* and he wrote of the divine truths in his *Loves of Divine Hymns.*[121] <Driven> by the *violent wind* of the spirit, he also compulsively published what he had seen in his rev-

ἐν ὀπτασίαις ὑπὲρ τὴν φύσιν γενόμενος ἐθεάσατο. Τῇ γὰρ
ἐνεργείᾳ τοῦ θείου πυρὸς ἐνεργούμενος, ὅλος πῦρ, ὅλος
φῶς καθ᾽ ἑκάστην γινόμενος, Θεὸς ἐχρημάτιζε θέσει, καὶ
ὡς υἱὸς Θεοῦ, ἀνακεκαλυμμένῳ ξενοτρόπως ἔνθεν ἤδη
προσώπῳ τῷ Πατρὶ καὶ Θεῷ κατὰ τὸν Μωσέα ὡμίλει, καὶ
τὰ τῆς ἐνεργείας τοῦ θείου πυρὸς μέλανι ἐν δακτύλῳ Θεοῦ
ὡς πλάκας [cf. Ex 31:18] ἐχάραττε. Πρὸς τούτοις ἐκτίθεται
καὶ τοὺς ἀπολογητικοὺς καὶ ἀντιρρητικοὺς αὐτοῦ λόγους
ἐνταῦθα δυνατοὺς δυνατῶς ἐν δυνάμει σοφίας κατὰ τῶν
ἀντιδιατιθεμένων [cf. 2 Tim 2:25] τούτους ἀναταξάμενος.

112

Ἀλλ᾽ οὐκ ἠρέμει²³⁶ ταῦτα ὁρῶν ὁ καὶ αὐτὸν ὡς τὸν Ἰὼβ
ἐξαιτησάμενος [cf. Lk 22:31] δαίμων [cf. Job 1:6–2:6]· ἐκμαί-
νει γὰρ τοὺς παρακειμένους τῇ μονῇ ἀγχιτέρμονας κατ᾽
αὐτοῦ, καὶ ποτὲ μὲν ὕβρεσιν αὐτὸν καὶ λοιδορίαις ἔπλυνον, καὶ πικρῶς κατωνείδιζον, ἔσθ᾽ ὅτε²³⁷ καὶ χεῖρας αὐτῷ
ἐπέβαλλον καὶ ταῦτα γέροντι ἤδη καὶ ἀδυνάτῳ ὄντι, καὶ
εἰς γῆν κατέρρασσον—ὦ τῆς ἀνοχῆς σου, Χριστέ μου, καὶ
τῆς ἀφάτου μακροθυμίας!—φονώσῃ χειρί, ποτὲ δὲ καὶ λίθοις ἐλιθοβόλουν τὸν δίκαιον. Τοίνυν καὶ τούτων εἷς ἐν
μιᾷ λίθον λαβών, ὅσον ἡ χεὶρ φέρειν ἠδύνατο, πέμπει δυνατῶς αὐτὸν κατὰ τὸν τόπον ἐν ᾧ καθέζεσθαι εἰώθει ὁ
ἅγιος καὶ γράφειν τὰ τῆς θείας χάριτος λόγια, καὶ τὸν

elation of God and what he witnessed in his visions when he had transcended his nature. Inspired by the energy of the divine fire, he became each day wholly fire, wholly light, and came to be God by adoption and as a son of God. As a result the person of God the Father was revealed to him in a wondrous fashion, and he conversed <with Him> like Moses, and inscribed in ink *by the finger of God* as on *the tablets* the energy of the divine fire. Furthermore, he also expounded his forceful statements of apology and refutation, composing them forcefully against *his opponents* with the force of wisdom.

Chapter 112

But the demon, who had also *demanded* Symeon *for trial* like Job,[122] did not remain quiet when he saw all this. He thus enraged the people who lived near the monastery against him. Sometimes they would heap insults and abuse upon Symeon and would criticize him bitterly, and at times they even laid hands on him (this despite the fact that he was already a feeble old man) and threw him to the ground with murderous hands—oh, my Christ, what forbearance and indescribable patience you have! At other times they would throw stones at the righteous Symeon. One day, indeed, one of them took a stone that was as big as he could hold in his hand and hurled this at the place where the saint used to sit and write his sayings of divine grace. The stone smashed

ὕελον συντρίψας ὁ λίθος διέρχεται κατὰ τοῦ μήνιγγος τοῦ
ἁγίου, καὶ ἀντικρὺ πίπτει τῆς αὐτοῦ ὄψεως, οὗ καὶ τῇ βιαίᾳ μόνον φορᾷ δίνης ἐπληρώθη ἡ αἰδέσιμος αὐτοῦ κεφα-
λή, ᾗτινι καὶ εἰ προσερράγη φερόμενος, οὐδὲν ἂν ἦν τὸ
κωλῦσον αὐθωρὸν παραπέμψαι τῷ θανάτῳ τὸν ἅγιον. Τί
οὖν ἐπὶ τούτοις ὁ μιμητὴς τοῦ εἰπόντος *οὐκ ἀποδώσεις
κακὸν ἀντὶ κακοῦ* [cf. Rom 12:17] πράττει; Ἀγαθοῖς πράγμασιν αὐτόν τε καὶ πάντας ἄλλους τοὺς κακοῦντας αὐτὸν
ἠμείβετο, διόπερ γαληνῷ τῷ φθέγματι φωνεῖ τὸν αὐτοῦ
μαθητὴν Συμεὼν καί φησιν· "Ὁρᾷς τὴν καθ' ἡμῶν ἀπει-
λήν, ἀδελφέ;" Ὑποδείξας αὐτῷ καὶ τὸν λίθον· "Ἀλλ' ἄπιθι
καὶ τὸν καθ' ἡμῶν τοῦ ἀνθρώπου θυμὸν σβέσον ἐλέῳ τῆς
εὐποιΐας, ἐκ τοῦ ὑστερήματος ἡμῶν τὰ πρὸς θεραπείαν
αὐτοῦ ἀφθόνως ἐπιχορηγήσας αὐτῷ."

113

Τοιοῦτος ἦν ὁ μέγας οὗτος τοῦ Χριστοῦ μαθητής, τὰ
μὲν ἐπαγόμενα αὐτῷ παρὰ δολίων ἀνδρῶν ὑπομένων, τοὺς
δὲ κακοῦντας ἀγαθοῖς ἀμειβόμενος. Ὅθεν καὶ ὡς ὁμότροπος τῶν ἀποστόλων καὶ μιμητὴς τοῦ Χριστοῦ *λοιδορούμε-
νος οὐκ ἀντελοιδόρει, πάσχων οὐκ ἠπείλει* [1 Pt 2:23], διωκό-
μενος ἠνείχετο, βλασφημούμενος *παρεκάλει* [cf. 1 Cor
4:12], καὶ ἔχαιρε *χαρὰν ἀνεκλάλητον* [cf. 1 Pt 1:8] ἐν ταῖς
θλίψεσιν, ὁρῶν ἑαυτὸν διερχόμενον διὰ τῶν μακαρισμῶν

through the glass in the direction of the saint's skull before falling right in front of his face. Its violent motion alone made the venerable man's head spin, and if it had reached the saint and struck his head, nothing could have stopped it from killing him outright. So what was Symeon's reaction? That imitator of the one who said *Do not repay evil with evil* repaid with good deeds both this man and all the others who did him wrong. In a calm voice he called his disciple Symeon[123] and said to him, "Do you see how I'm being threatened, brother?" and showed him the stone. "But go and soothe the man's anger at me with the mercy of charity, and supply him generously with aid from our meager resources."

Chapter 113

Such a man was this great disciple of Christ, enduring what was inflicted on him by deceitful people, but repaying with good deeds those who maltreated him. And so, since he was like the apostles and an imitator of Christ, *when he was abused he did not return the abuse, when he suffered he uttered no threats,* when he was persecuted he endured, when he was slandered *he encouraged* his slanderers, and he rejoiced with *unutterable joy* in his tribulations, for he saw himself fulfilling

τοῦ Χριστοῦ. Οὕτως οὖν ἔχων καὶ οὕτω βιοὺς ἀποστολικῶς κατὰ τὸ Εὐαγγέλιον ὁ μακάριος τοῦ Χριστοῦ μαθητὴς[238] ἐξέρχεται τῆς ἀπητηλῆς τοῦ κόσμου αἰσθήσεως,
καὶ τῷ μὲν σώματι συνεπορεύετο τοῖς ἀνθρώποις ἐπὶ τῆς
γῆς, τῇ δὲ ψυχῇ Θεῷ νοερῶς συνεγίνετο διὰ τοῦ θείου
φωτός, καὶ τοῖς ἀγγέλοις συνδιῃτᾶτο ἐν οὐρανοῖς.

2   Ὃν εἴ τις ἄγγελον ἐπίγειον καὶ ἄνθρωπον καλέσει
οὐράνιον, κρίνειν οἶδεν εὐστόχως καὶ[239] περὶ θείων πραγμάτων. Ὡς μὲν γὰρ οὐράνιος ἄνθρωπος τοῖς καλοῖς ἔλαμπεν
ἔργοις μέσον τῶν ἀνθρώπων τῆς γῆς, καὶ διὰ γνώσεως
οὐρανίου καὶ σοφίας Θεοῦ ἐφώτιζε τῶν ἐντυγχανόντων
αὐτῷ μετὰ πίστεως τὰς ψυχάς· ὡς δὲ ἐπίγειος ἄγγελος
προεώρα καὶ προεγίνωσκεν ἔσθ' ὅτε τὰ μέλλοντα, καὶ
προφητικῶς περὶ τούτων προέλεγε, καὶ τὸ πέρας ἐλάμβα-
νεν ἕκαστον ἐν τῷ ἰδίῳ καιρῷ. Καὶ μαρτυρεῖ τῷ λόγῳ ἡ
περὶ Ἰωάννου τοῦ περιβλέπτου ἐκείνου ἀνδρὸς ἐν βασιλείοις, ὃς ἐπὶ Βασιλείου τοῦ αὐτοκράτορος πρωτονοτάριος
τοῦ δρόμου ἐγένετο, προγνωστικὴ πρόρρησις τοῦ ἁγίου,
ὅπως παρρησίᾳ τὸν μέγαν ἐκεῖνον πειρασμὸν προεῖπε, καὶ
μετὰ παρέλευσιν χρόνων δέκα φοβερά τις κατὰ τοῦ ἀνδρὸς
ἐκ βασιλέως ἐξέβη ἀπόφασις, καὶ δριμυτάτη ποινὴ αὐτὸν
διεδέξατο· σὺν ταύτῃ δὲ καὶ ἡ τοῦ δεήσεων Ἰωάννου γαμ-
βροῦ πέλοντος τοῦ ἁγίου, ἃς καὶ ἐν τῷ κατὰ πλάτους βίῳ
αὐτοῦ πλατύτερον ὡς κατὰ μέρος ἐξέβησαν ἐξεθέμεθα.

3   Τοιοῦτος ἦν ὁ βίος αὐτοῦ καὶ τοιοῦτον τὸ ὀπτικὸν τῆς
καθαρωτάτης ἐκείνης ψυχῆς, ὡς ὁρᾶν αὐτὸν πρὸ χρόνων
πολλῶν τὰ μέλλοντα ἐν ἐσχάτοις γενέσθαι καιροῖς, καὶ
προγινώσκειν αὐτὰ καθά τις ἐν ταῖς χερσὶν[240] βίβλον

Christ's beatitudes. Being like this and living an apostolic life in accordance with the Gospel, Christ's blessed disciple Symeon passed beyond the deceptive perception of this world. For while in his body he was going about among people on earth, in his soul he was conversing intellectually with God through the divine light and was living with the angels in heaven.

A shrewd judge of divine affairs might well call him an 2 earthly angel and a heavenly man. For, as a heavenly man, he shone among people on earth as a result of his good deeds, and through his heavenly knowledge and wisdom about God he enlightened with faith the souls of those who talked to him. But as an earthly angel, he sometimes foresaw and had foreknowledge of the future and spoke about it prophetically in advance, and each prediction came to pass in its own proper time. Symeon's prognostic prediction about John, that celebrated man at the court who became *protonotarios tou dromou*[124] under the emperor Basil,[125] bears witness to my words. For Symeon openly foretold his great tribulation, and after ten years went by, a terrible sentence was indeed passed against that man by the emperor and he received a very harsh punishment. Along with this there is also Symeon's prediction concerning John, the master of petitions,[126] who was the saint's relative by marriage. But I have set these down at greater length and in detail, just as they happened, in the longer version of his *Life*.[127]

Symeon's way of life, then, and the visual acuity of that 3 purest of souls was such that he was able to see, many years ahead, what was going to happen in the end, and to know things in advance, just like someone who holds a book in his

κατέχων καὶ τῇ διηνεκεῖ ταύτης μελέτῃ ἐν γνώσει καθαρᾷ
τῶν ἐγκειμένων γινόμενος.

114

Ἀλλὰ γὰρ ἀναμνησθέντες καί τινων θαυμάτων αὐτοῦ,
οὗ θαῦμα μέγα ὅλος ὁ[241] βίος καὶ μᾶλλον ὁ λόγος τῆς σοφίας Θεοῦ καὶ τῆς γνώσεως, ὃν ἀποστολικῶς διὰ τῆς ἐπιπνοίας ὡς ἐκεῖνοι τοῦ Πνεύματος κατεπλούτησεν, ἐπὶ τὴν
μακαρίαν αὐτοῦ τελευτὴν τὸν λόγον ἰθύνωμεν.

2   Ὕδωρ οὐκ ἦν ἐν τῇ ὑπ' αὐτοῦ κτισθείσῃ μονῇ, καὶ
ἔκαμνον οἱ μαθηταὶ[242] πολλὰ τὸν κάματον ὑπομένοντες
διακομίζοντες κάτωθεν τοῦτο τοῖς νώτοις αὐτῶν. Τοῦτο
μεγάλως μᾶλλον ἐλύπει τὸν ἅγιον ἢ τοὺς αὐτοῦ μαθητάς.
Ὡς δὲ δυνατὸν οὐκ ἦν εὑρεθῆναι ὕδωρ ἐν τῷ χώρῳ ἐκείνῳ,
πέτρα γὰρ ἦν σχεδὸν ὅλος μία,[243] γνωρίζει Θεῷ διὰ προσευχῆς τῷ πάντα εἰδότι τὴν ὀδύνην αὐτοῦ μετὰ στεναγμοῦ
τῆς ψυχῆς [cf. Rom 8:26], τῶν κοπιώντων εἰς τὴν τοῦ ὕδατος ἀνακομιδὴν κατοικτείρας τὸν πόνον. Δεῖται οὖν γνωρίσαι αὐτῷ μυστικῶς τὸν τόπον, ἐν ᾧ ῥαγεῖσα ἡ πέτρα
βλύσει τοῖς διψῶσιν εἰς χρείαν τὸ ὕδωρ. Γνωρισθέντος οὖν
αὐτῷ τοῦ τόπου παρὰ Θεοῦ, τὴν δόξαν ἐκεῖνος φεύγων ἀεὶ
τῶν ἀνθρώπων, καὶ ἄκοντα ἔκρυπτεν ἑαυτόν.

3   Ἐπεὶ δὲ ἡ φύσις ἐζήτει λυθῆναι εἰς γῆρας ἐλάσασα
πολυχρόνιον καὶ ὅσον οὔπω μετὰ τὴν πολλὴν ἐκείνην

hands and by constantly studying it arrives at clear knowledge of its content.

Chapter 114

But now, after recalling some of Symeon's miracles (among which one great miracle was his life in its entirety and, even more so, the words of wisdom and knowledge about God which, like the apostles, he possessed in abundance through the inspiration of the Spirit), I shall turn my account directly to his blessed end.

There was no water in the monastery that Symeon 2 founded, and his disciples endured a lot of hard work as they toiled to carry it up on their backs from down below. This grieved the saint more than his disciples. As it was impossible to find water in that place (for the whole area was more or less one single rock), he made his distress known to God (who knows everything) through prayer with spiritual *groaning*, because he felt compassion for the labor of those who struggled to bring up the water. Symeon thus asked Him to let him know mystically the place where, if the rock were broken, water would gush forth for the use of those who were thirsting for it. This place was made known to him by God, but Symeon reluctantly kept the revelation hidden because he always avoided people's acclaim.

One day, however, when his physical nature, which had 3 reached advanced old age, was seeking release and he was

ὑπομονὴν τῶν πειρασμῶν ἔμελλεν ἀποδοῦναι καὶ τὴν
κοινὴν ὀφειλήν, προγνοὺς ὁ μακάριος τοῦτο καὶ ἤδη τῆς
τελευταίας ἁψαμένης²⁴⁴ αὐτοῦ νόσου, διὰ τοῦ φορείου φερόμενος ἐν μιᾷ, ἐπὶ τὸ ὕπαιθρον τῆς μικρᾶς ἐκείνης αὐλῆς
ἀπαγαγεῖν²⁴⁵ καὶ²⁴⁶ θεῖναι τοῖς φέρουσιν αὐτὸν ἐπισκήπτει.
Τούτου οὖν γεγονότος ζητεῖ διακομισθῆναι αὐτῷ γηπο-
νικὸν ἐργαλεῖον, ὃ κοινῶς τζαπίον καλεῖται, καὶ λαβὼν
αὐτὸ καὶ "Εὐλογητός," εἰπών, "ὁ Θεός," κρούει μέσον ὡς
εἶχε τοῦ ὑπαίθρου²⁴⁷ τρίς, καὶ τοῖς μοναχοῖς ἐντέλλεται
τοὺς ὀρύττοντας ἀγαγεῖν καὶ διὰ τάχους ὀρύξαι τὸν τόπον. Ὡς δὲ οἱ μὲν εἴχοντο τοῦ ἔργου θερμῶς, ὠρύχθη δὲ
βαθὺ καὶ ἦν οὐδαμοῦ ὕδωρ, ἀλλὰ περιτυχόντες ἄγαν ἀντι-
τύπῳ πέτρᾳ καὶ δεινῶς ὀξείᾳ, ἔστησαν τοῦ ἔργου κεκοπια-
κότες πολλὰ καὶ διαρρῆξαι μὴ δυνηθέντες αὐτήν.

4   Ἤκουσε ταῦτα ὁ ἅγιος ἄρτι τὰ περὶ τῆς ἐκδημίας καὶ
διαθήκης αὐτοῦ ὑπαγορεύων τῷ γράφοντι καί φησιν· "Εἴπατε τοῖς τὸ φρέαρ ὀρύττουσιν· Εἰς τὸ ἄκρον διαρρήξατέ
μοι τῆς πέτρας καὶ ἔτι κοπιάσετε οὐδαμῶς, εὐθὺς γὰρ ἀνα-
δοθῶσιν δαψιλῶς ἡμῖν ἐξ αὐτῆς αἱ πηγαί.'" Μίαν οὖν τὴν
φορὰν τῆς πληγῆς ποιήσαντες κατ' αὐτῆς οἱ ταύτην πολλάκις τετυφότες βαρέως καὶ μηδὲν ἀνύσαντες,²⁴⁸ εὐθὺς
ταύτην διέρρηξαν καὶ ἡ πέτρα ῥαγεῖσα καθαρώτατόν τε
καὶ ποτιμώτατον²⁴⁹ ὕδωρ ἐκ τῶν λαγόνων ἀνέδωκε, καὶ τὸ
ὄρυγμα εἰς φρέαρ ἐξ ἐκείνου γεγονὸς περίεστιν εἰς μαρτύριον ἧς ἔτυχε πρὸς Θεὸν²⁵⁰ παρρησίας. Οὕτως ἐπακούει
Θεὸς τῶν ὁσίων αὐτοῦ καὶ σιωπώντων τῶν ἀλαλήτων
φωνῶν [cf. 4 Mcc 10:18], καὶ ἄκοντας αὐτοὺς δημοσιεύει
διὰ τῶν ἔργων τῆς χάριτος.

about to pay the common debt after such great endurance of tribulations, the blessed Symeon (who foreknew this and was already suffering from his final illness) was being carried on his litter. He ordered his bearers to take him and set him down in the open enclosure of the little courtyard there. When this was done he asked them to bring him an agricultural tool (what is commonly called a mattock). He took hold of this and, saying "God be blessed," struck three times at the center of the enclosure where he was. Then he instructed the monks to bring in the <professional> diggers and dig quickly in that place. These men set to work enthusiastically and dug deep, but there was no water, and when they came to a very hard and terribly jagged rock, they stopped work because they were exhausted and could not break through it.

The saint heard about this just as he was dictating his last 4 will and testament to the scribe, and said, "Say to the men who are digging the well, 'Just break through the top of the rock for me and you will labor no longer, for it will immediately provide us with abundant streams <of water>.'" So the men, who had already struck that rock hard many times but had accomplished nothing, now hit it one single time and immediately broke through it. And when the rock broke, it produced the purest, freshest water from the cavities within it. The pit became a well from then on and it still exists as a witness to the close relationship that Symeon had with God. Thus *God listens* to His holy ones, *even to* the unspoken words of *the silent,* and He makes His holy ones known through His works of grace, even if they are reluctant.

LIFE OF SAINT SYMEON

115

Ἀλλ᾽ ἀναγκαῖον εἰπεῖν καὶ ὃ πρῶτον ἐμφανίσας ἑαυτὸν κατ᾽ ὄψιν Ἄννῃ τῇ τῆς Βαρδαίνης ἡγουμένῃ θαῦμα πεποίηκεν εἰς αὐτήν, ὡς ἐκείνη ζώσῃ φωνῇ διηγήσατο ἡμῖν οὕτως εἰποῦσα· "Λάβρῳ ποτὲ πυρετῷ συσχεθεῖσα δεινῶς ἐφλεγόμην τὰ σπλάγχνα, καὶ ὡς κηρὸς²⁵¹ ἐτηκόμην τὰς σάρκας, καὶ ὡσεὶ φρύγιόν μου τὰ ὀστᾶ συνεφρύγετο [cf. Ps 101(102):4], καὶ τὰς ἁρμονίας ὅλου διελυόμην τοῦ σώματος. Πλείστας οὖν ἡμέρας τῷ σφοδρῷ τηκομένης μου πυρετῷ καὶ μετρίας γοῦν τροφῆς γεύσασθαι μηδ᾽ ὁπωσοῦν δυναμένης, ἐπεὶ κραταιοτέραν τὴν νόσον τῶν ἰατρικῶν βοηθημάτων εἶδον οἱ ἰατροί, καὶ τὴν δύναμιν ἀποτεμνομένην ἑώρων τοῦ σώματος, τὰς σάρκας τε δεινῶς ἐκτακείσας, καὶ τὴν φωνὴν ἀποσβεσθεῖσαν τοῦ φθέγματος, ἀπεγνωκότες τὴν σωτηρίαν μου ὑπεχώρησαν μόνην με²⁵² μόνῃ τῇ μητρὶ ἔμπνουν νεκρὰν²⁵³ καταλείψαντες. Ἡ γοῦν μήτηρ, —καὶ τί γὰρ ἡ μήτηρ; —ὡς τοὺς μὲν ἰατροὺς ἀπειπόντας ἀκήκοε τὴν ζωήν μου, ἐμὲ δὲ κεκαλυμμένην ἔβλεπε τὰς ὁράσεις ἐν συνεχεῖ τῷ ἄσθματι πνέουσαν ἤδη τὰ ἔσχατα, λαβοῦσά με εἰς τοὺς κόλπους αὐτῆς ἐθρήνει πικρῶς, καὶ βρεχομένη τοῖς δάκρυσιν ἐξεδέχετο ἐκλειπούσης μου καλύψαι τοὺς ὀφθαλμούς.

2 "Οὕτως οὖν ἐγὼ ἔχουσα καὶ τῶν γινομένων εἰς ἐμὲ ἀναίσθητος μένουσα, ὁρῶ κατ᾽ ὄψιν τὸν μακάριον Συμεὼν δεξιὰν ὀρέγοντα τῷ ἁγίῳ τούτῳ πατρὶ Συμεώνῃ τῷ εὐλαβεῖ, καὶ μετὰ μεγάλης δόξης πρός με ἐρχόμενον. Ὡς δ᾽

268

Chapter 115

I have to tell the first miracle he performed, when he appeared in a vision to Anna the superior of Bardaine,[128] as she told me in her own words. This is what she said: "I once had a violent fever which caused my insides to burn terribly; my flesh was melting away like wax, *my bones were burned up like firewood,* and all the joints in my body were dissolving. I was consumed by this high fever for very many days and could not take even a bit of food. When the doctors realized my illness was stronger than their medical remedies and saw that my physical strength was failing, my flesh was melting away terribly, and I was losing my voice, they despaired of saving me and went away, leaving me behind as just a breathing corpse, completely alone with my mother. Then my mother—what else would a mother do?—when she heard the doctors despair of my life and saw me closing my eyes and, at the same time, already taking my last gasp, she took me to her bosom while lamenting bitterly and, soaked with tears, waited to close my eyes once I had passed away.

"But while I was in this state, lying there insensible to 2 what was happening to me, I saw in a vision the blessed Symeon, holding out his right hand toward his holy father Symeon Eulabes and coming toward me in great glory. When

ἤγγισέ²⁵⁴ μοι πραεία φησὶ τῇ φωνῇ·²⁵⁵ 'Χαίροις, ὦ κυρία
μου Ἄννα, τίς ἡ κατασχοῦσά σε δεινὴ ἀρρωστία, καὶ τί
ἔχουσα οὕτω συνέχῃ ἀσάλευτος ἐπὶ κλίνης κειμένη, μήτε
τῇ μητρὶ μήτε ἡμῖν ὁμιλοῦσα τοῖς φίλοις, μήτε τροφῆς
γευσαμένη καθόλου;' Ἀπὸ τῆς φωνῆς οὖν τοῦ ἁγίου ὥσπερ
εἰς ἐμαυτὴν ἐπανελθοῦσα ἀνέβλεψά τε ἅμα καὶ τὸ στόμα
διανοίξασα λεπτόν τι καὶ κατηναγκασμένον γνωρίσασα
τοῦτον ἔφην· Ἀποθνήσκω, πάτερ μου τιμιώτατε.'

3   "Ὁ γοῦν ἅγιος Συμεὼν ὁ Στουδιώτης στραφεὶς λέγει
τῷ μακαρίῳ τούτῳ καὶ ἁγίῳ Συμεώνῃ τῷ μαθητῇ αὐτοῦ·²⁵⁶
'Ἀνάστησον, κῦρι Συμεών, κρατήσας αὐτὴν ἀπὸ τῆς χειρός, καὶ δὸς αὐτῇ φαγεῖν [cf. Mk 5:41–43; Lk 8:54–55; Mt
9:25].' Ὁ δὲ τοῦτο πεποιηκὼς ἔδοξέ με τρέφειν, τροφὰς
παρὰ τῆς ἐμῆς ἐκζητήσας μητρός. Ὡς δὲ παρὰ τῶν ἁγίων
ἐκείνων ἐτράφην χειρῶν, εὐθὺς ἰσχὺν ὑγείας λαβοῦσα ἀνέ-
θορόν²⁵⁷ τε τῆς κλίνης, καὶ τὴν μητέρα καλέσασα, τὴν ὄψιν
αὐτῇ τε διηγησάμην ἅμα ἡ πρώην ἄφωνος καὶ νεκρά, καὶ
τροφὰς αἰτησαμένη παρ' αὐτῆς μάλα ἡδέως ἐτράφην, καὶ
ὅλη ὑγιὴς ἐξανέστην." Οὕτω καὶ νῦν τὸ ἱερὸν ἐνεργεῖ
Εὐαγγέλιον εἰς τοὺς κατὰ Θεὸν καὶ αὐτὸ τὸ Εὐαγγέλιον
ζῶντας καὶ τηροῦντας ἀπαραλείπτως τὰς αὐτοῦ ἐντολάς.

he drew near me he said in a gentle voice, 'Greetings, Lady Anna. What's this terrible illness you have? What's wrong with you that keeps you lying motionless in bed, not saying anything to your mother nor to us, your friends, and not eating any food at all?' At the saint's voice I returned to myself, as it were, and looked up, and at the same time I forced myself to open my mouth a little when I recognized him and said, 'I'm dying, my most venerable father.'

"Then holy Symeon the Stoudite [Eulabes] turned to his 3 blessed and holy disciple Symeon and said, 'Take her by the hand and make her stand up, Kyr Symeon, and give her something to eat.' When he had done this, he seemed to feed me with food he requested from my mother. When I had eaten from his holy hands I immediately became strong and healthy. I jumped out of bed and called my mother and narrated the vision to her at once, I who just before was speechless and dead. I asked her for food, ate with great pleasure, and arose in perfect health." Thus, even now, the holy Gospel works in those who live according to God and that same Gospel, and who keep its commandments without fail.

116

Ἀλλὰ τοῦτο μὲν τοιοῦτον. Φέρε δὲ καὶ πρὸς τὰς λοιπὰς τοῦ πατρὸς θαυματουργίας τὸν λόγον ἰθύνωμεν. Παρὰ τοῦ μακαρίου τούτου πατρὸς παιδίον ὢν²⁵⁸ ἀνετράφη ὁ Νικηφόρος²⁵⁹ ἐκεῖνος. Οὗτος τοίνυν μετὰ τὴν τοῦ ἁγίου κοίμησιν ἀποκαρεὶς ἐν τῇ μονῇ τῆς ἁγίας Μαρίνης, ἐκλήθη καὶ αὐτὸς Συμεών· αὐτόπτης δὲ θαυμάτων τινῶν γεγονὼς τοῦ πατρὸς ἐπὶ μάρτυρι Θεῷ ἱερεὺς ὢν ταῦτά μοι διηγήσατο οὕτως εἰπών·

2 "Ἔτι νέος," φησίν, "ὢν καὶ ἄρτι τὸν τεσσαρεσκαιδέκατον χρόνον ἀνύων τῆς ἐμῆς ἡλικίας, προσήχθην παρὰ τῶν ἐμῶν συγγενῶν τῷ ἁγίῳ, καὶ εἰς τοὺς ὑπηρετοῦντας κατετάγην αὐτοῦ. Ἐπεὶ δὲ ἡ ἐμὴ τῆς ὀρέξεως φύσις οὐκ οἶδ' ὅπως εἴπω τὴν τῶν ἰχθύων οὐ προσίετο βρῶσιν ἐξ ἁπαλῶν ὀνύχων αὐτῶν, εἴ τι γὰρ καὶ κατηναγκάσθην παρ' ὅτου λαβεῖν εἰς μετάληψιν καὶ μάλιστα ἐκ νεαρῶν καὶ οὐ τεταριχευμένων ἰχθύων, ἤμουν τε αὐτὸ ἐξαυτῆς καὶ ἀνετρέπετό μου ἡ φύσις καὶ ἀηδίας πάσης ἐγενόμην μεστός.

3 "Οὕτω τοίνυν ἔχοντός μου καὶ δεινῶς ὑπὸ τῆς ἀνορεξίας παθαινομένου, προτείνει ἐπὶ τραπέζης ποτὲ ὁ ἅγιος τὴν χεῖρα καὶ φαγεῖν ἐδίδου μοι μέρος ἰχθύος ὀπτοῦ. Ἐμοῦ δὲ παρισταμένου καὶ λαβεῖν ἐκεῖνο παραιτουμένου, ἐπεὶ τὴν αἰτίαν τῆς παραιτήσεως ἐρωτήσας ὁ ἅγιος ἔμαθε παρ' ἐμοῦ, συστείλας τὴν χεῖρα ἐσχόλασε βραχὺ καθ' ἑαυτόν, ὅσῳ γνωρίσαι τάχα δι' εὐχῆς τοῦτο²⁶⁰ τῷ τὰ²⁶¹ πάντα εἰδότι Θεῷ πρὸ γενέσεως [Susanna 35 OG]. Εἶτα μετὰ τὸ μυστικῶς αὐτὸν ἐντυχεῖν τῷ Θεῷ, ἐγγίσαι οἷ προστάττει μοι,

Chapter 116

So much for that. But now let me turn my account to the father's other miracles. As a boy, Nikephoros was raised by the blessed father. Then, when he was tonsured in the monastery of Saint Marina after the saint's death, he too was called Symeon. He was an eyewitness to some of the father's miracles, and as a priest and with God as his witness, he told me the following.

"When I was still a young boy and had just turned fourteen, I was brought to the saint by my relatives and installed as one of his servants. I don't know how to say this, but my natural constitution couldn't stand the taste of fish since I had been a baby; and so, if someone ever forced me to eat it, especially fresh, unsalted fish, I would immediately throw it up and my constitution would be upset and I would be filled with nausea.

"So then, with me having this condition and being badly afflicted by my dislike <of fish>, on one occasion at the refectory table the saint stretched out his hand and gave me a piece of baked fish to eat. When I just stood there and refused to take it, the saint asked me the reason. After he learned from me what this was, he drew back his hand and made himself still for a moment, long enough, probably, to make this known through prayer to *God who knows all things before their beginning.* Then, after his mystical consultation with God, he told me to approach him, and when I did so,

καὶ ἐγγίσαντι ἄρας τὴν χεῖρα ἐκεῖνος καὶ τὸ μέρος τοῦ
ἰχθύος εὐλογήσας ἐκεῖνο, δούς μοι τοῦτο φαγεῖν ἔφη·
Λαβὼν ἐν Χριστῷ τῷ Θεῷ μου φάγε καὶ ἔσῃ [cf. Mt 26:26;
Mk 14:22; 1 Cor 11:24] κατὰ φύσιν ἔχων ἀπό γε τοῦ νῦν
προσιεμένην τὴν ὄρεξιν ἃ ὁ Θεὸς δέδωκεν ἡμῖν εἰς μετάληψιν εἰπών· ἰδοὺ δέδωκα ὑμῖν πάντα ὡς λάχανα χόρτου
[Gen 9:3].' Ταῦτα τοῦ ἁγίου εἰπόντος καὶ ἐμοῦ φαγόντος
ἐν πίστει τὸ βρῶμα, εὐθὺς ἐν ἕξει ὀρέξεως πρὸς τὴν τῶν
ἰχθύων ἐγενόμην μετάληψιν Θεοῦ χάριτι καὶ εὐχαῖς τοῦ
πατρός, καὶ ἡδύτερον ἔκτοτε τούτους ἤσθιον μᾶλλον ἢ
πρώην τὰ κρέα λαϊκὸς ὤν. Τοῦτο πρῶτον σημεῖον τῆς
ἁγιωσύνης αὐτοῦ πεποίηκεν ὁ μακάριος εἰς ἐμέ, ὡς ὁ Ἰησοῦς καὶ Θεός μου τὸ ἐν Κανᾶ γάμῳ τῆς Γαλιλαίας σημεῖον [cf. John 2:11].

117

"Ἀλλὰ γὰρ ἐπεὶ συνήθης εἰς πάντα[262] ἐγενόμην τῷ
ἁγίῳ, καὶ πολλῆς ἀπήλαυον[263] παρ' αὐτοῦ τῆς ἀγάπης τε
καὶ κηδεμονίας τῆς κατὰ πνεῦμα,[264] οὐκ ἐδίδου χώραν
ἑτέρῳ τῶν συνόντων αὐτῷ μοναχῶν συνεῖναι καθόλου ἢ
συμμένειν αὐτῷ ἐν ἑνὶ καὶ τῷ[265] αὐτῷ κελλίῳ πλὴν ἐμοῦ,
εἴτε διὰ τὸ εἶναί με ἄκακον καὶ ἀπόνηρον εἰς παῖδας ἔτι τε-
λοῦντα· πολλὴ γὰρ ἡ φροντὶς ἦν αὐτῷ καὶ ἡ ἀκρίβεια διὰ
παντὸς[266] τοῦ μὴ παρά τινος γνωσθῆναί ποτε τὴν ἐργασίαν

he raised his hand, blessed the piece of fish, and gave it me to eat, saying, 'Take this in Christ my God and eat it, and from now on you will have a natural liking for what God has given us as food, for He said, Behold, *I have given to you all things, like the vegetables of the pasture.*'[129] When the saint had said this and I had eaten the food with faith, I immediately acquired a permanent appetite for fish by the grace of God and the father's prayers, and from then on I ate it with more pleasure than I previously used to eat meat when I was a layman. This was the first sign of his sanctity that the blessed one performed for me, like the sign that Jesus my God performed at the wedding at Cana in Galilee.

Chapter 117

"From the time I came to be very close to the saint and enjoyed much love and spiritual care from him," <continued Nikephoros,> "he wouldn't let any of his other fellow monks join him or stay in the same cell with him at all, except for me. I can't say whether this was because I was innocent and without guile, inasmuch as I was still a child (for he was always very careful and strict that no one should ever know what he did <in his cell>), or because he needed my help in

αὐτοῦ, εἴτε διὰ δουλείαν τινὰ τοῦ γήρως[267] αὐτοῦ ἢ καὶ
ἐξ οἰκονομίας αὐτοῦ τοῦ Θεοῦ, ὥστε φανερωθῆναι αὐτὸν
καὶ τὴν ἐργασίαν αὐτοῦ ὁποία τίς ἐστιν ἐν τῷ βίῳ μέσον
κόσμου καὶ πόλεως κατὰ τὴν παροῦσαν γενεάν, διὰ τὸ μέλ-
λειν αὐτὸν ὅσον οὔπω ἀναδραμεῖν εἰς Θεόν, οὐκ ἔχω λέγειν, ἕως τότε μηδενός ποτε ἐν τῷ κελλίῳ αὐτοῦ ἔνδον μεί-
ναντος μετ' αὐτοῦ.

2   "Τοιγαροῦν καὶ ὡς ἐν μιᾷ γωνίᾳ ἐκείμην ἐπὶ τοῦ ἐδάφους[268] τῆς κέλλης αὐτοῦ, ποτὲ κατὰ τὸ μεσονύκτιον ὡς
ὑπό τινος διυπνισθείς, εἶδον ὀφθαλμοῖς ἐγρηγορόσι
φρικτὸν θέαμα καὶ ἰδεῖν καὶ ἀκοῦσαι τηνικαῦτα τελεσθὲν
ἐπ' αὐτῷ. Ἐπειδὴ γὰρ ἡ Δέησις εἰκὼν μεγάλη τῇ στέγῃ
πλησιάζουσα τῆς κέλλης αὐτοῦ ὕπερθεν ἀπῃώρητο, καὶ
λύχνος ἦν καιόμενος ἔμπροσθεν τῆς εἰκόνος, εἶδον καὶ
ἰδοὺ κατὰ τὰ ἴσα τῆς εἰκόνος ἐκρεμᾶτο—μαρτυρεῖ μοι
Χριστὸς ἡ Ἀλήθεια—εἰς τὸν ἀέρα ὁ ἅγιος ὡσεὶ πήχεις τέσσαρας, τὰς χεῖρας ἔχων ὑψοῦ καὶ εὐχόμενος, ὅλος φωτὸς
καὶ ὅλος λαμπρότητος. Τοῦτο τὸ φρικτὸν ὡς εἶδον καὶ
ἐξαίσιον θαῦμα παιδίον ὢν καὶ ἄπειρος τοιούτων,[269] δεδοικὼς ὑπὸ τὸ στρῶμα εἰσῆλθον τὴν κεφαλὴν καὶ τὸ πρόσ-
ωπόν μου καλύψας. Πρωΐας δὲ γενομένης ὑπὸ τοῦ φόβου
συνεχόμενος εἶπον τῷ ἁγίῳ τὸ ὅραμα κατ' ἰδίαν. Ὁ δὲ μηδενὶ τοῦτο εἰπεῖν καθόλου ἐμβριμησάμενός με ἐπέσκηψεν.

his old age, or because it was a result of God's own planning (so that Symeon and the nature of his accomplishments in his life, right here in this world and this city in the present generation, might be made known, because he was just about to return to God), but until then no one had ever stayed in his cell with him.

"So, on one occasion when I was lying in a corner on the floor of his cell, I was awakened around midnight by something and I saw then, wide awake with my eyes wide open, a wonder occur involving him that was awesome to see and hear about. A large icon of the Deesis[130] hung high up there, close to the ceiling of his cell, and a lamp was burning in front of the icon. And behold, I saw the saint—Christ the Truth is my witness—suspended in the air at a height of around four cubits,[131] at the same level as the icon. He had his hands raised in prayer and was completely light, completely radiant. As I was a child and without any experience of such things, I was frightened when I saw this awesome and extraordinary miracle, and so I put my head under the mattress and hid my face. In the morning, because I was still afraid, I told the saint privately what I had seen. But he was angry and ordered me not to tell anyone at all about this.

118

"Ἐπεὶ δὲ οὐκ ἦν θέλημα τῷ Θεῷ ἕως τέλους λανθάνειν αὐτόν, ἀλλ᾿ ἔδει καὶ τὴν χάριν δημοσιεῦσαί ποτε ἑαυτήν, ἧς ἐκεῖνος πλουσίως ἀπήλαυσεν ἄνωθεν, κἂν μὴ βουλητὸν ὑπῆρχεν ἐκείνῳ· γύναιόν τι πενόμενον παιδίον ὡσεὶ χρόνων τεσσάρων παράλυτον ὁμοῦ καὶ ἀκίνητον ἐν ταῖς ἀγκάλαις ἐπιφερόμενον δεινῶς ἐκτεταριχευμένον τῇ νόσῳ καὶ μικροῦ μηδὲ ζῆν πιστευόμενον, ἐκ τῆς ἑστίας κινήσασα ἡ πάντα διοικοῦσα καὶ διευθύνουσα Πρόνοια, ἐπὶ τὴν μονὴν καὶ τὸν ἅγιον ἤγαγεν, ἥτις δύο μεριζομένη κακοῖς πενίᾳ καὶ νόσῳ βαρείᾳ τοῦ οἰκείου παιδός, ἔκαμνεν οὐ μικρῶς κατατρυχομένη καὶ δακρύων ποταμοὺς καταφέρουσα. Διὸ καὶ ἄνω γενομένη τῆς κλίμακος τῆς πρὸς τὸ εὐκτήριον τῆς ἁγίας Μαρίνης ἀνερχομένης τίθησι τὸν παῖδα λανθανόντως πρὸς τοὔδαφος, καὶ δρομαίως παλινοστήσασα ὑπεχώρησεν, ἵνα τῶν δύο κακῶν ὑφ᾿ ὧν ἐπιέζετο τὸ ἓν ἀποσκευασαμένη, μικρᾶς τινος αἴσθηται καὶ βραχείας ἀνακωχῆς.

2   "Ὡς δὲ οἱ περὶ τὴν μονὴν καὶ τὸν ἅγιον μοναχοὶ ἐξελθόντες εἶδον κείμενον τὸ παιδίον ὅλον ξηρόν, ὅλον ἀκίνητον, ἄφωνον, μόνον τοῖς ἀνεῳγμένοις ἀγρίως ὀφθαλμοῖς καὶ τῷ ἐγκοπτομένῳ συνεχῶς ἄσθματι γνωριζόμενον ὅτι ζῇ, ἀπαγγέλλουσιν ὡς φοβερόν τι πρᾶγμα καὶ ξένον ἰδεῖν ὀφθαλμοῖς τῷ ἁγίῳ. Ὁ δὲ τὴν ἐκ νάρθηκος αὐτοῦ βακτηρίαν λαβών, ὑφ᾿ ἣν ὑπεστηρίζετο καὶ ἐβοήθει τῷ γήρᾳ καὶ τῇ ἀδυναμίᾳ τοῦ ἰδίου σώματος, ἐξῆλθεν ἰδεῖν καὶ αὐτὸς τὸ τραγῴδημα καὶ οὐχὶ παιδίον ἐκεῖνο. Ὡς οὖν τοῖς

Chapter 118

"But because it was not God's will that Symeon should escape notice until the end, the grace which he enjoyed so richly from above did sometimes have to be made public, even if he didn't want this. Providence, which controls and guides everything, thus caused a poor woman to leave her home and led her to the monastery and the saint. She was carrying in her arms a child about four years old who was paralyzed, unable to move, terribly wasted by disease, and apparently with not long to live. Torn by the twin evils of poverty and the serious illness of her child, she struggled along, exhausted and shedding rivers of tears. After climbing the stairway that led up to the chapel of Saint Marina, she laid the child down on the ground without being seen and then left, hurrying away again, so that she might experience some minor and temporary relief by having rid herself of one of the two evils with which she was burdened.

"When the monks who lived in the monastery with the saint came out and saw the child lying there all shriveled up, completely motionless, not making a sound, with the only signs of life being his wildly staring eyes and his continual, gasping breaths, they went and told the saint about it as though it were some strange and horrible spectacle. Symeon, however, took the fennel-stalk staff which he used to support and help him in his old age and the infirmity of his body, and went out to see for himself this tragic spectacle that was not really a child. When he peered down at it with his most

συμπαθεστάτοις ἐκείνοις ἐναπέβλεψεν ὀφθαλμοῖς, καὶ
εἶδεν ὃ ἰδεῖν καὶ μόνον θέαμα ἦν τοῖς ὁρῶσι φρικτὸν καὶ
πάσης ἐκπλήξεως, ἐδάκρυσεν ἐπ' αὐτῷ, καὶ ἐκ βαθέων
καρδίας ἐστέναξεν, ἐκπλαγεὶς αὐτήν τε τὴν ὄψιν τοῦ ὁρω-
μένου, καὶ εἰς ὅσον ἡ ἐνέργεια τοῦ Πονηροῦ ἰσχύει κατὰ
τοῦ πλάσματος τοῦ Θεοῦ.

3   "Τοίνυν καὶ στραφεὶς πρὸς²⁷⁰ ἡμᾶς ὁ μακάριος κύκλῳ
φησὶ πάντων ἡμῶν παρισταμένων αὐτοῦ· Ὑμεῖς δὲ τί ἄρα
καὶ λογίζεσθε,' φησίν, 'ἢ καὶ βούλεσθε περὶ τοῦ παιδίου
τούτου;' Πάντων δὲ ἡμῶν ὡς ἐκ συνθήματος εἰρηκότων·
'Ταφῆναι χρὴ πάντως καὶ τῇ γῇ δοθῆναι, οἷα δὴ νεκρὸν
καὶ ὅσον οὔπω καὶ αὐτὴν μέλλον τὴν πνοὴν παραδοῦναι.'
'Οὐχ οὕτως,' ἔφη· 'οὐδὲ γὰρ λελογισμένως μοι δεδώκατε
τὴν ἀπόκρισιν.' Καὶ τὴν βακτηρίαν ἀποθέμενος, κύψας ὁ
γέρων καὶ ἅγιος, λαμβάνει αὐτὸ ταῖς οἰκείαις χερσὶ καὶ τί-
θησιν ὑπὸ τὸν θρόνον, ἐν ᾧ καθεζόμενος ἐν ταῖς συνάξεσιν
ἀνεπαύετο. Ἐπισκήψας δὲ ἡμῖν καταβιβάσαι τὸν λύχνον
τὸν ἐπίπροσθεν τῆς ἁγίας ἀπηωρημένον Μαρίνης, λαβὼν
ἔλαιον ἐκεῖθεν καὶ χρίσας τὸ ἐξηραμμένον δεινῶς ἐκεῖνο
παιδίον, ἐπευξάμενός τε καὶ τῇ χειρὶ σφραγίσας αὐτὸ—ὡς
ἐμεγάλυνας τοὺς ἁγίους σου, Χριστὲ Βασιλεῦ!—εὐθὺς εἰς
ἑαυτὸ παραδόξως ἐλθὸν ἀναζωπυρηθέν τε καὶ ἰσχὺν εὐρω-
στίας λαβὸν ἀπὸ μόνης τῆς τῶν χειρῶν ἐκείνων τῶν ὁσίων
ἐπιθέσεως, ἀνέστη ἐπὶ τοὺς πόδας αὐτοῦ ὃ ἐν ὅλῃ τῇ ζωῇ
αὐτοῦ κατακείμενον ἦν καὶ ἀκίνητον, καὶ τὸν θρόνον τοῦ
ἁγίου κρατῆσαν, εἶτα τὰ ἔνθεν τε κἀκεῖθεν τῆς ἐκκλησίας
σκάμνα χειραπτόμενον ἥλατό²⁷¹ τε καὶ ἐβάδιζε, καὶ τὰς

sympathetic eyes and saw this sight that was so horrible and really shocking just to look at, he wept to himself and groaned from the bottom of his heart, being struck both by the sight itself that he was seeing and by the extent of the power that the Evil One could exercise over that creature of God.

"Then that blessed man turned to us and said to all of us who were standing around him in a circle, 'What do you think about this? What do you want to do about this child?' And all of us, as though by agreement, replied, 'Without a doubt he should be buried and put in the ground, as he's almost dead already and is just about to stop breathing.' 'Not at all,' he said. 'You've given me your answer without considering it rationally.' And setting aside his staff, our elder, the saint, stooped down, took the child in his own hands and placed him on the seat where he used to sit to rest during the services. Then he ordered us to take down the lamp which hung before the icon of Saint Marina and, taking some oil from it, anointed that terribly withered child. He prayed and made the sign of the cross upon him with his hand, and immediately—oh Christ the King, how you have magnified your saints!—the child miraculously became himself again and was revived and received robust health simply from the imposition of those holy hands. That boy, who had been bedridden and immobile for his whole life, now stood up on his legs, took hold of the saint's chair, and then, holding on to the benches here and there in the church, walked and jumped about from one to another, looking for something 3

τροφὰς ὡς εἶχεν ἐζήτει, καὶ τραφὲν ὑγείας πάσης ἀπή-
λαυσε, καὶ τῇ μητρὶ ἀπεδόθη ἐργάτης τοῦ ἐράνου τῆς πε-
νίας καὶ τῆς δυστυχίας αὐτῆς. Καὶ ταῦτα μὲν τῆς αὐτοῦ
ἀναδείξεως.

119

"Γυνὴ δέ τις ἑτέρα ἄρτι καὶ αὐτὴ νεανίαν ἔχουσα τὸν
υἱὸν καὶ τὴν ἡλικίαν ὁρᾶσθαι ποθούμενον, ὑπὸ τοῦ φθόνου
πλεονεκτεῖται τοῦ Πονηροῦ καὶ κρουσθέντα ὑπὸ πνεύματος ἀκαθάρτου δαιμονῶντα καὶ ἀφρὸν ἀποπτύοντα ἐπεφέρετο. Αὕτη τοιγαροῦν ὑπὸ τῆς ἄνωθεν προνοίας καὶ χάριτος κινηθεῖσα φέρει τὸν υἱὸν ἐπὶ τὴν μονὴν καὶ τὸν ἅγιον,
καὶ τὴν κλίμακα ἀνελθοῦσα ἵστατο προσευχομένη ἐπίπροσθεν τῶν τῆς ἐκκλησίας θυρῶν καὶ ὑπὲρ τοῦ υἱοῦ τὸν Θεὸν
ἱκετεύουσα. Ἐπεὶ δὲ ὀφθῆναι καὶ ἰδεῖν τὸν ἅγιον ἐπεζή-
τησε, μηνύεται αὐτῷ ἡ τοῦ γυναίου ἀξίωσις. Ὁ δὲ πᾶσι χρι-
στομιμήτως εὐπρόσιτος ὢν ἀνδράσι, γυναιξί, παιδίοις, γέρουσι, νέοις, ξένοις, γνωρίμοις, ἀνθρώπῳ παντί, ἐξέρχεται
πρὸς αὐτὴν συνήθως τῇ βακτηρίᾳ ἐπιστηριζόμενος τῇ ἑαυτοῦ, γαληνῷ καὶ ἡσύχῳ ποδί. Ὡς οὖν ἐκείνη μὲν τὴν τιμὴν
τῆς γονυκλισίας ἀπένειμε τῷ ἁγίῳ μετὰ δακρύων καὶ πίστεως, ὁ νεανίας δὲ εἰς τὴν ὄψιν τῆς ἀγγελομόρφου θέας
αὐτοῦ τοῖς ἰδίοις ἠτένισεν ὀφθαλμοῖς, ῥίπτει αὐτὸν τὸ
ἀκάθαρτον πνεῦμα ἐπὶ τῆς γῆς, καὶ στρεβλῶσαν δεινῶς,

to eat. When he had eaten, he enjoyed complete health, and was given back to his mother. He was now able to work and help her out of her poverty and misfortune. This was how Symeon's grace was manifested.

Chapter 119

"On another occasion a woman also had a young son who, because he was good-looking, had attracted the envy of the Evil One. He had thus been afflicted with an unclean spirit and used to experience attacks of demonic possession and would foam at the mouth. Inspired by heavenly providence and grace, the woman brought her son to the monastery and the saint. After coming up the stairs she stood in prayer before the doors of the church, supplicating God on behalf of her son. When she asked to have an audience with the saint, her request was made known to him, and Symeon, who, in imitation of Christ, was accessible to all—men, women, children, old people, young people, strangers, acquaintances, everybody—came out to her, leaning on his staff as usual, at a calm and tranquil pace. But while she honored the saint by kneeling tearfully and with faith, the youth stared wide-eyed at the sight of Symeon's angelic appearance, and the evil spirit threw him to the ground. It twisted

κείμενον εἶχε καὶ τετριγότα τὰς μύλας, ἀφρὸν ἀποπτύοντα καὶ ὡς ἔριφον κράζοντα [cf. Mk 9:18; Lk 9:39].

2 Ὁ τοίνυν ἅγιος οὕτω θεασάμενος στρεβλούμενον ὑπὸ τοῦ δαίμονος τοῦ ἀκαθάρτου καὶ εἰς τὴν γῆν κυλιόμενον [cf. Mk 9:20] τὸν νεανίαν, οἰκτείρας αὐτὸν καὶ ἐκ βαθέων στενάξας ψυχῆς ἐπ᾽ αὐτῷ, δάκρυά τε κενώσας ἐνώπιον τοῦ χαρακτῆρος Ἰησοῦ Χριστοῦ τοῦ Θεοῦ ἄνωθεν ἐγγεγραμμένου τῆς πύλης, ἐμβριμησάμενός τε καὶ ἐπιτιμήσας τῷ πνεύματι, φησὶν ἀκουόντων ἡμῶν· Ἐπιτιμήσαι σοι Κύριος ὁ Θεός μου, πονηρὲ καὶ ἀκάθαρτε δαίμων· ἔξελθε ἀπὸ τοῦ πλάσματος τοῦ Θεοῦ [cf. Mk 9:25; Mt 17:18].᾽ Εἶπε, καὶ ἔλαιον ἀπὸ τοῦ λύχνου τῆς εἰκόνος λαβὼν καὶ ἀλείψας τὸν πάσχοντα, δοὺς αὐτῷ χεῖρα ἀνέστησε, καὶ ἀπέλυσεν αὐτὸν ὑγιᾶ μετὰ τῆς μητρὸς εἰς τὸν οἶκον αὐτοῦ μηκέτι ὀχληθέντα ὑπὸ τῆς ἐπηρείας τοῦ δαίμονος.

120

"Ποτὲ τοῦ ἁγίου ἐπὶ τὴν πατρίδα καὶ τὸν πατρικὸν οἶκον αὐτοῦ ἀπερχομένου, καὶ γενομένου αὐτοῦ ἐπὶ τὸν παρρρέοντα ποταμὸν τῆς Βιθυνῶν μέγιστον ὄντα τὸν Γάλλον,²⁷² ὁρᾷ ἐπὶ τὴν ὄχθην ἱστάμενον τοῦ ποταμοῦ ἁλιέα²⁷³ καὶ ἰχθύας τῷ καλάμῳ καὶ τῇ σαγήνῃ ἀγρεύοντα. Ὡς οὖν εἶδεν αὐτὸν ὁ ἅγιος, πυνθάνεται αὐτὸν εἰ ἄρα καὶ ἰχθύας ἔχει πιπράσαι αὐτῷ. Ὁ δέ· Πολλὰ κοπιάσας,᾽ φησίν,

him around terribly, and kept him lying there, grinding his teeth, foaming at the mouth, and bleating like a little goat.

"When the saint saw the youth being twisted about in 2 this way by the unclean demon and rolling around on the ground, he felt pity for him. He groaned for him from the depths of his soul and shed tears before the image of Jesus Christ our God that was painted over the gateway. Then he became angry and rebuked the spirit. In our hearing he said, 'My Lord God rebukes you, evil and unclean demon! Come out of this creature of God!' When he had said this, he took oil from the icon lamp and anointed the boy who was suffering in this way. Then he gave him his hand and made him stand up. Afterward Symeon sent him home with his mother, in good health, and no longer troubled by the demon's abuse.

Chapter 120

"Once, when the saint had gone away to his homeland and his family house, he came to the big river that flows through Bithynia, the Gallos. There he saw a fisherman standing on the riverbank, fishing with a pole and a net. When the saint saw him, he asked him if he had any fish to sell him. 'Venerable father,' said the man, 'I've been laboring

ἀπὸ βαθέος ὄρθρου μέχρι τοῦ νῦν, τίμιε πάτερ, ἐνάτης ὥρας οὔσης ὡς ὁρᾷς τῆς ἡμέρας, οὐδὲν οὐδαμῶς ἐπίασα ἢ ἐμαυτῷ πρὸς βρῶσιν ἢ ἑτέρῳ πρὸς πρᾶσιν.' Καὶ ὁ ἅγιος· 'Χάλασόν μοι τὸ ἄγκιστρον εἰς ἐμὸν ὄνομα, καὶ εἴ γέ τι κρατήσεις ἐπὶ Θεῷ,[274] λήψῃ παρ' ἐμοῦ ἀργύριον τιμῆς ἕνεκα τοῦ ἀγρευθέντος ἰχθύος, κἀγὼ τὸ ἀγρευθὲν ἀναλάβοιμι.'

2 "Ὁ οὖν ἁλιεὺς εὐθὺς ᾗ τάχους εἶχεν πρὸς τὸ μέσον τοῦ ποταμοῦ διαπετάζει τὸ ἄγκιστρον, καὶ—ὦ Χριστέ, τῶν θαυμάτων καὶ τῆς δυνάμεως τῶν ἁγίων σου!—οὐδὲ μικρὸν ἀναμείνας ἀνασπᾷ τοῦτο τῇ χειρὶ καὶ μέγιστον ἰχθὺν ἀναφέρει ἐκεῖθεν. Ὡς δὲ παρὰ προσδοκίαν πᾶσαν τὸν ἰχθὺν ὁ ἁλιεὺς ἐθεάσατο μέγαν παρ' αὐτοῦ ἀγρευθέντα, λαμβάνει αὐτὸν καὶ ὑπὸ τὸ ἴδιον φυλάττει ἱμάτιον. Καὶ ὁ ἅγιος· 'Λάβε,'[275] φησί, 'τὸ συμφωνηθέν σοι καὶ δός μοι τὸν εἰς τὸ ἐμὸν ὄνομα ἀγρευθέντα ἰχθύν.' Ὁ δέ· 'Χρῄζω τοῦτον,' φησίν, 'εἰς τὸν δεῖνα πατρίκιον, καὶ οὐ πιπράσκω αὐτόν.' Ὁ δὲ ἅγιος τὴν κακίαν ἐντεῦθεν[276] κατανοήσας αὐτοῦ καὶ τὸ ἄδικον τῆς ψυχῆς αὐτοῦ, καταλιπὼν αὐτὸν καὶ μικρὸν μεταβὰς ἐπηρᾶτο[277] τῷ ἀδίκῳ, καὶ παραχρῆμα ἀποσκευασάμενος ὁ ἰχθὺς τὸ ἱμάτιον καὶ εἰς ὕψος πηδήσας ἀκοντίζει ἑαυτὸν μέσον τοῦ ποταμοῦ, καὶ ἀφίησι τὸν ἀγνώμονα ὡς τὸ πρώην κενόν.

away from the crack of dawn until now (and as you see, it's
the ninth hour of the day),[132] and I've caught nothing at all,
either to feed myself or to sell to someone else.' The saint
replied, 'Drop your hook in for me, in my name, and if, by
the grace of God, you catch something, I'll pay you the price
of the fish you've caught and I'll take away the catch.'

"The fisherman immediately cast his hook into the mid-   2
dle of the river as fast as he could and—oh Christ, the miracles and power of your saints!—without waiting even a moment he drew it in with his hand and pulled out a very big
fish. But when the fisherman saw the big fish he had caught,
contrary to all his expectations, he took it and put it under
his coat. The saint said, 'Take what you agreed to and give
me the fish that was caught in my name!' But the fisherman
replied, 'I need this fish for Patrician So-and-so, and I'm not
selling it.' Then the saint realized how evil the fisherman
was and how unjust his soul. So he left him and, going a short
distance away, cursed the unjust man. Right away the fish escaped from the coat and, leaping up in the air, dove into the
middle of the river, leaving that hardhearted man as empty-
handed as before.

121

"Φίλος ἦν τῷ μακαρίῳ τούτῳ πατρὶ κατὰ τὸ ἐμπόριον τῆς Χρυσοπόλεως, ᾧ ὄνομα Ὀρέστης. Οὗτος ἱκανῶς ἔχων εἰς περιουσίαν καὶ εὐπορίαν χρημάτων ἀνενδεὴς τὰ πολλὰ ὑπῆρχεν ἀνήρ, καὶ μετὰ γυναικὸς καὶ παίδων εὐθυμῶν ἦν εἰς τὸν βίον καὶ τὴν οἰκίαν αὐτοῦ. Ἀλλὰ βασκήνας ὁ βάσκανος αὐτῷ δαίμων τῆς εὐθηνίας καὶ παραχωρηθεὶς κρούει ἀοράτως αὐτὸν κατὰ κόρρης δι᾽ ἐπιλήψεως, καὶ ὅλον ἐστράφη τὸ στόμα τοῦ ἀνδρὸς εἰς τὸ οὖς αὐτοῦ, καὶ ἀπεσβέσθη καὶ τὴν ἐνοῦσαν φωνήν. Φοράδην οὖν ἀναβαστάσαντες αὐτὸν ἀποκομίζουσιν εἰς τὴν οἰκίαν καὶ τοὺς παῖδας καὶ τὴν γυναῖκα. Ὡς δὲ τὸν ἄνδρα μὲν ἡ γυνή, οἱ παῖδες δὲ τὸν πατέρα οὕτω δεινῷ πάθει κατασχεθέντα εἶδον παρὰ πᾶσαν ἐλπίδα καὶ μηδὲ προσδοκώμενον ἐπιζῆσαι τῷ πάθει, θρήνοις[278] ἐκόπτοντο μετὰ πάντων τῶν συνόντων ἅμα καὶ φίλων, καὶ μεγάλα βοῶντες ἀπαράκλητα ἔκλαιον.

2   "Μηνύεται τοίνυν ἡ συμφορὰ τοῦ ἀνδρὸς τῷ πατρί, καὶ ὅτι ὁ φίλος Ὀρέστης ὅσον οὔπω τῆς παρούσης ζωῆς ἀπορρήγνυται. Ὁ δὲ οἷα δὴ τῷ Πνεύματι τὸ μέλλον προγνούς· 'Ἄγωμεν,' ἔφη τῷ μηνύσαντι, 'καὶ ὄψομαι τὸν φίλον ὁ φίλος ἐρχόμενος, καὶ ὀφθήσομαι ὑπ᾽ αὐτοῦ.' Λαβὼν οὖν τὴν βακτηρίαν αὐτοῦ ἥψατο τῆς πρὸς ἐκεῖνον ἀπαγούσης ὁδοῦ, κἀγώ," φησί, "τοῦ ἁγίου προώδευον. Ὡς οὖν ἐπὶ τὴν οἰκίαν ἦλθε τοῦ φίλου, καὶ ἡ γυνὴ τὸν ἅγιον ἐθεάσατο γοερὸν καὶ διωλύγιον[279] ὀλολύξασα· 'Ἰδού,' φησί, 'πάτερ, ὃν ἐφίλεις ὁ φίλος καὶ ὑφ᾽ οὗ θερμῶς ἐφιλήθης ἐκλείπει,

Chapter 121

"The blessed father had a friend called Orestes in the commercial district at Chrysopolis.[133] This Orestes was a man of considerable substance who had plenty of everything and wanted for nothing, including a happy life and home with his wife and children. But the jealous demon was jealous of his prosperity and, with God's permission, struck him in the head without being seen. As a result of this stroke the man's mouth was all twisted toward his ear and he also lost his speech. They lifted him up and carried him home to his wife and children on a stretcher. When the wife saw her husband, and the children their father, in this terrible and shocking state, they started mourning, lamenting with the whole household and their friends because they did not expect him to survive his illness. They cried loudly and wept inconsolably.

"The father [Symeon] was informed of his friend Orestes's misfortune and that he was on the point of departing this life. But Symeon, as though he foresaw the future through the grace of the Spirit, said to the man who had brought him the news, 'Let's go, and coming as a friend, I'll see my friend and he'll see me.' So the saint took his staff and set off down the road that led to Orestes's house, while I," said <Nikephoros,> "went ahead of him. When Symeon reached his friend's home and Orestes's wife saw the saint, she started wailing loudly. 'Look, father,' she said, 'the friend you loved and who loved you so warmly is leaving us, alas! At

αἰαῖ!²⁸⁰ Ὅσον οὔπω καὶ²⁸¹ χήρα τοῖς πᾶσιν ὀφθήσομαι, καὶ
τὰ ἐμὰ τέκνα ὀρφανὰ καὶ πατρὸς ἔρημα ἔσονται. Ἀλλὰ βο-
ήθει μοι ἀξιῶ τῇ σῇ δούλῃ, καὶ δεήθητι τοῦ Θεοῦ ἢ κἀμὲ
συναποψύξαι αὐτῷ καὶ μηδεμίαν ὥραν ὄπισθεν τοῦ ἀνδρὸς
ἐναπολειφθῆναι ἢ κἂν ἰδεῖν αὐτὸν εἰς τὸ²⁸² κατὰ φύσιν
ἀνορθωθέντα ποσῶς καὶ περὶ τῆς οἰκίας καὶ τῶν πραγμάτων διατασσόμενον.'²⁸³

122

"Ἀλλὰ ταῦτα μὲν ἡ γυνὴ πρὸς τὸν ἅγιον ἔλεγεν. Ὁ δὲ
ὡς εἶδεν οὕτω τὸν φίλον δεινῷ πάθει κατασχεθέντα ἄφω-
νόν τε καὶ τυφλὸν ἐπὶ τῆς κλίνης κείμενον καὶ μηδέν τι τῶν
γινομένων ἢ λεγομένων ἐπαισθανόμενον, δάκρυα συμπαθείας ἔχεεν ἐπ' αὐτῷ, καί· 'Οἴμοι, φίλε Ὀρέστα, οἶον,' φησί,
'πέπονθας! Οἶον εἰς σὲ ὁ βάσκανος δαίμων εἰργάσατο!'
Οὕτως εἰπὼν εἰς εὐχὴν ἐκτείνας τὰς χεῖρας, καὶ πρὸς
τὸν ὑπακούοντα Κύριον τῆς δεήσεως αὐτοῦ ἄρας τοὺς νο-
ητοὺς ὀφθαλμοὺς τῆς ψυχῆς, ἅπτεται τῆς κεφαλῆς τοῦ
ἀνδρὸς καὶ ποιήσας ἐπ' αὐτῷ τὴν τῶν νενοσηκότων εὐχὴν
σφραγίζει εὐθὺς τό τε στόμα καὶ ἅμα ὅλην αὐτοῦ τὴν κεφαλήν, καὶ παραυτίκα—ὦ τῆς ἀφάτου σου ἀγαθότητος, Κύριε!—εἰς τὸ κατὰ φύσιν ἀποκαθίσταται ὁ ἀνήρ, καὶ τὸ ἴδιον
στόμα ἐλεύθερον τῆς τοῦ Πονηροῦ ἀπολαβὼν ἐπηρείας
καὶ μάστιγος, ὁμιλίας ἀξιοῖ τὴν γυναῖκα καὶ τὸ χαῖρε τῷ
ἁγίῳ προσφθέγγεται.

any moment everyone will see me widowed, and my children are going to be fatherless orphans. But please, help me, your servant, and ask God either that I may die along with my husband and not linger after him even for an hour, or that I may see him somehow restored to his natural state and running his house and business again.'

Chapter 122

"This is what the woman said to the saint. As for Symeon, when he saw his friend in this terrible state, speechless, blind, and lying on his bed unaware of anything that was happening or being said, he shed tears of sympathy for him. 'Alas my friend Orestes,' he said, 'how you've suffered! Look what the jealous demon has done to you!' Saying this, he stretched out his hands in prayer and raised his spiritual gaze to the Lord, who was listening to his plea. Then he touched the man's head, said the prayer for the sick over him, and made the sign of the cross directly on his mouth and his whole head. Immediately—oh Lord, your unspeakable goodness!—the man was restored to his natural state and, with his mouth freed from the abuse and scourge of the Evil One, spoke with his wife and greeted the saint.

2   "Τοιγαροῦν καὶ οὐκ ἐνέλειπεν ἔκτοτε, ἕως ἐν τοῖς ζῶσιν
ἦν ὁ μακάριος, ὁ εὐεργετηθεὶς²⁸⁴ φίλος ἀποκομίζειν τὴν
καρποφορὰν τῷ ἁγίῳ καὶ τὴν εὐχαριστίαν ἀπονέμειν αὐτῷ.
Ἀλλ᾽ ὁ μὲν τὰ κομιζόμενα διὰ τὴν ἀγάπην ἐδέχετο, 'Εὐχαριστεῖν δέ,' ἔλεγεν, 'ἐπὶ πᾶσι μόνῳ Θεῷ, ἀδελφέ, τῷ δυ-
νατῷ ποιεῖν αὐτοῦ τὰ θαυμάσια ἐπὶ πᾶσι τοῖς ἠλπικόσιν εἰς
αὐτόν· αὐτοῦ γάρ ἐσμεν ποιήματα, καὶ παρ᾽ αὐτοῦ ἐκ τοῦ μὴ
ὄντος εἰς τὸ εἶναι γεγόναμεν, κτισθέντες ἐπὶ ἔργοις ἀγαθοῖς
[Eph 2:10] εἰς δόξαν τῆς αὐτοῦ ἀγαθότητος, ἄνθρωποι καὶ
αὐτοὶ ὄντες ὡς ὁρᾷς ἁμαρτωλοὶ καὶ ἀσθένειαν κατὰ πάντα
τὴν ἴσην ὑμῖν περικείμενοι. Οὐ μόνον δὲ ἀλλὰ καὶ τοῦ
οἰκείου βίου ἐπιμέλειαν χρὴ σπουδαίως ποιεῖσθαι μή τι
καὶ λανθανόντως ἢ καὶ ἑκουσίως τῶν μὴ ἀνηκόντων τῇ
θεοσεβείᾳ καὶ τῶν ἀναξίων τοῦ βουλήματος τοῦ Θεοῦ
πράττωμεν, καὶ διὰ τοῦτο χώραν διδόντες τῷ βασκάνῳ καὶ
πονηρῷ δαίμονι καθ᾽ ἡμῶν καὶ²⁸⁵ τοῖς τοιούτοις περιπί-
πτωμεν πειρασμοῖς. Ὅρα δὴ τοῦ λοιποῦ, ἀδελφέ, ὡς ὑγιὴς
τῇ χάριτι γέγονας τοῦ Θεοῦ, μηκέτι κατασχεθῇς κακο-
φροσύνῃ καὶ ἁμαρτίᾳ, ἵνα μὴ χεῖρόν τι τοῦ γεγονότος εἰς²⁸⁶
σὲ γένηται, καθά φησιν ὁ Θεὸς καὶ Λόγος οὐχὶ μόνον τῷ
παραλύτῳ [John 5:14], ἀλλὰ καὶ πᾶσι φιλαγάθως ἡμῖν.'

"From then on, for as long as the blessed Symeon was   2
alive, this friend who had received his help never failed to
bring offerings to the saint and express his thanks to him.
Symeon used to accept what he brought because of his love
<for Orestes>, but would say, 'You should thank God alone
for everything, brother, for it's He who has the power to
work these marvels for everyone who hopes in Him. People
like me *are His handiwork* and we've come into being from
nothing through Him, *created for good deeds* to glorify His
goodness. We're men too and, as you see, sinners who have
the same weakness in everything as you. Not just that, but
we too have to pay careful attention to our own conduct, so
that we do not act through negligence or even of our own
free will in a way that's inappropriate to our religious pre-
cepts and unworthy of God's will, and in that way give the
jealous and wicked demon an opportunity against us and
thus encounter the same sort of tribulations.[134] So look out
then, brother, now *you've been made well* by God's grace, that
you are no longer possessed by perversity and sin, *so that
nothing worse happens to you* than has happened already, as our
God and Word says, not only to the crippled man, but, in his
beneficence, to us all.'

123

"Ἀλλὰ γὰρ πῶς παραδράμω τὸ ἐν τοῖς διαπληκτιζομένοις αὐτῷ τηνικαῦτα τέρας φρικτόν, ὃ παρ' αὐτοῦ γέγονεν ἑνὶ τούτων τῶν ἀδελφῶν; ἀεὶ γὰρ τὸ προσυπαντῶν μοι τῶν ἐκείνου θαυμάτων μεῖζον τοῦ φθάσαντος δείκνυται, καὶ τὸν λόγον ἀνασειράζει τοῦ δρόμου ἐλθεῖν ἐπὶ τὸ τέλος ἀγωνιζόμενον, καὶ βιάζεται εἰπεῖν καὶ φανερὰ θεῖναι, ἃ Θεὸς κεκρυμμένα ὄντα νῦν ἡμῖν ἐφανέρωσεν. Ἔχει δὲ οὕτως τοῦ φρικτοῦ τούτου θαύματος ἡ διήγησις.

2   "Δύο ποτὲ ἄνδρες ἐκ τῶν προσοίκων ἀδελφοὶ ἐκ μητρικῶν τῶν ὠδίνων τῷ ἁγίῳ διὰ τὴν τῆς μονῆς κτῆσιν ἰσχυρῶς ὡς εἶχον διεπληκτίζοντο, ὕβρεσι καὶ ὀνειδισμοῖς βάλλοντες καὶ ἐπαπειλούμενοι δριμέως αὐτῷ. Ὡς δὲ ὁ μὲν προσηνῶς αὐτοῖς ἀπεκρίνατο, παρακαλῶν, δυσωπῶν, πάντα ποιῶν καὶ λέγων τὰ πρὸς εἰρήνην φέροντα αὐτῶν τὰς ψυχάς, οἱ δὲ τῇ ζέσει τοῦ θυμοῦ μᾶλλον καὶ μᾶλλον ἀνήπτοντο²⁸⁷ κατ' αὐτοῦ, καὶ ὕβρεσι τὸν ἅγιον ἔπλυνον, ἤρξατο αὐτοῖς προμαρτύρεσθαι τὸ φοβερὸν κρῖμα τοῦ Θεοῦ, οἷόν ἐστι κατὰ τῶν ὑβριστῶν καὶ διαλοιδορουμένων τοὺς δούλους τοῦ Θεοῦ. Ὁ οὖν εἷς ἐξ αὐτῶν, ᾧ ἦν ὄνομα Δαμιανός, μὴ ὑπενεγκὼν τὸ βάρος τοῦ ἀσχέτου θυμοῦ, ὠθεῖ τὸν ἅγιον τῇ παλαμναίᾳ καὶ βαναύσῳ χειρὶ τούτου καὶ καταρράσσει αὐτὸν κατὰ γῆς. Εἶτα δεδοικὼς μή ποτε ἡ ὀργὴ τοῦ Θεοῦ ἔλθῃ μετὰ θυμοῦ εἰς αὐτόν, μεταμεληθεὶς κύπτει διὰ τάχους καὶ ἀνιστᾷ τὸν ἅγιον τοῦ Θεοῦ ἱερέα ἀπὸ τῆς γῆς, ἀκηκοὼς ἐξ αὐτοῦ· ὁ Θεός,

Chapter 123

"But how can I pass over the terrible marvel that happened because of him to one of those brothers who were in dispute with him?" <Nikephoros continued.> "For with Symeon's miracles, the one that I've encountered most recently always seems greater than the one before it, and it draws my account (which I'm struggling to finish) off track and forces me to tell and clearly write down what was once concealed but that God has now revealed to us. So my narrative now includes this awesome miracle.

"Two of the neighbors, men who were brothers with the 2
same mother, were engaged in an extremely bitter dispute with the saint over the monastery's property, and were hurling insults and abuse at him and threatening him harshly. He would reply to them gently, asking them politely, treating them with respect, and doing and saying everything that would bring peace to their souls. But as they grew more and more inflamed by their boiling anger against the saint and heaped insults on him, he started to remind them how terrible God's judgment is against those who insult and vilify His servants. One of these men, who was called Damianos, could no longer contain the pressure of his uncontrollable anger, and with his violent, rough hand, he shoved the saint and knocked him to the ground. But then, terrified that the wrath of God might fall upon him in anger, the man repented. He quickly bent down and helped the holy priest of

ἀδελφέ, συγχωρήσει σοι καὶ μὴ στήσῃ σοι τὴν ἁμαρτίαν ταύτην [cf. Act 7:60].'

124

"Ὁ δέ γε ἕτερος, ᾧ ἦν Ἄνθης ὄνομα, εἰς πολὺν ὕθλον λοιδοριῶν τε καὶ ὕβρεων τὸ ἀναιδὲς μηκύνας αὐτοῦ τῆς ψυχῆς, καὶ μηδὲ μικρὸν φεισάμενος ἑαυτοῦ, μηδὲ κἂν ὅλως ἐπισχὼν τῆς ἐρεσχελίας ὁ δείλαιος ἐμπαροινεῖ τῷ ἁγίῳ, ὑποκριτὴν καὶ ἀχυροκάπνιστον καὶ ἀπατεῶνα τῶν ὑπαντώντων καὶ προσομιλούντων αὐτῷ ἀποκαλέσας αὐτόν. Ὁ οὖν μακάριος, ὡς εἶδεν αὐτοῦ τὴν ἄμετρον ἀναίδειαν εἰς πολὺ ἐκταθεῖσαν καὶ κατὰ τοῦ ναοῦ τοῦ Θεοῦ καὶ τοῦ Πνεύματος [cf. 1 Cor 3:16, 6:19], ὅστις ἦν αὐτὸς ἐκεῖνος, τὴν γλῶτταν τὸν ἀναιδῆ ἀκονήσαντα [cf. Ps 139(140):3], οὐ μόνον δέ, ἀλλὰ καὶ τὴν ζωοποιὸν νέκρωσιν ἣν ἐπεφέρετο ἐξ ἱερῶν ἀγώνων τῆς ἀρετῆς, ἀλλὰ καὶ τὴν ἐνέργειαν τῆς θείας χάριτος τὴν εἰς αὐτὸν μυστικῶς ἐνεργοῦσαν, τό τε ἦθος ἐκεῖνο τὸ γαληνόν, αὐτό τε τὸ ἀσκητικώτατον χρῶμα καὶ πάντα συλλήβδην εἰπεῖν τὰ καλά, ἃ φέρων εἶχεν ἐκ τῆς ἐπιπνοίας τοῦ Πνεύματος, ἐνυβρίσαντα, μιμεῖται τὸν Ἐλισσαιὲ ζῆλον, ὅν ποτε ἐκεῖνος κατὰ τῶν ἀκαθάρτων παίδων ἐκείνων ζήλῳ θείῳ κινούμενος ἔδειξε, βορὰν διὰ τῆς ἀρᾶς παραδοὺς τοῖς θηρίοις αὐτούς [4 Kings 2:24], καὶ ζήλου μεστὸς γεγονὼς ὑπὸ τοῦ Πνεύματος πυρποληθεὶς ἄνωθεν,

God up from the ground, while hearing him say, 'May God forgive you, brother, and *not hold this sin against* you.'

Chapter 124

"But the other man, who was called Anthes, unleashed a stream of nonsense from his shameless soul, full of vilifications and insults. The wretch had not the slightest concern for himself and did not hold back on his insults at all, but behaved toward the saint like some offensive drunk, calling him a fraud, someone who used chaff smoke,[135] and who deceived those who came to visit him and talk to him. The blessed Symeon saw that this man's boundless shamelessness was continuing to spread and that he was *sharpening* his shameless *tongue* against the temple of God and His Spirit (that was Symeon himself). Anthes was insulting not only the life-giving mortification[136] that had been conferred on Symeon by his holy struggles for virtue, but also the energy of divine grace that worked mysteriously in him, his mild manner, his most ascetic complexion, and, to put it briefly, all the good things that he had received through the inspiration of the Spirit. So Symeon imitated the indignation that Elisha once showed toward those unclean children when, moved by divine indignation, he fed them to the wild animals by his curse. Thus, filled with indignation and fired up by the Spirit from above, he said this to Anthes: 'If I'm a

τάδε φησὶ πρὸς αὐτόν· Εἰ τοίνυν, ὡς αὐτὸς σὺ διαβεβαιοῖ
τοῖς λόγοις, ὑποκριτὴς ἐγὼ ἄχυρα καπνιζόμενος καὶ τοῦτο
ἔχων ἐκεῖθεν τὸ χρῶμα πρὸς ἀπάτην, ὡς ἔφης, τῶν ἐμοὶ
προσυπαντώντων ἀνθρώπων καὶ ὁμιλούντων, ἀμὴν ἤδη
λέγω σοι ἐν ἀληθείᾳ, τοῦτο σὺ τὸ χρῶμα ποιήσεις ὀγκωθεὶς
τὴν γαστέρα, καὶ ἔσῃ πάντως καὶ αὐτὸς ὡς ἐγὼ τοὺς
ἀνθρώπους ἐξαπατῶν.'

2   "Εἶπε, καὶ—ὦ τῆς ἀφύκτου σου δίκης, Θεὲ τοῦ παν-
τός!—σὺν τῷ λόγῳ ταύτην[288] ἐκείνην τὴν τῆς ἡμέρας
ἑσπέραν ἀνακλιθεὶς ἐν τῇ ἑαυτοῦ κλίνῃ ὁ δυστυχὴς οὐκέτι
ἐξ αὐτῆς ἀναστῆναι ἴσχυσεν, ἀλλὰ νόσῳ βαρείᾳ ληφθεὶς
ὀγκωθείς τε εἰς ὑπερβολὴν καὶ κίτρῳ ἐοικὸς τὸ χρῶμα τῆς
ἰδίας ποιήσας ὄψεως, ἐν ῥηταῖς ἡμέραις ταύτῃ τῇ νόσῳ
ἐναπέψυξε καὶ τῇ φοβερᾷ ὀργῇ τοῦ Θεοῦ. Τοῦτο δὲ γέγονεν εἰς φόβον μὲν τῶν ἀπαιδεύτων καὶ ἀσυνέτων ἀνθρώπων, ἵνα μὴ τῶν ἁγίων καὶ τῆς ἐνοικούσης ἐν αὐτοῖς χάριτος καταφρονῶσιν, εἰς ἔκβασιν δὲ τοῦ εἰρημένου ὑπὸ τῶν
ἀποστόλων ἐν ταῖς αὐτῶν διατάξεσιν ἔνθα παραγγελίαν
ποιοῦνται περὶ τοῦ δεῖν τιμᾶν τοὺς πνευματικοὺς πατέρας
ἡμῶν ἐν τῷ λ΄ κεφαλαίῳ τοῦ δευτέρου βιβλίου κατὰ λέξιν
ἔχοντος οὕτως· *Οὗτοι, φησί, παρὰ Θεοῦ ζωῆς καὶ θανάτου
ἐξουσίαν εἰλήφασιν ἐν τῷ δικάζειν τοὺς ἡμαρτηκότας καὶ
καταδικάζειν εἰς θάνατον ζωῆς αἰωνίου καὶ λύειν ἁμαρτιῶν
τοὺς ἐπιστρέφοντας καὶ ζωογονεῖν αὐτούς.*

fraud, as you claim in your statements, and my skin is this color because I've used chaff smoke so as to deceive the people who come to visit and talk to me, as you allege, then so be it. But now I say to you in truth, you'll turn this color yourself when your stomach is all swollen up and then you'll no doubt be deceiving people yourself, just like I am!'

"Symeon said this and—oh, Your inescapable justice, God 2 of all!—at his word, that very evening, after that unfortunate man had lain down in his bed, he no longer had the strength to get up again but, stricken by a serious illness, became enormously distended. His face became the color of a lemon and he died within the number of days appointed by this illness and by the terrible wrath of God. Now this occurred partly to frighten ignorant and stupid men, so that they would not be contemptuous of the saints and the grace that dwells in them, and partly to fulfill the statement of the apostles in their *Constitutions* where, in the thirtieth chapter of the second book, they provide instruction about the need to honor our spiritual fathers. This reads as follows: *Those men,* it says, *have received from God the power of life and death in judging those who have sinned; they can condemn them to eternal death;*[137] *and those who repent, they can absolve from their sins and keep alive.*[138]

125

["]Ἐπεὶ δὲ καὶ ὁ χρόνος ἤδη πεπλήρωτο τῆς παρούσης ζωῆς τῷ ἁγίῳ καὶ ὁ ἀριθμὸς τῶν ἡμερῶν αὐτοῦ, καὶ τὸ τούτων πέρας ἐγνωρίσθη αὐτῷ, νόσῳ συσκευάζεται τῇ τελευταίᾳ, καὶ ἡ κλίνη αὐτὸν νοσηλευόμενον δέχεται· ἡ δὲ νόσος ῥύσις ἦν τῆς γαστρὸς τὴν οὐσίαν κενοῦσα καὶ τὸν σύνδεσμον τῶν συνδραμόντων στοιχείων εἰς ἕκαστον ἀπολύουσα. Ἔκειτο οὖν ὁ μακάριος ἐφ᾽ ἱκανὰς τὰς ἡμέρας τῇ νόσῳ κρατηθεὶς καὶ τὴν δύναμιν ὑπετέμνετο, τὰς σάρκας ἐτήκετο, καὶ τοῦ δεσμοῦ παρελύετο. Ἐς τοσοῦτον γὰρ ταριχευθεῖσαν ἔσχεν ὑπὸ τῆς ἀρρωστίας τὴν σάρκα, ὡς μὴ σαλευθῆναι δύνασθαι αὐτὸν ἀφ᾽ ἑαυτοῦ, εἰ μὴ πρότερον χεῖρα βοηθείας[289] δεδώκαμεν, καὶ διὰ μηχανῆς τινος ἔνθεν ἢ ἐκεῖθεν τοῦτον ἐστρέψαμεν.

2 "Οὕτω τοίνυν ἔχοντος αὐτοῦ καὶ ὑφ᾽ ἡμῶν βασταζομένου ἡνίκα καὶ πρὸς τὴν χρείαν ἡ φύσις ἠπείγετο,[290] ἐπισκήπτει μοι μόνῳ προσκαρτερεῖν καὶ προσμένειν αὐτῷ. Ἀλλ᾽ ἔτι νέος ὢν ἐγὼ καὶ δεινῶς εἰς βάθος ὑπὸ τοῦ ὕπνου κρατούμενος, φανερὸν τοῦτο ποιῶ τῷ ἁγίῳ, καὶ ὡς οὐκ ἐξικανοῦσαν ἔχω τὴν ἰσχὺν εἰς[291] θεραπείαν αὐτοῦ μόνος προσκαρτερεῖν, ὑπὸ τοῦ πάθους τούτου οἷα δὴ δοῦλος κυριευόμενος. Ὁ δὲ ἐν ταύτῃ· Δεῦρο τῇ θήκῃ,᾽ φησίν, ᾽ἣν ἄρκλαν κοινῶς ὀνομάζειν εἰώθαμεν, πεσὼν ἀναπαύθητι πλησίον ἐμοῦ, καὶ ῥᾷον ἕξεις[292] τοῦ πάθους.᾽ Τοῦτο πεποιηκότος ἐμοῦ κατὰ τὴν ἐκείνου," φησί, "πρόσταξιν, καὶ τῇ ἑσπέρᾳ, καθ᾽ ἣν τοῦτο προσέταξεν, ὑπνώσαντος ἐν αὐτῇ,

Chapter 125

"When the saint's time in this present life and the number of his days had been fulfilled, and he knew the end was close, he suffered his final illness. And when he fell ill, he became bedridden. The illness was dysentery, which emptied his body of its substance and gradually weakened the bonds that held together all its constituent parts. The blessed Symeon lay there for many days in the grip of this illness so that his strength dwindled, his flesh wasted away, and his muscles grew feeble. His flesh was so wasted by his sickness that he was unable to roll over by himself unless we first gave him a helping hand and turned him this way and that by means of a mechanical device.

"While he was in this state and we had to carry him whenever he received an urgent call of nature, he ordered me to attend to him and stay alone with him. I was still a young boy, however, and I used to sleep very deeply indeed. I let the saint know this, and that I didn't have sufficient strength to take care of him by myself because I was enslaved by this tendency to sleep so deeply. 'Here,' he said in response to this, 'lie on the chest (which we usually call an *arkla*)[139] and sleep close to me, and you'll be able to deal with this condition more easily.' I followed his instructions and did this," said <Nikephoros>, "and when I slept on it on the evening of the day he had given me these instructions, by the grace

2

οὐκέτι Θεοῦ χάριτι καθὰ καὶ πρώην τῷ ὕπνῳ κατεβυθίσθην, ὅλως ποτὲ ἢ²⁹³ τὴν ἀνάγκην εἶχον ἐκείνην καταφε-
ρόμενος ὑπ' αὐτοῦ· ἀλλ' ὥσπερ τι βαρὺ ἄχθος ἀποσεισάμενος αὐτὸν ἐγρηγορῶν ἤμην ἔκτοτε, οὐ μόνον ἔξυπνος
ὤν, ἀλλὰ καὶ καθεύδων, ταῖς πρεσβείαις αὐτοῦ κατὰ τὸ
εἰρημένον· 'ἐγώ,' φησί, 'κατεύδω, καὶ ἡ καρδία μου ἀγρυπνεῖ
²⁹⁴ [Ct 5:2].'

126

"Ἀλλὰ τούτοις πᾶσιν²⁹⁵ ἐπισυνάψας καὶ ὃ εἶδον σημεῖον," φησίν, "ἐν αὐτῷ κατὰ τὸν καιρὸν ἐκεῖνον τῆς αὐτοῦ
κατακλίσεως τοῦ περὶ τούτων δρόμου καταπαύσω τὸν λόγον. Ἐπειδὴ καθώσπερ ἔφθην εἰπὼν οὐδενὶ ἑτέρῳ πλὴν
ἐμοῦ συνεχώρει τὴν μετ' αὐτοῦ ἐν ἑνὶ καὶ τῷ αὐτῷ κελλίῳ
παραμονήν, ἐκείμην κατὰ τὸν καιρὸν τῆς αὐτοῦ κατακλίσεως ἐπάνω τῆς εἰρημένης θήκης ἐκείνης, καὶ τὴν ὅλην
νύκτα διεκαρτέρουν, ποτὲ μὲν ὑπνῶν, ποτὲ δὲ καὶ καθυπη-
ρετῶν αὐτῷ ὁπόταν²⁹⁶ ἐν χρείᾳ τινὸς ἐγένετο. Τοῦ χρόνου
δὲ τῆς ἀρρωστίας αὐτοῦ παριππεύσαντος, καὶ ἀπάρτι
δεινῶς κατεργασαμένης αὐτὸν τῆς νόσου, καὶ ὅσον οὔπω
λῦσαι τοῦτον φιλονεικούσης τῶν δεσμῶν τῆς σαρκός, ἐν
μιᾷ τῶν νυκτῶν ὡς ἤμην κείμενος ἐπάνω τῆς θήκης ἐκείνης
καὶ λεπτόν τι καὶ ἀδρανὲς ὕπνου μεταλαμβάνων, ὥσπερ
ὑπό τινος, καθὰ καὶ πρόσθεν εἰρήκαμεν, ἀφυπνίσθην, καὶ

of God I no longer sank into a deep sleep as I had done previously, when I was completely weighed down by the compulsion to sleep. It was as though some heavy burden had
been lifted from me, and from then on I remained watchful
over him through his prayers, not only when I was awake
but even while asleep, in accordance with the saying *I am
sleeping but my heart is keeping watch.*

Chapter 126

"Now, I'm going to add to all these miracles the sign
that I saw worked in Symeon when he was bedridden," said
<Nikephoros>, "and then I'll bring my account to a close. As
I've already said, Symeon permitted no one apart from me
to remain with him in his cell, and so, during the time he was
bedridden, I would lie on the chest I mentioned and spend
the entire night there, sometimes sleeping, sometimes helping him when he needed something. He had been sick for a
while then, and was very badly affected by his illness, which
was struggling to deliver him as soon as possible from the
bonds of the flesh. One night then, as I was lying on that
chest and dozing fitfully, it was as though I'd been woken up
by something, as I said before; and I saw that blessed and

ὁρῶ τὸν μακάριον καὶ ἰσάγγελον τοῦτον, ὃν μόλις μετὰ μη-
χανῆς τινος ἔνθεν ἢ[297] ἐκεῖθεν σαλεύοντες ἐπάνω τῆς κλίνης ἐστρέφομεν ὑπὸ τῆς ἀρρωστίας κατεργασθέντα—ὢ
τοῦ φρικτοῦ θαύματος!—ὑπὸ τὸν ἀέρα τῆς κέλλης κρεμάμενον αὖθις ὡσεὶ πήχεις ἀπὸ τῆς γῆς τέσσαρας ἢ καὶ πλέον,
καὶ προσευχόμενον τῷ Θεῷ αὐτοῦ ἐν ἀνεκλαλήτῳ φωτί.
Ὡς οὖν οὕτως εἶδον αὐτόν, ἐπεὶ καὶ ἀπὸ τῆς πρόσθεν θεωρίας μεμνημένος ὑπῆρχον ἀπάρτι τῆς μεγάλης ἁγιωσύνης
αὐτοῦ καὶ τῆς ἀγγελικῆς αὐτοῦ καταστάσεως, ἐθαύμαζον
ἐπ᾽ αὐτῷ κείμενος ἡσυχῇ καὶ φρίκης ὑπάρχων μεστός. Διε-
λογιζόμην δὲ καθ᾽ ἑαυτὸν[298] καὶ ἔλεγον· Ἆρα πῶς ὁ μὴ
χθὲς καὶ πρώην δυνάμενος ἀφ᾽ ἑαυτοῦ στραφῆναι τῆς κλίνης ἐπάνω ἢ κἂν ὅλως σαλευθῆναι καὶ ἀναστῆναι ἄνευ βοηθείας ἑτέρων χειρῶν, οὕτω μόνος ἐξανέστη τῆς κλίνης καὶ
οὕτως ἀεροβατῶν εὔχεται ὁ σάρκα φορῶν κάτω βρίθουσαν
καὶ ἄνθρωπος ὢν ὡς ἡμεῖς;᾽

127

"Ταῦτα τοίνυν στρέφων καθ᾽ ἑαυτὸν[299] καὶ θαυμάζων,
αὖθις καὶ μὴ βουλόμενος κατεβυθίσθην τῷ ὕπνῳ, ἔτι κρεμάμενον τὸν ἅγιον εἰς ἀέρα καταλιπών. Τοιγαροῦν καὶ μετ᾽
ὀλίγον αἴφνης ἀφυπνισθεὶς—εἶχον γὰρ πάλλουσαν τὴν
καρδίαν ἐπὶ τῷ παραδόξῳ ἐκείνῳ καὶ ξένῳ ὁράματι—ὁρῶ
τὸν ἅγιον ἤδη ἐπὶ τῆς κλίνης ἀνακλινόμενον καὶ τὴν

angelic man (whom, because of the effects of his sickness, we were turning over only with difficulty, using a mechanical device to roll him about this way and that on his bed), I saw this same man—oh, what an awesome miracle!—suspended once again in midair in his cell about four cubits or more off the ground, praying to his God in an indescribable light. I was amazed when I saw this and, since I was now already aware of his great holiness and angelic condition from the sight I had seen earlier, remained lying there quietly, filled with awe. And I thought to myself, 'How can this man, who yesterday or the day before couldn't turn himself over in bed, let alone move about or stand up without help from other people, rise up from his bed by himself in this way and pray while treading on thin air, when he has flesh which weighs him down and he is human like us?'

Chapter 127

"While I was pondering this and wondering about it, I fell asleep again even though I didn't want to, leaving the saint still suspended in midair. I woke up suddenly again a little while later—for my heart was racing at that strange and amazing vision—and I saw that the saint was now lying

σκέπην τοῦ σώματος ἀράμενον ἀφ᾿ ἑαυτοῦ καὶ σκεπόμενον, ὃ καὶ μᾶλλον[300] τῶν ἄλλων κατέπληξε καὶ ἐξέστησέ μου τὸν λογισμόν. Διὸ καὶ οὕτως ἔλεγον πρὸς ἐμαυτὸν θαυμάζων τὸ γεγονός· πῶς ὃν ἡ νόσος παρέλυσε καὶ ἀκίνητον ἀπειργάσατο, ἡ θεία χάρις ἡ πλουσίως ἐνοικήσασα εἰς αὐτὸν ἐν Πατρὶ καὶ Υἱῷ διὰ Πνεύματος Ἁγίου ὅλον ἐνίσχυσεν, ὅλον ἐνεδυνάμωσε[301] καὶ ἀπὸ γῆς ἥρπασεν εἰς ἀέρα πρὸς ὁμιλίαν αὐτῆς, καὶ ἧττον ἔσχε τῆς ἐνοικησάσης εἰς αὐτὸν ἐκ νεότητος θείας δυνάμεως ἡ τῆς νόσου καὶ τῆς ἀρρωστίας φθορά; Ἀλλὰ τοιοῦτον ἡ ἐξ ὕψους κατερχομένη δύναμις εἰς τοὺς ἁγίους καὶ ὁμοτρόπους τῶν ἀποστόλων δι᾿ ἐπιφοιτήσεως τῆς τοῦ Πνεύματος. Οὐ γὰρ νόσου μόνον καὶ φθορᾶς καὶ ἀρρωστίας, ὑφ᾿ ὧν οἶδεν ἡ σὰρξ λύεσθαί τε καὶ φθείρεσθαι καὶ εἰς γῆν ἀναλύεσθαι, ἀλλὰ καὶ βασάνων καὶ θανάτου καὶ μυχῶν ᾅδου ὑπερτέρα καὶ δυνατωτέρα καθέστηκεν.᾿ Ἐπεὶ δὲ καὶ ἡ ἡμέρα γένοιτο καὶ τῆς ὑπηρεσίας εἰχόμεθα τοῦ ἁγίου, θαρρήσας ἀποκαλύπτω καταμόνας αὐτῷ τὸ μυστήριον. Ὁ δέ· Δεσμὸν ἔχεις,᾿ φησίν, ᾿ἐκ Θεοῦ καὶ παρὰ τῆς ἐμῆς ταπεινώσεως μηδενὶ τὸ ὅραμα τοῦτο εἰπεῖν [cf. Mt 17:9], πρὶν ἂν ἴδῃς με ἀπὸ τῆς σαρκὸς ἐκδημήσαντα [cf. 2 Cor 5:8].᾿ Ὃ καὶ μέχρι τοῦ παρόντος ἐφύλαξα, καὶ οὐδενὶ δῆλον τοῦτο πεποίηκα." Ἕως ὧδε τὰ τοῦ Νικηφόρου τοῦ καὶ Συμεὼν πρὸς ἡμᾶς διηγήματα.

on his bed and that he'd pulled up the cover for his body by himself and covered himself up. This astounded and amazed me even more than anything else. And while I was wondering about what had happened, I said to myself, 'How did the divine grace, that dwells so abundantly in this man from the Father and the Son through the Holy Spirit, make him so strong and so powerful and take him up from the ground into the air to converse with It, when his illness has left him so weak and immobilized? How could the debilitation wrought by his illness and sickness be overcome by the divine power that has dwelled in him from his youth? But such is the power that descends from above on the saints and those who live like the apostles due to the intervention of the Spirit. For this has proved itself mightier and more powerful than not only illness and debilitation and sickness, by which the flesh is undone and debilitated and is dissolved back into earth, but also mightier than tortures and death and the innermost recesses of hell.' When day came and we were assisting the saint, I plucked up courage and revealed my secret to him when we were alone. But he said, 'By God and my humble self, you're bound to tell *no one about this vision* until you see that I've departed from my flesh.' And I've kept this promise until now and let no one know about it." And that is the end of the stories that Nikephoros, also called Symeon, told me.

128

Ἐπεὶ δὲ τρεῖς πρὸς τοῖς δέκα ἐν τῇ ὑπερορίᾳ πεποίηκε χρόνους, καὶ πολλοὺς ἐν ταύτῃ τοὺς πειρασμούς, πολλοὺς τοὺς πόνους καὶ τὰς θλίψεις ὁ γενναῖος τὴν ὑπομονὴν καθυπέστη, ἐζήτει δὲ τὴν λύσιν ἡ φύσις ἤδη πρὸς βαρὺ γῆρας ἐλάσασα, νόσῳ καὶ ἀρρωστίᾳ κάτοχος γίνεται. Ἐκτήξασα δὲ καὶ κατεργασαμένη τοῦτον εἰς τέλος, ἡ μὲν φύσις αὐτὴ τὰ ἑαυτῆς ἔπασχεν, εἰκὸς γὰρ ἦν· ἡ δὲ ψυχὴ ἐκείνου δι' ὅλου κεκολλημένη Θεῷ ὑπῆρχεν, ᾧ καὶ πρὸ τῆς λύσεως ἔζη καὶ ἐθεολόγει καὶ συνεγίνετο. Διὸ καὶ τὴν ἀπὸ τοῦ σώματος λύσιν ἐδεῖτο ταχεῖαν γενέσθαι [cf. Phlp 1:23], ἵνα πρὸς οὐρανοὺς κουφισθῇ τῷ τῶν ἀρετῶν ἅρματι [cf. 4 Kings 2:11], καὶ εἰς ἀκηράτους σκηνώσεις ἐπαναπαύσηται [cf. 2 Cor 5:1–4].

2   Ὅθεν αὐτὸς ἑαυτὸν καὶ τοὺς ἰδίους στηρίζων μαθητὰς τῇ παρακλήσει τοῦ λόγου παρεμυθεῖτο, ὁμοῦ τε τὴν ὥραν καὶ τὴν ἡμέραν τῆς ἀπὸ τοῦ σώματος ἐκδημίας προλέγων αὐτοῖς, καὶ μὴ πρὸ καιροῦ καὶ μετὰ καιρὸν ἀφιλοσόφως ὥσπερ οἱ μὴ ἔχοντες ἐλπίδα [1 Th 4:13] οὕτω κόπτεσθαι καὶ θρηνεῖν ἐπισκήπτων, καὶ ἅμα προφητείᾳ φρικτῇ τὸ

9. *Symeon's Death; Niketas Stethatos's Role in Preserving His Memory and Writings*

Chapter 128

After the noble Symeon had spent thirteen years in exile and, in the course of this, endured many tribulations and many labors and afflictions, his mortal nature sought its deliverance, for he had now reached a very advanced age and was overcome by illness and sickness. Thus his mortal nature, which had wasted him away and finally overpowered him, suffered its own proper fate, as was to be expected. But throughout, his soul remained united with God, with whom it used to live and converse and associate, even before his deliverance. It thus sought a swift deliverance from his body in order that it might soar up to heaven in the chariot of the virtues and take its rest in those undefiled pavilions.[140]

For this reason he strengthened his own resolve and that of his disciples and consoled them with words of comfort. He also predicted to them the day and the hour when he would depart from his body, and thus told them not to mourn or to lament in a way that was inappropriate to Christian philosophy either beforehand or afterward, like *those who have no hope.* At the same time, with this terrible proph-

τέλος ἐπισφραγίζων τοῦ βίου αὐτοῦ. Ὡς γὰρ πρὸς τοὺς θρηνοῦντας τὴν ὀρφανίαν³⁰² ἐμβλέψας εἶδε, "Τί με λείποντα ὀδύρεσθε;" εἶπεν. "Πέμπτην ἰνδικτιῶνα τάφῳ³⁰³ καλύπτετε θνῄσκοντα, εἰς πέμπτην με πάλιν ὄψεσθε ἰνδικτιῶνα καὶ ἐξιόντα τοῦ τάφου καὶ ὑμῖν συνεσόμενον τοῖς ποθοῦσιν." Ταῦτ' εἰπών, ἐπεὶ καὶ ἡ ὡρισμένη κατὰ τὴν δωδεκάτην τοῦ Μαρτίου ἐνειστήκει, ἐν μεθέξει τῶν ἀχράντων τοῦ Χριστοῦ μυστηρίων ὥσπερ ἔθος αὐτῷ καθ' ἑκάστην ὁ ἀοίδιμος γεγονὼς καὶ τὸ "ἀμὴν" εἰπών, ᾄδειν τὰ ἐπιτάφια τοῖς ἑαυτοῦ προετρέπετο μαθηταῖς.

129

Οἱ μὲν οὖν ἦδον ἡμμέναις λαμπάσι καὶ δεδακρυμένοις ὄμμασι, ὁ δὲ ὑψοῦ τὰς ἱερὰς αὐτοῦ χεῖρας ἐπάρας καὶ κατὰ τὴν ἐνοῦσαν ἔτι δύναμιν μικρὸν προσευξάμενος, εἶτα ἐπὶ σχῆμα τυπώσας αὐτὰς καὶ ὅλον ἑαυτὸν ἐντίμως συστείλας, κατὰ τὸ μέσον τῆς ὑμνῳδίας, "Εἰς χεῖράς σου, Χριστὲ Βασιλεῦ, τὸ πνεῦμά μου παρατίθημι [Ps 31(32):5; Lk 23:46]" ἠρέμα καὶ γαληνὸν ἐπειπών, χαίρων ὁ περιβόητος καὶ πολύαθλος ἀθλητὴς τοῦ Χριστοῦ τοῦ καρτερικοῦ καὶ πολυάθλου σώματος αὐτοῦ ἐξεδήμησεν, ἐν φαιδροῖς τοῖς ἄθλοις ἐκδημήσας πρὸς Κύριον [cf. 2 Cor 5:8] ὁλοκαυτωθεὶς καὶ ὑπὸ τοῦ πυρὸς τοῦ παμφάγου³⁰⁴ ἐν τῷ καιρῷ τοῦ θανάτου ὡς ἱερεῖον ἄμωμον καὶ εὐπρόσδεκτον τῷ Θεῷ [cf. Lv

ecy, he confirmed that his life was at its end. When he looked at them then and saw them mourning the fact that they were being orphaned, he said, "Why are you mourning my passing? In the fifth indiction I'll be dead and you'll bury me in my grave, but then, again in the fifth indiction, you'll see me emerging from that grave to be with you who yearn for this."[141] These were his words. Then, when the appointed day arrived on March 12, after he had participated in the immaculate mysteries of Christ (as he used to do every day) and said the "Amen," the celebrated Symeon ordered his disciples to chant the funeral service.

Chapter 129

While the monks sang this with the lamps lit and their eyes filled with tears, Symeon lifted up his holy arms and prayed with the little strength he had left, then he crossed his arms and gathered himself together in a dignified way.[142] In the middle of the hymn, that renowned competitor for Christ who had competed so much said in a soft and calm voice, "*Into your hands,* Christ the King, *I commend my spirit.*" Thus he departed from his long-suffering body that had competed so much. Surrounded by the glittering prizes from his contests, he *departed to the Lord,* wholly consumed at the time of his death by the all-consuming fire as an unblemished sacrifice acceptable to God, in the manner I have also

22:18–21; Rom 15:16], καθὼς ἐν τῷ ἐπιταφίῳ αὐτοῦ τὸν τρόπον ἀνεγραψάμεθα. Προστίθεται οὖν τοῖς δικαίοις ὁ δίκαιος, ὁ ὅσιος τοῖς ὁσίοις, τοῖς θεολόγοις ὁ θεολόγος, ὁ
ἱερομάρτυς καὶ ὁμολογητὴς καὶ μέγας διδάσκαλος τῆς
ἐκκλησίας Χριστοῦ τοῖς ὁμολογηταῖς καὶ διδασκάλοις καὶ
ἱερομάρτυσι, ἐν ἄθλοις ὁμολογίας τε καὶ ἀσκήσεως.³⁰⁵

2   Ἀλλὰ γὰρ τριάκοντα χρόνων μετὰ τὴν τελευτὴν τοῦ
ἀοιδίμου τούτου πατρὸς διεληλυθότων, κατὰ τὴν προφητείαν αὐτοῦ προμηνύεται ἡ ἀνακομιδὴ τῶν ἱερῶν τούτου
λειψάνων διὰ σημείου, τυπωθέντος ἀρρήτῳ λόγῳ τοῦ πέμ-
πτου στοιχείου ἐν μαρμάρῳ τῆς κέλλης τοῦ αὐτοῦ μαθητοῦ Νικήτα τοῦ Στηθάτου τελείαν ὑποστιγμὴν ἔχοντος
ὥσπερ γέγραπται καὶ παρὰ πολλῶν ἐθεάθη. Τοίνυν καὶ
τῆς πέμπτης τελειωθείσης ἰνδίκτου κατὰ τὸ ˏϛφξ΄ ἔτος,
ἀνακομίζονται ἀπροσδοκήτως τὰ πάσης ἔμπλεα³⁰⁶ χάριτος
καὶ εὐωδίας αὐτοῦ λείψανα καὶ ὑπὲρ γῆν λάμποντα, συγ-
καλοῦντα πολλούς, καὶ τοὺς φίλους αὐτοῦ³⁰⁷ μαθητὰς τῇ
προσψαύσει³⁰⁸ καὶ τῷ ἀσπασμῷ ἁγιάζοντα.

130

Τοιοῦτος ἦν, ἀδελφοί, ὁ τρισόλβιος καὶ τρισμακάριστος
πατὴρ ἡμῶν Συμεών, μέγας μὲν κατὰ τὸ κρυπτόμενον τῷ
Θεῷ, τοῖς ἀνθρώποις δὲ ἀγνοούμενος, ἀποστολικὸς τοῖς
ἔργοις καὶ τὴν διάνοιαν, ζῶν ἀληθῶς ὥσπερ εἴρηται κατὰ

recorded in his memorial oration.[143] That righteous man was thus united with the righteous <in heaven>, that holy one with the holy ones, that mystical theologian with the theologians, that holy martyr and confessor and great teacher of the Church of Christ with the confessors and teachers and holy martyrs, surrounded by his prizes for confession and asceticism.

Then, thirty years after the death of this celebrated father, a sign foretold the translation of his holy relics in accordance with his prophecy. For the fifth letter of the alphabet was <discovered> imprinted (in a way that can't be rationally explained) in a piece of marble in the cell of his disciple Niketas Stethatos. It had a clear mark after it indicating that it was a numeral,[144] just as if it had been written, and many people saw it. Thus, at the end of the fifth indiction in the year 6560,[145] his relics, fragrant and full of grace, were unexpectedly returned <to Constantinople>.[146] Now that they are resplendent above ground, they attract many people and sanctify his dear disciples when they touch and kiss them.

Chapter 130

Such, my brothers, was our thrice happy, thrice blessed father Symeon. He was secretly great in God's eyes but was himself unknown to men, like an apostle in his deeds and thought, a man who truly lived, as I have said, according to

τὸ Εὐαγγέλιον τοῦ Χριστοῦ καὶ Θεοῦ. Ὅθεν καὶ ζῶν ἐδό-
ξασεν ἐν ἑαυτῷ τὸν Θεὸν [cf. John 13:32] καὶ μετὰ θάνατον,
λάμψας ἐνώπιον τῶν ἀνθρώπων³⁰⁹ ταῖς ἀγαθαῖς πράξεσι
[cf. Mt 5:16]. Διὸ³¹⁰ εἰκότως ἐδοξάσθη καὶ αὐτὸς ὑπ' αὐτοῦ
[cf. John 13:32; 1 Kings 2:30].

2   Ὅτι δὲ τοῖς ἀποστόλοις ὁμότροπος ἦν τοῦ Χριστοῦ καὶ
τῆς αὐτῆς καὶ οὗτος ἀπήλαυσε³¹¹ χάριτος, δῆλον οὐ μόνον
ἐξ ὧν πεποίηκε θαυμάτων καὶ ἐκ τοῦ λόγου τῆς σοφίας,
θεολογήσας ἀγράμματος ὢν [cf. Act 4:13] καὶ εἰς ὀπτασίας
καὶ ἀποκαλύψεις Κυρίου κατὰ τὸν Παῦλον ἐλθών [Act 12:1],
ἀλλὰ καὶ ἀπὸ τοῦ χρωτὸς τῶν ἱματίων αὐτοῦ, καθὰ καὶ περὶ
ἐκείνων ἀκούομεν [Act 19:12]. Καὶ γὰρ ὥσπερ³¹² αἱ σκιαὶ
τῶν ἀποστόλων Χριστοῦ θαύματα ξενοτρόπως ἐποίουν
[Act 5:15], οὕτω καὶ τῶν ἱματίων τούτου ἡ εὐώδης ὀδμὴ
εὐφροσύνην ἐδίδου καὶ ψυχῆς ἀγαλλίασιν [Ps 44(45):15, 50
(51):8; cf. Is 51:11] τοῖς ἁπτομένοις αὐτῶν, μύρου τινὸς ξέ-
νου καὶ παραδόξου εὐωδίαν ἀποπεμπόντων· καὶ εἰκότως,
διαδοθείσης γὰρ ἐν αὐτοῖς τῆς ἔνδοθεν κατοικησάσης ἐν
αὐτῷ τοῦ Πνεύματος χάριτος, τῶν ἐγγιζόντων αὐτῷ μετὰ
πίστεως εὐφροσύνης καὶ ἀγαλλιάσεως ἀπὸ τῆς ἐκπεμπομένης ἐξ αὐτῶν εὐωδίας ἐπλήρου τὰς καρδίας ὁμοῦ καὶ τὰ
πνεύματα.

3   Ταύτης τοίνυν τῆς χάριτος οὐ μόνον ὁ συγγραφεὺς
αὐτὸς ἐγὼ καὶ μαθητὴς ἐκείνου ἐν μεθέξει ἐγενόμην πλου-
σίᾳ, ἀλλὰ καὶ ἕτερός μοι τῶν αὐτοῦ μαθητῶν ὁ Θεόδουλος
τοιοῦτόν τι διηγήσατο· "Ποτέ μοι," φησίν, "ὁ ἅγιος ἕνα
τῶν χιτωνίσκων αὐτοῦ ἐδωρήσατο, ἐγὼ δὲ ὡς ἐδεξάμην
αὐτὸν μετὰ πίστεως, εὐθὺς ἀποδυσάμενος τὰ ἱμάτια καὶ

the Gospel of Christ and God. While he was alive and after his death Symeon thus glorified God in himself, shedding light before men with his good deeds, so it is fitting for him to be glorified by Him.

That Symeon was indeed like the apostles of Christ and enjoyed the same grace as they is clear from the miracles that he performed and from the wisdom of his words, for although he was uneducated he was a theologian and *went on to visions and revelations of the Lord* like Paul. Not only that, but it is also clear from the clothes *that had been in contact with his skin,* just as we hear about them. And in the same way that the shadows of Christ's apostles worked miracles in an extraordinary way, so the fragrant scent of Symeon's clothes also gave *joy and* spiritual *gladness* to those who touched them, for they exuded the fragrance of an exotic and marvelous perfume. And rightly so, for the grace of the Spirit that dwelled within him had spread to his clothes and would fill the hearts and spirits of those who approached him in faith with *joy* and *gladness* at the fragrance emanating from them.

I myself, Symeon's disciple and hagiographer, was not alone in having rich experience of this grace, for another of his disciples, Theodoulos, also told me something similar. "The saint," he said, "once gave me one of his undershirts. I accepted it with faith and immediately took off my clothes,

τὸν οἰκεῖον ἀποθέμενος χιτῶνα περιεβαλλόμην αὐτὸν
γυμναῖς ταῖς σαρξί. Τοιγαροῦν καὶ ὡς ἦλθον πεσεῖν ὑπὸ
τὴν ἰδίαν κλίνην καὶ τραπῆναι εἰς ὕπνον, τοσαύτης ἠσθόμην ὡς ἀπὸ μύρου πολυτίμου³¹³ τῆς εὐωδίας, ὡς χαλάσαι
ἀπὸ τῆς ὥας ἐντὸς αὐτοῦ τὴν ἐμὴν κεφαλὴν καὶ ἀπολαύειν
αὐτῆς καὶ κόρον μὴ λαμβάνειν με τῆς ἐκπεμπομένης
εὐφροσύνης ἐκεῖθεν. Πολλάκις δέ μου αὐτὸν ἀποπλύναν-
τος καὶ ἀνακαθάραντος, ἔμεινε τὴν αὐτὴν εὐωδίαν ἔχων,
μέχρις οὗ κατεκόπη καὶ εἰς λεπτὰ διῃρέθη παλαιωθείς."
Καὶ ταῦτα μὲν περὶ τούτων, καὶ τῆς ἐνοικησάσης ἐν αὐτῷ
τοῦ Πνεύματος χάριτος.

131

Χρεὼν δὲ εἰπεῖν καὶ γραφῇ παραδοῦναι καὶ ἃ κἀμοὶ οὐ
μόνον διὰ νυκτερινῆς ὄψεως περὶ τῶν αὐτοῦ συγγραμμάτων ἐπέσκηψεν, ἀλλὰ καὶ ἃ προφητικῶς οἷα δὴ τὰ ἐσόμενα
μακρόθεν προβλέπων διὰ γραφῆς ἀπεφθέγξατο πρός με
περὶ αὐτῶν, ὅπως δι' ἐμοῦ καὶ πᾶσιν ἄλλοις γενέσθαι μέλ-
λουσι φανερὰ εἰς ὠφέλειαν³¹⁴ τῶν ἐντυγχανόντων αὐτοῖς.

2   Ἔτι περιόντος τοῦ μακαρίου ἐν τῇ παρούσῃ ταύτῃ ζωῇ
καὶ τὰ ὑπὸ τοῦ θείου Πνεύματος χορηγούμενα μυστήρια
τῷ νοῒ αὐτοῦ καὶ ἄκοντος αὐτοῦ γράφοντος ἐν νυκτὶ καὶ
ἡμέρᾳ (οὐδὲ γὰρ ἦν αὐτῷ ἄνεσις ἢ καθόλου ἐδίδοτο παρὰ
τοῦ σφύζοντος ἐν αὐτῷ καὶ ἀλλομένου Πνεύματος, ἕως οὗ

set aside my own undershirt, and put Symeon's on next to my skin. Then, when I went to bed and was falling asleep, I sensed a fragrance like that of some very expensive perfume, and so I slid my head down inside its hem to enjoy it and I couldn't get enough of the joy that emanated from it. Even though I often washed and cleaned this shirt, it kept the same fragrance until it became threadbare and fell to pieces when it was worn out." That's <all I have to say> about this and the grace of the Spirit that dwelled in Symeon.

Chapter 131

Now I must also recount and set down in writing not only the instructions he gave me about his literary compositions in a nocturnal vision, but also those that he communicated to me in a letter concerning them. He did so prophetically, as though he could see far into the future, indicating how, through me, his writings would be made known to everyone else for the benefit of those who read them.

While the blessed Symeon was still alive, he would write 2 down compulsively, day and night, the mysteries that the divine Spirit supplied to his intellect. For the Spirit that pulsed and throbbed within him would give him no respite at all until he had set down in writing what It said and in-

ἃ ἐκεῖνο λαλοῦν ἦν καὶ ἐνεργοῦν ἔνδοθεν αὐτοῦ γραφῇ
παραδέδωκεν), ἐδίδου κἀμοὶ τὰ σχεδιαζόμενα ὑπ' αὐτοῦ,
καὶ μετέγραφον ταῦτα εἴς τε βεμβράνας βιβλίων καὶ κον-
τάκια ἕτερα. Ἐπεὶ δὲ μετὰ τὸ ταῦτα μεταπῆξαι ἀντέστρε-
φον πάλιν αὐτὰ πρὸς αὐτόν, ἔδοξέ μοι ἐν μιᾷ ποτε παρ'
ἐμαυτῷ ἓν παρακατασχεῖν τῶν κοντακίων. Ὡς δὲ ὁ ἀποκο-
μίσας ἐρωτώμενος παρ' ἐκείνου περὶ τοῦ λείποντος οὐκ
εἶχε λελογισμένως ἀπολογήσασθαι ἀγνοῶν περὶ τούτου,
ὥσπερ ἠγανάκτησε κατ' αὐτοῦ, καὶ αὐτὸν ἀπεπέμψατο.

3   Τοῦτο τοίνυν ἀκηκοὼς ἐγὼ ᾤμην ὅτι δόλον τινὰ ὑπ-
έλαβε κατ' ἐμοῦ ὁ μακάριος, ἐπεὶ κατέσχον παρ' ἐμαυτῷ
τὸ κοντάκιον, καὶ λύπῃ[315] ληφθεὶς ἀπελογησάμην[316] αὐτῷ
περὶ τούτου διὰ γραφῆς. Ὁ δὲ θείῳ διηνεκῶς κινούμενος
Πνεύματι, καὶ τὸ μέλλον ἐκβῆναι ἐν ὑστέροις καιροῖς βουλόμενος γραφῇ καὶ ἀκοαῖς παραδοῦναι, καὶ τὸ προφητικὸν
τῆς ψυχῆς αὐτοῦ ἐνδείξασθαί τε ὁμοῦ καὶ πιστώσασθαι
τοῖς ἐσχάτοις ἐρχομένοις καιροῖς, ἐν ἁπλαῖς οὕτω πως καὶ
ἰδιωτικαῖς λέξεσιν ἐπιστέλλει μοι, καί φησι·

132

"Τὸ πιττάκιόν σου, πνευματικὸν ἡμῶν τέκνον, ἐδεξά-
μεθα μέν, οὐκ ἀπεδεξάμεθα δέ, ἀλλὰ καὶ πολλῆς σου τῆς
εὐηθείας κατέγνωμεν, ὅτι δὴ καὶ τοιαῦτα ὅλως ἐλογίσω
περὶ ἡμῶν, ὡς δόλῳ ποτέ τινι ἢ περιεργίᾳ πρὸς τὸ λυπῆσαί

spired in him. He would then give me his rough drafts and I would copy them out onto parchment in books or otherwise onto scrolls.[147] When I had transcribed these I would return them to him. On one occasion, however, I decided to keep one of the scrolls with me. Symeon asked the person who was bringing them back to him about the missing item, but the man was unable to provide a reasonable explanation because he didn't know anything about it. As a result, Symeon was angry with him and sent him away.

When I heard this, I thought that the blessed one had assumed I had played some sort of trick by keeping the scroll with me, and being very upset, I offered him an explanation of the matter in writing. But Symeon, who was constantly inspired by the divine Spirit, wanted to pass on (both in writing and orally) what was going to come about at a later time and thus demonstrate the prophetic nature of his soul while providing proof of it to those who would live later on. He thus sent me a letter, written in rather simple and ordinary terms, which said this:

Chapter 132

"Although I received your note, my spiritual child, I did not welcome it. In fact I disapproved of your great foolishness in even having such thoughts about me—as though I would ever conceive the idea or think that you kept the pa-

με τὸ χαρτίον σὺ ἀπεκράτησας ἐνεθυμήθην τοῦτο ἢ ἐλογισάμην ἐγώ! Ποῖος γὰρ ἐν τούτῳ δόλος ἢ ποία θλῖψίς μοι προσγενήσεταί ποτε, εἰ καὶ φαίνομαι περὶ πολλοῦ ταῦτα ποιούμενος; Ἀλλ᾽ ὅτι πάντως ἠγνόουν σε τοῦτο ἔχειν, καὶ ὑπέλαβον ἐκ καταφρονήσεως τοῦ ὑπουργοῦντός μοι ἴσως τοῦτο ἀπολεσθῆναι ἢ κατὰ τὴν ὁδὸν ἢ καὶ ἄλλως πως, καὶ εἰς τοῦτο³¹⁷ ἐλυπήθην, ἐπεὶ εἰς σέ, ὃν ὡς ἐμαυτὸν ἔχειν ἅπαξ καθωμολόγησα, καὶ πάντα τὰ ἐμά σοι ἐθάρρησα, καὶ διὰ σοῦ καὶ πᾶσιν ἄλλοις ἐλπίζω³¹⁸ φανερὰ γενήσεσθαι, καθὼς ὁ Χριστὸς τοῖς ἑαυτοῦ μαθηταῖς ἔλεγεν· *ἃ εἰς τὸ οὖς ἠκούσατε, κηρύξατε ἐπὶ τῶν δωμάτων* [Mt 12:27], ποίαν ὑπόληψιν πονηρὰν κατὰ σοῦ εἶχον ἀναλαβέσθαι; Ἐγὼ γὰρ διὰ τοῦτό σε καὶ παρακαλῶ ἐν τετραδίοις μεταγράψαι αὐτά, ἵνα τὰ σχέδη πάντα σοι καταλείψω. Καὶ πῶς με τοιαῦτα λογίσασθαι ὑπέλαβες κατὰ σοῦ;

2 "Ὅμως ὁ Θεὸς συγχωρήσει σοι τὴν ἁμαρτίαν ταύτην, ὅτι ἔξω τῆς ἀγάπης ἡμᾶς εἶναι ἔκρινας τῆς πάντα ὑπομενούσης καὶ μηδέποτε ἐκπιπτούσης [cf. 1 Cor 13:7–8], ἐὰν μή τις ἑκουσίως ταύτης ἀποσπασθῇ· ἐκείνη δὲ μένει ἄτμητος, ἀδιαίρετος, πάντας τοὺς βουλομένους ἐπιστρέφειν καὶ πάλιν κολλᾶσθαι αὐτῇ εὐμενῶς προσδεχομένη καὶ γνησίως προσκολλωμένη, πολλάκις δὲ καὶ τοὺς μὴ βουλομένους ἑλκύουσα καὶ προσκαλουμένη πρὸς ἑαυτήν, ᾗ καὶ σὲ τέκνον εὔχομαι κολληθῆναι καὶ ἑνωθῆναι, ἵνα δύνασαι μὴ λογίζεσθαι τὸ κακὸν ἢ τὸ ὂν ἢ καὶ τὸ μηδόλως ὄν, ἀλλὰ μένειν σε διηνεκῶς *ἐν παντὶ καὶ ἐν πᾶσι* [Php 4:12] πρὸς ἡμᾶς καὶ πρὸς πάντας ἀσκανδάλιστον. Ἀμήν."

per as some sort of fraud or trick to upset me! For what trick
or affliction would ever have that effect on me, even if I do
seem to care a lot about these things? Because I was completely unaware that you had the paper, I imagined that my
servant had been careless and had perhaps lost it on the way
or in some other fashion, and that is why I was upset. For
how could I entertain any suspicion of wrongdoing on your
part when I have pledged once and for all to treat you like
myself,[148] and have entrusted you with all my writings, and
hope that they become known to everyone else through
you, just as Christ said to His disciples, *what you hear whispered you must shout from the house tops?* That's why I ask you
to copy what I write into notebooks, so that I may leave
all the drafts to you. So how can you suspect me of such
thoughts about you?

"All the same, God will forgive you this sin, which is that   2
you thought you had lost my love when, in fact, this endures
all things and never ends, unless someone separates himself
from it of his own accord. My love remains entire and undi-
vided. It graciously welcomes and truly becomes one with
everyone who wants to turn back and be united with it
again,[149] and on many occasions it even draws to itself and
calls to itself those who don't want to. So I beg you, my child,
to be made one with my love and united with it again, so
that you may be incapable of thinking evil of anything
(whether it really is or isn't), but may rather *in any and all circumstances* never give offense to me or anyone else. Amen."

133

Ταῦτα τοιγαροῦν πρὸς ἐμὲ γεγραφώς, ἐπεὶ ἔτι νέος ὢν ἐγὼ καὶ ἀτελὴς τὸν λόγον τῆς γνώσεως ἄρτι τὸν ἴουλον ἐπανθοῦντα ἐπιφερόμενος, τὴν δύναμιν τῶν ῥημάτων αὐτοῦ γνῶναι μὴ δυνηθείς, γραφῇ τέως ταύτην τε τὴν ἐπιστολὴν καὶ ἃς ἐπέστειλε διαφόρως πρός με παρέδωκα, ἄνωθεν οἶμαι καλῶς κινηθεὶς ἐπὶ τοῦτο. Χρόνων δὲ παρεληλυθότων ἑκκαίδεκα καὶ πολλοῖς μαχόμενος καὶ προσπαλαίων, ὡς ἄνωθεν εἴρηται, διὰ μέσου τοῖς πειρασμοῖς, οὐ μόνον ταύτης λήθην ἔλαβον τῆς ἐπιστολῆς, ἀλλὰ καὶ πάντων ἄλλων τῶν θεοπνεύστων αὐτοῦ συγγραμμάτων.

2   Ποτὲ δὲ τῆς ἀγαθότητος τοῦ Θεοῦ³¹⁹ (ταῖς ἐκείνου δεήσεσιν) ἐπισκεψαμένης καὶ πρὸς τὰς θλίψεις καὶ τὰς ἀνάγκας [cf. 2 Cor 6:4] ἡμῶν ἰδούσης (ἃς ὑφιστάμεθα πρὸς ἔκτισιν τῶν ἁμαρτημάτων ἡμῶν ἐν τούτῳ τῷ βίῳ), καὶ τὴν εἴσοδον αὖθις ἀκώλυτον ἡμῖν ποιησάσης ἐν τῇ θεοσώστῳ ποίμνῃ ἡμῶν τῇ τοῦ Στουδίου (πάντων δηλαδὴ τῶν πολεμούντων ἡμᾶς ἀποσοβηθέντων παρ' αὐτῆς καὶ ἠσθενηκότων), ὡς εἶχον ἐπισκεπτόμενος ἐξαυτῆς ἐμαυτὸν διὰ τῆς φίλης ἐμοὶ μετανοίας καὶ ἡσυχίας καὶ τῶν δακρύων, ἐπαπολαύων τε καὶ τῆς δωρεᾶς τοῦ Θεοῦ, ἥτις ἐστὶν ἡ παράκλησις λέγω τοῦ Πνεύματος τοῦ Ἁγίου [Act 9:31] ἡ διὰ τῆς γλυκυτάτης κατανύξεως γινομένη ἐν τῇ καρδίᾳ, —καλὸν γὰρ εὐγνωμονεῖν καὶ ἀνακηρύττειν εἰς πάντας τὸ ἔλεος τοῦ Θεοῦ—, ἔκστασίς με λαμβάνει τις καὶ ἀλλοίωσις αἴφνης ἀλλοιώσεως τῆς δεξιᾶς τοῦ Ὑψίστου [Ps 76(77):10],

Chapter 133

When Symeon wrote this to me, I was still young and my education not yet complete, for I was just growing my first beard, so I was unable to grasp the importance of his words. But, being happily inspired from above to do so, I guess, I wrote out a copy of this letter, and those that he had sent me at various times.[150] But sixteen years went by during which, as I've stated above, I was fighting and struggling with many people. In the midst of these trials I forgot not only all about the letter but also about all of Symeon's other divinely inspired compositions.

However, once God's goodness (as a result of Symeon's supplications) took notice of my distress and my hardship (which I endured as payment for my sins in this life), and enabled me to reenter the divinely protected monastery of Stoudios without any opposition (that is, after all my opponents had been scared away and enfeebled by that goodness), I immediately began to focus on myself as best I could by means of the penitence, spiritual tranquillity, and tears that are so dear to me. I also had the benefit of God's gift, by which I mean *the comfort of the Holy Spirit,* that arises in the heart through most sweet compunction—for one should acknowledge with gratitude God's mercy and proclaim it to all. Then, in the second week of Lent, I suddenly had an experience of ecstasy and spiritual transformation, *a transfor-*

δευτέρας οὔσης ἑβδομάδος τηνικαῦτα τῶν νηστειῶν, ὑπὸ
φρικτῆς ὄπισθεν κατὰ τὴν πρώτην τῆς ἑβδομάδος ἡμέραν
καταληφθέντα ὁράσεως.

3   Τοιγαροῦν καὶ πάσας ἀλλοιώσασα τὰς αἰσθήσεις μου
πᾶσαν ὁμοῦ τὴν φύσιν τὰς φρένας, τὰς κινήσεις μου πάσας
τοῦ σώματος, ἐπιλαθέσθαι με πεποίηκε κατὰ τὸν θεῖον
Δαυὶδ καὶ τὸν ἄρτον μου φαγεῖν [Ps 101(102):4]· ὅλος γὰρ
ἐγενόμην—μαρτυρεῖ μοι Χριστὸς ἡ Ἀλήθεια!—ὡς μὴ περικείμενος σῶμα [cf. 2 Cor 12:2–3]· κοῦφον γὰρ ἐδόκουν καὶ
ὡς πνευματικὸν αὐτὸ περιφέρειν, μὴ πεινῶν, μὴ διψῶν, μὴ
κόπων³²⁰ καὶ ἀγρυπνίας³²¹ ἐπαισθανόμενος, ἐκ τῆς ἐν ἐμοὶ
γενομένης ἐλευθερίας τε καὶ κουφότητος, δι᾽ ἀπορρήτου
σιγῆς τῶν δυνάμεων τῆς ψυχῆς καὶ τῶν λογισμῶν τῆς διανοίας καὶ διὰ γαλήνης ἀφράστου τῆς καρδίας μου. Ἡ γὰρ
ἀγάπη τοῦ Θεοῦ ἐκχυθεῖσα εἰς αὐτὴν τὰς αἰσθήσεις μου
τῆς ψυχῆς ἦρεν ἅμα πάσας εἰς οὐρανοὺς καὶ ἤμην ἐν γαληνῷ φωτὶ ὥς τις ἀσώματος, καὶ ἦν ἐν ἡδονῇ πολλῇ καὶ
ἀφράστῳ χαρᾷ ἐν ὅλαις ἡμέραις ἑπτὰ ἡ ψυχή μου ὑπ᾽
οὐδενὸς ὀχλουμένη πάθους ἢ λογισμοῦ ἢ ἀνάγκης εἰπεῖν
φυσικῆς, τῆς αἰσθήσεως ἀπ᾽ ἐμοῦ πάσης ἅμα φυγούσης
τοῦ κόσμου ἢ ξενωθείσης ἢ χωρησάσης εἰς τὸ μὴ ὄν.

mation that was from the right hand of the Most High, for, on the first day of the week, I unexpectedly received an awesome vision.

This transformed all my senses, along with my entire nat-   3
ural constitution, my mind, and all my physical movements, and made me *forget to eat my bread* (as the divine David has it). It was as though I no longer had a body around me at all—Christ the Truth is my witness!—for I seemed to be sur-rounded by a body that was subtle and somehow spiritual. I wasn't hungry or thirsty and had no feeling of weariness or sleeplessness, due to the sense of freedom and subtlety I had within me that arose from an indescribable silence that <stilled> the forces of my soul and the thoughts of my mind and from an unutterable calmness in my heart. For the love of God had been poured into it and so raised all the sensa-tions of my soul up to heaven. Like an incorporeal being, I remained in that tranquil light and my soul experienced much pleasure and unutterable joy for seven whole days. My soul was untroubled by anything, whether passion, thought, or physical need, so to speak, for every perception of this world had entirely left me and had either been banished or turned into nothingness.

LIFE OF SAINT SYMEON

134

Ὡς δὲ οὕτως ὑπὸ τοῦ μακαρίου τούτου πάθους εἰχό-
μην, ἔτι ἡσυχάζων καὶ ὢν ἐν τοῖς ὑπερῴοις τοῦ Προδρο-
μικοῦ καὶ μεγάλου ναοῦ, κινεῖται μετὰ γλυκυτάτης³²² κατανύξεως ἡ ψυχή μου εἰς τὴν ἀγάπην τοῦ μακαρίου τούτου
καὶ ἁγίου μου πατρὸς Συμεὼν τοῦ ἐμὲ φωτίσαντος καὶ εἰς
τὴν ὁδόν με τῆς ζωῆς ἐμβιβάσαντος. Ἠσθόμην γὰρ ὥσπερ
τινὸς μυστικῶς ἀναμιμνήσκοντός μου τὸν νοῦν καὶ ὑποτι-
θεμένου ὧν εἰς παντελῆ λήθην ἦλθον, οἷον τὴν εὐσέβειαν
τοῦ μακαρίου τούτου πατρός, τὴν ἀπαράμιλλον αὐτοῦ
ἐργασίαν τῆς ἀρετῆς, τὴν διηνεκῆ κατάνυξιν, τὰ καθημε-
ρινὰ δάκρυα, τὴν ταπείνωσιν, τὴν πραότητα, τὴν ἀγάπην
ἐκείνην τὴν ἀνυπόκριτον [Rom 12:9; 2 Cor 6:6], τὴν ἀθόλω-
τον καὶ ἀέννατον προσευχήν, τὴν ἐγκράτειαν, τὴν νηστεί-
αν, τὴν ὁλόνυκτον ἀγρυπνίαν, τὴν τῶν πειρασμῶν ὑπομο-
νήν, τὴν ἐν πᾶσιν οἷς ὑπέμενε θλιβεροῖς καθ᾽ ἑκάστην
εὐχαριστίαν, τὴν ἐλεημοσύνην, τὴν εἰς τοὺς δεομένους
μετάδοσιν, τὴν συμπάθειαν, τὴν μακροθυμίαν, τὴν χρη-
στότητα τῶν ἠθῶν, τὴν ἀγαθοσύνην καὶ εὐθύτητα τῆς
ψυχῆς, τὸ ἀταπείνωτον τοῦ φρονήματος, τὸ ὑπὲρ τοῦ δικαίου καὶ τῆς ἀληθείας ἐνστατικόν, τὸ ἄμαχον, τὸ νηφάλι-
ον, τὸ σῶφρον, τὸ ἐπιεικές, τὸ δίκαιον, τὸ ὀρθόδοξον, τὸ
φιλάδελφον, τὸ γαληνόν, τὸ καθαρὸν τῆς καρδίας δι᾽ ὃ
καθ᾽ ἑκάστην μετεῖχε τῶν θείων μυστηρίων τοῦ Χριστοῦ,
τὸ πεφωτισμένον τοῦ λόγου, τὸ ἡδὺ τῆς ἐντεύξεως, τὸ
λαμπρότατον καὶ καθαρώτατον τῆς ψυχῆς ὅθεν εἶχε τὸ

326

Chapter 134

While I was having this blessed experience and was still in a state of spiritual tranquillity in the gallery of the great church of the Prodromos,[151] my soul turned with the sweetest compunction to the love of this blessed man, my holy father Symeon, who had enlightened me and set me on the path of life. I felt as though someone was mysteriously bringing back memories to my mind and presenting things that I had completely forgotten, like that blessed father's piety, his unrivaled practice of virtue, his continuous compunction, his daily tears, his humility, his mildness, his *genuine love,* his untroubled and unceasing prayer, his abstinence, his fasting, his all-night vigils, his endurance of trials, his daily thanksgiving during all the tribulations he endured, his almsgiving, his charity to those in need, his sympathy, his patience, the correctness of his behavior, the goodness and rectitude of his soul, the unbending quality of his resolve, his determination for righteousness and truth, his lack of aggression, his temperance, his self-control, his fairness, his justice, his orthodoxy, his brotherly love, his calmness, the purity of his heart (as a result of which he participated every day in Christ's holy mysteries), the enlightenment of his words, the pleasure of his conversation, the great brilliance and purity of his soul (that made his face shine like the sun),

LIFE OF SAINT SYMEON

πρόσωπον φαιδρὸν ὥσπερ ἥλιον, τὸ ἥμερον, τὸ ἥσυχον, τὸ
καρτερικὸν ἐν ταῖς θλίψεσι, τὸ ἀφιλάργυρον, τὸ ἀφιλέν-
δεικτον, τὸ ἀκενόδοξον, τὸ ἀπόνηρον, τὸ ταπεινόν, τὸ
ἁπλοῦν, τὸ μέτριον, τὸ φιλεύσπλαγχνον, τὸ φιλάγαθον,³²³
τὸ φιλόπτωχον, τὸ φιλόστοργον ἐν τοῖς τέκνοις αὐτοῦ, τὸ
ἀμνησίκακον ἐν τοῖς κακοποιοῦσιν αὐτόν, τὸ ἱλαρόν, τὸ
χάριεν, τὸ φιλόκαλον, τὸ φιλάρετον.

2   Καὶ πρὸς τούτοις τὰ τούτων ἔτι τελεώτερά τε καὶ ὑψηλότερα, τὴν σοφίαν τοῦ λόγου, τὴν γνῶσιν τῶν ἀπορρή-
των τοῦ Θεοῦ μυστηρίων, τὸ ὕψος τῆς θεολογίας αὐτοῦ,
τὸ βάθος τῆς ταπεινοφροσύνης αὐτοῦ, τὰς φρικτὰς ὀπτασίας (κατὰ τὸν μακάριον Παῦλον [cf. 2 Cor 12:1]), τὰς μυ-
στικὰς ἀποκαλύψεις, τὴν τοῦ ἀπείρου καὶ θείου φωτὸς
θεωρίαν, τὸ χερουβικὸν ἐν τῇ παραστάσει τῆς λειτουργίας τῶν φρικτῶν τοῦ Χριστοῦ μυστηρίων (ἐν ᾗ καθαρῶς
τὸ Πνεῦμα τὸ Ἅγιον ἔβλεπε κατερχόμενον καὶ ἁγιάζον
αὐτὸν καὶ τὰ δῶρα), τὰς προγνώσεις, τὰς προφητείας, τὸ
προορατικόν· ἔτι δὲ τὰς νουθεσίας, τὰς κατηχήσεις, τὸν
ἔμπρακτον καὶ διδακτικὸν λόγον, τὰ τούτου συγγράμματα, τὰς ἑρμηνείας τῆς θείας γραφῆς, τοὺς ἠθικοὺς καὶ
κατηχητικοὺς λόγους ἐκείνους, τὰς ἐπιστολάς, τοὺς ἀπολογητικοὺς αὐτοῦ λόγους, τοὺς ἀντιρρητικούς, τῶν θείων
ὕμνων τοὺς ἔρωτας.

his gentleness, his spiritual tranquillity, his patience in tribulations, his freedom from avarice, from ostentation, from vanity, from wickedness, his humbleness, his simplicity, his moderation, his compassion, his love of goodness, his love for the poor, his affection for his spiritual children, his willingness to forgive those who wronged him, his cheerfulness, his grace, his love of what is good, his love of virtue.

And, in addition, also things about him that were even more perfect and sublime: the wisdom of his words, his knowledge of the ineffable mysteries of God, the sublimity of his theology, the profundity of his humility, his awesome visions (like those of the blessed Paul), his mystical revelations, his contemplation of the infinite and divine light, his cherubic appearance at the liturgy of Christ's awesome mysteries (in which he used to see plainly the Holy Spirit descending and blessing him and the gifts), his foreknowledge, his prophecies, his foresight. And still others: his exhortations, his instructions, his practical and informative advice, his written compositions, his studies of holy scripture, his *Ethical*[152] and *Catechetical Discourses,* his *Letters,*[153] his apologetics, his refutations, and his *Loves of Divine Hymns.*

135

Τούτων οὖν ὑπομιμνησκόμενος πάντων τὴν μεγαλειότητα, ὡς ἐγένετο τοσούτων ἀγαθῶν θησαυρός, ὡς ἐγένετο σκεῦος ἐκλογῆς [Act 9:15] τοῦ Θεοῦ καὶ πεπλούτηκε πᾶσαν ἀρετήν, ὅλον τὸν πλοῦτον τῶν χαρισμάτων τοῦ Πνεύματος [cf. 1 Cor 12:4–11], ἐπειδὴ πεφίληκε καὶ ἡρμόσατο [2 Cor 11:2] ἑαυτῷ τὴν Σοφίαν [cf. Wis 8:2] διὰ ὑπερβολὴν καθαρότητος, οὐκ εἶχον, ἄπειρος ὢν ἔτι τῆς θαυμαστῆς ταύτης τοῦ Πνεύματος ἐνεργείας, ὅπως ἀκριβῶς ὑπολάβω, πόθεν μοι ταῦτα καὶ παρὰ τίνος μυστικῶς ἐνηχοῦνται, καὶ τίς ἐστιν ὁ ταῦτα λέγων ἐν τῇ καρδίᾳ μου καὶ κινῶν τὴν ψυχήν μου εἰς τὴν ἐκείνου ἀγάπην, ἕως οὗ διαπορούμενόν με ἰδοῦσα ἡ τοῦ Θεοῦ χάρις καὶ ζητοῦντα μαθεῖν τὴν αἰτίαν ὅθεν παραδόξως ταῦτά μοι λέγονται, προσέθετο εἰπεῖν εἰς τὸ οὖς μου· "Ταῦτά ἐστιν ἐκ τῆς τοῦ Πνεύματος ἐπιδημίας καὶ παρακλήσεως, καθὼς λέγει ὁ Χριστὸς καὶ Θεὸς τοῖς ἀποστόλοις αὐτοῦ καὶ δι᾽ αὐτῶν πᾶσιν ὑμῖν τοῖς πιστοῖς· *ὁ δὲ Παράκλητος τὸ Πνεῦμα τὸ Ἅγιον, ὃ πέμψει ὁ Πατὴρ ἐν τῷ ὀνόματί μου, ἐκεῖνος ὑμᾶς διδάξει πάντα, καὶ ὑπομνήσει ὑμᾶς πάντα ἃ εἶπον ὑμῖν* [John 14:26]."

2   Ταῦτα πάντα ὥσπερ εἴρηται ὑπομιμνησκόμενος καὶ εἰς τὴν ἀγάπην πλατυνόμενος [cf. Ps 118(119):32; 2 Cor 6:11] τοῦ τρισολβίου τούτου πατρός, ἠναγκαζόμην—ἐπὶ μάρτυρι Θεῷ—ὥσπερ ὑπό τινος ἔνδοθεν κινούμενός τε καὶ νυσσόμενος[324] με τὴν ἐνάρετον ἐγκωμιάσαι πολιτείαν αὐτοῦ καὶ ὕμνους τινὰς ἐπαξίους τῷ ὕψει τῆς ἁγιωσύνης

Chapter 135

As I was reminded of the magnificence of all these attributes, I realized how Symeon had come to be a treasury of such good things and how he had become a *chosen instrument* of God filled with every virtue, with the entire wealth of the gifts of the Spirit, because he had loved and *betrothed* himself to Wisdom through his outstanding purity. But since I was still inexperienced in this marvelous activity of the Spirit, I had no clear understanding of the source of all these memories, who was making these mysterious utterances, and who was speaking in my heart and inspiring my soul with such love for Symeon. But then the grace of God saw that I was confused and trying to discover the reason for these extraordinary revelations to me, and it chose to whisper to me, "These memories are the result of the arrival and advocacy[154] of the Holy Spirit, just as Christ our God says to His apostles and through them to all you faithful people, *Your Advocate, the Holy Spirit whom the Father will send in my name, will teach you everything and will call to mind everything I have told you.*"

When I remembered all this, as I have said, and was 2 opened up to the love of this thrice-blessed father, I felt compelled—God is my witness—just as though I were being urged and prodded from within by someone, to celebrate his virtuous way of life and compose some hymns to sing his praises that would be worthy of the sublimity of his holiness.

αὐτοῦ συντάξαι εἰς ὑμνῳδίαν αὐτοῦ. Ἐμοῦ δὲ ἐπὶ πολλὰς
ἀναβαλλομένου ἡμέρας διὰ τὸ μὴ πεῖραν ἐσχηκέναι ποτὲ
τῆς ἐπὶ τὸ γράφειν τὰ τοιαῦτα τέχνης (οὐ γὰρ ἔφθασα τῇ
θύραθεν γνώσει καταπυκνωθῆναι καλῶς καὶ στομωθῆναι
τοῖς λόγοις νέος καὶ τεσσαρεσκαιδεκαέτης τὴν ἡλικίαν τῷ
βίῳ καὶ τοῖς θορύβοις ἀποταξάμενος, καὶ τὴν διατριβὴν
τῶν μαθημάτων ἀπολιπών). Οὐκ ἦν μοι νύκτα καὶ ἡμέραν
ἀνάπαυσις ὑπὸ τοῦ ἐμπυρίζοντός με Πνεύματος ἔνδοθεν
καὶ ἐπὶ τοῦτο σφόδρα με νύσσοντος καὶ κινοῦντος.

136

Διὰ δὴ τοῦτο καὶ μὴ φέρων ἐπὶ πολὺ τὴν ἀνάγκην,
πρῶτα μὲν ὕμνους κανόνων ἐκτίθημι εἰς τὸν ἐν ἁγίοις πατέρα ἡμῶν καὶ ὁμολογητὴν Θεόδωρον τὸν Στουδιώτην
εἰς γυμνασίαν τοῦ λόγου καὶ τοῦ πρὸς αὐτὸν πόθου ἐκπλή-
ρωσιν, εἶτα τοῖς λόγοις καθάπερ ὑφ' ἡδονῆς ἀρρήτου γλυ-
κανθεῖσά μου ἡ διάνοια ἐξεθέμην καὶ εἰς τὸν μακάριον
τοῦτον καὶ μέγαν πατέρα ἡμῶν Συμεώνην ἐπιτάφιον λόγον καὶ ὕμνους ᾄδεσθαι καὶ ἐγκώμια, πηγαζούσης μου τῆς
διανοίας ὥσπερ ἀπὸ πηγῆς τινος καθαρᾶς τῶν νοημάτων
ἀφθόνως καὶ ἀκωλύτως τὰ νάματα, μὴ ἐξικανούσης μου
τῆς χειρὸς τῇ ταχυτῆτι τοῦ τὸν λόγον ἐπιχορηγοῦντός μοι
ἔνδοθεν. Ταῦτα τοιγαροῦν ἐκθέμενος, ἀνακαθάρας τε καὶ
εἰς χάρτην μεταπηξάμενος, ὑπέδειξά τινι τῶν πολλὴν

I put off doing this for a long time, however, because I had never had any experience of the art of writing this sort of thing (I had not managed to accumulate very much secular learning or develop my command of language, as I had renounced the life of the world and its clamor when I was young and was only fourteen years old, and had abandoned my schoolwork). But there was no respite for me, night and day, from the Spirit which inflamed me from within and kept forcefully prodding and urging me to do this.

Chapter 136

For this reason then, when I could not bear this pressure any longer, I first wrote some hymns[155] on our holy father and confessor Theodore the Stoudite. I did this to practice my writing and to express my affection for him. Then, since my mind had been sweetened with words as though by some indescribable pleasure, I also wrote a memorial oration for our great and blessed father Symeon,[156] as well as hymns for singing and eulogies of him. My mind was gushing with ideas like water flowing abundantly and ceaselessly from a pure spring, and my hand could not keep up with the pace at which the words were being supplied from within me. I thus wrote these down, and after I had edited them and transcribed them onto paper, I showed them to someone who had a lot of experience in both secular and sacred knowledge. When he told me that my compositions were not in-

ἐχόντων τῆς τε θύραθεν καὶ τῆς ἔσωθεν γνώσεως πεῖραν,
καὶ ἀκηκοὼς παρ' αὐτοῦ ὡς οὐκ ἔλαττόν εἰσι τῶν παλαιῶν
ὑμνογράφων καὶ τοῦ ἐκκλησιαστικοῦ χαρακτῆρος, ἐκπεράσας καὶ ἀπελθὼν ἐν τῇ σορῷ τοῦ μακαρίου τούτου
πατρὸς ὕμνησα μεθ' ἑτέρων ἀνδρῶν εὐλαβῶν τὸ ὕψος τῆς
ἁγιωσύνης αὐτοῦ, καὶ τὸν ἐπιτάφιον λόγον ἀνέγνων, ἀφο-
σιούμενος αὐτῷ τὴν κατὰ δύναμιν τιμήν τε καὶ ὑμνῳδίαν.
Πόθῳ τοίνυν καὶ πίστει πολλῇ ταῦτα πεποιηκὼς εἰς αὐτόν,
ὄψις με τοιαύτη ἐν μιᾷ τῶν νυκτῶν ἀναδέχεται.

137

Ἐδόκουν ὡς ὑφ' ἑτέρου καλούμενος καὶ οὕτω λέγοντος
πρός με· "Φωνεῖ σε ὁ πνευματικὸς πατήρ, ἀδελφέ,³²⁵ καὶ
ἔρχου ἀκολουθῶν μοι!" Καὶ αὐτὸς ἀκούσας ἠρξάμην³²⁶
ἕπεσθαι αὐτῷ σὺν χαρᾷ πάσῃ καὶ προθυμίᾳ ψυχῆς, οὐ γὰρ
ἤμην ἀξιωθεὶς ἀφ' οὗπερ πρὸς Θεὸν ἐνεδήμησεν ἰδεῖν
αὐτὸν ἕως τότε. Ὡς δ' ἐγενόμην πλησίον εἰς οἴκημά τι
βασιλικὸν καὶ λαμπρότατον, ὃ κουβούκλειον οἶδε καλεῖν
ἡ συνήθεια, ἐπέτρεψέ μοι τὴν εἴσοδον ὁ καλέσας διαπετάσας τὰς θύρας, καὶ ἰδοὺ θεωρῶ ἐπὶ πολυτίμου³²⁷ κλίνης καὶ
ὑψηλῆς ὕπτιόν πως τὸν ἅγιον κείμενον καὶ οἷά τινα βασι-
λέα περίδοξον ἀναπαυόμενον, λαμπρὸν τὸ πρόσωπον
ἔχοντα καὶ ὥσπερ ἐπιμειδιῶντα καὶ βλέποντα εἰς ἐμέ· καὶ
ὡς κατ' ὄψιν αὐτοῦ ἐγενόμην, νεύει με³²⁸ τῇ χειρὶ καὶ τῷ

ferior to those of the ancient hymnographers and were of ecclesiastical standard, I crossed over \<the Bosporus\> and visited our blessed father's tomb. There, along with some other pious men, I sang in praise of the sublimity of Symeon's holiness and read his memorial oration aloud, showing my respect for him and singing his praises to the best of my ability. And then one night, after I had done this with love and much faith in him, I had the following vision.

Chapter 137

Someone seemed to be calling me and saying, "Your spiritual father is asking for you, brother. Come, follow me!" When I heard this I began to follow him, full of joy and spiritual eagerness, for until then I had not been permitted to see Symeon since his departure to God. When I drew near a magnificent imperial chamber (what is usually called a *koubouklion*),[157] the man who had called me opened the doors and told me to enter. And, lo and behold, there I saw the saint reclining on his back on a very costly raised couch, reposing like some famous emperor. His face was shining and he was smiling as he looked at me. When I came into his presence, he gestured to me with his hand, indicating that I

335

νεύματι προσεγγίσαι αὐτῷ. Καὶ εὐθὺς ἐγὼ σὺν εὐφροσύνῃ
καρδίας πολλῇ ἔδραμον, καὶ κλίνας τὸ γόνυ τὴν τιμὴν ἀπ-
ένειμον ὡς εἶχον αὐτῷ μετ᾽ αἰδοῦς πάσης καὶ εὐλαβείας.

2   Ὁ δέ, ἐπεὶ ἀναστὰς προσῆλθον αὐτῷ, ἐνηγκαλίζετό με
καὶ κατησπάζετο εἰς τὸ στόμα, καὶ οὕτω μοι ἱλαρῷ καὶ
γλυκεῖ τῷ φθέγματι ἔλεγεν· "Ἀνέπαυσάς με, τέκνον μου
ποθεινὸν καὶ φιλούμενον." Λαβόμενος δέ μου καὶ τῆς δεξιᾶς χειρός, τέθεικεν αὐτὴν ὑπὸ τὸν μηρὸν αὐτοῦ τὸν δε-
ξιόν, τῇ δὲ ἑτέρᾳ αὐτοῦ χειρὶ δεικνύων μοι ἦν ἡπλωμένον
καὶ γεγραμμένον χαρτίον ἐν ταύτῃ κατέχων αὐτό, καὶ ἔλε-
γεν· "Ἵνα τί δὲ καὶ ἐπελάθου τοῦ λέγοντος· *ταῦτα παράθου
πιστοῖς ἀνθρώποις, οἵτινες ἱκανοὶ ἔσονται καὶ ἑτέρους διδάξαι*
[2 Tim 2:2];" Ὡς δὲ ταῦτα μὲν ἐκεῖνος εἶπεν, ἐγὼ δ᾽ εὐθὺς³²⁹
σὺν τῷ λόγῳ ἔξυπνος γέγονα (ὁ καθ᾽ὕπαρ καὶ οὐ καθ᾽
ὕπνους τοῦτο ἰδών), ἐν τοσαύτῃ χαρᾷ εὗρον ἐμαυτὸν καὶ
εὐφροσύνῃ ψυχῆς καὶ τὸ στόμα τὸ ἐμὸν³³⁰ γέμον γλυκύτητος, καὶ ἀγαλλιάσεως τὴν καρδίαν μου, ὥστε ἀπὸ τῆς
ἄγαν ἡδονῆς καὶ τῆς τοῦ Πνεύματος εὐφροσύνης ἀπο-
δύσασθαι τὸ σῶμα ἐζήτουν καὶ γυμνῇ τῇ ψυχῇ γενέσθαι
ἔνθα ἡ κατοικία ἐκείνῳ ἐδόθη μετὰ πάντων τῶν ἀπ᾽ αἰῶνος
ἁγίων ἐν τῇ ἀΰλῳ μακαριότητι.

should approach him. I immediately hurried forward, my
heart filled with happiness, and knelt, treating him with as
much deference as I could to show my respect and reverence.

After I had stood up and approached him, he embraced   2
me, kissed me on the mouth,[158] and said to me in a cheerful,
pleasant voice, "You've put me at rest, my dear and beloved
child." Then he took my right hand and placed it upon his
right thigh,[159] while with his other hand he showed me an
open scroll with writing on it that he was holding. "Why," he
said, "have you forgotten the one [Paul] who said, *put this
into the charge of men you can trust, who will also be able to teach
others?*" But as soon as he had said this to me, I woke up
(I who saw this while I was wide awake and not sleeping). I
found myself in such a state of spiritual joy and happiness,
while my mouth was so filled with sweetness and my heart
with such exaltation, that I longed to strip off my body because of this great pleasure and happiness from the Spirit
and go, with my soul naked,[160] to that place where Symeon
had been given his abode along with all the saints from every
age in immaterial blessedness.

138

Ὅτι δὲ ὅρασίς ἐστιν ἀληθὴς καὶ οὐκ ἐνύπνιον τοῦτο, πείθει με καὶ ἡ γενομένη τηνικαῦτα χαρὰ ἐν ἐμοὶ μετ' εὐφροσύνης ἀρρήτου καρδίας, καὶ ἅμα ἡ ἐντυπωθεῖσα τῷ νοΐ μου ἀνεξάλειπτος περὶ τούτου μνήμη. Τὰ γὰρ φαντάσματα ὅμου τε κατὰ φαντασίαν τῇ ψυχῇ ἐπιγίνονται καὶ τοῦ φαντασθέντος ἀφυπνισθέντος³³¹ ἄδηλα καὶ ἀμνημόνευτα καθόλου τῷ νοΐ γίνονται· οὐχ οὕτω δὲ ἔχει ἐπὶ τῶν ὄψεων τῆς ἀληθείας, ἀλλ' εἰς μακροὺς χρόνους καὶ μέχρι τέλους ἐπιμένουσι τῷ νοΐ ὡς ἐδείχθησαν.

2 Πείθει δέ με καὶ ὁ θεολόγος Γρηγόριος εἰς Καισάριον οὕτω γράφων καὶ τὴν γενομένην αὐτῷ περὶ τούτου ὄψιν ὡς ἀλήθειαν ἀποδεξάμενος καὶ οἷς γράφει πιστούμενος· τότε, φησί, Καισάριον ὄψομαι μηκέτι ἐκδημοῦντα, μηκέτι φερόμενον, μηκέτι ἐλεούμενον, λαμπρόν, ἔνδοξον, ὑψηλόν, οἷός μοι καὶ κατ' ὄναρ ὤφθης πολλάκις, ὦ φίλτατε ἀδελφῶν ἐμοὶ καὶ φιλαδελφότατε. Οὐ μόνον δέ, ἀλλὰ καὶ περὶ τῆς μητρὸς ἀσθενούσης τοιοῦτόν τι θεασαμένου, ἀληθὴς τῆς ὄψεως ἡ ἔκβασις γέγονε, καὶ πιστοῦται ταύτην ἐν οἷς οὕτω γράφων καὶ πείθει με ταύτην ὅρασιν ἀληθείας εἶναι καὶ οὐ φαντασίαν ἐνυπνίου τινά· φησὶ γάρ· πῶς οὖν τρέφει ταύτην Θεός; Οὐ 'μάννα βρέξας' [Ps 77(78):24; cf. Nm 11:6–9; Dt 8:3, 16; Jos 5:12] ὡς τὸ πάλαι τῷ Ἰσραήλ. Καὶ μετ' ὀλίγα· τίνα δὲ τρόπον; ἔδοξεν ἐμὲ τὸν αὐτῇ φίλτατον (προετιμᾶτο γὰρ ἡμῶν ἄλλος οὐδ' ἐν ὀνείρῳ), ἀθρόως ἐπιστάντα νυκτὸς μετὰ κανοῦ καὶ ἄρτων λαμπροτάτων, ἐπευξάμενόν τε αὐτοῖς

Chapter 138

The joy that came over me then and the indescribable feeling of happiness in my heart convinces me that this was a true vision and not just a dream, as does the fact that the memory of it has been imprinted indelibly in my mind. For apparitions are generally produced in the soul by the imagination, and the mind completely forgets what has been imagined as soon as this fades from view. But this is not the case with true visions, for they remain in the mind for a long time, even until the end of one's life, just as they first appeared.

I am also convinced of this by Gregory the Theologian 2 when he writes about Kaisarios,[161] for he accepts that the vision he had of this man was true and provides proof in what he writes: *Then I will see you, Kaisarios, no longer departed <from this life>, no longer being carried <on a bier>, no longer pitiable, but instead brilliant, glorious, and eminent, as I have often seen you in my dreams, my dearest and most beloved of brothers.*[162] Not only this, but he also saw something similar concerning his mother when she was ill. The outcome was true to the vision, and he provides proof of this in what he writes, convincing me that this was a true vision and not just some fantasy he saw in a dream. For he says, *How did God feed my mother? Not by 'raining manna,' as for Israel long ago,*[163] and then a little later, *But how? She thought that I, who was her favorite (for even in a dream she did not prefer another one of us), was suddenly there in the night with a basket of brightly shining bread. She*

καὶ σφραγίσαντα, ὥσπερ φίλον ἡμῖν, θρέψαι τε καὶ ῥῶσαι καὶ συναγαγεῖν τὴν δύναμιν. Καὶ ἡ τῆς νυκτὸς ὄψις ἔργον ἦν ἀληθείας· ἐξ ἐκείνου γὰρ ἑαυτῆς γίνεται καὶ τῆς χρηστοτέρας ἐλπίδος, τῷ τοῦτο δῆλον ἐναργῆ καὶ φανερὸν γενέσθαι γνωρίσματι. Καὶ ὅτι μὲν ὅρασις ἀληθείας καὶ οὐ φαντασία τις ἄλογος καὶ τὸ ἐμοὶ³³² δειχθὲν ὑπάρχει, ἱκανῶς διὰ πάντων τῶν εἰρημένων ἡμῖν ἐδείξαμεν.

139

Τὴν γοῦν τῆς ὄψεως κρίσιν κατ᾽ ἐμαυτὸν ἐκζητῶν καὶ ἀνακρίνων, ὥσπερ τις μυστικώτερον ἐμυσταγώγει με ταύτην. Πλὴν ὅμως καὶ παλαιῷ σοφωτάτῳ τὰ θεῖα καὶ τὰ ἀνθρώπινα δεῖν ἔγνων ταύτην ἀνακαλύψαι, ὃς ἅμα τῷ συμβαλεῖν τοῖς λεγομένοις, καὶ τὰ αὐτὰ ἰσοφώνως τῇ γενομένῃ³³³ μοι περὶ ταύτης μυσταγωγίᾳ ὑπολαβὼν ἔλεγε·

2 "Διὰ μὲν τοῦ εἰπεῖν τὸν ἅγιον," φησί, "πρὸς σέ, 'Ἀνέπαυσάς με, τέκνον μου ποθεινὸν καὶ φιλούμενον,' τὴν τῶν ὕμνων ἀποδοχὴν καὶ τῶν ἐγκωμίων τῶν πρὸς αὐτὸν ὑπεσήμαινε, δεικνὺς ὅτι τῶν ὕμνων καὶ τῶν ἐγκωμίων τῶν πρὸς αὐτοὺς οἱ ἐν θεῷ ζῶντες ἅγιοι καὶ μετὰ θάνατον χαίροντες ἀντιλαμβάνονται μετὰ πάσης ἀποδοχῆς. Τοῦτο γὰρ καὶ Διονύσιος ὁ Ἀρεοπαγίτης ἐμφαίνει ἐν τῷ μυστηρίῳ καὶ τῇ θεωρίᾳ τῶν κεκοιμημένων, ὡς διαβαινούσης

saw me bless the loaves and make the sign of the cross, as I liked
to do, and then feed her so that she felt better and recovered her
strength. And her nocturnal vision did truly happen, for she became
herself again from that moment and her prospects improved, some-
thing that was obviously made clear and evident by this token.[164]
So, I have done enough to demonstrate by everything I have
said that what was shown me was a true vision and not some
irrational fantasy.

Chapter 139

Anyway, as I was searching for the meaning of this vision
and asking myself about it, it was as though someone explained its mysteries to me in some mystical way. Nevertheless, I thought I should also disclose it to an elder who was
extremely wise in divine and human matters, but in fact, as
soon as he heard what I said, he responded with exactly the
same words as the mystical explanation of this that I had received myself. This is what he said:

"By saying to you, 'You've put me at rest, my dear and   2
beloved child,' the saint is indicating his acceptance of the
hymns and eulogies you have written in his honor. He thus
demonstrates that the saints who live with God after their
death joyfully receive the hymns and eulogies written in
their honor and find them completely acceptable. Indeed,
Dionysios the Areopagite also indicates this in his *Mystery*
and *Contemplation of the Deceased*,[165] for <he asserts that> the

τῆς δόξης πρὸς τὸν Θεὸν καὶ αὐτῆς δηλονότι τῆς ὠφελείας τῶν ἀκροωμένων βελτιουμένων ἀπὸ τῆς ἀκροάσεως
καὶ τὴν πολιτείαν τῶν ἁγίων καὶ τὰς πράξεις μιμουμένων
αὐτῶν. Διὰ δὲ τοῦ ἀσπασμοῦ τὴν ἐντεῦθεν γινομένην³³⁴
οἰκείωσιν πρὸς αὐτοὺς καὶ τὴν ἐξ ἐκείνων διδομένην χάριν
τοῖς ταῦτα γράφουσιν ὑπεδήλου.

3   "Τὸ δὲ θεῖναι τὴν δεξιάν σου χεῖρα εἰς τὸν μηρὸν αὐτοῦ
τὸν δεξιὸν τὸν ὅρκον, ὃν ἀπήτησεν Ἀβραάμ ποτε τὸν οἰκο-
γενῆ καὶ ἐπίτροπον αὐτοῦ οὕτως εἰπών· θὲς τὴν χεῖρά σου
ὑπὸ τὸν μηρόν μου, καὶ ὅμοσόν μοι τὸν Θεὸν τοῦ οὐρανοῦ
καὶ τῆς γῆς [Gen 24:2–3, 9], ὑπηνίττετο, ὅρκον ἀπαιτῶν σε
περὶ τῶν γεννημάτων τοῦ πνεύματος, ὧν συνελάβετο ἐν
γαστρὶ διανοίας αὐτοῦ ἐν φόβῳ Θεοῦ καὶ ἐκύησεν ἐπὶ τῆς
γῆς ἤγουν τῆς γενεᾶς ταύτης τῶν ἀνθρώπων, —λέγω δὴ
περὶ τῶν αὐτοῦ συγγραμμάτων τῶν χορηγηθέντων αὐτῷ
παρὰ τοῦ Πνεύματος ἄνωθεν, ὡς ἂν³³⁵ ταῦτα γραφῇ καὶ
πιστοῖς ἀνθρώποις παράθῃ³³⁶ εἰς ὠφέλειαν τῶν ἐντυγχανόντων, καθώς σοι διὰ τοῦ ἀποστολικοῦ καθυπέμνησε ῥή-
ματος· ταῦτά, φησί, παράθου πιστοῖς ἀνθρώποις, οἵτινες
ἱκανοὶ ἔσονται καὶ ἑτέρους διδάξαι [2 Tim 2:2], καὶ τὸν χάρτην ἡπλωμένον καὶ γεγραμμένον ὑπέδειξεν."

honor <contained in such writings> is transferred to God and these are thus of obvious benefit to those who hear them, since these people are improved by hearing about and imitating the lives and deeds of the saints.[166] The kiss implies the kinship with the saints that results from such writings, as well as the grace given by the saints to those who write these compositions.

"Putting your right hand on his thigh alludes to the sworn 3 pledge that Abraham once demanded from his house slave and steward when he said, *place your hand under my thigh, and* swear to me *by the God of heaven and earth.* This demands an oath from you concerning Symeon's spiritual offspring,[167] those whom he conceived in the womb of his mind in the fear of God and whom he bore on earth, or rather, among the present generation of men—I mean an oath concerning the compositions that were provided to him by the Spirit from above. You are thus sworn to write these down and make them known to the faithful so that they may benefit those who read them. Symeon reminded you of this with the quotation from the apostle, *put this into the charge of men you can trust, who will also be able to teach others,* and when he showed you the unrolled paper with writing on it."

140

Οὕτω τοιγαροῦν τῆς ὄψεως τὴν κρίσιν ὑπὸ τοῦ διανοί-
γοντος ἡμῶν τὸν νοῦν εἰς τὸ συνιέναι τὰς γραφὰς καὶ ὑπὸ
τοῦ παλαιοῦ τῶν ἡμερῶν [Dn 7:9, 13, 22] σοφωτάτου γέροντος μυσταγωγηθείς, ἐμνήσθην αὐτίκα καὶ τῆς πρός μέ
ποτε γενομένης γραφῆς παρὰ τοῦ ἁγίου καὶ τῶν θεοπνεύστων συγγραμμάτων αὐτοῦ καὶ καθὼς τηνικαῦτα προ-
φητικώτατα γέγραφε πρός με, οὕτω πάντα εἰς τὸν ἴδιον
ἐξέβη καιρόν, πιστεύω δὲ ὅτι καὶ ἔτι ἐκβήσεται, πάντων
δηλαδὴ τῶν συγγραμμάτων αὐτοῦ ἐλθόντων εἰς τὰς ἐμὰς
χεῖρας ὑπ᾽ ἄλλου δυσκόλου κεκρατημένων καὶ ὥσπερ βα-
σιλικοῦ θησαυροῦ φυλαττομένων ἐπὶ χρόνοις τρισκαίδε-
κα, ὡς καὶ ἑνὸς βιβλίου διαπραθέντος ἀπὸ τῶν συγγραμμάτων αὐτοῦ πρὸς ἐμὲ διακομισθῆναι καὶ ἐπισυναφθῆναι
τοῖς ὑπολοίποις.

2   Ἔνθεν τοι καὶ κατὰ τὴν αὐτοῦ προφητείαν καὶ τὸ ἱερὸν
αὐτοῦ ἐπιστόλιον κληρονόμος γενόμενος τοῦ πλούτου
τῶν χαρισμάτων αὐτοῦ, ὃν ἐδωρήσατο αὐτῷ ὁ Θεὸς ὡς
τοῖς αὐτόπταις τοῦ Λόγου [cf. Lk 1:2] διὰ τῆς τοῦ Πνεύματος δωρεᾶς, πανταχοῦ τοῦτον ἀνακηρύττω καὶ πᾶσιν
ἀφθόνως εἰς εὐεργεσίαν καὶ ὠφέλειαν ψυχῆς χορηγῶν
προτίθημι τὰς θεολογίας αὐτοῦ, κἂν οἱ βασκαίνοντες τοῖς
κακοῖς διὰ τὴν ἧτταν οὐ βούλονται· περὶ οὗ καὶ τὴν ἀντι-
μισθίαν ἐκ χειρὸς Κυρίου ἔνθεν τε κἀκεῖθεν ἐλπίζω λαβεῖν
διὰ τῶν τοῦ μακαρίου τούτου καὶ ἁγίου δεήσεων, ὅτι αὐτός
ἐστιν ὁ εἰπὼν ἀψευδῶς· ὁ δεχόμενος δίκαιον εἰς ὄνομα

Chapter 140

Once I had been given this explanation of how to interpret my vision, both by Him who opens our mind to the understanding of scripture and by that *ancient of days*, that extremely wise elder, I also immediately remembered the letter that the saint had written to me and his divinely inspired compositions. And just as he had written prophetically to me then, so everything came about in its own good time, and, I believe, will still come about. For all his compositions that had been taken and guarded like some royal treasure for thirteen years by another difficult man have indeed come into my hands, and one book of his compositions that had been sold off has been restored to me and is now back together with the rest.

And so, in accordance with his prophecy and his holy letter to me, I have inherited the wealth of spiritual gifts that God gave him, just as He gave it to those <apostles> *who were eyewitnesses of the Word* through the gift of the Spirit. I am thus making his legacy known everywhere and I am publishing his divine writings for everyone, making sure that they are readily available to help and benefit their souls, even if those who are jealous in their wickedness, because they have been defeated, do not want this to happen. And I am hoping to receive my reward for doing so from the Lord's hand in this world and the next, through the intercessions of this blessed saint, because it is He who says truthfully, *Whoever receives a righteous man as a righteous man will be given*

δικαίου μισθὸν δικαίου λήψεται [Mt 10:41]. Καὶ αὖθις· ὁ δεχόμενος ἅγιον εἰς ὄνομα ἁγίου μισθὸν ἁγίου λήψεται, καὶ
ὁ δεχόμενος προφήτην εἰς ὄνομα προφήτου μισθὸν προφήτου
λήψεται [Mt 10:41]. Καὶ αὖθις· ὁ δεχόμενος ὑμᾶς ἐμὲ δέχεται,
ὁ δὲ ἐμὲ δεχόμενος δέχεται τὸν ἀποστείλαντά με [Mt 10:40;
cf. Mk 9:37; John 13:20]. Ἀλλὰ τούτων μὲν ἅλις.

141

Τί δαί; Καταλείψομεν ἀμνημόνευτα καὶ ἃ μετὰ τὴν
αὐτοῦ κοίμησιν ἕτερα ὁ θεολογικώτατος καὶ ὁμολογητὴς
πατὴρ ἡμῶν Συμεὼν ἐποίησέ τε καὶ ποιεῖ θαύματα ἐτησίως; Καὶ πῶς οὐκ εἰσπραχθησόμεθα δίκας ἐνδίκως παρὰ
Θεοῦ περὶ τούτου ὡς καταφρονηταὶ τῶν θείων πραγμάτων; Ἀλλὰ δεῦτε καὶ διηγήσομαι ὑμῖν τοῖς πιστοῖς, λόγον
μηδένα τῶν Ἰουδαιοφρόνων ἀνδρῶν καὶ βασκάνων ποιούμενος, ὅσα ἐποίησεν ὁ Θεὸς [cf. Ps 65(66):16] μετὰ τῶν
πατέρων ἡμῶν, καὶ ὅσα τῇ δυνάμει τοῦ Πνεύματος μετὰ
πότμον ὁ ἁγιώτατος πατὴρ ἡμῶν ἐποίησε θαύματα εἰς δόξαν Θεοῦ τοῦ δοξάσαντος αὐτὸν μέσον τῆς ἐκκλησίας
αὐτοῦ.

2   Ἱερεύς τις καὶ μονάζων ἄρτι ἐξ ὄρους ὁρμώμενος Λά-
τρου καὶ πρὸς ξενιτείαν ἐκδοὺς ἑαυτόν, τόπους πολλοὺς

346

a righteous man's reward, and again, whoever receives a saint because he is a saint will be given a saint's reward, and *whoever receives a prophet as a prophet will be given a prophet's reward,* and again, *Whoever receives you receives me and whoever receives me receives the One who sent me.* But enough of this.

10. Symeon's Posthumous Miracles

Chapter 141

What now? Shall I let the other miracles be forgotten that our father Symeon, the great theologian and confessor, performed after his death and still performs every year? Would I not be justly punished by God for neglecting divine matters if I did so? But *come then,* and, taking no notice of those Jewish-minded people who are jealous <of Symeon>, *I will tell* you faithful ones *what* God *did* with our fathers, and what miracles our most holy father performed after his death in the midst of his church by the power of the Spirit to the glory of God who glorified him.

An ordained monk had recently set out from Mount 2 Latros[168] and had devoted himself to traveling. After he had

ἱστορήσας καὶ διελθὼν καταπαύει τῆς ἄλης ἐν τῷ μικρῷ ποιμνίῳ τῆς ἁγίας Μαρίνης τῷ κατὰ τὴν Χρυσόπολιν ὑπὸ τοῦ ἁγίου κτισθέντι. Ἐπεὶ δὲ παρὰ τῶν ἐκεῖσε μοναζόντων ὁ εἰρημένος ἱερεὺς ἐξενίσθη, ἀρεσθεὶς ἐκεῖνος εἰς τὴν τοῦ μικροῦ ποιμνίου καταμονήν, συνδιάγειν καὶ συζῆν[337] ᾑρετίσατο τοῖς αὐτοῦ μοναχοῖς καὶ τοὺς ἀσκητικοὺς σύναμα πόνους καθυπομένειν· ὃν καὶ οἱ τηνικαῦτα ὄντες ἐκεῖσε μονάζοντες ἀποδεξάμενοι, ὥσπερ εἴρηται, τάττουσι τῇ αὐτῶν ἀδελφότητι, καὶ εἷς τῆς ἐκείνων οὗτος ὁμηγύρεως γίνεται.

3   Ὡς οὖν ἐν πάσαις ταῖς τελουμέναις ἐν τῷ εὐκτηρίῳ δοξολογίαις συνέψαλλε πᾶσιν ὁ ἀνὴρ καὶ τῆς θείας λειτουργῶν ἀντείχετο λειτουργίας, ἐπεὶ κατὰ τὸ κέρας τοῦ βήματος ἐπίπροσθεν τοῦ θυσιαστηρίου ὁ χαρακτὴρ τῆς εἰκόνος τοῦ ἁγίου πατρὸς Συμεὼν ἀπηώρητο, ἀπιστίας ἐκεῖνος βληθεὶς λογισμοῖς ἐνδοιάζειν ἤρξατο καθ᾽ ἑαυτὸν καί· "Πόθεν ἄρα οὗτος," ἔλεγε, "καὶ ἐκ ποίων σημείων καὶ θαυμάτων ὡς οἱ πάλαι τὴν ἁγιωσύνην αὐτοῦ ἐπιστώσατο, ἵνα γνοὺς καὶ αὐτὸς ἐγὼ ἔξω νῦν αὐτὸν ὡς ἅγιον, οἷα δὴ πιστωθεὶς ἐκεῖθεν, ὥσπερ τοὺς παλαιοὺς ἔχει ἔκπαλαι τῶν χρόνων ἐκ τῶν τοιούτων ἡ τῶν πιστῶν ἐκκλησία;"

seen and visited many places, he stopped his wandering at the little flock of Saint Marina that had been founded by the saint near Chrysopolis. Since this priest had been received as a guest by the monks who lived there and had enjoyed his stay with the little flock, he decided to remain there and live with the monks in the monastery and join them in the performance of ascetic labors. The monks who were living there at the time accepted him, as has been said, and made him a member of their brotherhood, and he joined their community.

The man thus used to join everyone else in the chanting 3 of all the services performed in the chapel and served as a celebrant at the divine liturgy, but since the icon depicting the holy Symeon was suspended from the crossbeam of the sanctuary in front of the altar,[169] he was assailed by a lack of faith and started to have doubts in his mind. "How and by what signs and miracles like <those performed by> the <saints of> old," he said to himself, "has this man's holiness been attested, so that I myself may now know for sure that he is a saint, convinced by the same sort of <signs and miracles> as the church of the faithful has had from ancient times for the <saints of> old?"

142

Οὕτω τοίνυν αὐτοῦ τοῖς τοιούτοις ἐνδοιάζοντος λογισμοῖς ὡς ὑπὸ πνεύματος ἀπιστίας ἐνεργουμένου, ἐν μιᾷ τῶν ἡμερῶν ὡς ἡ ἑωθινὴ παρὰ πάντων ἐτελέσθη δοξολογία καὶ οἱ μοναχοὶ πάντες τοῦ εὐκτηρίου ἐξῆλθον καὶ πρὸς τὰς ἑαυτῶν ἐχώρησαν κέλλας, ἐκεῖνος ἑκουσίως μονώτατος ἐν τῷ εὐκτηρίῳ χλευάσων³³⁸ ἐπὶ κακῷ μόρῳ τῆς ἑαυτοῦ κεφαλῆς τὸν ἅγιον ἐναπέμεινε. Σκοτισθεὶς οὖν ὑπὸ τοῦ Διαβόλου ὁ ἄθλιος προσέρχεται τῇ τοῦ ἁγίου εἰκόνι, καὶ ὡς πλησίον γένοιτο ταύτης, ἐκτείνει ὁ ἀναιδὴς ἀναιδῶς κατὰ τῆς εἰκόνος τὴν ἑαυτοῦ δεξιὰν καί φησιν *ἐν ὑπερηφανίᾳ καὶ ἐξουδενώσει* [Ps 30(31):18]· "Τοῦτον ἐγὼ ἡγήσομαί ποτε καὶ δοξάσω ἢ τὸ σύνολον προσκυνήσω ἀσυνέτως ὡς ἅγιον;" Καὶ σὺν τῷ λόγῳ ἔτι ταύτης τῆς φωνῆς *οὔσης ἐν τῷ στόματι αὐτοῦ, καὶ ὀργὴ τοῦ Θεοῦ ἀνέβη ἐπ᾽ αὐτόν* [cf. Ps 77(78):30–31]· αὐτὴν γάρ, ἣν κατὰ τῆς ἁγίας εἰκόνος ἐξέτεινε χεῖρα, εὐθὺς ὁ μάταιος ἐξηράνθη, καὶ οὕτως ἐπὶ σχήματος ἔστη ἐκτεταμένην ἔχων, μὴ πρὸς ἀγκῶνα συσταλῆναι παρ᾽ ἐκείνου ἰσχύουσαν. Ἀλλὰ βληθεὶς ἐντεῦθεν ὁ ἀνόητος εἰς δριμείας ὀδύνας, ἄκων καὶ μὴ βουλόμενος, μὴ μεταβῆναι δυνηθεὶς ὅλως ἐκεῖθεν, ταῖς γοεραῖς φωναῖς ἑαυτὸν τοῖς πᾶσιν ἐδημοσίευσεν.

2   Ὑπὸ τῆς βοῆς οὖν ἐκείνου θροηθέντες οἱ μοναχοὶ καὶ εἰς τὸ εὐκτήριον εἰσδραμόντες, εὗρον κρίσει δικαίᾳ Θεοῦ τιμωρούμενον τοῦτον, ὡς δεδεμένον οἷάπερ ἀπὸ τῆς δεξιᾶς χειρός, καὶ πρὸς τὸν ἀέρα κρεμάμενον τῆς εἰκόνος

Chapter 142

With such doubts in his mind, as though moved by a spirit of disbelief, one day when everyone had finished the morning service and all the monks had left the chapel and gone off to their own cells, this man stayed behind of his own volition all by himself in the chapel <with the idea of> jeering at the saint, <but in fact bringing down> a miserable fate upon his own head. Blinded by the Devil, the wretch approached the saint's icon, and when he was close to it, that shameless man shamelessly stretched out his right arm against the icon and said *with pride and contempt,* "Why would I ever accept and praise or stupidly venerate this man as a saint in any way at all?" At his words, with the sound of them still *in his mouth, God's wrath rose against* him, for the very arm that that foolish man had stretched out against the holy icon was immediately paralyzed, and it stayed stretched out in this position so that he was unable to bend it at the elbow. Then, when the foolish man was, as a result, assailed with sharp pains, he reluctantly and unwillingly made his plight known to everyone with cries of distress, since he was completely incapable of moving from there.

Alarmed by his shouts, the monks rushed into the chapel 2
and found him being punished by a just judgment of God. For it was just as though he had been bound by his right hand and suspended in the air in front of the icon, and, with

ἐπίπροσθεν, καὶ βοαῖς γοεραῖς πρὸς ἔλεον αὐτοῦ κάμπτοντα τοὺς εἰς αὐτὸν ὁρῶντας μονάζοντας. Οἱ γοῦν συνδραμόντες τῶν μοναχῶν, ἐπεὶ τὴν αἰτίαν ἐξ ἐκείνου μάθοιεν τῆς εἰς αὐτὸν τοιαύτης ὀργῆς τοῦ Θεοῦ, πολλὰ τῆς αὐτοῦ καταστενάξαντες τόλμης καὶ ἅμα τοῦτον κατελεήσαντες, ἐδέοντο τοῦ Θεοῦ καὶ τοῦ θεσπεσίου πατρὸς Συμεὼν λυθῆναι τὸν ἄθλιον τῆς δεινῆς τιμωρίας ἐκείνης. Διὸ καὶ ἀπὸ τοῦ λύχνου τῆς εἰκόνος αὐτοῦ λαμβάνοντες ἔλαιον καὶ τὴν ἐξηραμένην ὅλην αὐτοῦ χεῖρα, ὑφ' ἧς εἰς ἀέρα ἐκρέματο, ἀπὸ τοῦ ὤμου καὶ μέχρι δακτύλων ἀλείφοντες, μόλις ἴσχυσαν ἀπὸ πρωΐας καὶ μέχρις ἡλίου δυσμῶν εἰς ἔλεον αὐτοῦ κάμψαι Θεὸν καὶ τὸν ἅγιον, τοῦ λυθῆναι τὴν τολμηρὰν αὐτοῦ χεῖρα τῶν ἀφύκτων καὶ ἀοράτων δεσμῶν τῆς ὀργῆς τοῦ Θεοῦ. Καὶ τοῦτο μὲν τοιοῦτον τὸ θαῦμα φρικτὸν καὶ παράδοξον.

143

Τούτου δὲ παρόμοιον καὶ ἐν ἄλλῳ γέγονεν ἀπιστίας λογισμοῖς καθυποβληθέντι κατὰ τὴν τοῦ ἁγίου πανήγυριν ὡς οὐκ ὤφελεν. Ἔστι δὲ τοιοῦτον· τελουμένης τῆς τοῦ ἁγίου ἡμῶν[339] πανηγύρεως κατὰ τὴν τοιαύτην μονήν, ἐπεὶ πλῆθος οὐκ ὀλίγον συνῆλθεν ἐν ταύτῃ, ἦσαν δὲ καὶ ἀπὸ τῆς βασιλικῆς μονῆς τοῦ Κοσμιδίου μονάζοντες, εἰς τούτων ὁ καλλίφωνος ἐκεῖνος Ἰγνάτιος, κατὰ τὴν ἀγρυπνίαν

shouts of distress, was begging for mercy from the monks who were looking at him. When the monks who thus rushed in together learned from him why God was so angry with him, they were greatly saddened at his audacity but at the same time pitied him, so that they begged God and His wondrous father Symeon to release the wretch from that awful punishment. They thus took oil from the lamp <in front> of Symeon's icon and anointed the monk's whole paralyzed arm, by which he was hanging in the air, from the shoulder right up to the fingers. Only after they did this from early morning to sunset were they able to move God and His saint to mercy and thus free that man's audacious hand from the inescapable and invisible bonds of God's wrath. So that's the story of that frightful and extraordinary miracle.

Chapter 143

Something similar to this also happened to another man who was assailed inappropriately by doubts at the saint's festival. This is what happened. Our holy father's festival was being celebrated at that monastery and a large crowd had gathered there, including some monks from the imperial monastery of Kosmidion,[170] one of whom was that professional singer Ignatios.[171] During the dawn vigil, while he

τοῦ ὄρθρου ὡς τὸ πρὸς τὸν ἅγιον γραφὲν ἡδυφώνως ᾖδε
κοντάκιον, καὶ τοὺς περὶ αὐτὸ[340] οἴκους λιγυρᾷ διήρχετο
τῇ φωνῇ, ἐνεργείᾳ καὶ φθόνῳ τοῦ Σατανᾶ ἀπιστίας καὶ
αὐτὸς ἐβλήθη λογισμοῖς κατὰ τοῦ τρισολβίου πατρός, ἀτενῶς ὁρῶν πρὸς τὴν αὐτοῦ θείαν εἰκόνα εἰς τὸ κέρας ὡς
εἴρηται κρεμαμένην τοῦ βήματος. Ὑπὸ τῶν τοιούτων οὖν
λογισμῶν ἀφανῶς τοῦ ἀνδρὸς ἐνεργουμένου, βουληθεὶς ὁ
ἅγιος θεραπεῦσαι τὴν ἐκείνου ψυχὴν ὑπὸ τοῦ φθόνου βλα-
πτομένην τοῦ Διαβόλου, καὶ τοῖς συνάδουσιν αὐτῷ πᾶσι
χάριτος μεταδοῦναι καὶ ὠφελείας, ἔτι ᾄδοντος ἡδυφώνως
αὐτοῦ, αἴφνης κατ᾽ ὄψιν αὐτοῦ τε καὶ τοῦ ὑπαγορεύοντος
αὐτοῦ Μεθοδίου ἀπὸ τῆς τῶν Στουδίου δραμόντος μονῆς,
ὥσπερ ἀπανθρακωθεῖσα κατὰ τὸ πρόσωπον ἡ τοῦ ἁγίου
εἰκὼν καὶ φλογοειδὴς γενομένη ἤρξατό πως[341] κυμαίνε-
σθαι καὶ ὧδε κἀκεῖσε φέρεσθαι κατὰ τὸ κέρας τοῦ βήματος, ἐν ᾧ ἀπῃώρητο.

2   Τοῦτο τοίνυν ὡς Ἰγνάτιος ἐθεάσατο τὸ παράδοξον
θαῦμα, εὐθὺς ἐσβέσθη τε αὐτοῦ ἡ φωνὴ καὶ ἐνεὸς[343] καὶ
ἄναυδος καὶ ἄλαλος ἔστη. Ὡς δ᾽ οἱ[343] μελῳδοῦντες καὶ
πανηγυρίζοντες ἅμα τὸν μὲν ἄλαλον εἶδον αἰφνίδιον, τὴν
δὲ τοῦ ἁγίου εἰκόνα κυμαινομένην καὶ σειομένην καθ᾽ ἑαυτήν, ἐπυνθάνοντο τί συνέβη τῷ ᾄδοντι καλλιφώνῳ, τίς τε
ἡ αἰτία τῆς ἐκείνου κωφεύσεως, καὶ τί λογιζόμενος τοῦτο
πέπονθεν ὁ καλλίφωνος. Ὁ δὲ ἀληθὴς ὢν καὶ ἐπιγνώμων,
κατανυγεὶς τὸν τῆς ἀπιστίας ἐξωμολογήσατο λογισμὸν
τῆς ψυχῆς αὐτοῦ, καὶ ὅπως ἀτενίζων πρὸς τὴν τοῦ ἁγίου
εἰκόνα φλογὶ ἐοικυῖαν εἶδε τὴν ὄψιν αὐτῆς ἐπισείουσαν
οἷον αὐτῷ, καὶ τρανῶς διὰ τῆς κινήσεως τὴν ἐνοικοῦσαν

was sweetly chanting a hymn[172] written to the saint and, in his clear voice, was going through the stanzas about Symeon and gazing directly at his holy icon which hung, as I've said, from the crossbeam of the sanctuary,[173] he too was stricken with doubts about our thrice-blessed father, due to the activity and envy of Satan. Because the man was secretly influenced by such thoughts, the saint wished to heal his soul, which had been harmed by the Devil's envy, and also provide grace and benefit to everyone who was singing with him. And so, while Ignatios was still singing sweetly, right before his eyes and those of the choir director Methodios (who had come from the monastery of Stoudios), the face of the saint's icon turned burning red and fiery and the icon somehow began to sway about and move here and there on the crossbeam of the sanctuary from which it was hanging.

When Ignatios saw this extraordinary miracle, he immediately lost his voice and he stood there struck dumb, speechless and mute. And as the singers and the people celebrating the festival saw him suddenly unable to speak and at the same time saw the saint's icon swaying about and moving to and fro by itself, they began to ask what had happened to the professional singer, what had made him fall silent, and what he had been thinking when this happened to him. And Ignatios, being a man of true understanding, was stung to repentance and confessed the doubt that was in his soul, and how, when he was gazing at the saint's icon, he had seen that its face was like flame, as though it were menacing him. The icon thus clearly showed by its movement the

ἐν αὐτῇ τοῦ Ἁγίου Πνεύματος χάριν δεικνύουσαν, καθά
ποτε καὶ διὰ γλωσσῶν πυρίνων ἐπὶ τῶν ἀποστόλων ταύτην ὑπέδειξε τοῖς λαοῖς ὁ Θεός [Act 2:3], καὶ τοὺς μὲν ὑπο-
βληθέντας λογισμοῖς ἀπιστίας τούτῳ τῷ τρόπῳ πιστοὺς
διαφερόντως εἰργάσατο.

144

Ἀλλ' εἰ δοκεῖ καὶ ἐφ' ἕτερον θαῦμα τοῦ Θεολόγου
πατρὸς ἔλθωμεν. Τῶν καθυπηρετούντων τῷ μαθητῇ τοῦ
ἁγίου, λέγω δὴ τῷ Στηθάτῳ Νικήτᾳ, εἷς ἦν καὶ ὁ Μανασ-
σῆς ἐκεῖνος. Οὗτος τοιγαροῦν εἰς δυσεντερίας[344] περι-
πεσὼν νόσημα, ὃ λέγεται ἰλεός, καὶ ἐπὶ πεντεκαίδεκα ἡμέρας τὰ σῖτα μὲν συνήθως λαμβάνων[345] τοῦ σώματος εἰς
διατροφήν, ἔξοδον δὲ τῶν περιττευμάτων αὐτοῦ μηδόλως
ποιούμενος, περὶ τὴν ἑαυτοῦ ζωὴν ἐκινδύνευε, καθ' ἑκάστην ὡς εἰπεῖν τὸν θάνατον ἐκδεχόμενος, διὰ τὸ καὶ τὴν
δυσωδίαν τῆς γαστρὸς παρὰ φύσιν ἐκ τοῦ στόματος τούτου ἐξέρχεσθαι. Ἐπεὶ τοίνυν πᾶσαν ἰατρικὴν μέθοδον καὶ
πᾶν φάρμακον ἰατρικὸν ἄπρακτον ἐπὶ τὸν ἄνδρα τοῦτον ἡ
νόσος ἤλεγχεν αὕτη, καὶ τῆς παρούσης παρὰ τῶν ἰατρῶν
ἀπεγνώσθη ζωῆς, αὐτὸς τῶν ἄλλων πάντων ἀλογήσας, δι'
ὧν παραμυθεῖται τὸ σῶμα νοσηλευόμενον, καταφεύγει διὰ
μετανοίας καὶ προσευχῆς εἰς Θεόν.

grace of the Holy Spirit that dwelled in it, just as God also once demonstrated this to the people through tongues of fire on the apostles, and in this way it thus made believers especially out of those who had been assailed by doubts.

Chapter 144

But now, if you agree, let us turn to another miracle of our father the Theologian. Among those who were serving in obedience to the saint's disciple (I'm referring to Niketas Stethatos) was that man Manasses. He fell victim to an internal malady of the type called ileus [intestinal obstruction]. Thus, although he took food as usual for fifteen days to nourish his body, he evacuated none of his excrement at all and was in danger of losing his life. Each day, so to speak, he was awaiting death, because the stench from his belly was also coming out of his mouth in an abnormal way. Since this illness had thus proved every medical technique and every medicinal remedy useless to the man, and the doctors had despaired of his life, he paid no heed to any other means by which he might relieve his sick body, but took refuge in God with repentance and prayer.

2   Διὸ καὶ ἐξ ἀθυμίας πολλῆς δακρύων λιβάδας καταγα-
γών, καὶ εἰς ὕπνον ἐντεῦθεν τραπείς, ὁρᾷ κατ' ὄψιν νυκτὸς
τὸν ῥηθέντα μαθητὴν τοῦ ἁγίου (ᾧ καὶ καθυπηρέτει ὡς
εἴρηται), φωνοῦντα καὶ προσκαλούμενον τοῦτον καὶ ἐπίπροσθεν παρεστῶτα τῆς τοῦ ἁγίου εἰκόνος καὶ οὕτως εἰπόντα πρὸς αὐτόν· "Μανασσῆ, ἄρας τὸν λύχνον τῆς εἰκόνος τοῦ ἁγίου πατρὸς πίε ὡς ἔχεις αὐτόν, καὶ ῥᾷον ἕξεις
τῆς νόσου." Ὁ δὲ ὡς ἤκουσε, σὺν τῷ λόγῳ λαβὼν τοῦτον
καὶ ὅλον κατ' ὄναρ πιών, εὐθὺς ἔτι κατεχόμενος τῷ ὕπνῳ
νύσσεται τὴν γαστέρα, καὶ τὸν ὕπνον ἀποτιναξάμενος τῆς
κλίνης ὡς εἶχεν ἐκπεπηδηκώς, τῶν πεντεκαίδεκα ἡμερῶν
τὸν ἐναποκείμενον φορυτὸν τῆς γαστρὸς ἐξέχεέ τε ἅμα ἐν
μιᾷ, καὶ καθαρᾶς τῆς ὑγιείας ἀπήλαυσεν.[346]

3   Οὕτως οὖν ἐκ παραδόξου τῆς θεραπείας τετυχηκώς, ἧς
οὐκ ἴσχυσε πρὸ τούτου διὰ φαρμάκων ἰατρικῶν τυχεῖν
προσδραμὼν ἰατροῖς, εὐχαριστεῖ θερμῶς τῷ ἁγίῳ τῇ θείᾳ
προσπεσὼν τούτου μετὰ δακρύων εἰκόνι, καὶ ἡδέως τὸ γεγονὸς εἰς αὐτὸν παρ' αὐτοῦ ἐκδιηγούμενος τὴν τούτου
πρὸς Θεὸν παρρησίαν καὶ ἁγιότητα τρανῶς τοῖς[347] πᾶσιν
ἐκήρυττε. Καὶ τοῦτο μὲν ἤδη τοιοῦτον.

145

Ἄνδρες δὲ δύο τινὲς εὐλαβεῖς, ὧν ὁ μὲν Ἰωάννης, ὁ δὲ
Φιλόθεος ἐκαλεῖτο, κατὰ τὴν θείαν τοῦ Κυρίου ἐντολὴν

And so, after shedding streams of tears in his great de- 2
spair, he fell asleep and saw in a nocturnal vision the saint's
aforesaid disciple [Niketas] (whom, as has been mentioned,
he was serving in obedience), calling to him and summoning
him while standing in front of the saint's icon. Niketas said
to him, "Manasses, take the lamp from the holy father's icon
and drink as much as you can from it and you will get better
from your illness." As soon as he heard this Manasses took
the lamp and drank all the lamp oil in his dream. Immediately, while he was still fast asleep, he felt a pain in his belly
and, shaking off his sleep, leaped out of bed as quickly as he
could and excreted from his belly all at one time the waste
that had been stored up for fifteen days. And he then enjoyed perfect health.

After he had received a cure in this extraordinary way, a 3
cure that he had previously been unable to obtain by going to doctors for medicinal remedies, Manasses fervently
thanked the saint, prostrating himself before his divine icon
with tears. Happily narrating what had happened to him
through Symeon, he plainly proclaimed to everyone the latter's holiness and access to God. So much for that story.

Chapter 145

Two pious men, one of whom was called John, the other
Philotheos, were in agreement in the world, according to

καὶ ἀπόφασιν συμφωνήσαντες ἐν τῷ κόσμῳ [cf. Mt 18:19], καὶ τούτου τὴν ἀποταγὴν³⁴⁸ φρονίμως ἅμα πεποιηκότες, τὸ ἱερὸν τῶν μοναζόντων ἐνεδύσαντο σχῆμα, καὶ πρὸς ἀσκητικοὺς ἀγῶνας αὐθαιρέτως ἐχώρησαν. Ἐπεὶ δὲ διὰ τῶν ἀνδρῶν τούτων ἀσκητικὸν καταγώγιον ἔμελλεν ἀνεγεῖραι³⁴⁹ ἡ Πρόνοια εἰς γυμνασίαν ἀρετῆς τῶν ἀποτάξασθαι βουλομένων τῷ κόσμῳ καὶ διὰ πόνων εὐσεβείας τῶν μοναζόντων εὐαγγελικοῦ βίου ἀντιποιεῖσθαι, κινεῖ τούτους ἄνωθεν καὶ ταῦτα πενίᾳ συζῶντας καὶ ἀπορίᾳ καὶ μηδὲ τῆς ἐφημέρου εὐποροῦντας τροφῆς, καὶ μονὴν ἀνεγείρουσιν ἱερὰν ἀσκητῶν συνεργείᾳ Θεοῦ καὶ δυνάμει, κατὰ τὸν Ἀνάπλουν τῆς Προποντίδος τοῦ Βυζαντίου, οὕτω σεμνὴν καὶ ὡραίαν, οὕτω περικαλλῆ καὶ χαρίτων μεστήν, ὡς ἐξίστασθαι τοὺς τὴν τῶν ἀνδρῶν εἰδότας πενίαν ὁμοῦ καὶ εὐτέλειαν, ὁρῶντας τὴν τῆς μονῆς πολυέξοδον κτῆσιν καὶ τὴν ταύτης κατασκευήν.

2   Μετὰ γοῦν τὸ τὴν τοιαύτην ἀπαρτίσαι μονὴν ὁ μὲν αὐτῶν θεόφιλος ὢν καὶ θερμὸς εἰς ἀγῶνας πνευματικοὺς ὁ καὶ φερωνύμως κληθεὶς Φιλόθεος, κελλίον ἡσυχαστικὸν ἑαυτῷ κατασκευάσας εἰς ἔγκλειστρον, ὑπεισέρχεται τοῦτο, καὶ κλείει πᾶσαν πρόοδον, καὶ τοὺς τελεωτέρους τῆς ἡσυχίας ἀγῶνας ἡρετίσατο προθύμως μετέρχεσθαι· ὁ δὲ ἀσθενὴς ὢν τὰς δυνάμεις τοῦ σώματος οἷα δὴ εὐνοῦχος ὁ Ἰωάννης, τὴν τῆς μονῆς οἰκονομίαν ὑπεισέδυ, καὶ ταύτης ὡς φρόνιμος μετήει οἰκονόμος [Lk 12:42].

the Lord's divine commandment and decree. They wisely effected the renunciation of the world at the same time and, putting on the holy habit of monks, withdrew of their own free will into ascetic contests. Now, through these men, Providence was going to construct an ascetic abode as a gymnasium of virtue for those who wished to renounce the world and through labors of piety seek for themselves instead the monastic life of the Gospel. Providence thus inspired these men from on high, and although they were living together in poverty and privation and did not even have enough to eat every day, with the cooperation and power of God they constructed a holy monastery for ascetics at Anaplous on the Byzantine Bosporus.[174] This was so stately and beautiful, so very well made and full of grace, that those who knew about the men's poverty and their destitution were astounded when they saw the lavish foundation of the monastery and its construction.

After the completion of this monastery, one of the two, 2 who loved God and was fervent for spiritual contests (the one who had been properly given the name Philotheos),[175] prepared a cell suitable for spiritual tranquillity as a hermitage for himself. He entered into this, closed off all access, and chose to eagerly pursue more advanced contests of tranquillity. But the other, John, who was physically weaker since he was a eunuch, undertook the administration of the monastery and managed it as a *wise steward*.

146

Ἀλλὰ γὰρ ὁ Φιλόθεος ὡς ἔκρινεν εἰσελθεῖν εἰς τὸ τῆς ἡσυχίας σεμνὸν ἐργαστήριον, σκέπτεται προτοῦ πρὸς τὴν βασιλεύουσαν εἰσελθεῖν καὶ τὰς εὐχὰς αὐτοῦ εἰς τοὺς ἐκεῖσε πανσέπτους ναοὺς ἀποδοῦναι, καὶ ἰδεῖν καὶ ὁμιλῆσαι καὶ βουλεύσασθαι περὶ τοῦ σκοποῦ τούτου ἀνδράσι πνευματικοῖς, καὶ οὕτω πᾶσι συντάξασθαι καὶ πρὸς τὴν τοῦ κελλίου ἐκείνου ἡσυχίαν χωρῆσαι μετὰ Θεόν. Τοίνυν καὶ εἰς Κωνσταντινούπολιν εἰσελθὼν καὶ τοὺς ἐν αὐτῇ πανσέπτους ναοὺς προσκυνήσας, καὶ ἀποδοὺς ἐν τούτοις τὰς εὐχὰς τῷ Θεῷ, ἔρχεται καὶ πρὸς τὴν περίφημον μονὴν τοῦ Στουδίου, Νικήταν ἐκεῖνον ἀσπάσασθαι (ᾧ ἐπώνυμον ὁ Στηθάτος) καὶ τούτῳ περὶ τοῦ τοιούτου σκοποῦ συμβουλεύσασθαι.

2   Ἐπεὶ δὲ ὁ ῥηθεὶς οὗτος ἀνὴρ μαθητὴς τοῦ Θεολόγου τούτου πατρὸς διάπυρος ἐχρημάτιζε, τῷ Φιλοθέῳ προσομιλῶν καὶ τὸν βίον τοῦ ἁγίου ἐκδιηγούμενος, ποίους τε πειρασμοὺς καὶ ὅσας θλίψεις διὰ τὴν πρὸς[350] Χριστὸν ἀγάπην καὶ τὸν πατέρα ὑπέμεινεν, οἵας τε χάριτος ἄνωθεν ἐπίσης ἠξιώθη τοῖς ἀποστόλοις, ὅπως δὲ θείῳ ἐθεολόγησε Πνεύματι ἀμαθὴς τῶν θύραθεν ὢν μαθημάτων, καὶ διδασκαλίας λόγους συνεγράψατο εἰς οἰκοδομὴν τῆς ἐκκλησίας Χριστοῦ, εἰς θερμὸν ἔρωτα τοῦ ἁγίου τὴν τοῦ ἀνδρὸς ψυχὴν εἰκότως διήγειρε. Τοίνυν καὶ ζητήσαντι βίβλον ἐγχειρίσας αὐτῷ μίαν τῶν θεοπνεύστων συγγραμμάτων καὶ τῆς διδασκαλίας αὐτοῦ, ἀπέλυσε χαίροντα τοῦτον

Chapter 146

When Philotheos decided to enter that holy workshop of spiritual tranquillity, he thought he should first visit the imperial city and offer his prayers at the most holy churches there, as well as seeing and speaking with spiritual men and seeking their advice about his plan; then, after he had said goodbye to everyone, he would withdraw into the spiritual tranquillity of that cell, alone with God. So he went into Constantinople, and after worshipping at its most holy churches and offering his prayers to God in them, he also went to the famous monastery of Stoudios to greet Niketas (who is called Stethatos) and ask his advice about his plan.

Since this Niketas was a fervent disciple of our father the 2 Theologian, he described the saint's life while he was speaking with Philotheos: what trials and how many tribulations Symeon endured out of his love for Christ and his spiritual father; what grace he was accorded from above like the apostles; and how he became a theologian through the divine Spirit, even though he was uneducated in secular learning, and composed books of instruction for the edification of Christ's church. In this way Niketas suitably roused the man's soul to a fervent love for the saint. When the man asked for a book, Niketas handed him one containing Symeon's divinely inspired compositions and his teaching, and

ὑπεισελθεῖν τὸ ἔγκλειστρον καὶ τοὺς ἱδρῶτας ἐκεῖσε κενῶσαι τῆς ἀρετῆς.

3 Ὁ γοῦν θεοφιλὴς ἐκεῖνος Φιλόθεος, πρὸ τοῦ εἰσελθεῖν[351] ἐν τῷ τῆς ἡσυχίας ἐργαστηρίῳ,[352] ὡς τῶν ἱερῶν ἀγώνων σπουδαίως ἀντείχετο, λογισμοὶ φροντίδος ὥσπερ ἦν εἰκὸς ἐπεισήεισαν τῆς ἐν τῇ ἐγκλείστρᾳ βιαίας ἀσκήσεως καὶ τῶν ἐν αὐτῇ τάχα ἱδρώτων καὶ παλαισμάτων· τοιοῦτον γὰρ πάντως ψυχὴ ἐναγώνιος πόνους ἐπὶ τούτοις ἀεὶ προστιθέναι ζητοῦσα, ὡς ἐπ᾽ αὐτῇ πληροῦσθαι προδήλως τὸ σοφὸν ἐκεῖνο λόγιον· *ὁ προστιθεὶς γνῶσιν προστίθησιν ἄλγημα* [Ecl 1:18].

147

Τοιγαροῦν καὶ ὡς οὕτως εἶχεν ὁ ἀνὴρ καὶ θερμῶς ἐδέετο τοῦ Θεοῦ ὑπομονὴν αὐτῷ καὶ ἰσχὺν καὶ σύνεσιν ἐπιβραβεῦσαι τοῦ τὰς θλίψεις καὶ τὴν στένωσιν τοῦ ἐγκλειστηρίου φερεπόνως καθυπομεῖναι, γίνεταί πως καθ᾽ ὕπαρ ἐν μιᾷ τῶν νυκτῶν, καὶ ἀκούει κρούοντος ὥσπερ ἐν τῷ πυλῶνί τινος. Ὡς δ᾽ ἔσπευσεν[353] ἰδεῖν τίς ὁ κρούων ἐστίν, ὁρᾷ τὴν πύλην ἀνοίξας πολιὸν ἄνδρα καὶ αὐτὸν εὐνοῦχον εὐσχήμονά τε καὶ σεμνοπρεπῆ καὶ τὸ εἶδος ἀγγελικὸν ὡς τὰ μάλιστα, χάριτος θείας πλῆρες τὸ πρόσωπον φέροντα, καί φησι πρὸς αὐτόν· "Τίς εἶ, τίμιε πάτερ; Καὶ τίνα ζητεῖς,

then sent him off rejoicing to enter into his hermitage and there shed the sweat of virtue.

But before he entered the workshop of spiritual tranquil- 3 lity to zealously withstand the holy contests, that God-loving Philotheos was shaken, as was to be expected, by anxieties over the violent asceticism <in which he would engage> in his hermitage and the sweat-inducing labors and contests <he would have to endure> in it. For thus it always is for a battle-hardened soul that constantly seeks to add to its labors, as it manifestly fulfills in itself that wise saying, *Those who increase knowledge increase suffering.*

Chapter 147

The man was thus in this state and was fervently begging God to grant him endurance and strength and intelligence to bear patiently the tribulations and the confinement of his hermitage. While he was awake one night then, he heard what sounded like someone knocking at the door. As he was eager to see who was knocking, he opened the door and saw a gray-haired man, a respectable and dignified-looking eunuch with a particularly angelic appearance and a face full of divine grace. Philotheos said to him, "Who are you, venerable father? Whom are you looking for by coming to visit

ἐπιδεδημηκὼς πρὸς τὴν ἡμετέραν ταπείνωσιν;" Ὁ δὲ μει-
λιχίῳ τῷ φθέγματι· "Ἐγώ," φησί, "Συμεών εἰμι ὁ κατὰ τὴν
Χρυσόπολιν καὶ τὴν ἐκεῖσε μονὴν τῆς ἁγίας Μαρίνης τὰς
οἰκήσεις ποιούμενος, καὶ ἦλθον ἐνταῦθα εἶναι καὶ συνοι-
κήσων ὑμῖν." Ὁ δὲ Φιλόθεος· "Καὶ τίς σου," φησί, "τὸν
χιτῶνα διέρρηξε, πάτερ;" Εἶδεν γὰρ διερρωγότα τοῦτον
χιτῶνα φοροῦντα. Ὁ δὲ ἅγιος· "Πονηροί τινες ἄνθρωποι
τοῦτό μοι πεποιήκασι δωρεάν [cf. Ps 34(35):19]· ἀλλὰ τί
ἔχων, φίλε Φιλόθεε, φροντίζεις καθ᾽ ἑαυτόν; Περὶ ὧν δεῖν
μεριμνᾶν καὶ φροντίζειν, εἰκότως ἔσο τοῦτο πρῶτον εἰδώς,
ὅτι ὁ μέλλων ἐν κοινωνίᾳ γενέσθαι τῶν φρικτῶν μυστηρίων, ἀποτάσσεσθαι ὅτι μάλιστα πολυποσίᾳ καὶ δείπνοις
ὀφείλει, καὶ μόνοις ἑσπέρας τρισὶ ποτηρίοις εἰς πόσιν
χρῆσθαι καὶ παραμυθίαν τοῦ σώματος, καὶ μετὰ τὴν μετ-
ουσίαν αὐτῶν τοῖς αὐτοῖς ὡσαύτως ἀρκεῖσθαι ἐν διαίτῃ
καὶ τραπέζῃ λιτῇ."

2   Τί προοιμιαζόμενος καὶ ἐμφαίνων αὐτῷ διὰ τούτων;[354]
"Ὅτι," φησί, "δέον εἰδέναι σε ἀγώνων τοιούτων ἁπτόμενον ἀσκήσεως καὶ ἡσυχίας, οὕτω δεῖ καθαίρειν ἑαυτὸν δι᾽
ἐγκρατείας καὶ δακρύων καὶ προσευχῆς, ὡς ἕτοιμον γίνεσθαι καθ᾽ ἑκάστην εἰς τὴν ὑποδοχὴν τῶν τοῦ Χριστοῦ μυστηρίων, δι᾽ ἧς ἡσυχάζων καὶ προσευχόμενος ἀρεμβάστως,
πεφωτισμένον ἕξεις τὸν νοῦν ἐκ πλουσίας μετουσίας τοῦ
Ἁγίου Πνεύματος καὶ θεωριῶν τῶν κεκρυμμένων μυστηρίων τοῦ Θεοῦ, ὡς γέγραπται· τὸ Πνεῦμα πάντα ἐρευνᾷ καὶ
τὰ βάθη τοῦ Θεοῦ [1 Cor 2:10]."

my humble self?" In a gentle voice the visitor said, "I'm Symeon, the one who lives near Chrysopolis in the monastery of Saint Marina there, and I've come to be here and live with you." But Philotheos said, "Who has torn your tunic, father?" For he saw he was wearing a torn tunic. The saint replied, "Some wicked men did this *without cause,* but why, my dear Philotheos, are you worrying yourself <over that>? You should know that the first of your worries and concerns should probably be about this: that someone who's going to partake of the awesome mysteries should renounce in particular excessive drinking and eating. In the evening you should only have three cups to drink to sustain your body, and after having these, you should be satisfied with a similarly frugal diet and meal."

What was Symeon getting at and indicating to Philotheos 2 by this? "That," he said, "you should understand, when you're engaging in such contests of asceticism and spiritual tranquillity, you have to purify yourself through abstinence and tears and prayer, so as to be ready every day for the reception of Christ's mysteries. As a result you'll be in a state of spiritual tranquillity and, praying without distraction, you'll have your mind enlightened through rich communication with the Holy Spirit and by visions of the hidden mysteries of God, as it has been written, *the Spirit explores everything, even the depths of God.*"

148

Ὡς γοῦν οὕτως ὁ ἅγιος ὡμίλει τῷ Φιλοθέῳ, βάλλει τὴν χεῖρα αὐτοῦ ἔσωθεν τῶν ἱματίων ἐκείνου, καὶ ἅπτεται γυμνοῦ τοῦ στομάχου ἐν τῇ κλίνῃ κειμένου, καὶ κρατῶν αὐτοῦ ὥσπερ ἐμέτρει τοῦτον κινῶν τὴν χεῖρα, καὶ τοῖς δακτύλοις ἐν[355] τῇ παλάμῃ συνέσφιγγε χωρητικὸν οἱονεὶ ὀλίγων τροφῶν ἀπεργαζόμενος. Διὸ καὶ τὸν Φιλόθεον ἀσπασάμενος, "Εἰ βούλει," ἔφη, "πρὸς τὴν ἡμετέραν ξενίαν ἐκπεράσας ἐλθέ, καὶ ὀψόμεθα πάλιν καὶ ἀσπασόμεθά σε τὸν φίλον Φιλόθεον." Ταῦτ' ἐκεῖνον εἰπόντα καὶ τοῦτον ἀκούσαντα,[356] ὁμοῦ μὲν ἤρθη ὁ ἅγιος τῆς θεωρίας τοῦ Φιλοθέου, καὶ πρὸς ἑαυτὸν ὁ Φιλόθεος γεγονὼς εὐθυμίας πάσης τὴν ψυχὴν αὐτοῦ εὗρε πεπληρωμένην, καὶ φυσικὴ ἔκτοτε ἡ ἐγκράτεια ἐγένετο αὐτῷ μετ' ὀλιγοδείας καὶ τραπέζης λιτῆς διεξιόντι τὴν αὐτοῦ ἐγκεκλεισμένην ζωήν, ὁμοῦ δὲ καὶ χαίρων διηγεῖτο τοῖς συνοῦσι τὴν ὀπτασίαν καὶ τὴν τοῦ ἁγίου πρὸς αὐτὸν ἐπιδημίαν τε καὶ ἐμφάνειαν.

2   Ἀλλὰ γὰρ ὡς ᾔσθετο τινος ἀντιλήψεως ἐκεῖθεν ὁ σεμνὸς τὰ πάντα Φιλόθεος, θείαν εἶναι κρίνας τὴν ὅρασιν καὶ οὐκ ἀπάτην, ἔγνω δεῖν τὴν εὐγνωμοσύνην ἐνδείξασθαι. Τοίνυν καὶ μετὰ τῶν συνόντων αὐτῷ ἀδελφῶν πρὸς ἀναζήτησιν τοῦ ἁγίου ἐξέρχεται, καὶ δὴ πρὸς τὴν καθ' ἡμᾶς ἐκπεράσας Χρυσόπολιν κατὰ τὴν πρὸς αὐτὸν τοῦ ἁγίου ἐπίσκηψιν, ζητεῖ τὴν ῥηθεῖσαν τοῦ ἁγίου μονήν, καὶ εὑρών, ἐπεὶ τὴν σορὸν τῶν λειψάνων τοῦ ἁγίου ὑπέδειξαν αὐτῷ οἱ ἐκεῖσε

Chapter 148

W hile the saint was speaking with Philotheos in this way, he put his hand inside the latter's clothes and touched his bare stomach as he was lying in bed. The saint took hold of his stomach and, moving his hand as though he was measuring it, squeezed it with his fingers and his palm as if enabling it to contain less food. Then, when he was giving Philotheos a farewell embrace, he said, "Cross over to my place of exile, if you want, and I'll see you again and embrace you, my dear Philotheos." When Symeon had said these words and Philotheos had heard them, the saint disappeared from Philotheos's sight. Coming to himself, Philotheos found his soul filled with good cheer. From then on abstinence came naturally to him and he lived out his enclosed life with minimal needs and a frugal table. He also enjoyed recounting to his companions his vision of the saint's visit and appearance to him.

But since Philotheos (who was good in every way) felt he   2
had received a certain amount of help from this source, and decided that this had been a divine vision, not a false one, he thought he should demonstrate his gratitude. And so, along with his fellow brethren, he set out to look for the saint. When he had crossed over to our Chrysopolis, in accordance with the saint's instructions, he looked for the monastery that the saint had mentioned. When he found it, the monks who were living there showed him the tomb with

μονάζοντες, πίπτει πρηνὴς ἐν αὐτῇ καὶ τῷ Θεολόγῳ πατρὶ
Συμεὼν ἀφοσιοῦται μετ᾽ εὐχαριστίας καὶ τιμῆς πάσης τὴν
προσκύνησιν ὡς εἰκὸς ἦν. Λαβὼν οὖν[357] ἔκτοτε τὴν τοῦ
ἁγίου εἰκόνα καὶ τὰ εἰς αὐτὸν γραφέντα ἐγκώμια παρὰ τοῦ
ῥηθέντος μαθητοῦ τοῦ ἁγίου, ἀλλὰ καὶ τὰς θεοπνεύστους
διδασκαλίας αὐτοῦ, ἔχει τε ὅλον τὸν ἅγιον ἐν ἑαυτῷ καὶ
πᾶσι τοῖς ἐκεῖσε συνδιάγει ὁ ἅγιος. Διὸ καὶ τὴν τοῦ πατρὸς
μνήμην ἐτησίως πανηγυρίζει εὐφραινόμενος ἐν αὐτῇ, καὶ
προκοπὰς καὶ ἀναβάσεις ἐν καρδίᾳ ὁσημέραι ψαλμικῶς δια-
τίθεται [Ps 83(84):5]. Καὶ ταῦτα μὲν τὰ πρὸς ἑτέρων παρὰ
τοῦ ἁγίου ὠφέλειαν.

149

Τίνα δὲ καὶ πρὸς τὸν αὐτοῦ γνήσιον μαθητὴν μετὰ
πότμον εἰργάσατο, εἰ δοκεῖ, ἀκουσώμεθα. Κατὰ τὸν καιρὸν
τῶν πανσέπτων ποτὲ τῆς ἁγίας τεσσαρακοστῆς νηστειῶν
ὁ ῥηθεὶς τοῦ ἁγίου γνήσιος μαθητὴς Νικήτας ὁ καὶ Στηθάτος, τῶν ἱερῶν συνήθως ἀγώνων ἐχόμενος, πνεύματι
πορνείας οἰκονομικῶς τῆς χάριτος συσταλείσης καθυπο-
βάλλεται. Συνετὸς οὖν ὑπάρχων ὡς τὰ μάλιστα ὁ ἀνὴρ καὶ
βίον ἐναγώνιον ἔχων ἐν ἀσιτίᾳ καὶ πάσῃ κακοπαθείᾳ, καθ᾽
ἑαυτὸν ἐξίστατο ἀπορῶν. Διὸ καὶ ζητῶν πόθεν καὶ ἐκ ποίας αἰτίας ὑπεισέδυσαν αὐτῷ οἱ ῥυπαροὶ καὶ ἀκάθαρτοι

the saint's remains, and he fell flat upon it and devoted the proper veneration to our father Symeon the Theologian with thanks and every honor. Then he took away from there an icon of the saint and the encomia written about him by the saint's previously mentioned disciple, together with his divinely inspired teachings. He thus possessed the saint completely in himself, even though the saint <still> lives with everyone there <in Chrysopolis too>. He also celebrates the father's memory every year, rejoicing in it, and every day he makes progress and *ascents in his heart,* in the words of the psalm. So this was what the saint did to benefit others.

Chapter 149

But let us also hear, if you agree, what he did for his true disciple after his death. Once, at the time of the most solemn forty-day fast of holy Lent, Niketas Stethatos (the previously mentioned true disciple of the saint) was assailed by a spirit of lust while he was engaged in his usual way in the sacred contests, for grace was withdrawn from him by divine purpose. As this man <thought himself> very smart and led a life engaged in spiritual combat through fasting and every kind of mortification, he was astonished at this and was at a loss. He tried to determine how and why these dirty and unclean thoughts had slipped into him at such a time, when his

λογισμοὶ ἐν τοιούτῳ καιρῷ, ἐν ᾧ τεταριχευμένον τὸ σῶμα
ἐκ τῶν ἀγώνων ἔφερε τῆς νηστείας καὶ σχεδὸν ἀπονενε-
κρωμένον εἰπεῖν ἄγαν ἐξ ἄκρας ἀσιτίας καὶ ἀγρυπνίας, μὴ
εὑρίσκων, σφόδρα τῇ λύπῃ καὶ τῇ ἀθυμίᾳ ἐβάλλετο, μὴ
ἔχων ὅ τι καὶ δράσει εἰς θεραπείαν τοῦ πάθους.

2   Τῇ οὖν λύπῃ συνεχόμενος δέησιν πρὸς[358] Θεὸν καὶ τὸν
ἅγιον ποιεῖται θερμῶς, καὶ δὴ οὕτω παρακαλῶν καὶ δεό-
μενος τοῦ Θεοῦ καὶ τοῦ ἁγίου, ἐν μιᾷ τῶν ἡμερῶν μετὰ τὸ
τῆς ἀπραγματεύτου τραπέζης ἐκείνης μεταλαβεῖν καὶ μετρίας τροφῆς, εἰς τὸ ἀσκητικὸν αὐτοῦ χαράδριον ἀνακλί-
νεται μετὰ λύπης, ὑποχθόνιον ἔχων ἔτι καὶ ὑπὸ θόλους τὴν
οἴκησιν. Ὡς δ' ἔδοξεν ὑπνοῦν μήπω κλείσας τοὺς ὀφθαλμούς, ὁρᾷ καθ' ὕπαρ ὡς γρηγορῶν ἔκειτο ἐλθόντα τὸν
ἅγιον φανερῶς καὶ πρὸς τὴν τούτου κλίνην καθίσαντα,
εἶτα τοῦ ἱματίου ἁψάμενον καὶ καλοῦντα τοῦτον πρὸς
ὄνομα· φησὶ δέ· "Οὐκ οἶδας, τέκνον ἐμόν, ὅθεν σοι οὗτοι
καὶ ἐκ ποίας αἰτίας παρεισέδυσαν οἱ ἐμπαθεῖς λογισμοί;"
Ὁ δὲ ὡς αἴφνης εἶδε καὶ ἤκουσε τοῦ ἁγίου, συσταλεὶς πρὸς
ἑαυτὸν μετὰ φόβου πρὸς αὐτὸν ἀποκρίνεται· "Πᾶσαν περὶ
τούτου," φησίν, "ἔρευναν, ἅγιε τοῦ Θεοῦ, ποιησάμενος
οὔπω τὴν αἰτίαν τῆς τοιαύτης ὀχλήσεως ἠδυνήθην εὑρεῖν."
Καὶ ὁ ἅγιος· "Ἀλλ' ἐγώ σοι ταύτην[359] μηνύσων ἦλθον καὶ
τοῖς ἐμοῖς λόγοις πρόσεχε! Ἴσθι ταύτην εἶναι, τέκνον, ἐξ
ὑπερηφανίας τε καὶ οἰήσεως τοῦ λογιστικοῦ μέρους τῆς
σῆς βεβαίως ψυχῆς· ταπείνωσόν σου τὸ φρόνημα παρα-
μετρῶν ἑαυτὸν καὶ τὰ σὰ ταῖς τοῦ Χριστοῦ ἐντολαῖς, καὶ
ταχέως φεύξεται ἀπὸ σοῦ!"

body was wasted away through the contests of fasting and practically deadened, so to speak, due to his extreme abstinence from food and keeping vigil. But as he could not discover the cause, he was assailed by extreme grief and despair, since he was unable to do anything to cure his passion.[176]

Still consumed with grief, then, he fervently entreated 2 God and the saint [Symeon]. One day while he was thus beseeching and imploring God and the saint, after he had partaken of his scant meal and meager nourishment, he lay down sorrowfully on his ascetic mat,[177] for he was still living in some subterranean vaults. As he was thinking about going to sleep but had not yet closed his eyes, while he was lying there wide awake, in a waking vision he clearly saw the saint come and sit beside his bed and then touch his clothes and call him by name. Symeon said, "You don't know, do you, my child, where these passionate thoughts are coming from, and the reason why they are insinuating themselves?" When Niketas suddenly saw and heard the saint, he shrank back out of fear and replied to him, "I've tried everything to find out about them, holy one of God, but so far I've been unable to discover the cause of this trouble." The saint said, "But I've come to reveal this to you, so pay attention to my words! Know then, my child, that this trouble is certainly due to arrogance and conceit in the rational part of your soul. Humble your presumption by measuring yourself and your deeds against Christ's commandments, and this trouble will swiftly leave you!"

3   Ταῦτ᾽ εἰπὼν εὐθὺς ἐκρύβη τῆς ἐκείνου ὁράσεως. Ὁ δὲ
πρὸς ἑαυτὸν ἐλθὼν καὶ διὰ σπουδῆς τοῦ χαραδρίου ἐξανα-
στάς, ἐδίωκεν ὀπίσω τοῦ ἁγίου καὶ τὸν καθυπηρετοῦντα
ἠρώτα· "Εἶδες τῶν ὧδε τὸν ἅγιον Συμεὼν ἐξελθόντα;" Ἔνθεν τοι καὶ τὸ λογιζόμενον ἀκριβῶς ἐξερευνήσας αὐτοῦ,
εὗρε σαφῶς τὴν αἰτίαν ὡς πρὸς αὐτὸν ὁ ἅγιος ἔφη δι᾽ ἧς
τὸ πάθος ἐνέσκηψε τῇ ἐκείνου ψυχῇ παρὰ προσδοκίαν καὶ
τοιοῦτον καιρόν. Διὸ καὶ τὸ φρόνημα ταπεινώσας αὐτοῦ,
ἑνὶ παθήματι τῶν[360] Χριστοῦ τῷ ἐμπτύσματι παραμετρή-
σας τὰ δῆθεν ἑαυτοῦ κατορθώματα, εὐθὺς τῆς τῶν λογισμῶν καὶ τοῦ πάθους ἠλευθηρώθη ὀχλήσεως, καὶ
παράκλησις τοῦτον τοῦ Ἁγίου Πνεύματος διεδέξατο διὰ
δακρύων καὶ κατανύξεως, εὐχαριστοῦντα μεγαλῶς τῷ
Θεολόγῳ πατρί, καὶ πίστιν ἐν ἀγάπῃ πρὸς αὐτὸν προσ-
τιθέμενον. Καὶ τοῦτο μὲν τοιοῦτον.

150

Θέλων δὲ[361] δεῖξαι ὁ Θεός, ὅτι εὐαπόδεκτόν ἐστιν αὐτῷ
τε καὶ τῷ τούτου θεράποντι Συμεὼν καὶ πρὸς ὠφέλειαν
τῆς τῶν πιστῶν ἐκκλησίας, εἰ τῶν θεοπνεύστων αὐτοῦ λόγων μεταγραφὴ γένοιτο, δεικνύει καὶ νῦν, ὥσπερ πάλαι τῷ
μαθητῇ Πρόκλῳ τοῦ Χρυσορρήμονος, τὴν ὄψιν τοιάνδε
Ἰωάννῃ μαθητῇ τῷ τοῦ Στηθάτου. Ἐπειδὴ γὰρ ἐξ ἀποκαλύψεως προτραπείς ποτε παρὰ τοῦ ἁγίου ὁ εἰρημένος

With these words, Symeon immediately disappeared   3
from Niketas's sight. When he came to himself, Niketas got
up quickly from his mat and chased after the saint and asked
the monk who was serving him, "Did you see the holy
Symeon coming out of here?" Then he carefully examined
his thoughts and, just as the saint had said to him, clearly
found out the reason why the passion had assailed his soul
so unexpectedly and at such a time. And so, after Niketas
humbled his presumption and began to compare his accomplishments with but one of Christ's sufferings, namely how
He was spat upon, he was immediately freed from this trouble and his passionate thoughts. He thus received the comfort of the Holy Spirit through tears and compunction, and
gave great thanks to our father the Theologian, and increased his faith in his love for him. And so much for that
story.

Chapter 150

Since God wanted to show that the transcription of Symeon's divinely inspired words would be acceptable to Him and
to His servant Symeon and beneficial to the church of the
faithful, He now also showed the following vision to
Stethatos's disciple John, just as He did to Chrysostom's disciple Proklos in the old days.[178] For when the aforesaid Niketas Stethatos (who had once been urged by the saint in a

Νικήτας οὗτος ὁ καὶ Στηθάτος—καθὼς ἐν τῷ διὰ πλάτους ἀναγέγραπται τοῦ ἁγίου βίῳ—τὰς θεοπνεύστους διδασκαλίας καὶ τὰς ἐπωφελεῖς αὐτοῦ συγγραφὰς μεταγράψαι, εἴχετο σπουδαίως τῆς τούτων ἐν μεμβράναις γραφῆς ὁ ἀνήρ, βλέπει ὁ μαθητὴς αὐτοῦ ὄψιν κατ' ὄναρ τοιαύτην·

2   Ἔδοξε γὰρ κατὰ τὴν συνήθειαν ὁ Ἰωάννης εἰσελθεῖν ἔσω τῆς κέλλης τοῦ εἰρημένου ἀνδρὸς τοῦ ζητῆσαι καὶ ἀκοῦσαί τι περὶ ὠφελείας ψυχῆς· ὡς δ' ἤγγισε δῆθεν τῇ θύρᾳ τοῦ δωματίου, ἐν ᾧ ἦν ὁ Στηθάτος τῇ ἡσυχίᾳ σχολάζων, ἐπεὶ πρὸς αὐτὸν ὥρμησεν εἰσελθεῖν, ὁρᾷ μὲν αὐτὸν καθήμενον καὶ τὴν γραφίδα κινοῦντα καὶ σπουδαίως διαπονούμενον εἰς τὴν τῶν θεοπνεύστων λόγων τοῦ ἁγίου μετάπηξιν, τὸν δὲ θεσπέσιον καὶ Θεολόγον πατέρα Συμεώνην ἀντικρὺ τούτου καθήμενον καὶ αὐτόν, καὶ τῇ μὲν μιᾷ χειρὶ βακτηρίᾳ ἐπιστηριζόμενον, τὴν δεξιὰν δὲ ἐκτεταμένην πρὸς αὐτὸν ἔχοντα, καὶ ὥσπερ τὰ τῶν ἰδίων σχεδῶν ὑποδεικνύοντα τούτῳ, καὶ γνησίως στόμα πρὸς στόμα περὶ τούτων διαλεγόμενον καὶ μυσταγωγοῦντα αὐτὸν[362] τὰ βάθη τῆς ὑψηλῆς αὐτοῦ θεωρίας τῶν λόγων καὶ τῆς μυστικῆς θεολογίας τὰ δόγματα, ἃ θεολογήσας ἐπίσης τοῖς πάλαι θεολόγοις πηγὴν ἀειζώων ναμάτων εἰς ἴαμα ψυχῶν τῇ τοῦ Χριστοῦ ἐκκλησίᾳ κατέλιπε.

3   Τοῦτο τοίνυν ὡς εἶδεν ὁ Ἰωάννης γνωρίσας τὸν ἅγιον, καίτοι μὴ εἰδὼς αὐτὸν ἐν τοῖς ζῶσι, καὶ δυσωπηθεὶς τὸν ἀγγελοειδῆ τοῦ πατρὸς χαρακτῆρα, συνεστάλη πρὸς ἑαυτὸν φόβῳ ληφθεὶς καὶ οὐκ ἔδοξεν εἰσελθεῖν· εἶτα μετ' ὀλίγον τοῦ ἁγίου ἐξελθόντος ἐκεῖθεν καὶ ἀνωφερῆ ὁδὸν γαληνῷ βαδίζοντος τῷ ποδί, ἀκούειν αὐτοῦ ἔδοξε πρὸς ὄνομα

revelation—as has been written in the fuller *Life* of the saint[179]—to copy out his divinely inspired teachings and beneficial writings) was thus busy writing these works out on parchment, his disciple saw the following vision in a dream.

John thought he would go into Niketas's cell as usual to 2 seek and hear something spiritually beneficial, but when he reached the doorway of the room in which Stethatos was practicing his spiritual tranquillity, and started to go in, he saw him sitting there, using his pen and working busily at the transcription of the saint's divinely inspired words. But then he also saw, sitting opposite him, father Symeon the divine Theologian, supporting himself on his staff with one hand and reaching out with his right hand toward Niketas as though he was indicating to him points from his own drafts. He truly was discussing these points face-to-face and initiating Niketas into the profundities of the sublime contemplation of his words and the tenets of his mystical theology, which he had composed like the theologians of old and left behind as a spring of constantly flowing waters to cure the souls in Christ's church.

When John saw this, he recognized the saint, even though 3 he had never seen him in real life, and, being abashed by the father's angelic appearance, he shrank back gripped with fear, and decided not to go in. After a little while, when the saint came out of there and was walking slowly on the way

καλοῦντος αὐτὸν καί φησιν· "Ἰωάννη, εἶπον τῷ ἐμῷ Νι-
κήτᾳ· ᾽σπεῦσον, τέκνον, τελειῶσαι τὴν τῶν ἐμῶν πονημά-
των μετάπηξιν, καὶ ὃ ζητεῖς γενηθήσεταί σοι πάντως καὶ
πληρωθήσεται.'" Καὶ τὰ μὲν πρὸς τὸν αὐτοῦ μαθητὴν τὸν
Στηθάτον Νικήταν τοιαῦτα τοῦ ἁγίου μετὰ τὴν αὐτοῦ κοίμησιν.

151

Πῶς δὲ παραδράμω κἀκεῖνο, ὅπερ καὶ ἀκουόμενον
ἐξιστᾷ τοὺς ἀκούοντας; συνάψω δ' ὅμως καὶ τοῦτο τοῖς
φθάσασιν εἰς δόξαν Θεοῦ καὶ ὠφέλειαν καὶ εὐφροσύνην
τῆς ἐκκλησίας αὐτοῦ.

2   Τῆς ἑορτῆς ποτε τοῦ ἁγίου τελουμένης κατὰ τὴν γ΄ τοῦ
Ἰανουαρίου μηνὸς (καθ' ὃν[363] ἑορτάζομεν τὴν ἐξορίαν
αὐτοῦ), εἷς τῶν συνεορταζόντων καὶ Κοσμᾶς ὁ εὐλαβέστα-
τος μοναχὸς καὶ καθηγούμενος τοῦ ἁγίου Στεφάνου τοῦ
κατὰ τὸν βουνὸν τοῦ ἁγίου Αὐξεντίου ἔτυχεν εἶναι. Ἐπεὶ
οὖν ἡ πανήγυρις μετ' ἐγκωμίων ἐγένετο τοῦ ἁγίου καὶ
χαρὰ μετ' εὐφροσύνης τοὺς συνεορτάζοντας πάντας εἶχεν
ἐν τῷ δοξάζεσθαι τὸν Θεὸν ἐν αὐτῇ καὶ πένητας τρέφε-
σθαι καὶ φωταγωγεῖσθαι ναούς, ζῆλος ὑπεισῄει Θεοῦ τῷ
εἰρημένῳ ἀνδρὶ καὶ κατὰ νοῦν ἐμέμφετό πως ἑαυτόν, ὅτι
μὴ καὶ αὐτὸς τὰς θεοπνεύστους διδασκαλίας ἔχων καὶ τὰ
συγγράμματα τοῦ ἁγίου πανηγυρίζει ὁμοίως τὰ τῆς ἑορτῆς
τοῦ Θεολόγου πατρός.

up, John seemed to hear Symeon call his name and say, "John, tell my Niketas this: 'Hurry up and finish the transcription of my works, my child, and all that you seek will come to pass and be fulfilled.'" These are the miracles the saint performed after his death involving his disciple Niketas Stethatos.

Chapter 151

But how can I pass over this one, for just hearing it amazes listeners? So I will nevertheless add this one as well to the miracle stories that have already been told, to the glory of God and the benefit and joy of His church.

Once, when the feast of the saint was being observed on January 3 (on which day we celebrate his exile), one of those participating in the celebration was Kosmas, that most pious monk and superior of the monastery of Saint Stephen on Mount Saint Auxentios.[180] So when the festival was taking place with encomia of the saint and everyone celebrating together was full of joy and gladness at the way God was glorified in this way and the poor were being fed and the churches illuminated, the zeal of God entered into this Kosmas. He began blaming himself in his own mind, as it were, for not possessing the divinely inspired teachings and writings of the saint himself and so not being able to celebrate our father the Theologian's feast in a similar way.

3   Τοίνυν καὶ παράκλησιν ἐποιήσατο πρὸς τὸν πολλάκις
ῥηθέντα τοῦ ἁγίου μαθητὴν τοῦ λαβεῖν ἐξ αὐτοῦ τὴν τοῦ
Θεολόγου πατρὸς εἰκόνα, ἔτι δὲ καὶ τοὺς ἐκείνῳ γραφέν-
τας ὕμνους ὁμοῦ καὶ τὰ ἐγκώμια, ὡς ἂν³⁶⁴ καὶ αὐτὸς ἐτησίως πανηγυρίζῃ κατὰ τὴν ἰδίαν μονὴν τὴν τοῦ ἁγίου μνήμην καὶ τὴν εὐλογίαν κατὰ τὸ γεγραμμένον κομίζηται
ἄνωθεν· *οἱ εὐλογοῦντές σε, φησί, εὐλογηθήσονται, καὶ οἱ
καταρώμενοί σε κεκατήρανται* [cf. Nm 24:9]. Ἔνθεν τοι
καὶ δυσωπήσας αὐτὸν ὁ ἀνὴρ ὥσπερ εἴρηται καὶ μίαν τῶν
εἰκόνων λαβὼν ἐξ αὐτῶν μετὰ πίστεως τοῦ μεγάλου
πατρὸς ἡμῶν Συμεών, ἐγχειρίζει ταύτην ἑνὶ τῶν μοναχῶν
τῆς αὐτοῦ μονῆς τοῦ διασῶσαι αὐτὴν ἐν τῇ ῥηθείσῃ τοῦ
ἁγίου Στεφάνου μονῇ, προάγειν τε αὐτῷ ἐπισκήπτει καὶ
τῆς ἐπὶ τὸν βουνὸν φερούσης ἔχεσθαι. Λαβὼν οὖν ὁ μοναχὸς ἐκεῖνος τὴν τοῦ ἁγίου εἰκόνα καὶ καταφρονήσας
τῶν ὑπὸ τοῦ ἡγουμένου ῥηθέντων αὐτῷ παραινέσεων περὶ
τῆς εἰκόνος, δίδωσιν αὐτὴν Σκύθῃ τινὶ δούλῳ γεγονότι
ποτὲ τοῦ ῥηθέντος ἡγουμένου τοῦ φέρειν αὐτὴν ἐπὶ τὸν
βουνὸν ἀνερχομένῳ σπουδαίως καὶ ἕπεσθαι.

152

Ὁ δὲ βάρβαρος ἐκεῖνος κλὼψ αὐτόχρημα καὶ δραπέ-
της ὤν, τὴν εἰκόνα λαβὼν καὶ εἰς τοὐπίσω χωρήσας καὶ εἰς
ἀκάτιόν τι³⁶⁵ ἀπὸ Χαλκηδόνος εἰσελθών, διαπερᾷ τὴν

Kosmas thus asked for the help of the frequently men- 3
tioned disciple of the saint [Niketas] in obtaining from him
an icon of our father the Theologian, and also the hymns he
wrote and likewise his encomia, so that he too might celebrate the saint's memory every year in his own monastery
and might receive blessing from heaven according to the
scripture, *Blessed will be those who bless you and cursed are those
who curse you.* But then when, as has been said, this man
[Kosmas] had asked Niketas and had received with faith
from the monks one of the icons of our great father Symeon,
he entrusted it to a monk from his monastery to take safely
to the aforementioned monastery of Saint Stephen, and he
told this man to go ahead and set out on the road to the
mountain. That monk took the saint's icon but then disregarded his superior's instructions about the icon. Instead he
gave it to a Scythian[181] who had once been a slave of the said
superior, <and told him> to go quickly and carry it up the
mountain, while he followed.

Chapter 152

That barbarian, who was, however, really a thief and a
runaway, took the icon and turned back. He then got onto a
boat at Chalcedon, crossed the Bosporus, and, going into

Προποντίδα, καὶ πρὸς τὴν βασιλεύουσαν εἰσελθὼν πιπρά-
σκει αὐτὴν Βενετίκῳ.³⁶⁶ Ὡς δ᾽ ἐπὶ τὴν ἰδίαν μονὴν ὁ ἡγούμενος ἔφθασε, ζητεῖ τὸν μοναχόν, ᾧ τὴν εἰκόνα παρέθετο,
καὶ οὐδαμοῦ ἡ εἰκών, οὐδαμοῦ ἐκεῖνος ὁ βάρβαρος, ᾧ δέδωκεν ὁ μοναχὸς ἐξ ἀφροσύνης τὴν τοῦ ἁγίου εἰκόνα. Οὐ
πολλαὶ διῆλθον ἡμέραι, καὶ ἐπεὶ λύπη καὶ ἀθυμία περὶ τοῦ
γεγονότος τὸν ἡγούμενον κατεῖχε, τῷ ἀναψηλαφῶντι ὁ
δοῦλος παρὰ Θεοῦ παραδίδοται. Ὁ δὲ ὁμολογεῖ ἐταζόμε-
νος πεπρακέναι τὴν εἰκόνα εἰς Βενετίκους.³⁶⁷ Δίδοται ἡ
τιμὴ τῷ ἀγοραστῇ, ἣν λαβὼν ὁ δοῦλος ἐκδεδαπάνηκεν.
Ἀνασώζουσιν οἱ τὴν τοῦ Θεολόγου πατρὸς λαβόντες εἰκόνα ἐν τῇ τοῦ ἁγίου Στεφάνου μονῇ, σύναμα τῷ δραπέτῃ
δούλῳ ἐκείνῳ καὶ μαστιγίᾳ.

3   Ὡς δ᾽ ἡ ἁγία εἰκὼν ἐσώθη—ὦ τῆς ἀφύκτου δίκης τοῦ
Θεοῦ!—ἡνίκα εἰς τὸ ἐκκλησιαστήριον ἀπετέθη κατὰ τὸ
κέρας τοῦ βήματος, *καὶ ἡ ὀργὴ τοῦ Θεοῦ ἀνέβη* [Ps 77(78):31]
ἐπὶ τὸν κεκλοφότα καὶ τολμητίαν ἐκεῖνον· δαίμονι γὰρ
ἀλάλῳ καὶ δεινῷ κρουσθεὶς δικαίᾳ κρίσει ὁ δείλαιος εὐθὺς
ὕπτιος ἐπίπροσθεν πάντων ἔπεσε τετρυγὼς τοὺς ὀδόντας
καὶ τοὺς ἀφροὺς ἀποπτύων καὶ κράζων οἷα δὴ τράγος τὰ
παρακεκομμένα καὶ ἄσημα. Ἀλλ᾽ ἐφ᾽ ἱκανὰς τῇ παιδείᾳ
ταύτῃ ἐπιμείνας ἡμέρας ὁ ἄθλιος μόλις ἀφείθη τῆς τοῦ
δαίμονος μάστιγος τῇ τοῦ ἁγίου Συμεὼν συμπαθείᾳ, καὶ
ἰάσεως ἔτυχεν. Οὕτω τοίνυν *δοξάζει τοὺς δοξάζοντας
αὐτὸν ὁ Θεὸς* [cf. 1 Kings 2:30] καὶ σεβασμίους πᾶσιν
αὐτοὺς ἐν τῇ ἑαυτοῦ ἀποδείκνυσιν ἐκκλησίᾳ. Ὅτι αὐτῷ ἡ
δόξα εἰς τοὺς αἰῶνας τῶν αἰώνων. Ἀμήν.

the imperial city, sold it to a Venetian. When the superior reached his monastery he sought out the monk to whom he had entrusted the icon, but the icon was nowhere to be found, nor was that barbarian to whom the monk in his foolishness had given the saint's icon. Before many days had passed, however, when the superior had been stricken with grief and despair over what had happened, the slave was delivered by God to the investigating authorities. After being interrogated, he confessed to having sold the icon to Venetians. The purchaser was reimbursed for the price that the slave had received and then spent. And so they recovered the icon of our father the Theologian and took it to the monastery of Saint Stephen along with that runaway slave who deserved a flogging.

But when the holy icon had been saved—oh, the inescapable vengeance of God!—and it was placed on the crossbeam of the sanctuary[182] in the chapel, *the wrath of God rose up* against that thieving and audacious fellow. For the wretch was struck by a terrible demon of muteness, in just condemnation, and immediately fell on his back in front of everyone, grinding his teeth, spitting up foam, and making inarticulate and unintelligible cries like a billy goat. The miserable fellow endured this punishment for many days and was only released with difficulty from the demon's scourge due to the holy Symeon's compassion, and received healing. God thus glorifies those who glorify Him and shows that they are worthy of reverence by all in His church, because to Him is the glory forever and ever. Amen.

Note on the Text

The Greek text in this volume is based on Irénée Hausherr's 1928 critical edition,[1] supplemented with revisions established by Symeon Koutsas in his 1994 critical edition.[2] Hausherr based his text on the only two manuscripts available to him, *Parisinus* 1610 and *Coislin* 292 of the Bibliothèque Nationale in Paris, both of the fourteenth century.[3] While Koutsas was able to draw on a further eight manuscripts, seven of which come from libraries on Mount Athos,[4] only two are as early as those employed by Hausherr. Koutsas's edition thus has the advantage of thoroughly established accuracy, but in fact it does not differ substantially from that of Hausherr; almost all variants are minor and very few indeed have any real effect on the sense or translation. The present edition notes only the variant readings between the texts of Hausherr and Koutsas and does not note those between individual manuscripts, since this information is readily available in the previous critical editions.

I have made a few minor tacit corrections to the punctuation and accentuation of the Greek text.

Notes

1 Hausherr, *Vie*.
2 Koutsas, *Life*.
3 Hausherr, *Vie*, xii–xv.
4 Koutsas, *Life,* 38–43.

Notes to the Text

1   ἐραστὴς Κ
2   Οὗτος Κ om. Η
3   θερμότερον Κ θερμοτέρως Η
4   τῷ βίῳ ad. Η
5   αἴφνης Κ αἴφνως Η
6   οὕτω Κ οὕτως Η
7   τελεώτερον Κ τελεωτέρως Η
8   σεμνοτάτῃ καταστολὴ Κ σεμνότητα τῇ καταστολῇ Η
9   ἐξ αὐτῆς Κ ἐξαυτῆς Η
10 ἄρτι Κ ἔτι Η
11 θείου Κ θεϊκοῦ Η
12 ᾠδῆς Κ ᾠδῶν Η
13 τούτῳ Κ ταῦτα Η
14 κατὰ βραχὺ Κ καταβραχὺ Η
15 ἑαυτό Κ ἑαυτὸν Η
16 τούτῳ Κ τούτου Η
17 ὑπὲρ ἀρετῆς Κ ὑπ' ἀρετῆς Η
18 νεκρῶν Κ om. Η
19 προσαραχθείσας Κ προσαχθείσας Η
20 τανυσμῷ Κ τανισμῷ Η

21	ἀναισθησίας Κ ἀναισθήσεως Η
22	γὰρ ad. Η
23	ἐκνικήσαντος Κ νικήσαντος Η
24	δὲ Κ τε Η
25	Στουδίου Κ στουδίων Η
26	εἰ βούλει σωθῆναι Κ εἰς σωθῆναι βούλει Η
27	πλείονας Κ πλέον Η
28	δουλώσας Κ δουλεύσας Η
29	ἀτιμοτέρας ad. Η
30	ἀμφοτέρωθεν Κ ἀμφωτέρωθεν Η
31	προξενεῖ Η προξένει Κ
32	ἀντιπίπτων αὐτοῦ Κ αὐτοῦ ἀντιπίπτων Η
33	διὰ καρτερίας αὐτῷ Κ αὐτῷ διὰ καρτερίας Η
34	προσαποδύεσθαι Κ προσαποδύσασθαι Η
35	εὐφροσύνην Κ εὐφροσύνη Η
36	τοῦ ad. Η
37	τῶν Κ τὸν Η
38	προσβαλεῖν Κ προσβάλλειν Η
39	αὐτοῦ ad. Η
40	τοῖς Κ ταῖς Η
41	τοῖς Κ ταῖς Η
42	ἀπειθείᾳ Κ ἀπαθείᾳ Η
43	θαρρῶν Κ θάρρων Η
44	δὲ Κ om. Η
45	τοῦτον ἐκείνων Κ τούτων ἐκεῖνον Η
46	δεινότερον Κ δεινοτέρως Η
47	δὲ ad. Η
48	δώματος Κ δόματος Η
49	ἐκείνου Κ ἐκεῖνον Η
50	παρ' ἐλπίδα Κ παρὰ ἐλπίδα Η
51	καταχέων Κ καταφέρων Η
52	σωφροσύνης Κ εὐφροσύνης Η
53	γραφῶν ad. Η
54	ἐλάμπετο Κ ἐλλάμπετο Η
55	ἕως Κ μέχρι Η
56	ἐπάξιον Κ ἄξιον Η

57	τῆς K om. H
58	ἐξιστάμενον K ἐξιστάμενος H
59	καθ' ὅλον K καθόλου H
60	ὑπερκύψας K ὑπερκόψας H
61	τὸν ad. H
62	ὑποκρύβειν K ἀποκρύβειν H
63	ἔσωθεν K ἔνδοθεν H
64	δὲ K τε H
65	τῷ τούτου σώματι K τούτου τῷ σώματι H
66	φωτεινὴν K φωτινὴν H
67	ἁγίων K ἁγίαις H
68	τοῖς K om. H
69	ἐπαυξάνεται K ἐπαυξάνετο H
70	Καὶ πᾶσαν μὲν K Πᾶσαν μὲν δὴ H
71	πῇ K πὴ H
72	πῇ K πὴ H
73	τελεσθείσης K τελεισθείσης H
74	παλλία K πάλλια H
75	καὶ τὸν ἅγιον K τὸν μακάριον H
76	τὴν K om. H
77	ἀπήλαυσεν K ἀπέλαυσεν H
78	ἔπασχε K ἐπάσχετο H
79	τῷ K om. H
80	οὕτω K οὕτως H
81	αὐτὸν ad. H
82	ἔνδον K ἔνδοθεν H
83	ὡς ἂν K ὡσὰν H
84	αὐτὴ K αὕτη H
85	ἔμαθε K ἐπεὶ μάθοι H
86	ἀπειθείας K ἀπειθίας H
87	τῆς K om. H
88	ἀπειθείᾳ K ἀπειθίᾳ H
89	τὴν K om. H
90	καθ' ἑαυτὸν K κατὰ σεαυτὸν H
91	βαλὼν K βάλλων H
92	δεῖξαι K διδάξαι H

93 ὡς ad. H
94 ἀφύκτων K ἀνεφίκτων H
95 παρ' ἐλπίδα K παρὰ ἐλπίδα H
96 ἀνεψιὸν K ἀνέψιον H
97 ἐμεμαθήκει K μεμαθήκει H
98 ἐναλλαγῆς K ἀπαλλαγῆς H
99 σπηλαίοις K σπληλαίοις H
100 πάτερ, φησίν K φησι πάτερ H
101 ἰδίου K οἰκείου H
102 τὸν ἡμίονον K τῶν ἡμιόνων H
103 ὑπομένει K ὑπομενεῖ H
104 ὑπολάβῃ K ὑπολάβοι H
105 δ' ἐπιθυμῶν K δὲ ἐπιθυμῶν H
106 τε K om. H
107 καί εἴ ποτε K εἰ καί ποτε H
108 εὑρέθη K εὑρεθῇ H
109 τρισόλβιος K τρισόσιος H
110 ἐκείνου K αὐτοῦ H
111 ἐπώνυμον K ἐπωνύμων H
112 ἐπαπολαύειν K ἐπαπολαβεῖν H
113 ἡγουμενείας K ἡγουμενίας H
114 μὲν K om. H
115 ὡς ἂν K ὡσὰν H
116 πολυτόκον K πολύτοκον H
117 γε K om. H
118 ὀξίνην K ὄξυνον H
119 πάσας K πάντα H
120 τοῦ K om. H
121 γὰρ ad. H
122 μόνην K μόνως H
123 ἐμβριμώμενος K ἐμβριμούμενος H
124 ὡς ἂν K ὡσὰν H
125 ἐν ad. H
126 δὲ K δὴ H
127 ἀπ' ἀρχῆς K ἀπαρχῆς H
128 ἑξήκοντα K ἑβδομήκοντα H

129	φανερῶς Κ φανερῶσ‹ιν› Η
130	αὐτῶν Κ αὐτοῦ Η
131	δὲ ad. Η
132	πραττομένοις καὶ λεγομένοις Κ λεγομένοις καὶ πραττομένοις Η
133	αὐτῷ Κ om. Η
134	κατεληλυθότι Κ om. Η
135	τῇ τοῦ Χριστοῦ χάριτι Κ παρὰ Χριστοῦ Η
136	κῦριν Κ κύριον Η
137	ὑμῖν Κ ἡμῖν Η
138	ὑμᾶς Κ ἡμᾶς Η
139	ἅγιος Κ ἐν ἁγίοις Η
140	δ' ad. Η
141	αὐτοῦ Κ αὐτῷ Η
142	ἐκεῖθεν Κ ἔγγυθεν Η
143	ἁπτόμενον Κ ἁψάμενον Η
144	τοίνυν ὥρας οὕτω Κ ὥρας οὕτω τοίνυν Η
145	ἀκαταπαύστως Κ ἀκατασπάστως Η
146	αὐτὸν Κ αὐτῷ Η
147	ἐκείνοις Κ ἐκείνων Η
148	τὸν Κ om. Η
149	ἐξυμνεῖν Κ ἀνυμνεῖν Η
150	αὐτὸν Κ αὐτῷ Η
151	ὡς ἂν Κ ὡσὰν Η
152	Οὐμενοῦν Κ Οὔμενουν Η
153	ὡς ἂν Κ ὡσὰν Η
154	σοφώτατε Κ σοφώτατον Η
155	ἐνδότερα Κ ἐνδότατα Η
156	‹ὡς› ad. Η
157	ὠφέλεια Κ ὠφέλειαν Η
158	πλείους Κ πλείονες Η
159	ὡς ἂν Κ ὡσὰν Η
160	αὐτῷ Κ αὐτοῦ Η
161	τὴν ad. Η
162	καὶ τὴν εἰκόνα αὐτοῦ ἀνιστορήσας προσκυνεῖ Κ om. Η
163	πατρὸς Κ πατέρος Η

164   περὶ τὴν Κ περιττὴν Η
165   σπουδὴν Κ om. Η
166   ἀπελογήσω Κ ἀπελογίσω Η
167   ἔφη Κ ἔφης Η
168   παρορμώσας Κ παρορμήσας Η
169   τῷ εὐαγγελίῳ Κ τῶν εὐαγγελίων Η
170   σου Κ om. Η
171   καὶ τῆς ἁγίας καὶ ἱερᾶς εὐχαριστίας μετόχους ποιήσαντας Κ om. Η
172   κατοιχομένους Κ κατηχομένους Η
173   συνιόντας Κ συνιέντας Η
174   εὐωδεῖν Κ εὐωδιάζειν Η
175   τοὺς ad. Η
176   κατήγορος πικρὸς μόνος ἦν Κ πικρὸς ἦν μόνος κατήγορος Η
177   αὐτῷ ad. Η
178   καταντήσασα Κ καταυτήσασα Η
179   ἀποσεισάμενος Κ ἀποσπασάμενος Η
180   ἡμῶν ad. Η
181   τιμωρίας Κ τιμωρίαν Η
182   Ταῦτ' εἰπὼν Κ Ταῦτα εἰπὼν Η
183   ἐπὶ Κ ἐν Η
184   ἠμπέσχετο Κ ἠμπέχετο Η
185   ὡς ἂν Κ ὡσὰν Η
186   συγκοινωνὸς Κ κοινωνὸς Η
187   τῶν Κ om. Η
188   Θεόν Κ Χριστόν Η
189   τοῦ Κ om. Η
190   τε Κ δὲ Η
191   ὁ Κ om. Η
192   καὶ ad. Η
193   τῆς μεγάλης ταύτης Κ ταύτης τῆς μεγάλης Η
194   τῶν χρήσεων εὐαρμοστίᾳ σὺν ἀκμῇ καὶ σφοδρότητι ἐν ἀξιωματικῇ τοῦ λόγου ἰδέᾳ καὶ τῇ λαμπρότητι τῆς ἀληθείας Κ ἐν ἀξιωματικῇ τοῦ λόγου ἰδέᾳ καὶ τῇ λαμπρότητι τῶν χρήσεων εὐαρμοστίᾳ σὺν ἀκμῇ καὶ σφοδρότητι τῆς ἀληθείας Η
195   διαπεράναντα Κ διαπεράνασαν Η

196 ηὐχαρίστει K εὐχαριστεῖ H
197 ἐκχεῶ K ἐκχέω H
198 ἐπέβλεπον K ἔβλεπον H
199 ἐνέπλησαν K ἔπλησαν H
200 δὲ K τε H
201 εὐχαριστεῖν τε καὶ ὑπερεύχεσθαι K εὐχαριστῶν τε καὶ ὑπερευ-
χόμενος H
202 ὕφος K ὕψος H
203 ἀγῶνας καὶ K om. H
204 ἴσην K ἴσον H
205 παρ' ᾧ K παρ' ὧν H
206 δριμύτερον K δριμυτέρως H
207 χρόνοις K χρόνους H
208 ὡς K om. H
209 τὸ K τῶ H
210 διώκτην K διωκτήν H
211 ἄλας K ἄλες H
212 περιήστραπτε K περιήστραπται H
213 ἢ K ὡς H
214 καθ' ἑαυτοῦ K κατὰ ἑαυτοῦ H
215 συμπλέκονται K συμπλέκοντες H
216 τοῦ ad. H
217 τελείωσε K τελευθείσης H
218 ὑμῶν K ἡμῶν H
219 ἔφορος K εὔφορος H
220 κατὰ φιλίαν K om. H
221 δεσπότης K δέσποτα H
222 οὕτω λέγων K om. H
223 βαστάσει καὶ K καὶ βαστάσει H
224 τῷ K om. H
225 ὁμολογῶν K ὁμολογῶ H
226 καθ' ἑαυτὸν K κατὰ σεαυτὸν H
227 ὑπεραγαπήσεις K ὑπεραγαπήσας H
228 προβιβάζεις K προσβιβάζεις H
229 εἴπωμεν K εἴπομεν H
230 ἐπειδὴ K ἐπεὶ H

231 τοῖς λόγοις τοῖς ἡμετέροις ἐδείχθης Κ ἐδείχθης τοῖς λόγοις τοῖς ἡμετέροις Η

232 τοὺς Κ om. Η

233 προσηύξατο Κ προσεύξατο Η

234 τὰ ad. Η

235 τελεώτερον Κ τελεωτέρως Η

236 ἠρέμει Κ ἠρεμεῖ Η

237 ἔσθ' ὅτε Κ ἔστι δ' ὅτε Η

238 μαθητὴς Κ om. Η

239 καὶ Κ om. Η

240 ταῖς χερσὶν Κ ταῖν χεροῖν Η

241 ὁ Κ om. Η

242 μαθηταὶ Κ μηθηταὶ Η

243 μία Κ μίᾳ Η

244 ἁψαμένης Κ ἁψάμενος Η

245 ἀπαγαγεῖν Κ ἀπαγαγοῦσι Η

246 καὶ Κ om. Η

247 ὑπαίθρου Κ ὑπαιθρίου Η

248 ἀνύσαντες Κ ἀνοίσαντες Η

249 ποτιμώτατον Κ πότιμον Η

250 θεὸν Κ θεοῦ Η

251 κηρὸς Κ κηρὸν Η

252 με Κ om. Η

253 νεκρὰν Κ νεκρὸν Η

254 ἤγγισέ Κ ἔγγισέ Η

255 πραεία φησὶ τῇ φωνῇ· χαίροις Κ πραεία τῇ φωνῇ· χαίροις φησίν Η

256 τούτῳ καὶ ἁγίῳ Συμεώνη τῷ μαθητῇ αὐτοῦ Κ τούτου μαθητῇ τούτῳ δὴ τῷ ἁγίῳ Συμεώνη Η

257 ἀνέθορόν Κ ἀνέσφηλά Η

258 ὧν Κ om. Η

259 ἀνετράφη ὁ Νικηφόρος Κ ὁ Νικηφόρος ἀνετράφη Η

260 τάχα δι' εὐχῆς τοῦτο Κ τοῦτο δι' εὐχῆς τάχα Η

261 τὰ Κ om. Η

262 πάντα Κ πάντας Η

263 ἀπήλαυον Κ ἀπέλαβον Η

264 τε καὶ κηδεμονίας τῆς κατὰ πνεῦμα K καὶ προσπαθείας H
265 τῷ K om. H
266 καὶ ἡ ἀκρίβεια διὰ παντὸς K διαπαντὸς καὶ ἀκρίβεια H
267 γήρως K γήρους H
268 ἐπὶ τοῦ ἐδάφους K ὑπὸ τὸ ἔδαφος H
269 τοιούτων K τούτων H
270 πρὸς K εἰς H
271 ἤλατό K ἤλλατό H
272 Γάλλον K Γάλον H
273 τοῦ ποταμοῦ ἁλιέα K ἁλιέα τοῦ ποταμοῦ H
274 θεῷ K θεοῦ H
275 λάβε K λαβέ H
276 ἐντεῦθεν K ἐκεῖθεν H
277 ἐπηρᾶτο K ἐπαρᾶτο H
278 θρήνοις K θρήνους H
279 διωλύγιον K διολύγιον H
280 αἰαῖ K αἴ αἴ H
281 ὅσον οὔπω καὶ K καὶ ὅσον οὔπω H
282 τὸ K τὰ H
283 διατασσόμενον K διαταξάμενον H
284 ὁ εὐεργετηθεὶς K εὐεργετηθεὶς ὁ H
285 καὶ K om. H
286 εἰς K ἐπὶ H
287 ἀνήπτοντο K ἀπήπτοντο H
288 ταύτην K καὶ κατ' αὐτὴν H
289 βοηθείας K βοηθείαν H
290 ἠπείγετο K ἐπείγετο H
291 τὴν ad. H
292 ἕξεις K ἔξεις H
293 ἢ K ἡ H
294 ἀγρυπνεῖ K γρηγορεῖ H
295 τούτοις πᾶσιν K πᾶσι τούτοις H
296 ὁπόταν K ὁπότ' ἂν H
297 ἢ K καὶ H
298 καθ' ἑαυτὸν K κατ' ἐμαυτὸν H
299 καθ' ἑαυτὸν K κατ' ἐμαυτὸν H

300	μᾶλλον K πλέον H
301	ἐνεδυνάμωσε K ἐδυνάμωσεν H
302	ὀρφανίαν K ὀρφανείαν H
303	με ad. H
304	παμφάγου K πανφάγου H
305	ἀσκήσεως K ἰάσεως H
306	ἔμπλεα K om. H
307	καὶ ad. H
308	προσψαύσει K παρουσίᾳ H
309	ἐν ad. H
310	καὶ ad. H
311	ἀπήλαυσε K ἀπέλαυσε H
312	Καὶ γὰρ ὥσπερ K Ὥσπερ γὰρ καὶ H
313	πολυτίμου K πολυτιμίου H
314	ὠφέλειαν K ὠφελίαν H
315	λύπῃ K λυπῇ H
316	ἀπελογησάμην K ἀπελογισάμην H
317	τοῦτο K τοῦτον H
318	ἐλπίζω K ἐλπίζων H
319	καὶ ad. H
320	κόπων K κόπον H
321	ἀγρυπνίας K ἀγρυπνίαν H
322	τῆς ad. H
323	τὸ ἁπλοῦν, τὸ μέτριον, τὸ φιλεύσπλαγχνον, τὸ φιλάγαθον, K om. H
324	κινούμενός τε καὶ νυσσόμενος K κινοῦντος καὶ νύσσοντός H
325	ὁ πνευματικὸς πατήρ, ἀδελφέ, K ὁ πατήρ, ἀδελφέ, ὁ πνευματικός H
326	Καὶ αὐτὸς ἀκούσας ἠρξάμην K om. H
327	πολυτίμου K πολυτιμίου H
328	με K μοι H
329	δ' εὐθὺς K δὲ εὐθὺς H
330	τὸ ἐμὸν K om. H
331	ἀφυπνισθέντος K om. H
332	ἐμοὶ K κἀμοὶ H
333	γενομένῃ K γενομένη H
334	γινομένην K γενομένην H

335 ὡς ἂν Κ ὡσὰν Η
336 παράθῃ Κ παράθῃς Η
337 συζῆν Κ συνζῆν Η
338 χλευάσων Κ χλευάζων Η
339 πατρὸς ad. Η
340 αὐτὸ Κ αὐτὸν Η
341 πως Κ om. Η
342 ἐνεὸς Κ ἐννεὸς Η
343 δ᾽ οἱ Κ δὲ οἱ Η
344 δυσεντερίας Κ δυσεντερίαν Η
345 συνήθως λαμβάνων Κ λαμβάνων συνήθη Η
346 ἀπήλαυσεν Κ ἀπέλαυσεν Η
347 τοῖς Κ om. Η
348 ἀποταγὴν Κ ἀποτογὴν Η
349 ἀνεγεῖραι Κ ἀνεγείρειν Η
350 τὸν ad. Η
351 εἰσελθεῖν Κ ὑπεισελθεῖν Η
352 ἐν τῷ τῆς ἡσυχίας ἐργαστηρίῳ Κ τὸ τῆς ἡσυχίας ἐργαστή-
     ριον Η
353 ἔσπευσεν Κ ἔσπευδεν Η
354 καὶ ἐμφαίνων αὐτῷ διὰ τούτων Κ διὰ τούτων καὶ ἐμφαίνων
     αὐτῷ Η
355 ἐν Κ καὶ Η
356 Ταῦτ᾽ ἐκεῖνον εἰπόντα καὶ τοῦτον ἀκούσαντα Κ Ταῦτ᾽ ἐκείνου
     εἰπόντος καὶ τούτου ἀκούσαντος Η
357 οὖν Κ γοῦν Η
358 τὸν ad. Η
359 ἤδη ad. Η
360 τῶν Κ om. Η
361 δὲ Κ om. Η
362 αὐτὸν Κ αὐτῷ Η
363 καθ᾽ ὃν Κ καθ᾽ ἣν Η
364 ὡς ἂν Κ ὡσὰν Η
365 τι Κ τε Η
366 Βενετίκῳ Κ βενετικῷ Η
367 Βενετίκους Κ βενετικούς Η

Notes to the Translation

ABBREVIATIONS

BMFD = J. Thomas and A. C. Hero, eds. *Byzantine Monastic Foundation Documents*. 5 vols. (Washington, D.C., 2000)

CFHB = Corpus Fontium Historiae Byzantinae

Catechetical Discourses = B. Krivochéine and J. Paramelle, eds. *Syméon le Nouveau Théologien, Catéchèses*. Vol. 1 (Discourses 1–5), SC 96 (Paris, 1963); vol. 2 (6–22), SC 104 (Paris, 1964); vol. 3 (23–34), SC 113 (Paris, 1965)

DOP = *Dumbarton Oaks Papers*

Ethical Discourses = J. Darrouzès, ed. *Syméon le Nouveau Théologien, Traités Théologiques et Éthiques*. Vol. 1 (Theol I–III; Eth I–III), SC 122 (Paris, 1966); vol. 2 (Eth IV–XV), SC 129 (Paris, 1967)

Hymns = *Syméon le Nouveau Théologien, Hymnes*. Ed. J. Koder, trans. J. Paramelle and L. Neyrand. Vol. 1, SC 156 (Paris, 1969); vol. 2, SC 174 (Paris, 1971); and vol. 3, SC 196 (Paris, 1973)

Janin, *CP* = R. Janin. *La géographie ecclésiastique de l'empire byzantin, 1: Le siège de Constantinople et le patriarcat oecuménique, 3: Les églises et les monastères*. 2nd ed. (Paris, 1969)

Koutsas, *Life* = S. Koutsas. Ἅγιος Συμεών ὁ Νέος Θεολόγος (Nea Smyrne, 1994)

Lampe, *A Patristic Greek Lexicon* = G. W. H. Lampe, ed. *A Patristic Greek Lexicon* (Oxford, 1961)

Mystical Life = Symeon the Theologian. *On the Mystical Life: The Ethical Discourses*. Trans. A. Golitzin. 3 vols. (Crestwood, N.Y., 1995–1997)

OC = Orientalia Christiana (Rome, Pontificium Institutum Orientalium Studiorum)

ODB = A. P. Kazhdan et al., eds. *Oxford Dictionary of Byzantium*. 3 vols. (New York, 1991)

PG = J.-P. Migne, ed. *Patrologiae cursus completus, series Graeca*. 161 vols. (Paris, 1857–1866)

Philokalia = *The Philokalia: The Complete Text Compiled by St. Nikodimos of the Holy Mountain and St. Makarios of Corinth.* Trans. G. E. H. Palmer, P. Sherrard, and K. Ware. 4 vols. (London, 1979–1995)

SC = Sources Chrétiennes. (Paris, Les Éditions du Cerf.)

v. Ant. = G. J. M. Bartelink, ed. *Athanase d'Alexandrie. Vie d'Antoine*. SC 400, 2nd ed. (Paris, 2004)

1   The chamberlain or *koitonites* (κοιτωνίτης) was a courtier who held an evidently influential position close to the emperor. See *ODB* s.v.

2   The term *porphyrogenitos* (πορφυρογέννητος), "born in the purple," is used of an imperial child born to a reigning emperor. See further *ODB* s.v. Basil II (b. 958) and his younger brother Constantine VIII (b. 960/61) were the sons of Romanos II. Although both were crowned at a very young age, neither assumed real power until sometime later, Basil in 985 and Constantine after his brother's death in 1025.

3   The *spatharokoubikoularioi* were evidently imperial escorts. One possible implication of the term is that Symeon was a eunuch, but this is debated; see Alfeyev, *St. Symeon*, 30 n. 90.

4   The senate was a largely ceremonial and evidently numerous body in this period. It is thus possible that Symeon, who, according to information provided in the following chapter, can have been no more than thirteen or fourteen at this time, could have been made a senator despite his youth.

5   Symeon's own account of all this appears in his *Catechetical Discourses* 22:22–128.

6   Marcus Eremita, *De lege spirituali* 69, *PG* 65.913C; trans. *Philoka-*

lia 1.115. The quotation here differs slightly from the standard text. Cf. *Catechetical Discourses* 22:31–43, where the book is attributed only to Mark and this quotation is the first of three that are singled out. As Hausherr notes, *Vie,* 7, the inclusion of Diadochos here seems to be a simple error on the part of Stethatos. Both Mark the Hermit (an Egyptian ascetic) and Diadochos of Photike lived in the fifth century and wrote influential works of spiritual, theological, and monastic guidance.

7   While "Lord, have mercy" (Kyrie Eleison) was a common liturgical prayer, more importantly here it represents the briefest version of the "Jesus prayer," the constant recitation of which formed a vital element in the Byzantine mystical tradition.

8   There is an English translation of this chapter in Deno J. Geanakoplos, *Byzantium: Church, Society, and Civilization Seen though Contemporary Eyes* (Chicago, 1984), p. 182.

9   Cf. John of Damascus, *Homilia in transfigurationem* 3:6–7, *Die Schriften des Johannes von Damaskos,* ed. B. Kotter, vol. 5 (Berlin, 1988), p. 439; and *Analecta Hymnica Graeca, Canones Decembris* Day 22 Canon 45 Ode 9:3–4, *Analecta hymnica graeca e codicibus eruta Italiae inferioris,* ed. A. Kominis and G. Schirò, vol. 4 (Rome, 1976), pp. 188–89. Niketas uses the same phrase below in Chap. 10.

10   The *Scala paradisi* or *Ladder of Paradise* by John Klimax, ed. *PG* 88.631–1161, trans. Colm Luibheid and Norman Russell, *John Climacus, The Ladder of Divine Ascent* (Mahwah, N.J., 1982). The *Ladder,* an essential work of Byzantine and Orthodox spirituality, dates from the first half of the seventh century.

11   Niketas here echoes Athanasios of Alexandria, *Vita Antonii.* Cf. *v. Ant.* 8:2.

12   Klimax, *Scala paradisi,* 18, *PG* 88.932B.

13   Several phrases in this chapter and at the start of the next again allude to Athanasios of Alexandria, *Vita Antonii.* Cf. *v. Ant.* 8:2, 156–57; 42:7, 250–51.

14   Cf. Genesis 19:17–26.

15   This is the first occurrence of the wrestling and athletics metaphor that Niketas, following a long tradition, uses throughout the *Life.*

16   Cf. above, Chap. 6.

17   That is, the novice's habit.

18   This exact phrase appears in *Catechetical Discourses* 26:78–79. The following instructions summarize material included in the first half of that *Discourse,* which is directed at monastic beginners.

19   Here and in the rest of the chapter Niketas again echoes Athanasios of Alexandria, *Vita Antonii:* cf. *v. Ant.* 9:5, 160–61; 24:1, 200–201; 51:3, 274–75.

20   See *Catechetical Discourses* 16:54–107 for Symeon's own version of material in this and the following chapter.

21   The broader passage describing the presentation at the temple and the Song of Simeon from which this phrase is taken in Luke 2 is significant for the present context.

22   See Daniel (Susanna) 45–64.

23   The monastery of Saint Mamas was located in southwestern Constantinople not far from the Xylokerkos gate (now the Belgrad Kapı) and thus probably less than half a mile to the northwest of Stoudios. Although its foundation probably dates back to the sixth century, the *Life* reveals below (Chap. 34) that it was in poor condition by this time.

24   The same word (θεωρία) used for Symeon's visions of light.

25   Arsenios the Great, a Byzantine noble who became an exemplary hermit in Egypt in the first half of the fifth century. Arsenios would sleep at dawn. On his praying all night, see the *Apophthegmata patrum* 30, *PG* 65.97C. Cf. also Theodore of Stoudios, *Oratio* 12.15, *PG* 99.864BC.

26   The *kathisma* was the communal reading in church of one of the twenty sections into which the psalter was divided. See Koutsas, *Life,* 101 n. 13, and *ODB* s.v. "Kathisma" (2).

27   Literally, "When the wood was struck": the hammering of the gong or sounding board used to signal the start of services and other occasions in the monastic and liturgical day.

28   Very early in the morning.

29   Nicholas II, patriarch of Constantinople, 984–996.

30   A version of this section of the chapter is preserved in Chap. 153 of the *One Hundred and Fifty-Three Practical and Theological Texts*

ascribed to Symeon preserved in the *Philokalia, PG* 120.685D–88A; trans. *Philokalia* 4.62–63.

31   A very similar version of this answer is also to be found in Chap. 153 in the *Philokalia, PG* 120.685 CD; trans. *Philokalia* 4.62.

32   The immediate reference here is to the priest's chair (καθέδρα) in the sanctuary.

33   The *omophorion* was a long scarf of white wool decorated with crosses. It was one of the traditional vestments worn by bishops in the Byzantine church and symbolic of episcopal authority. The point here is that Symeon was neither a bishop nor a patriarch in earthly terms.

34   As Koutsas, *Life,* 115 n. 20, indicates, Niketas is quoting here from the third *sticheron* or hymn of vespers for the feast of the Transfiguration.

35   Maurice ruled from 582 to 602.

36   I take this as a reference to a type of window design common in middle and later Byzantine churches in which narrow arched apertures contained a series of disks made by blowing and turning molten glass in a cylindrical mould.

37   A traditional saying first attested in Philo, *De specialibus legibus* 4.156, *Philonis Alexandrini opera quae supersunt,* ed. L. Cohn, vol. 5 (Berlin, 1906), p. 244; and in Christian literature in Origen, *Commentarii in evangelium Joannis* 13.46 (303) ll.28–29, *Origène. Commentaire sur saint Jean,* ed. C. Blanc, vol. 3, SC 222 (Paris, 1975), pp. 198–99. The phrase "art of arts" is also used of the monastic life by Symeon: *Catechetical Discourses,* 26:9.

38   The idea of an individual becoming an instrument played by the Spirit is relatively common in patristic writing, especially in exposition of the psalms. For an early parallel to the passage here see Clement of Alexandria, *Paedagogus* 2.4.41.5, *Clément d'Alexandrie. Le pédagogue,* ed. M. Harl, H.-I. Marrou, C. Matray, and C. Mondésert, vol. 2, SC 108 (Paris, 1965), pp. 90–93.

39   *Hymns.* The most recent English translation is Griggs, *Divine Eros.* See also below, Chap. 111. On the title, see Koder, *Hymnes* 1:50–52.

40   *Catechetical Discourses.* English translation: de Catanzaro, *Symeon the New Theologian.*

41   The implication is that the monks accuse Symeon of blas-
        phemy.

42   Sisinnios II, 996–998.

43   This picks up the passage quoted above in Chap. 34: "He who
        does not gather with me scatters."

44   The term *katechoumena,* by this period, indicates marginal areas
        of churches, such as the galleries, to which the unbaptized had
        at one time been confined during services.

45   The same verb is used to describe the consequences of Pan-
        dora's opening of her notorious box in Hesiod, *Works and Days,*
        95.

46   Symeon had himself been a monk in the monastery of Stoudios
        in Constantinople (above, Chaps. 11–21), while Niketas was a se-
        nior figure there, and perhaps its superior. The monastery evi-
        dently had a considerable influence at this time on the role and
        patterns of Byzantine monasticism. See particularly Krausmül-
        ler, "Stoudios and St. Mamas," 67–85.

47   There are two wordplays here that are impossible to render ef-
        fectively in English. The same verb (αὐξάνω) is used to describe
        both Symeon's development or growth and the increase of his
        flock. At the same time, the verb used for the tonsuring of his
        disciples (ἀποκείρω) is also one used of the shearing of sheep—
        Symeon tonsures his followers and shears his flock.

48   The name Arsenios means "masculine" or "virile" in Greek. Ar-
        senios the monk is both physically and spiritually "manly" de-
        spite being a eunuch.

49   The Greek would equally well be understood as "he keeps me
        warm in the hollow of his womb." Niketas deliberately employs
        an ambiguous phrase here to imply a woman's anatomy for
        Symeon as the spiritual mother of Arsenios.

50   The Greek term μῆνιγξ refers literally to any membrane but es-
        pecially that enclosing the brain.

51   The Greek title *patrikios* was a high-ranking dignity that could
        be granted to court officials, governors, and generals.

52   On Arsenios the Great, see n. 25.

53   An identical or similar expression is used on a number of occa-
        sions by Theodore the Stoudite in his letters. See, e.g., *Epist.* 277

l.14–15, *Theodori Studitae Epistulae,* ed. G. Fatouros, CFHB 31, vol. 2.

54   There is a word play in the Greek here between the name Hierotheos (Ἰερόθεον) and the description "priest of God" (ἱερέα ... Θεοῦ).

55   The Greek word used here, σαλός, refers specifically to holy fools.

56   An area in southwestern Constantinople which was the site of the forum and column of Arcadius. It was approximately half a mile from the site of the monastery of Saint Mamas.

57   The same phrase is used above, Chap. 34.

58   Symeon was following the tradition of Platon, the superior of the monastery of Sakkoudion, who had handed over responsibility to his nephew Theodore of Stoudios in 794.

59   Sergios II was patriarch of Constantinople from 1001 to 1019.

60   From this point on the exhortation to Arsenios in Chaps. 60–63 closely parallels, and in some sections reproduces exactly, material from the later paragraphs of Symeon's eighteenth *Catechetical Discourse.* See *Catechetical Discourses,* vol. 2, 302.464–310.569.

61   Two versions of the ninth-century *Rule* of the Monastery of Saint John of Stoudios have survived, along with Theodore of Stoudios's own *Testament.* See *BMFD* 1, 67–119. In this immediate context, Chaps. 22 and 23 of Theodore's *Testament* (p. 79) are most relevant, but it is to be noted that there is surprisingly little general correlation between these documents and the present set of instructions to the superior.

62   The *Rule* for Stoudios, Chap. 25, expressly forbids punishment with the whip as having been "properly judged unacceptable by the fathers." See *BMFD,* 1, 108.

63   Probably a reference to Canon 73 of the *Canons of the Holy Apostles. Fonti, Fascicolo IX, Discipline générale antique (IVe–IXe s.),* ed. Périclès-Pierre Joannou, vol. 1.2 (Grottaferrata, 1962), p. 45.

64   Cf. above, Chap. 37.

65   The saying comes from John Klimakos, *Scala Paradisi* 4, PG 88.618B, but is also found in a considerable number of monastic *typika* in the context of rules and advice concerning confession.

66   See Basil of Caesarea, *Asceticon magnum sive Quaestiones (regulae fusius tractatae)*, Chap. 27, *PG* 31.988B.

67   Significantly here, the passage at 1 Thessalonians 4:17 continues ". . . in the clouds to meet the Lord in the air."

68   Symeon the Theologian, *Theological, Gnostic, and Practical Chapters,* ed. with French translation, Darrouzès, *Syméon le Nouveau Théologien, Chapitres théologiques, gnostiques et pratiques.*

69   See above, Chap. 4.

70   These works have not survived.

71   See above, Chap. 59.

72   The verb ἡσυχάζω is that used for the pursuit of spiritual tranquillity *(hesychia)* by Symeon and other Byzantine saints.

73   For more on Stephen, see Introduction, pp. xiv–xv.

74   Stephen held the title of *synkellos* (σύγκελλος), the close adviser of the patriarch who usually lived with him and was seen as his designated successor. See further *ODB* s.v.

75   Basil of Caesarea, *Epist.* 356. *Saint Basile. Lettres,* ed. Y. Courtonne, vol. 3 (Paris, 1966), p. 218.

76   The Greek term θεώρημα contains the sense of both "doctrine" and "vision" as well as "speculation." Stephen is clearly meant to be seen as mocking Symeon by its use.

77   Symeon's composition is preserved as his Hymn 21: *Hymns,* vol. 2, 130–69. See further here the detailed discussion of the piece in Alfeyev, *St. Symeon,* 39–40, 151–54.

78   Or "his (own) verbal skill and spirit."

79   The whole verse in Psalm 139 (140) reads, "They make their tongue sharp as a serpent's, and under their lips is the poison of vipers." For Niketas, Stephen is worse than simply sharp-tongued.

80   Cf. Gregory of Nazianzus, *Or. 21, In laudem Athanasii, PG* 35.1097.

81   Or "the cause of the righteous man."

82   Only Mark's version of the story uses the term "righteous" (δίκαιος) of John. It was Herodias's daughter who performed the actual dance that resulted in John's execution.

83   This statement echoes the somewhat more explicit description of Symeon Eulabes's exceptional dispassion in Symeon's Fif-

teenth Hymn: *Hymns* 15, 294–95, ll.205–19. For more on that passage, see Derek Krueger, "Homoerotic Spectacle and the Monastic Body in Symeon the New Theologian," in *Toward a Theology of Eros: Transfiguring Passion at the Limits of Discipline,* ed. Virginia Burrus and Catherine Keller (New York, 2006), pp. 116–17.

84   *Apostolic Constitutions* 7.9, ed. B. M. Metzger, *Les constitutions apostoliques,* vol. 3 (Paris, 1987), p. 38.

85   *Apostolic Constitutions* 2.33, ed. B. M. Metzger, *Les constitutions apostoliques,* vol. 1 (Paris, 1985), pp. 252–54. The passage has been changed from the second to the third person.

86   John Chrysostom, *In beatum Philogonium, PG* 48.747–49.

87   John Chrysostom, *Hom. 36, Encomium in sanctum apostolum Paulum, PG* 63.839.

88   A late third-century martyr from Caesarea in Cappadocia, the seat of Basil's bishopric.

89   Basil, *Hom. 18, In Gordium martyrem, PG* 31.492AB, 493A. The quotation omits two short passages from the original.

90   The well-known theologian and archbishop of Alexandria (295–373).

91   Gregory of Nazianzus, *Or. 21 in laudem Athanasii, 5, PG* 35.1088A.

92   The Greek could also mean that the icon in question itself contained a number of figures and depicted Symeon along with other saints and Christ Himself.

93   The Greek is ambiguous. It is unclear whether Niketas refers to Symeon Eulabes or the younger Symeon.

94   This idea, found quite commonly in discussions concerning the theology of icons, is first recorded in Basil of Caesarea, *de Spiritu Sancto* 18.45. *Basile de Césarée. Sur le Saint-Esprit,* ed. B. Pruche, 2nd ed. (Paris, 1968), p. 406.19–20.

95   John of Damascus, *Expositio fidei,* IV.15. *Die Schriften des Johannes von Damaskos,* ed. B. Kotter, vol. 2 (Berlin, 1973), pp. 202–3.

96   The two terms are found together not only at Colossians 1:16 but also at Revelations 13:2, where they are used in relation to the powers of one of the beasts of the apocalypse, an allusion that would surely not be missed by Symeon's audience.

97   Cf. Gregory of Nazianzus, *Or. 43, Funebris oratio in laudem Basilii*

NOTES TO THE TRANSLATION

Magni Caesareae in Cappadocia episcopi, 28.2. *Grégoire de Nazianze. Discours funèbres en l'honneur de son frère Césaire et de Basile de Césarée,* ed. F. Boulenger (Paris, 1908), pp. 118–21.

98   John of Damascus, *Oratio II de Imaginibus* 11:1–30. *Die Schriften des Johannes von Damaskos,* ed. Bonifatius Kotter, vol. 3 (Berlin, 1975), pp. 101–2.

99   The emperor Constantine V (741–755), notorious and vilified in Orthodox circles for his enforcement of iconoclasm.

100   Theophilos was archbishop of Alexandria ca. 384–415. His opposition to Chrysostom for his alleged Origenist views was at least partially responsible for the latter's deposition from the patriarchate of Constantinople in 403 and subsequent exile in 404.

101   Cf. above, Chap. 37.

102   The usual route across the Bosporus from Constantinople. Although the Greek term "Propontis" usually refers to the Sea of Marmara, it is used here and elsewhere in the *Life* to refer to the southern end of the Bosporus: cf. Chaps. 100, 145, and 152. Chrysopolis, which was a suburb of Chalcedon, is to be identified with modern Üsküdar. Paloukiton is otherwise unknown but is assumed to be close to Chrysopolis.

103   This monument is otherwise unattested and its significance unknown. McGuckin's translation of this passage ("Symeon the New Theologian," 30) has a reference to "the column of the condemned prince"; this and his consequent attempt to associate it with the failed bid for power by Bardas Phokas in 976 appears to result from a misunderstanding of Horn's French translation, *dauphin.*

104   See Raymond Janin, *Les églises et les monastères des grands centres byzantins* (Paris, 1975), pp. 25–26.

105   It was thus midafternoon.

106   The verb καταβάλλω also contains the sense here of "depositing" or "storing up." Niketas is thus mocking the *synkellos,* who suspected that Symeon had deposited gold beneath his cell, when all he had actually "deposited" there was the sweat of his ascetic labors.

107   The Greek word ἀμπεχόνη can mean specifically a shawl or

prayer shawl and more generally clothing. Here it seems to indicate some sort of light outer garment.

108   There is a play on words here. The name Stephen (Stephanos) in Greek means "crown."

109   The Greek word φάρμακον, translated here as "remedy," generally refers to curative medicines but may also contain the sense of poison or magical potion, something Symeon/Niketas is surely playing upon.

110   This phrase might also be translated "Because the news about Symeon struck everyone who heard about it like a bolt of lightning."

111   See above, Chaps. 54–55, 57.

112   The term *sekreton* (σέκρετον) evidently refers in this context to the hall in which the patriarchal court met.

113   Here and in the rest of the exchange to Chap. 108 the verb πειθαρχέω is translated as "to be convinced" rather than its usual sense of "obey" or "be obedient." In these highly charged circumstances, the patriarch is clearly interested in leaving Symeon room to do as he wishes without incurring a charge of direct disobedience.

114   Symeon/Niketas is likely thinking of Theodore the Stoudite, who was exiled on a number of occasions between 795 and 821.

115   As Koutsas notes, this phrase commonly introduces the rulings of the Ecumenical Councils; *Life,* 268–69.

116   Cf. above, Chap. 44 and n. 46. Over the centuries the monastery had become known for its resistance to official policy in a number of matters but especially that of iconoclasm.

117   Or perhaps "Afterward he crossed over to his beloved place of solitary contemplation, as he wished to build a cell there."

118   The λαοσυνάκτης was a church official who gathered the congregation for services.

119   A *metochion* (μετόχιον) was a subsidiary monastery attached to a larger one, often acting as a base for supervising distant estates or for monks visiting a town.

120   The Greek carries profound implications that it is impossible to render in succinct English. On one level Symeon's unity or oneness with God broadens his practical command of words, his

ability to reason, and his grasp of spiritual matters. On another
level he is united rationally and spiritually with the Word and
Holy Spirit of God.

121   See above, Chap. 37 n. 39.

122   See above, Chap. 72.

123   Most likely the disciple Nikephoros/Symeon, on whom see below, Chaps. 116–27.

124   An important court official who served as deputy to the *logothetes
tou dromou,* the senior minister in charge of a range of responsi-
bilities that included court ceremonial, imperial security, information gathering, and some aspects of foreign affairs.

125   Basil II (976–1025).

126   The *deeseon* (more commonly *epi ton deeseon*) was a senior court
official responsible for dealing with requests made to the emperor.

127   Niketas refers here and in Chap. 150 to a longer version of the
Life. This has not survived.

128   This convent was probably founded by a woman of the Bardas
family. It is otherwise unattested. See Janin, *CP,* 57.

129   The verse begins, "And every creeping thing that is alive you
shall have for food."

130   An icon, usually by this period of intercession, depicting Christ,
who is sometimes enthroned between the Virgin and John the
Baptist, who entreat Him.

131   Roughly six feet.

132   Midafternoon.

133   See above, Chap. 95. As this story shows, the monastery of Saint
Marina was evidently close by.

134   The Greek term, πειρασμός, likely carries the sense of "temptation" as well as "tribulation" in this passage. Given Orestes's
wealth, the author may well have 1 Timothy 6:9 in mind.

135   The allegation is evidently that Symeon was using chaff smoke
to darken or dirty his face. Chaff was known to produce choking
black smoke when burned and was used as a means of torture in
the Byzantine period.

136   The ascetic concept that mortification of the flesh and its
earthly desires brings eternal life to those who practice it.

Symeon expounded his ideas on this topic in his twenty-eighth Catechetical Discourse (*Catechetical Discourses,* vol. 3, 128–63) and his eleventh Ethical Discourse (*Ethical Discourses,* vol. 2, 328–83).

137 Literally, "death of eternal life."

138 *Apostolic Constitutions* 2.33. *Les constitutions apostoliques,* ed. B. M. Metzger, vol. 1 (Paris, 1985), p. 254, with minor variations.

139 From the Latin *arcula,* meaning a small box or casket.

140 Given the wording of the passage in 2 Corinthians 5:1–4, there is probably an intentional wordplay here between ἀκήρατος, "undefiled," "inviolate," "untouched," "unfading," and ἀχειρο- ποίητος, "not made with hands."

141 The Byzantine "indiction" was a fifteen-year cycle, each year of which began on September 1. The "fifth indiction" thus refers to the fifth year of the current cycle. The second part of Symeon's prediction evidently refers to the translation of his relics, which will take place in the corresponding year of a future cycle. See also the following chapter.

142 The Greek verb συστέλλω carries a range of meaning that is hard to convey in English. The implication is that Symeon withdraws into himself, as the *Life* has said earlier that he was accustomed to do in meditation, but also braces himself for death. At the same time the original audience would be well aware in this context that the verb also has the sense of enshrouding.

143 This has not survived. See also below, Chap. 136.

144 Greek uses the letters of the alphabet for numbers. This use is indicated by the punctuation mark (ὑποστιγμή) mentioned here.

145 August 1052 CE.

146 The verb ἀνακομίζω here could simply indicate "translation," but the implication is that Symeon's relics were returned to Constantinople, a move that was significant in a number of ways.

147 The term *kontakion* in Byzantine sources most usually refers to a type of hymn or, earlier, verse sermon, and thus this passage might also be translated: "I used to copy out these and other verses [*kontakia*] onto book parchment." This is Horn's under-

standing in his French translation (Hausherr, *Vie,* 189–91), and is logical since Symeon's substantial literary oeuvre included much hymnography. However, as Koutsas (*Life,* 320 n. 72) points out, the term may also indicate the wooden spool around which a scroll was wrapped and hence, by extension, the papyrus scroll itself. The flow of the Greek seems to support this latter interpretation, as does the use of χαρτίον for the same item in the following chapter.

148   The verb καθωμολόγησα also contains the sense of "betrothal" as well as "pledge." Cf. Exodus 21:8–9.

149   Cf. Genesis 2:24; Matthew 19:5; Mark 10:7; Ephesians 5:31, where the passive of the verb προσκολλάω is used of a man becoming one with, or joined with, his wife.

150   The start of the previous chapter indicates that Niketas's letter to Symeon was sent on an erasable writing tablet (πιττάκιον). Presumably Symeon's response was in the same form.

151   John the Baptist. The large basilica of Saint John at Stoudios was originally constructed in the mid-fifth century. Turned into a mosque by the Ottomans, known as Imrahor Camii, it is today largely in ruins.

152   *Ethical Discourses.* See Golitzin, *Mystical Life.*

153   See Turner, *Epistles of St. Symeon.*

154   Or "consolation," "encouragement." The terms παράκλησις and its cognate παράκλητος, cf. John 14:16, have quite a broad range of meaning that is impossible to capture in one word.

155   Literally "hymns for canons." In the liturgical context a canon was a set of linked verses sung at the early morning service of *orthros* (matins). It was composed of eight or nine odes based on biblical canticles with additional hymns sung between the three sections into which it was divided.

156   See also above, Chap. 129.

157   An imperial bedchamber (from the Latin *cubiculum*).

158   It was customary to give the kiss of peace on the mouth. See Robert Taft, *The Great Entrance* (Rome, 1978), pp. 390–92, and cf. Alice-Mary Talbot, ed., *Holy Women of Byzantium* (Washington, D.C., 1996), pp. 26, 90.

159   Compare the potentially homoerotic imagery found here and

below in this chapter with passages in the parable that Symeon
tells in his Tenth Ethical Discourse of the repentant rebel who is
embraced by the emperor (*Ethical Discourses* 10, vol. 2, 235–73;
Golitzin, *Mystical Life,* 150–51). And see Krueger, "Homoerotic
Spectacle," (as in n. 83) pp. 99–118.

160   The concept of the "naked soul" is used and explored on a number of occasions in Symeon's own writings. See, e.g., *Ethical Discourses* 5, vol. 2, 84–85, ll.63–65; *Catechetical Discourses* 21, 362–63,
ll.144–47; 28, 154–55, ll.330–31.

161   Gregory of Nazianzus was commonly known as Gregory the
Theologian. His younger brother, Kaisarios, died in 369 CE.

162   Gregory of Nazianzus, *Or. 7, Funebris in laudem Caesarii fratris,* 21,
PG 35.784B. The quotation is exact except for the omission of
one word in the middle, but Niketas omits the final phrases of
the original passage to make it support his argument.

163   Gregory of Nazianzus, *Or. 18, Funebris oratio in patrem, praesente
Basilio,* 30, *PG* 35.1021C. In the original context Gregory's
mother is close to death because an illness has prevented her
from eating.

164   Ibid., 1024A, with minor variations in the last sentence.

165   Dionysios the Areopagite, *De ecclesiastica hierarchia,* 7.3.2, *Myste-
rium super his qui sancte obdormierunt,* and 7.3.3, *Contemplatio, PG*
3.556–69. The name of Dionysios the Areopagite, an Athenian
nobleman who was converted to Christianity by Saint Paul and
who became the first bishop of Athens, was adopted by the later
(fifth/sixth century) author of a significant corpus of theological
works.

166   Cf. the passages from Chrysostom and Basil cited by Symeon in
his speech to the synod, above, Chaps. 84–85.

167   The oath in Genesis 24:2, 9 requires the servant to find a wife
(Rebecca) for Abraham's son, Isaac.

168   An important monastic center near Miletos on the west coast
of Asia Minor. Latros developed in the eighth century and flour-
ished from the tenth to the late thirteenth century.

169   The phrase τὸ κέρας τοῦ βήματος appears to be unique to this
work. It is understood here by Koutsas (*Life,* 359) and Horn
(Hausherr, *Vie,* 209) as indicating "the corner of the sanctuary."

In Chap. 152, where it recurs, Koutsas (*Life,* 389) takes it as "the top of the sanctuary." A location in the corner of the sanctuary would not, however, place the icon "in front of the altar," and I thus take κέρας as indicating the "cross" or "transverse beam" of the iconostasis (or perhaps some projection from it), following Lampe, *A Patristic Greek Lexicon,* s.v. κέρας 2a.

170   See Janin, *CP,* 296–300.

171   The term *kalliphonos* indicates a professional singer or chanter: see, e.g., *Typikon* of Theodora Palaiologina for the Convent of Lips in Constantinople, 39, *BMFD* 3, 1277, cf. 1257; *Testament* of Constantine Akropolites for the Monastery of the Resurrection (Anastasis) in Constantinople, 7, *BMFD* 4, 1380, cf. 1376.

172   More specifically, a *kontakion.* Cf. above, Chap. 131 n. 147.

173   Cf. above, Chap. 141.

174   Anaplous (modern Arnavutköy) was located on the European shore of the Bosporus some six miles north of the center of Constantinople. See further Janin, *CP,* 338, 340.

175   Philotheos in Greek means, literally, "loving God."

176   The Greek term πάθος has here the sense not only of passion, in terms of spiritual temptation, but also physical illness, affliction, and suffering.

177   I take χαράδριον here as "mat" with Lampe, *A Patristic Greek Lexicon,* s.v. However both Koutsas (*Life,* 379–81) and Horn (Hausherr, *Vie,* 223) understand it as a "cave" or "lair."

178   See Symeon Metaphrastes, *Life of John Chrysostom,* 23, *PG* 114.1104B ff.

179   And in the present *Life:* see above, Chaps. 137–40. On the longer version see also above, Chap. 113.

180   Auxentios (modern Kayışdağ) was a holy mountain some seven miles southeast of Chalcedon and thus quite close to Symeon's monastery of Saint Marina. Saint Stephen the Younger founded a monastery there in the eighth century. Although destroyed during the second period of iconoclasm, the monastery had evidently been restored or refounded by this time.

181   The term is used to indicate nomadic ethnicity.

182   See above, Chap. 141.

Bibliography

EDITIONS OF THE GREEK TEXT

Hausherr, Irénée, and Gabriel Horn. *Un grand mystique byzantin, vie de Syméon le Nouveau Théologien (949–1022) par Nicétas Stéthatos*. Orientalia Christiana 12. Rome, 1928.

Koutsas, Symeon. *Ἅγιος Συμεών ὁ Νέος Θεολόγος*. Nea Smyrne, 1994.

SELECTED MODERN EDITIONS, TRANSLATIONS, AND STUDIES

Alfeyev, Hilarion. *St. Symeon the New Theologian and Orthodox Tradition*. Oxford, 2000.

Christou, Panagiotes. *Νικήτα Στηθάτου μυστικὰ συγγράμματα*. Thessalonike, 1957.

———. *Συμεὼν τοῦ Νέου Θεολόγου· Βίος, Κεφάλαια, Εὐχαριστίαι*. Thessalonike, 1983.

Darrouzès, Jean, ed. *Nicétas Stéthatos, Opuscules et lettres*. SC 81, Paris 1961.

———, ed. *Syméon le Nouveau Théologien, Traités théologiques et éthiques*. Vol. 1, SC 122, Paris, 1966; vol. 2, SC 129, Paris, 1967.

Darrouzès, Jean, and Louis Neyrand, eds. *Syméon le Nouveau Théologien, Chapitres théologiques, gnostiques et pratiques*. SC 51bis, Paris, 1980.

de Catanzaro, Carmino J. *Symeon the New Theologian—The Discourses*. Mahwah, N.J., 1980.

Fraigneau-Julien, Bernard. *Les sens spirituels et la vision de Dieu selon Syméon le Nouveau Théologien*. Paris, 1986.

Golitzin, Alexander. *St. Symeon the New Theologian. On the Mystical Life: The Ethical Discourses*. 3 vols. Crestwood, N.Y., 1995–1997.

Griggs, Daniel K. *Divine Eros: Hymns of St. Symeon the New Theologian*. Crestwood, N.Y., 2011.

Koder, Johannes. "Ὁ Συμεών ὁ Νέος Θεολόγος καὶ οἱ Ὕμνοι του." In *Τέσσερα κείμενα για την ποίηση του Συμεών του Νέου Θεολόγου,* edited by Athanasios Markopoulos, 1–35. Athens, 2008.

Koder, Johannes, Joseph Paramelle, and Louis Neyrand. *Syméon le Nouveau Théologien, Hymnes.* Vol. 1, SC 156, Paris, 1969; vol. 2, SC 174, Paris, 1971; and vol. 3, SC 196, Paris, 1973.

Krausmüller, Dirk. "The Monastic Communities of Stoudios and St. Mamas in the Second Half of the Tenth Century." In *The Theotokos Evergetis and Eleventh-Century Monasticism,* edited by Margaret Mullett and Anthony Kirby, 67–85. Belfast, 1994.

———. "Private vs. Communal: Niketas Stethatos's *Hypotyposis* for Stoudios, and Patterns of Worship in Eleventh-Century Byzantine Monasteries." In *Work and Worship at the Theotokos Evergetis 1050–1200,* edited by Margaret Mullett and Anthony Kirby, 309–328. Belfast, 1997.

Krivochéine, Basil. *In the Light of Christ: Saint Symeon the New Theologian (949–1022); Life—Spirituality—Doctrine.* Translated by Anthony Gythiel. Crestwood, N.Y., 1986.

Krivochéine, Basil, and Joseph Paramelle, eds. *Syméon le Nouveau Théologien, Catéchèses.* Vol. 1 (Discourses 1–5), SC 96, Paris, 1963; vol. 2 (6–22), SC 104, Paris, 1964; vol. 3 (23–34) SC 113, Paris, 1965.

Maloney, George A. *Hymns of Divine Love by St. Symeon the New Theologian.* Denville, N.J., 1976.

———. *The Mystic of Fire and Light: St. Symeon the New Theologian.* Denville, N.J., 1975.

Markopoulos, Athanasios, ed. *Τέσσερα κείμενα για την ποίηση του Συμεών του Νέου Θεολόγου.* Athens, 2008.

McGuckin, John A. "St. Symeon the New Theologian (949–1022): Byzantine Spiritual Renewal in Search of a Precedent." In *The Church Retrospective,* edited by R. N. Swanson, Studies in Church History 33, pp. 75–90. Woodbridge, Eng., 1997.

———. "Symeon the New Theologian (d. 1022) and Byzantine Monasticism." In *Mount Athos,* edited by Anthony Bryer and Mary Cunningham, 17–35. Aldershot, Eng., 1996.

McGuckin, Paul. *Symeon the New Theologian: The Practical and Theological Chapters and the Three Theological Discourses.* Kalamazoo, Mich., 1982.

Oikonomides, Nikos. "How to Become a Saint in Eleventh Century Byzantium." In Οἱ Ἥρωες τῆς Ὀρθόδοξης Ἐκκλησίας. Οἱ Νέοι Ἅγιοι, 8ος–16ος αἰ., edited by Eleonora Kountoura-Galaki, 473–91. Athens, 2004.

Paschalides, Symeon A. "Ὁ ἀνέκδοτος λόγος τοῦ Νικήτα Στηθάτου Κατὰ ἁγιοκατηγόρων καὶ ἡ ἀμφισβήτηση τῆς ἁγιότητας στὸ Βυζάντιο κατὰ τὸν ιι° αἰώνα." In Οἱ Ἥρωες τῆς Ὀρθόδοξης Ἐκκλησίας. Οἱ Νέοι Ἅγιοι, 8ος–16ος αἰ., edited by Eleonora Kountoura-Galaki, 493–518. Athens, 2004.

The Philokalia: The Complete Text Compiled by St. Nikodimos of the Holy Mountain and St. Makarios of Corinth. Translated by G. E. H. Palmer, Philip Sherrard, and Kallistos Ware. 4 vols. London, 1979–1995.

Turner, Henry J. M. *St. Symeon the New Theologian and Spiritual Fatherhood.* Leiden, 1990.

———. *The Epistles of St. Symeon the New Theologian.* Oxford, 2009.

Völker, Walther. *Praxis und Theoria bei Symeon dem neuen Theologen: Ein Beitrag zur byzantinischen Mystik.* Wiesbaden, 1974.

Index

Note: chapter numbers in parentheses are passages where the person or place is not specifically mentioned by name but alluded to.